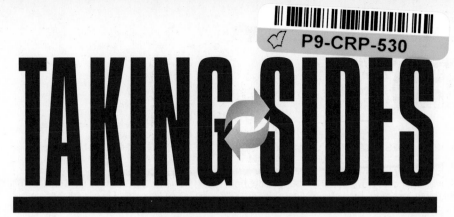

TAKING SIDES

Clashing Views in

Life-Span Development

THIRD EDITION

Selected, Edited, and with Introductions by

Andrew M. Guest
University of Portland

Mc Graw Hill

Connect
Learn
Succeed™

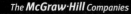

TAKING SIDES: CLASHING VIEWS IN LIFE-SPAN DEVELOPMENT, THIRD EDITION

Published by McGraw-Hill, a business unit of The McGraw-Hill Companies, Inc., 1221 Avenue of the Americas, New York, NY 10020. Copyright © 2011 by The McGraw-Hill Companies, Inc. All rights reserved. Previous edition(s) 2009, 2007, and 2005. No part of this publication may be reproduced or distributed in any form or by any means, or stored in a database or retrieval system, without the prior written consent of The McGraw-Hill Companies, Inc., including, but not limited to, in any network or other electronic storage or transmission, or broadcast for distance learning.

Some ancillaries, including electronic and print components, may not be available to customers outside the United States.

Taking Sides® is a registered trademark of the McGraw-Hill Companies, Inc.

Taking Sides is published by the **Contemporary Learning Series** group within the McGraw-Hill Higher Education division.

1 2 3 4 5 6 7 8 9 0 DOC/DOC 1 0 9 8 7 6 5 4 3 2 1 0

MHID: 0-07-804995-4
ISBN: 978-0-07-804995-8
ISSN: 1559-2642

Managing Editor: *Larry Loeppke*
Director, Specialized Production: *Faye Schilling*
Senior Developmental Editor: *Jill Meloy*
Editorial Coordinator: *Mary Foust*
Production Service Assistant: *Rita Hingtgen*
Permissions Coordinator: *Lenny J. Behnke*
Editorial Assistant: *Cindy Hedley*
Senior Marketing Manager: *Julie Keck*
Senior Marketing Communications Specialist: *Mary Klein*
Marketing Coordinator: *Alice Link*
Project Manager: *Erin Melloy*
Design Specialist: *Brenda Rolwes*
Cover Graphics: *Rick D. Noel*

Compositor: *MPS Limited, A Macmillan Company*
Cover Image: © *Design Pics/Punchstock*

Editors/Academic Advisory Board

Members of the Academic Advisory Board are instrumental in the final selection of articles for each edition of TAKING SIDES. Their review of articles for content, level, and appropriateness provides critical direction to the editors and staff. We think that you will find their careful consideration well reflected in this volume.

TAKING SIDES: Clashing Views in LIFE-SPAN DEVELOPMENT

Third Edition

EDITOR

Andrew M. Guest
University of Portland

ACADEMIC ADVISORY BOARD MEMBERS

Preface

We all have a vested stake in the study of life-span development because we are all experts in the ages and stages of our own lives. Yet our experiences, and our understandings of those experiences, vary dramatically from person to person. Where some of us are sure that our childhood interactions with our parents shaped everything about the way we function in the world, others are convinced that we are living out a biologically or genetically determined destiny. While many people see childhood as a period of risks and challenges, others appreciate the joy and opportunity of being young. Where we often focus on adulthood as defined by careers and family, we also recognize that well-being in adulthood depends upon abstract qualities such as happiness and success. In one sense, these types of contrasts show how the study of life-span development is inherently controversial. The purpose of this book is to make that controversy useful by providing educated and intelligent perspectives on issues that are important to everyone's life, not to mention being important to academic study of the life-span.

This third edition of *Taking Sides: Clashing Views on Controversial Issues in Life-Span Development* presents 20 issues that challenge students and scholars to think deeply about issues confronted throughout the ages and stages of our lives. Seven of these issues are entirely new to this edition, while several other reading selections have been updated from previous editions. In all cases, each issue is framed by a question about what, why, or how we develop, and each question is addressed from two distinct perspectives selected from previously published work. These 40 selections represent the perspectives of a broad group of scholars and experts. Each of the 20 issues also has an introduction with an explanation of how and why it is important for the larger study of life-span development and a postscript providing challenge questions to elaborate on the issue along with suggestions for further reading.

The materials and ideas dealt with in this book derive from diverse fields of study including psychology, sociology, biology, cognitive science, gerontology, and pediatrics. In fact, one appealing aspect of studying life-span development is that it is an interdisciplinary subject focused on answering interesting questions. Thus, while the materials provided with each issue allow an understanding of what experts in diverse subjects think, the challenge for readers is to use the evidence and opinions to answer the questions for themselves. The book explains, for example, why understanding how much our development depends upon our parents is important, but it is up to readers to take that explanation and the available evidence to establish their own educated position.

Although the perspectives presented in this book represent educated thinking on these issues, the reason the issues are controversial is because that thinking is still evolving. Researchers are always developing new techniques for studying human development, individuals are always adapting to the different challenges faced at each stage of life, and societies are always changing the way they treat children, adults, and the elderly. Likewise, readers of this book, as experts in their own life-span development, will have valuable experiences and perspectives that complement those discussed in the book. In the end, what is most important is to have a point of view on these issues that is educated and informed—sometimes that point of view will match earlier beliefs, other times it will represent a dramatic change. In all cases, however, the most valuable understandings derive from using controversy as an opportunity to think through the challenges of our lives.

A word to the instructor An *Instructor's Resource Guide with Test Questions* (multiple-choice and essay) is available through the publisher for the instructor using Taking Sides in the classroom. A general guidebook, *Using Taking Sides in the Classroom*, which discusses methods and techniques for integrating the pro-con approach into any classroom setting, is also available. An online version of *Using Taking Sides in the Classroom* and a correspondence service for Taking Sides adopters can be found at http://www.mhhe/cls.

    Taking Sides: Clashing Views in Life-Span Development is only one title in the Taking Sides series. If you are interested in seeing the table of contents for any of the other titles, please visit the Taking Sides Web site at http://www.mhhe.com/cls.

Acknowledgments I greatly appreciate the opportunities for learning about the life-span provided by my former teachers and colleagues at the University of Chicago's Committee on Human Development and by my current students at the University of Portland (who allowed me the opportunity to draft all the material with an intelligent and critical audience). Beyond those groups, I owe the most thanks to Sara Guest for her support and understanding.

Contents In Brief

UNIT 1 General Issues in the Study of Life-Span Development 1

Issue 1. Does the Cultural Environment Influence Lifespan Development More than Our Genes? 2

Issue 2. Are Peers More Important than Parents during the Process of Development? 24

Issue 3. Do Significant Innate Differences Influence the Career Success of Males and Females? 47

UNIT 2 Prenatal Development and Infancy 73

Issue 4. Is Drinking Alcohol While Pregnant an Unnecessary Risk to Prenatal Development? 74

Issue 5. Is There a "Myth of the First Three Years"? 87

Issue 6. Are There Good Reasons to Allow Infants to Consume Electronic Media, Such as Television? 99

UNIT 3 Early Childhood and Middle Childhood 133

Issue 7. Is Advertising Responsible for Childhood Obesity? 134

Issue 8. Does Emphasizing Academic Skills Help At-Risk Preschool Children? 159

Issue 9. Is Attention Deficit Disorder (ADD/ADHD) a Legitimate Medical Condition That Affects Childhood Behavior? 182

UNIT 4 Adolescence 201

Issue 10. Should Contemporary Adolescents Be Engaged in More Structured Activities? 202

Issue 11. Does the Adolescent Brain Make Risk Taking Inevitable? 219

UNIT 5 Youth and Emerging Adulthood 239

Issue 12. Is There a "Narcissism Epidemic" Among Contemporary Young Adults? 240

Issue 13. Are College Graduates Unprepared for Adulthood and the World of Work? 256

Issue 14. Is There Such a Thing as "Emerging Adulthood"? 270

UNIT 6 Middle Adulthood 291

Issue 15. Is the Institution of Marriage at Risk? 292

Issue 16. Is Religion a Pure Good in Facilitating Well-Being during Adulthood? 316

Issue 17. Are Professional Women "Opting Out" of Work by Choice?   339

UNIT 7   Later Adulthood   363

Issue 18. Is More Civic Engagement Among Older Adults Necessarily Better?   364

Issue 19. Is "Mild Cognitive Impairment" Too Similar to Normal Aging to be a Relevant Concept?   384

Issue 20. Should the Terminally Ill Be Able to Have Physicians Help Them Die?   402

Contents

Preface   iv

Correlation Guide   xv

Introduction   xvii

UNIT 1   GENERAL ISSUES IN THE STUDY OF LIFE-SPAN DEVELOPMENT   1

Issue 1.   Does the Cultural Environment Influence Lifespan Development More than Our Genes?   2

YES: **Paul Ehrlich and Marcus Feldman,** from "Genes and Cultures: What Creates Our Behavioral Phenome?" *Current Anthropology* (February 2003)   *4*

NO: **Gary Marcus,** from "Making the Mind: Why We've Misunderstood the Nature-Nurture Debate," *Boston Review* (December 2003/January 2004)   *13*

Stanford University professors of biology Paul Ehrlich and Marcus Feldman argue that human behavior exhibits such complexity that genetic programs simply can't explain the way people develop. Psychologist and researcher Gary Marcus asserts that research clearly demonstrates how a relatively small number of genes influence our environmental learning by "cascading" to determine the paths of our behavioral development.

Issue 2.   Are Peers More Important than Parents during the Process of Development?   24

YES: **Judith Rich Harris,** from "How to Succeed in Childhood," *Wilson Quarterly* (Winter 1991)   *26*

NO: **Howard Gardner,** from "Do Parents Count?" *New York Times Book Review* (November 5, 1998)   *35*

Developmental psychology writer Judith Rich Harris presents a strong and provocative argument suggesting that parents do not influence child development to any significant degree, while peers and social groups have a primary influence. Harvard psychologist Howard Gardner reviews Harris's work and suggests her argument is overstated and misleading— parents do matter.

Issue 3.   Do Significant Innate Differences Influence the Career Success of Males and Females?   47

YES: **Steven Pinker,** from "The Science of Gender and Science: Pinker vs. Spelke: A Debate," *Edge: The Third Culture* (May 2005)   *49*

NO: **Elizabeth Spelke,** from "The Science of Gender and Science: Pinker vs. Spelke: A Debate," *Edge: The Third Culture* (May 2005)   *60*

After the Harvard president controversially suggested innate gender differences may play a role in men's disproportionate representation in science careers, cognitive psychologist Steven Pinker suggested that research does find clear innate differences between men and women in some basic cognitive abilities relevant to success. Harvard psychologist Elizabeth Spelke draws on research into cognitive development to suggest that the major reasons for any differences in career success lie in social, rather than genetic, forces.

UNIT 2   PRENATAL DEVELOPMENT AND INFANCY   73

Issue 4.   Is Drinking Alcohol While Pregnant an Unnecessary Risk to Prenatal Development?   74

YES: **Phyllida Brown**, from "Drinking for Two," *New Scientist* (July 1, 2006)   *76*

NO: **Julia Moskin**, from "The Weighty Responsibility of Drinking for Two," *The New York Times* (November 29, 2006)   *81*

Science writer Phyllida Brown reviews contemporary research about the effects of alcohol exposure during prenatal development and concludes that total abstinence from drinking is the smart option during pregnancy. Journalist Julia Moskin finds the evidence against light drinking lacking, and argues that women should be allowed to decide for themselves if an occasional alcoholic beverage is harmful.

Issue 5.   Is There a "Myth of the First Three Years"?   87

YES: **Gwen J. Broude**, from "Scatterbrained Child Rearing," *Reason* (December 2000)   *89*

NO: **Zero to Three: National Center for Infants, Toddlers and Families**, from "Zero to Three: Response to *The Myth of the First Three Years*," http://www.zerotothree.org/no-myth.html   *93*

Gwen J. Broude, who teaches developmental psychology and cognitive science at Vassar College, reviews, supports, and augments John Bruer's idea that a "myth of the first three years" has falsely used neuroscience to claim that infancy is the only critical developmental period. Zero to Three, a national organization devoted to promoting healthy infant development, contradicts Bruer's idea by asserting that a great deal of diverse research supports the idea that the first three years are critical to development and success in adulthood.

Issue 6.   Are There Good Reasons to Allow Infants to Consume Electronic Media, Such as Television?   99

YES: **Victoria Rideout, Elizabeth Hamel, and the Kaiser Family Foundation**, from "The Media Family: Electronic Media in the Lives of Infants, Toddlers, Preschoolers and their Parents" A Report from the Kaiser Family Foundation (May 2006)   *101*

NO: **Ellen Wartella and Michael Robb**, from "Young Children, New Media" *Journal of Children and Media* (Issue 1, 2007)   *120*

Victoria Rideout, Elizabeth Hamel, and the Kaiser Family Foundation find that television and electronic media allow families to cope with busy schedules and are of value to parents of infants. Ellen Wartella and Michael Robb, who are scholars of children and the media, describe limitations on infant's ability to learn from electronic media and note concerns about the diminishing of direct infant to parent interactions.

UNIT 3   EARLY CHILDHOOD AND MIDDLE CHILDHOOD   133

Issue 7.   Is Advertising Responsible for Childhood Obesity?   134

YES: **The Kaiser Family Foundation,** from "The Role of Media in Childhood Obesity," *Issue Brief* (February 2004)   *136*

NO: **The Federal Trade Commission Bureau of Economics Staff,** from "Children's Exposure to Television Advertising in 1977 and 2004: Information for the Obesity Debate," *Federal Trade Commission Bureau of Economics Staff Report* (June 1, 2007)   *150*

In a review of research on media exposure and childhood obesity, the Kaiser Family Foundation concludes that exposure to advertising, more than inactivity, best explains the increasing rates of childhood obesity. In contrast, the Federal Trade Commission Bureau of Economics Staff specifically evaluated television advertising to children and found that increasing rates of childhood obesity do not correspond with increasing exposure to food advertising.

Issue 8.   Does Emphasizing Academic Skills Help At-Risk Preschool Children?   159

YES: **U.S. Department of Health and Human Services,** from *Strengthening Head Start: What the Evidence Shows* (June 2003)   *161*

NO: **C. Cybele Raver and Edward F. Zigler,** from "Another Step Back? Assessing Readiness in Head Start," *Young Children* (January 2004)   *173*

The U.S. Department of Health and Human Services argues that preschool programs can help young children most by emphasizing academic and cognitive skills. Professors C. Cybele Raver and Edward F. Zigler argue that overemphasizing academic and cognitive skills at the expense of social, emotional, and physical well-being is a mistake dependent on misguided efforts to make the entire educational system focused on concrete assessment.

Issue 9.   Is Attention Deficit Disorder (ADD/ADHD) a Legitimate Medical Condition That Affects Childhood Behavior?   182

YES: **Michael Fumento,** from "Trick Question" *The New Republic* (February 2003)   *184*

NO: **Rogers H. Wright,** from "Attention Deficit Hyperactivity Disorder: What It Is and What It Is Not," in Rogers H. Wright and

Nicholas A. Cummings, eds., *Destructive Trends in Mental Health: The Well-Intentioned Path to Harm* (Routledge, 2005)   *191*

Science journalist and writer Michael Fumento suggests that despite the extensive political controversy, it is clear that ADHD is a legitimate medical condition disrupting childhood. Psychologist Rogers Wright argues that ADHD is a transitory condition and fad diagnosis rather than an enduring disease.

UNIT 4   ADOLESCENCE   201

Issue 10.   Should Contemporary Adolescents Be Engaged in More Structured Activities?   202

YES: Joseph L. Mahoney, Angel L. Harris, and Jacquelynne S. Eccles, from "Organized Activity Participation, Positive Youth Development, and the Over-Scheduling Hypothesis," *Social Policy Report* (August 2006)   *204*

NO: Alvin Rosenfeld, from "Comments on 'Organized Activity Participation, Positive Youth Development, and the Over-Scheduling Hypothesis'," *212*

Psychologist Joseph Mahoney and colleagues recognize the concern about "over-scheduling" but present research suggesting that the benefits to structured activities outweigh any costs. Child psychiatrist Alvin Rosenfeld asserts that all of the data suggest that most youth and adolescents need less structured activity and more balance.

Issue 11.   Does the Adolescent Brain Make Risk Taking Inevitable?   219

YES: Laurence Steinberg, from "Risk Taking in Adolescence: New Perspectives From Brain and Behavioral Science," *Current Directions in Psychological Science* (April 2007)   *221*

NO: Michael Males, from "Does the Adolescent Brain Make Risk Taking Inevitable?: A Skeptical Appraisal," *Journal of Adolescent Research* (January 2009)   *227*

Although adolescent risk-taking has proved difficult to study and explain, psychology professor Laurence Steinberg claims brain science is now demonstrating that basic biological changes explain much about the issue. Sociologist Michael Males rejects "biodeterminism" as an oversimplification that exaggerates the effects of brain age and ignores the realities of social and economic differences.

UNIT 5   YOUTH AND EMERGING ADULTHOOD   239

Issue. 12   Is There a "Narcissism Epidemic" Among Contemporary Young Adults?   240

YES: Jean M. Twenge and Joshua D. Foster, from "Mapping the scale of the narcissism epidemic: Increases in narcissism 2002–2007 within ethnic groups." *Journal of Research in Personality* (December 2008)   *242*

NO: M. Brent Donnellan, Kali H. Trzesniewski, and Richard W. Robins, from "An emerging epidemic of narcissism or much ado about nothing?" *Journal of Research in Personality* (June 2009)   *247*

Jean M. Twenge and Joshua D. Foster present evidence from surveys of college students that reinforces their claim of a "narcissism epidemic." Research psychologists M. Brent Donnellan, Kali H. Trzesniewski, and Richard W. Robins take the evidence used by Twenge and colleagues and draw different conclusions, arguing claims of an epidemic are greatly exaggerated.

Issue 13.   Are College Graduates Unprepared for Adulthood and the World of Work?   256

YES: Mel Levine, from "College Graduates Aren't Ready for the Real World," *The Chronicle of Higher Education* (February 18, 2005)   *258*

NO: Frank F. Furstenberg et al., from "Growing Up Is Harder to Do," *Contexts* (Summer 2004)   *263*

Professor of pediatrics, author, and child-rearing expert Mel Levine argues that contemporary colleges are producing a generation of young adults who are psychologically "unready" for entering adulthood and the world of work. Sociologist Frank Furstenberg and colleagues assert that major social changes have extended the transition to adulthood, and college graduates are the group most apt to cope with these social changes.

Issue 14.   Is There Such a Thing as "Emerging Adulthood"?   270

YES: Jeffrey Jensen Arnett, from "Emerging Adulthood: What Is It, and What Is It Good For?" *Child Development Perspectives* (December 2007)   *272*

NO: Leo B. Hendry and Marion Kloep, from "Conceptualizing Emerging Adulthood: Inspecting the Emperor's New Clothes?" *Child Development Perspectives* (December 2007)   *280*

Developmental psychologist Jeffrey Jensen Arnett has earned wide acclaim among scholars for defining an "emerging adulthood" as a distinctly modern stage of the life-span. Life-span research scholars Lew B. Hendry and Marion Kloep argue that defining emerging adulthood as a discrete stage provides a misleading account of the age period between the late teens and the mid- to late twenties.

UNIT 6   MIDDLE ADULTHOOD   291

Issue 15.   Is the Institution of Marriage at Risk?   292

YES: Andrew J. Cherlin, from "The Deinstitutionalization of American Marriage," *Journal of Marriage and Family* (September 2004)   *294*

NO: Frank Furstenberg, from "Can Marriage Be Saved?" *Dissent Magazine* (Summer 2005)   *308*

Sociologist Andrew J. Cherlin suggests that the institution of marriage is losing its preeminence and may become just one of many relationship options for couples. Frank Furstenberg, on the other hand, proposes that the institution of marriage will persist with appropriate government policies and support to families.

Issue 16. Is Religion a Pure Good in Facilitating Well-Being during Adulthood? 316

YES: **David G. Myers**, from "Wanting More in an Age of Plenty," *Christianity Today* (April 2000) *318*

NO: **Julie Juola Exline**, from "Stumbling Blocks on the Religious Road: Fractured Relationships, Nagging Vices, and the Inner Struggle to Believe," *Psychological Inquiry* (vol. 13, 2002) *327*

Psychologist and author David Myers asserts that religion is an antidote to the discontent many adults feel despite incredible relative material wealth. Professor of psychology Julia Juola Exline asserts that research suggesting religion to be a pure good for adult development neglects to account for the fact that it can also be a source of significant sadness, stress, and confusion.

Issue 17. Are Professional Women "Opting Out" of Work by Choice? 339

YES: **Linda Hirshman**, from "Homeward Bound," *The American Prospect Online* (November 21, 2005) *341*

NO: **Pamela Stone**, from "The Rhetoric and Reality of 'Opting Out'," *Contexts* (Fall 2007) *351*

Scholar Linda Hirshman identifies as a feminist, but is frustrated with findings suggesting that successful and well-qualified women have put themselves in situations where it makes sense to prioritize parenthood over work. Sociologist Pamela Stone interviewed a different but also very successful sample of women who sacrificed careers for parenthood and found that while they perceived themselves to be making a choice, in fact they were tightly constrained by traditional gender roles and inflexible workplaces.

UNIT 7 LATER ADULTHOOD 363

Issue 18. Is More Civic Engagement Among Older Adults Necessarily Better? 364

YES: **Sheila R. Zedlewski and Barbara A. Butrica**, from "Are We Taking Full Advantage of Older Adults' Potential?" *Perspectives on Productive Aging* (Number 9, December 2007) *366*

NO: **Marty Martinson**, from "Opportunities or Obligations? Civic Engagement and Older Adults," *Generations* (Winter 2006–2007) *375*

Urban Institute researchers Sheila R. Zedlewski and Barbara A. Butrica, writing as part of a broader project to investigate the changing nature of retirement, argue that promoting civic engagement is good for both individuals and society. Critical gerontologist Marty Martinson acknowledges that promoting civic engagement in old age can be useful, but suggests that it also serves to shift attention away from broader social problems and responsibilities toward individuals who may or may not benefit from conventional civic engagement.

Issue 19. Is "Mild Cognitive Impairment" Too Similar to Normal Aging to be a Relevant Concept? 384

YES: **Janice E. Graham and Karen Ritchie,** from "Mild Cognitive Impairment: Ethical Considerations for Nosological Flexibility in Human Kinds," in *Philosophy, Psychiatry, & Psychology* (March 2006) *386*

NO: **Ronald C. Petersen,** from "Mild Cognitive Impairment Is Relevant," in *Philosophy, Psychiatry, & Psychology* (March 2006) *395*

Philosophers Janice E. Graham and Karen Ritchie raise concerns that rigidly defining Mild Cognitive Impairment (MCI) as a disorder associated with aging artificially creates the harmful impression that the conditions of old age are merely biomedical problems. Medical doctor and researcher Ronald C. Petersen has been a prominent proponent of defining MCI as an intermediate stage between normal aging and Alzheimer's disease. In this selection he counters Graham and Ritchie by emphasizing the usefulness of MCI as a diagnosis.

Issue 20. Should the Terminally Ill Be Able to Have Physicians Help Them Die? 402

YES: **Richard T. Hull,** from "The Case for Physician-Assisted Suicide," *Free Inquiry* (Spring 2003) *404*

NO: **Margaret A. Somerville,** from "The Case against Euthanasia and Physician-Assisted Suicide," *Free Inquiry* (Spring 2003) *408*

Philosopher Richard T. Hull claims that allowing physician-assisted suicide will appropriately give control over dying to patients and families rather than medical professionals. Ethicist Margaret Somerville instead asserts that allowing euthanasia oversimplifies the complex issues at the end of life, and allows people to ignore the imperative of providing appropriate care.

Contributors   414

Correlation Guide

The *Taking Sides* series presents current issues in a debate-style format designed to stimulate student interest and develop critical thinking skills. Each issue is thoughtfully framed with an issue summary, an issue introduction with points and counterpoints, and challenge questions. The pro and con essays—selected for their liveliness and substance—represent the arguments of leading scholars and commentators in their fields.

Taking Sides: Clashing Views in Life-Span Development, 2/e is an easy-to-use reader that presents issues on important topics such as *childhood obesity, self-esteem, and successful aging.* For more information on *Taking Sides* and other *McGraw-Hill Contemporary Learning Series* titles, visit www.mhcls.com.

This convenient guide matches the issues in **Taking Sides: Life-span Development**, 2/e with the corresponding chapters in two of our best-selling McGraw-Hill Life-Span Development textbooks by Santrock.

Taking Sides: Life-Span Development, 2/e	A Topical Approach to Life-Span Development, 4/e by Santrock	Essentials of Life-Span Development, 1/e by Santrock
Issue 1: Does the Cultural Environment Influence Life-Span Development More Than Our Genes?	**Chapter 2:** Biological Beginnings	**Chapter 4:** Socioemotional Development in Infancy
Issue 2: Are Peers More Important than Parents During the Process of Development?	**Chapter 15:** Peers and the Sociocultural World	**Chapter 10:** Socioemotional Development in Adolescence
Issue 3: Do Significant Innate Differences Influence the Career Success of Males and Females?	**Chapter 12:** Gender and Sexuality	
Issue 4: Does Prenatal Exposure to Drugs Such as Cocaine Create "Crack Babies" With Special Developmental Concerns?	**Chapter 2:** Biological Beginnings	**Chapter 2:** Biological Beginnings
Issue 5: Is There a "Myth of the First Three Years?"		**Chapter 5:** Physical and Cognitive Development in Early Childhood
Issue 6: Are There Good Reasons to Allow Infants to Consume Electronic Media, Such as Television?	**Chapter 15:** Peers and the Sociocultural World	**Chapter 6:** Socioemotional Development in Early Childhood
Issue 7: Is Advertising Responsible for Childhood Obesity?	**Chapter 4:** Health	

(Continued)

Taking Sides: Life-Span Development, 2/e	A Topical Approach to Life-Span Development, 4/e by Santrock	Essentials of Life-Span Development, 1/e by Santrock
Issue 8: Does Emphasizing Academic Skills Help At-Risk Preschool Children?	**Chapter 16:** Schools, Achievement, and Work	**Chapter 5:** Physical and Cognitive Development in Early Childhood
Issue 9: Is Attention Deficit Disorder (ADD/ADHD) a Legitimate Medical Condition That Affects Childhood Behavior?	**Chapter 16:** Schools, Achievement, and Work	**Chapter 7:** Physical and Cognitive Development in Middle and Late Childhood
Issue 10: Are Efforts to Improve Self-Esteem Misguided?	**Chapter 11:** The Self, Identity, and Personality	**Chapter 8:** Socioemotional Development in Middle and Late Childhood
Issue 11: Should Contemporary Adolescents Be Engaged in More Structured Activities?		
Issue 12: Does Violent Media Cause Teenage Aggression?	**Chapter 13:** Moral Development, Values, and Religion **Chapter 15:** Peers and the Sociocultural World	**Chapter 6:** Socioemotional Development in Early Childhood
Issue 13: Are Contemporary Young Adults More Selfish than Previous Generations?		
Issue 14: Are College Graduates Unprepared for Adulthood and the World of Work?	**Chapter 16:** Schools, Achievement, and Worky	**Chapter 11:** Physical and Cognitive Development in Early Adulthood
Issue 15: Is the Institution of Marriage at Risk?	**Chapter 14:** Families, Lifestyles, and Parenting	**Chapter 12:** Socioemotional Development in Early Adulthood
Issue 16: Can Lesbian and Gay Couples Be Appropriate Parents for Children?	**Chapter 14:** Families, Lifestyles, and Parenting	**Chapter 6:** Socioemotional Development in Early Childhood
Issue 17: Is Religion a Pure Good in Facilitating Well-Being During Adulthood?	**Chapter 13:** Moral Development, Values and Religion	**Chapter 13:** Physical and Cognitive Development in Middle Adulthood
Issue 18: Can We Universally Define "Successful Aging"?	**Chapter 15:** Peers and the Sociocultural World	**Chapter 16:** Socioemotional Development in Late Adulthood
Issue 19: Are Brain Exercises Unhelpful in Preventing Cognitive Decline in Old Age?	**Chapter 7:** Information Processing	**Chapter 15:** Physical and Cognitive Development in Late Adulthood
Issue 20: Should the Terminally Ill Be Able to Have Physicians Help Them Die?	**Chapter 17:** Death, Dying, and Grieving	**Chapter 17:** Death, Dying, and Grieving

Introduction

Thinking about Change

The study of life-span development centers on a question of great intuitive interest: Do people ever really change? Can an introverted child who is full of worry become a confident and composed adult? Might an apathetic student go on to become successful in the world of work? Do relationships with those we care about inevitably shift across the years?

These types of questions weighed heavily on my mind many years ago when I was a 17-year-old preparing to leave the only home I had ever known to attend college. On the night I was leaving, I rode to the airport with my father, a well-educated and thoughtful man. We were rushing so that I could board an overnight flight from the West Coast to the East Coast, bringing with me all my worldly possessions in two suitcases. As with so many adolescents going off to college, I was both excited and overwhelmed by possibilities. My imagination flowed with ideas about who and what I might become, and most of those ideas centered on a hope that I could change for the better. I loved the idea of self-improvement; I was devoted to developing into a "better person." As I talked with my father, expressing my hopes in anxious tones, he listened calmly. Finally, when we arrived at the gate and it was time for me to board my plane, my father looked at me casually and said, "You know, in my experience, people don't really change." I was stunned.

From his perspective as a mature adult, using the wisdom accumulated through his life, my father told me that while people might change the things they do, the places they live, the details of their daily routine, they do not change who they are in deep and substantive ways. With youthful idealism, I firmly disagreed. I felt deeply that people could change across the life-span, so much so that understanding aspects of that change became my life's work. Now, as a developmental psychologist, I've studied, read, and investigated many aspects of how people do and don't change. And in looking back I have to admit that in ways my father was right: in certain ways people don't change. But the story is much more complicated and wonderful than that. And that story is told through the study of life-span development: the study of patterns in human thought, feelings, and behavior in relation to particular ages, with general attention to change over time.

The study of life-span development makes clear that even the continuities in life, the things that do not change, take place in shifting contexts: changing social environments, changing physical capacities, changing psychological perspectives. As such, I've come to appreciate, and be fascinated by, the necessary interaction of change and continuity in people through their lives—how can people be both the same and different? That question involves inherent contradictions and inherent controversy, which suggests that the study of life-span development is particularly well-suited to the nature of this book: it advances by taking conflicting perspectives on complex and important issues regarding change and continuity through life.

History of the Study of Life-Span Development

Historically the question of how people do (or do not) change through their lives has evoked opposing perspectives. Many ancient societies assumed that people were created with a pre-determined character that was destined through some supernatural power. Yet those beliefs were tempered by the realization that what people experience matters. Parents, societies, and philosophers have long negotiated between an assumption that people have an inherent developmental destiny, and the knowledge that what happens to people in the social world can alter that destiny.

While these positions have an extensive history, in academic circles they are most commonly identified with 17th and 18th century European philosophers Jean-Jacques Rousseau and John Locke. Rousseau suggested that infants were "noble savages" born with an inherent nature that is only corrupted by society. Locke, in contrast, is known for the famous claim that people come into the world as a *tabula rasa*, or blank slate, to be shaped entirely by experience. In a recent book about the history of child rearing advice in America, Ann Hulbert argues this opposition plays itself out in many subsequent historical epochs: one group argues that people have potent natural dispositions guiding development with a strong hand, while another group asserts that people develop entirely through social experiences. The recurring nature of this opposition shows one way in which those who are concerned with life-span development have always been "taking sides."

Taking a scientific, rather than philosophical or parental, approach to understanding development has only become a widespread endeavor in recent centuries. In fact, the idea of childhood as a distinct life-span stage, rather than as just adulthood in miniature, may be a relatively recent invention. In a famous and controversial book titled *Centuries of Childhood,* French historian Philippe Aries argued that Western societies only began treating children as different from adults in the 15th and 16th centuries, and such treatment did not become commonplace until the 19th and 20th centuries. This theory has generated strong reactions, with many scholars responding to say that childhood has always been associated with distinct characteristics. Nevertheless, the idea that contemporary perspectives on childhood are historically exceptional has much support: the transition to worlds of adulthood with work and responsibility happens later than ever. Partially as a result, we now take for granted that people advance through different stages of life. Further, scholars and scientists from diverse fields of study recognize that the life-span needs to be understood within the context of those stages.

So what are the stages? That question turns out to be more complicated than many people expect. While we are always talking about "children," or "youth," or "middle-age," or the "elderly" the characteristics of such stages are not entirely distinct. Much of how we understand these stages depends upon earlier schemes.

Perhaps the most famous such scheme was presented by Sigmund Freud. In the late 19th century Freud provoked and dismayed Western society by proposing that unconscious experiences in very early childhood, often of a sexual nature, formed personality throughout the rest of the life-span. Freud further asserted that the formative experiences cohered around different foci at different ages: infants were concerned with oral gratification—being able to suck and bite, toddlers with anal functions and toilet training, young children with phallic organs—learning about gender roles, and teenagers with genital functions—experiencing puberty and a blossoming sexuality. For Freud, the way a person negotiated those foci influenced them for the rest of their lives. While there is a general consensus that Freud placed far too much emphasis on sexuality as the axis of all development, his theory contributed much. We now take for granted that early experiences shape later life, and we recognize that those experiences occur in a stagewise progression.

While Freud focused on personality development, another influential scientist working in the early and middle part of the 20th century turned scholarly attention to stages of cognitive development: the Swiss psychologist Jean Piaget virtually founded modern developmental psychology through his recognition that the way children think progresses in orderly patterns. Piaget based his provocative insight on rigorous observations suggesting that children's cognitive functioning (the way they think) develops naturally through a series of detached steps. In a way, Piaget provided enduring support for stage models, suggesting that children's thinking is not just less sophisticated than that of adults—it is qualitatively different. Thus, when children make assumptions about toy dolls being alive, or about objects only existing when they can see them, they are not making "errors" but instead are demonstrating patterns of thought that meaningfully represent their age. Piaget's work is still the standard for much research in child development, though some of his specific claims have become controversial. As such, several issues in this book explicitly reference the work and legacy of Piaget.

A third giant in the history of the study of life-span development was a student of Freud's named Erik Erikson. In the middle part of the 20th century Erikson took Freud's basic insights about personality, built on the increasing popularity of stage models for the life-span, and outlined an influential framework for understanding life-span development—a framework that guides the organization of this book. Erikson's model of the life-span had two major advantages over previous models. First, in contrast to Freud, Erikson reduced the emphasis on sexuality, focusing on psychosocial challenges rather than psychosexual stages. Second, in contrast to both Freud and Piaget, Erikson asserted that developmental stages continue throughout life, rather than ending after adolescence.

Though this now seems somewhat obvious—of course adults continue to develop—for much of the 20th century scholars paid little attention to anything other than child development. The implicit assumption was that the life-span included a period of rapid growth during childhood, a period of decline at the end of life, and was largely at stasis in the many years of adulthood. In recent decades, however, scholars have recognized that a great deal of patterned development and change occurs during the long years of adulthood.

Finally, Erik Erikson was influential because he recognized the "biopsychosocial" nature of life-span development. While biology, psychology, and society are often studied separately, biological factors (such as physical health, sexual maturation, and genetic predispositions) interact with psychological factors (such as personality, attitudes, and cognitive appraisals), which interact with social factors (such as schools, peer networks, the media, and cultural meaning systems) to craft our individual lives. Some of the issues addressed in this book involve all three of these types of influences, while some emphasize one or the other. Overall, however, the collection of issues as a whole represents diverse and interacting influences.

Modern advances in technology and research methods allow us to study biological, psychological, and sociological influences on the life-span with increasing depth and accuracy. But the contemporary issues covered in this book still rely upon some fundamental insights from history, and as such are organized by an idea shared by all the major scholars of life-span development: different ages associate with meaningfully different patterns of thought and behavior. Beyond that shared idea, however, no stage model proposed by any one leading scholar is perfect: the nature and definition of the stages remains controversial. Perhaps the only thing about stages of the life-span that we can say with certainty is that they are only as meaningful as the society in which they are used. Thus, it is important to consider the stages of life-span in their own historical and cultural context.

Stages of the Life-Span in Context

Representations of the life-span as a series of stages exist across centuries and across cultural traditions. These representations are interesting to consider both for their diversity and for their similarity. There is something universal about patterns of development, but there are also tremendous local differences in how those patterns look.

From an Eastern tradition, stages are represented in a parable about how Confucius, who lived between 551–479 BC, reflected on his life:

> At 15 I set my heart upon learning.
> At 30 I had planted my feet firmly upon the ground.
> At 40 I no longer suffered from perplexities.
> At 50 I knew what were the biddings of heaven.
> At 60 I heard them with docile ear.
> At 70 I could follow the dictates of my own heart; for what I desired no
> longer overstepped the boundaries of right.

From classic Western literature, Shakespeare articulated the life-span in his play "As You Like It" as different ages of man:

> At first the infant, Mewling and puking in the nurse's arms.
> And then the whining school-boy, with his satchel
> And shining morning face, creeping like snail
> Unwillingly to school.

And then the lover,
Sighing like furnace, with a woeful ballad
Made to his mistress' eyebrow.
Then a soldier,
Full of strange oaths and bearded like the pard,
Jealous in honour, sudden and quick in quarrel,
Seeking the bubble reputation
Even in the cannon's mouth.
And then the justice,
In fair round belly with good capon lined,
With eyes severe and beard of formal cut,
Full of wise saws and modern instances;
And so he plays his part.
The sixth age shifts
Into the lean and slipper'd pantaloon,
With spectacles on nose and pouch on side,
His youthful hose, well saved, a world too wide
For his shrunk shank; and his big manly voice,
Turning again toward childish treble, pipes
And whistles in his sound.
Last scene of all,
That ends this strange eventful history,
Is second Childishness and mere oblivion,
Sans teeth, sans eyes, sans taste, sans everything.

From one of the great books of religion, "The Sayings of the Fathers" in the *Talmud* set out the life-span as marked by specific ages:

5 years is the age for reading;
10 for Mishnah (the laws);
13 for the Commandments (moral reasoning);
15 for Gemara (Talmudic discussions—abstract reasoning);
18 for Hupa (wedding canopy);
20 for seeking a livelihood;
30 for attaining full strength;
40 for understanding;
50 for giving counsel;
60 for becoming an elder;
70 for white hair;
80 for Gevurah (new, special strength of age);
90 for being bent under the weight of the years;
100 for being as if already dead and passed away from the world

And finally in modern society, beyond academia, we represent the life-span in advertising and different consumer choices—as in advertisements for Farmers' Insurance suggesting that the stages of the life-span focus on:

Buying a Car,
Buying a Home,
Getting Married,
Having a Baby,

Beginning Driver,
Sending a Child to College,
Starting a Business,
Planning your Retirement.

Regardless of the source or the historical period, most people find something that resonates in all of these representations. Yet history also teaches us that stages are not universal; in fact, the life-span could easily be represented simply as one continuous stage. There are, however, several reasons that dividing the life-span into multiple stages proves useful. For one thing, the life-span is extraordinarily complex, and categorizing information into smaller groups helps make it feel more manageable and less daunting. Likewise, learning about ordered change that seems consistent across different people and groups helps to make sense of what is fundamental in development. If, for example, we find that the teen years are tumultuous and stressful in all societies then we can reasonably suspect that there is something fundamental about development during that age.

As it turns out, in the case of adolescence, many components of development vary significantly in different societies—adolescence is not tumultuous for all teens around the world, and thus it seems that the "storm and stress" of adolescence is at least partially a social and cultural construction. In fact, even the definition of stages is not as simple as it might first appear. Adolescence, for example, was not considered a major stage of the life-span until the end of the 19th century, when the broadening of educational opportunities created a longer transition between childhood and adulthood. In contemporary Western society some scholars have proposed that the continuing expansion of higher education and longer transition to independent adulthood has created another "new stage" of something like "emerging adulthood." In some senses, then, the very nature of the stages in the life-span is controversial.

Even placing the term "life-span" in front of the word "development" generates disagreement. The notion of a life-span suggests a progressive and constrained period of time that some scholars feel unfairly minimizes the disjointed and social nature of development. Thus, some people prefer the term "life-course" as more accurately representing the twists and turns of development that necessarily occurs in a social world. Still others prefer the term "life-cycle" as more accurately representing the sequential process that brings people through a full circle of growth and decline.

Ultimately, despite viable alternatives, this book is organized into seven parts. The first part covers general issues in the study of life-span development and the other six parts invoke a basic set of life-span stages: prenatal and infancy, early and middle childhood, adolescence, youth and early adulthood, middle adulthood, and later adulthood. The issues discussed in relation to these stages can, however, equally be considered topically. Though there are multiple ways of topically organizing the issues in this book, several possible examples include:

- Focusing on the topic of cognitive development and intellectual ability by combining Issue 3 (regarding the cognitive abilities of men and women), Issue 8 (regarding the types of abilities necessary to help at-risk preschool children), and Issue 19 (regarding brain exercises and cognitive decline in old age).

- Focusing on physical health and development by combining Issue 4 (regarding consumption of alcohol during pregnancy), Issue 7 (regarding childhood obesity), Issue 10 (regarding the importance of structured activities for adolescents), and Issue 18 (regarding civic engagement among older adults).

- Focusing on parenting by combining Issue 2 (regarding the relative influence of parents and peers upon development), Issue 6 (regarding whether infants should be exposed to electronic media), and Issue 17 (regarding women "opting out" of work to focus on parenting).

Fundamental Questions

Regardless of how the issues are organized, several questions underlie the topics in this book. First is a question that runs across the social sciences, but that is particularly relevant to thinking about development: the question of nature or nurture? Is life-span development more a product of natural and biological dispositions, or is development the result of nurturing experiences in the world? This question has become particularly contentious with the advent of modern technology that allows researchers to map genetic codes and produce detailed images of mental activity. It is clear that human thought, feeling, and behavior all originate in a biological organ: the brain. Yet scientists are actively debating what aspect of the brain activity that guides such thought, feeling, and behavior comes from biological programs and what comes from learned concepts. It is obvious that we are products of both nature and nurture, but the necessary balance for life-span development is the subject of tremendous controversy. This question is implicit in most of the issues in this book, while being explicitly addressed in Issue 1 (regarding the relative influence of culture and genes), Issue 5 (regarding the importance of external stimulation during the first three years), and Issue 9 (regarding the nature of Attention Deficit Disorder), and Issue 11 (regarding the cause of adolescent risk taking).

A second fundamental question relates to the role of culture. While cultural differences and diversity are genuine, it is not clear whether culture fundamentally alters patterns of development. Can we apply research about human development in a city in the United States to human development in rural India? Could we even apply research from urban cities to the rural United States? Could we apply knowledge equally to males and females? Implicit in many studies of life-span development is the idea that there is a "best" pattern of development. But what if there is no one best pattern of development, only patterns of development that are more or less appropriate to different cultural settings and groups? Does that invalidate the effort of finding general principles of life-span development? This question is fundamental to most of the issues in this book, being directly addressed in Issue 2 (regarding the influence of parents on development), Issue 12 (regarding generational changes in narcissism, and Issue 15 (regarding general changes in the institution of marriage).

A third fundamental question fits best with the issue raised at the start of this introduction: do people really change? As noted earlier, development is a process of both continuity and change. Yet, the above models of stages in the life-span suggest that each stage is a discrete entity. But are they? Where does one stage begin and another end? When teaching about the life-span I often ask my traditionally college-aged undergraduate students whether they are adults—they usually are not entirely sure. They are kind of adults, kind of adolescents, kind of kids. So when do they become adults? Do they just wake up one day and there they are? Of course not; becoming an adult is a slow and gradual process. Further, the very idea that what happens to us as children has a direct impact on how we turn out in later life suggests a continuous process of development. If it were not, we wouldn't care so much about the quality of schools, parenting, and programs for children.

Yet when we step back we can all acknowledge that there are clear differences between children and adults, and between younger adults and older adults. Those differences are not just physical; there are differences in the way people think, and the contexts in which they live their lives. The question of whether it is best to conceptualize the life-span as one continuous process, or as a series of discrete stages, is particularly important in our increasingly specialized society where products, services, and interactions are guided by understandings of people at specific ages. The question also influences numerous scholarly debates, and as such it orients several of the issues in this book including Issue 5 (regarding the developmental importance of infancy), Issue 8 (regarding academic skills for at-risk preschool children), and Issue 13 (regarding the preparation of college graduates for adulthood).

The Uses of Controversy

The fundamental questions for the study of life-span development continuously manifest themselves in different and specific topical controversies. While this process can be occasionally confusing and frustrating to those who want to know the "right" answers about development, controversy is how our knowledge of the life-span advances. Over time, controversies spark knowledge and ideas that are central to all of our lives. There are several prominent historical examples of how this works.

One example comes from the start of the life-span: what happens to newborn babies? Prior to advances in medical technology during the 20th century, an extraordinarily high number of babies died before reaching their first birthday (sadly, this is still the case in many parts of the developing world—but that is a slightly different issue). When the germ theory of disease became prominent, doctors and scientists realized that inadequate hygiene and unnecessary exposure to germs caused many infant deaths. In a well-intentioned effort to keep babies safe and healthy, many hospitals started keeping babies in sterile conditions separate from human contact. Over time, such efforts were extended to children born to mothers who were considered deviant, such as those convicted of crimes. The logic in all these cases was that of contagion: certain types of human contact were too risky for vulnerable infants.

Fortunately, this logic was controversial, and researchers studying the earliest stages of life began to challenge the new scientifically based practices. Studies of children removed at birth from their mothers demonstrated remarkable physical, social, and psychological deficits. Researchers began to hypothesize that something about human contact, and forming an attachment bond, was virtually essential to healthy human development. For many years controversy raged; with one side suggesting that infants needed to be kept safely away from excessive contact, and the other suggesting that human contact was exactly what made infants safe. Eventually the evidence became overwhelming in favor of the latter position; the debate promoted scholarship demonstrating irrefutably that babies have an innate need for attachment, contact, and simple touch. Without any controversy we would not possess that essential knowledge.

In a more contemporary example, recent decades have brought increasing attention to the role of self-esteem in life-span development. Due to a confluence of historical and social conditions, the idea that feeling good about one's self is a foundation for healthy development became received wisdom in the 1970s and 1980s. Numerous social service agencies, schools, activity programs, and therapists made promoting self-esteem the centerpiece of efforts to facilitate healthy development. While self-esteem is still extremely popular— as it is indeed nice to feel good about one's self—scholars have generated controversy by raising important questions about the evidence for self-esteem as a cure for social and personal ills. Despite massive research attention, the evidence that self-esteem alone provides a direct foundation for healthy development is sorely lacking. Though a virtual industry of self-esteem promoters has resisted the challenge, the controversy continues to have important implications for schools, counselors, parents, and programs. And for scholars the controversy has generated a much more nuanced and realistic perspective on how and why feeling good about one's self might matter.

In both of these examples, and in most of the issues discussed in this book, controversy provides useful knowledge when scholars and individuals combine a genuine interest in facilitating healthy life-span development with a concern for tangible evidence. In the case of infant attachment and touch, both sides cared about healthy babies and both sides deeply believed their side was right. In the case of self-esteem and positive development, both sides care about reducing social ills and both sides believe in what they are doing. Ultimately, however, resolving these issues, and resolving other controversies in social science, requires intelligent interpretations of evidence that go beyond taken-for-granted beliefs.

Our taken-for-granted beliefs are strong and pervasive, partially because many of the issue questions in this book relate to issues people confront in their daily lives; we are all experienced in our own process of development. As such, when considering these questions it is natural to have instinctive reactions and beliefs. The material in this book will, however, be most useful when readers get beyond initial beliefs to carefully consider the points and the evidence. In fact, when I teach about these issues I do not allow my students to make statements that start with "I believe . . . " or "In my opinion . . . " While

I value the importance of students' beliefs and opinions, the controversies that we study must be evaluated primarily in regard to available evidence. Evidence is the foundation of scientific understanding, even though it may contradict deeply held beliefs. But much educational value lies in the space between evidence and beliefs: I hope that both my students, and those who read this book, are able to learn what scholars know and apply that knowledge to form educated positions on issues of great importance in contemporary society.

Conclusion

Ultimately, focusing on evidence and carefully considering intelligent positions from all viewpoints is how I have dealt with the challenge posed by my father when I was starting my own college experience: concluding that people do indeed change. While my own approach has focused on developmental psychology, the evidence and intelligent positions in this book come from diverse sources because the study of life-span development takes many perspectives. A partial list of the academic disciplines that both contribute to and draw from the study of life-span development might include: psychology, sociology, anthropology, education, social work, biology, history, cognitive science, geriatrics, and pediatrics. Thus, the readings and positions in this book represent quality work from many fields. Clear and quality thinking about controversial issues is not limited to any particular academic approach.

As you consider the issues in this book, reflecting on the questions raised in this introduction may facilitate your own clear and quality thinking. Ask yourself, for example, about how each issue relates to what you know or imagine from your own experience regarding each stage of the life-span? Ask yourself how much nature and nurture play a role in influencing the different developmental issues? Ask yourself about the social and policy implications of taking specific positions on each issue. And keep in mind that vexing question raised by so many people starting to learn about life-span development: Do people really change?

Engaging with these issues has certainly helped me change: I've become a better scholar of life-span development, and my hope is that readers will have a similar experience. I'd like for readers to experience some small level of change in their own development by earnestly confronting the different sides of these controversial issues. By keeping in mind the history of the field, the useful but historically particular nature of defining life-span stages, the fundamental questions underlying most controversies, and the value of controversy for advancing knowledge, readers should indeed be able to experience change firsthand.

Internet References . . .

Developmental Psychology Resources

This Web site provides academic resources and links related to developmental psychology.

http://www.psy.pdx.edu/PsiCafe/Areas/Developmental/

The American Psychological Association

The American Psychological Association is a general resource for many of the issues most pertinent to developmental psychology and life-span development.

http://www.apa.org/

Nature Versus Nurture

This provides an overview of the debate on whether nature or nurture, culture or genes, is more influential in life-span development.

http://en.wikipedia.org/wiki/Nature_versus_nurture

The American Academy of Pediatrics

The American Academy of Pediatrics is a professional organization focused on the health of children. Their Web site provides featured articles, books, and other reference materials on children's health topics.

http://www.aap.org/

The Nurture Assumption

This Web site provides extensive links related to the controversial argument that parents do not matter as much in development as most people think.

http://home.att.net/~xchar/tna/

Future of Children

Future of Children is a digital journal, providing an example of developmental research aimed at promoting effective policies and programs for families and children.

http://www.futureofchildren.org/

General Issues in the Study of Life-Span Development

*A*lthough this book organizes development into a series of stages, several issues central to understanding the life-span are not exclusive to one particular age. These issues relate to larger questions about the nature of development: what forces and characteristics shape us into the people we become? The issues in this section deal with this larger question, and provide a foundation for thinking about specific stages, by directly addressing the role of culture, genes, parents, and sex/gender in shaping the thoughts, feelings, behaviors, and experiences that make us human.

- Does the Cultural Environment Influence Lifespan Development More than Our Genes?

- Are Peers More Important than Parents during the Process of Development?

- Do Significant Innate Differences Influence the Career Success of Males and Females?

ISSUE 1

Does the Cultural Environment Influence Lifespan Development More than Our Genes?

YES: Paul Ehrlich and Marcus Feldman, from "Genes and Cultures: What Creates Our Behavioral Phenome?" *Current Anthropology* (February 2003)

NO: Gary Marcus, from "Making the Mind: Why We've Misunderstood the Nature-Nurture Debate," *Boston Review* (December 2003/January 2004)

ISSUE SUMMARY

YES: Stanford University professors of biology Paul Ehrlich and Marcus Feldman argue that human behavior exhibits such complexity that genetic programs simply can't explain the way people develop.

NO: Psychologist and researcher Gary Marcus asserts that research clearly demonstrates how a relatively small number of genes influence our environmental learning by "cascading" to determine the paths of our behavioral development.

$\mathbf{P}$erhaps the most central question in the study of lifespan development is whether nature or nurture exerts more influence on our developing thoughts, feelings, and behavior. Even in daily life, we regularly wonder about people—do they act that way because of things in their experience (nurture), or is it just the way they were born (nature)? This debate takes many different forms, and it underlies many of the important topics of study within lifespan development.

Most reasonable people agree that both nature and nurture, both genes and culture, shape development. Thus, the debate is mostly about the relative influence of each: does nature overwhelm nurture, or does nurture trump nature. Historically, the pendulum of popular opinion has tended to swing back and forth between trusting nature or emphasizing nurture.

In recent years, with advanced technology and research methods, the pendulum seems to have swung in favor of nature. With the ability to identify

2

individual genes and image activity in the brain, scientists have made regular claims about how diverse aspects of behavior and development—everything from political affiliation to sexual behavior—are controlled by innate biology.

In the first of the following selections, however, renowned biologists Paul Ehrlich and Marcus Feldman argue that biological determinism, the idea that evolved predispositions determine behavior beyond the influence of the environment, does not make biological sense. Drawing from the recent mapping of the human genome, they claim there are simply too few genes and too much variation in human development. They take particular aim at claims that gender differences are biological, which has been an important part of this debate because gender differences often seem to persist despite diverse environments. Ehrlich and Feldman, however, claim that in looking at the grand scheme of history the clear variations in behavior patterns belie a biological explanation.

In contrast, New York University professor of psychology Gary Marcus claims that the dominant influence of genes on development has only become more clear in recent research. While acknowledging that genes and the environment always interact, Marcus draws on extensive research with animals demonstrating that small genetic manipulations have dramatic influences on behavior. He also responds to the claim that there are not enough genes to control complex behaviors by insisting that relationships between genes and behavior don't have to be one to one. Genes often interact, or "cascade," in various patterns that account for a massive number of developmental outcomes.

POINT

- There are simply too few genes to explain all of the complexity in human development.
- While gender differences are frequently cited as having a genetic base, there is actually significant historical variation in what is considered "normal" behavior for each gender.
- Focusing on the genetic causes of behavior and development has led to horrible social policies such as those of the Nazis during World War II.

COUNTERPOINT

- Genes do not influence behavior individually, but rather through nearly infinite combinations.
- Small genetic differences in animals create large differences in behavior patterns.

- While our brains are "plastic" in the sense of changing through development, those changes are constrained by genetic limits.

YES ←

Paul Ehrlich and
Marcus Feldman

Genes and Cultures: What Creates Our Behavioral Phenome?

The recent publication of the first draft of the human genome has brought to public attention the relationship between two concepts, genotype and phenotype—a relationship that had previously been discussed largely by academics. The genotype of an organism is encoded in the DNA that is held in chromosomes and other structures inside its cells. The phenotype is what we are able to observe about that organism's biochemistry, physiology, morphology, and behaviors. We will use the term "phenome" to circumscribe a set of phenotypes whose properties and variability we wish to study. Our focus will be on that part of the human phenome that is defined by behaviors and especially on the behavioral phenome's connection with the human genome.

Our understanding of human behavioral traits has evolved; explanations of the control of those traits offered 50 years ago differ from those most common today. In prewar decades genetic determinism—the idea that genes are destiny—had enormous influence on public policy in many countries: on American immigration and racial policies, Swedish sterilization programs, and, of course, Nazi laws on racial purity. Much of this public policy was built on support from biological, medical, and social scientists, but after Hitler's genocidal policies it was no longer politically correct to focus on putative hereditary differences. The fading of genetic determinism was an understandable reaction to Nazism and related racial, sexual, and religious prejudices which had long been prevalent in the United States and elsewhere. Thus, after World War II, it became the norm in American academia to consider all of human behavior as originating in the environment—in the way people were raised and the social contexts in which they lived.

Gradually, though, beginning in the 1960s, books like Robert Ardrey's *Territorial Imperative* and Desmond Morris's *The Naked Ape* began proposing explanations for human behaviors that were biologically reductionist and essentially genetic. Their extreme hereditarian bias may have been stimulated by the rapid progress at that time in understanding of the role of DNA, which spurred interest in genetics in both scientists and the public. But perhaps no publication had broader effect in reestablishing genetic credibility in the behavioral sciences than Arthur Jensen's article "How Much Can We Boost IQ?" Although roundly criticized by quantitative geneticists and shown to be based on the fraudulent data of Sir Cyril Burt, Jensen's work established a tradition

From *Current Anthropology*, vol. 44, no. 1, February 2003, pp. 87–89, 92–95. Copyright © 2003 by University of Chicago Press via the Copyright Clearance Center. Reprinted by permission.

that attempts to allocate to genetics a considerable portion of the variation in such human behaviors as for whom we vote, how religious we are, how likely we are to take risks, and, of course, measured IQ and school performance. This tradition is alive and well today.

Within the normal range of human phenotypic variation, including commonly occurring diseases, the role of genetics remains a matter of controversy even as more is revealed about variation at the level of DNA. Here we would like to reexamine the issue of genetics and human behavior in light of the enormous interest in the Human Genome Project, the expansion of behavioral genetics as described above, and the recent proliferation of books emphasizing the genetic programming of every behavior from rape to the learning of grammar. The philosopher Helena Cronin and her coeditor, Oliver Curry, tell us in the introduction to Yale University Press's "Darwinism Today" series that "Darwinian ideas . . . are setting today's intellectual agenda." In the *New York Times*, Nicholas Wade has written that human genes contain the "behavioral instructions" for "instincts to slaughter or show mercy, the contexts for love and hatred, the taste for obedience or rebellion—they are the determinants of human nature."

Genes, Cultures, and Behavior

It is incontrovertible that human beings are a product of evolution, but with respect to behavior that evolutionary process involves chance, natural selection, and, especially in the case of human beings, transmission and alteration of a body of extragenetic information called "culture." Cultural evolution, a process very different from genetic evolution by natural selection, has played a central role in producing our behaviors.

This is not to say that genes are uninvolved in human behavior. *Every* aspect of a person's phenome is a product of interaction between genome and environment. An obvious example of genetic involvement in the behavioral phenome is the degree to which most people use vision to orient themselves— in doing everything from hitting a baseball to selecting new clothes for their children. This is because we have evolved genetically to be "sight animals"— our dominant perceptual system is vision, with hearing coming in second. Had we, like dogs, evolved more sophisticated chemical detection, we might behave very differently in response to the toxic chemicals in our environment. The information in our DNA required to produce the basic morphology and physiology that make sight so important to us has clearly been molded by natural selection. And the physical increase in human brain size, which certainly involved a response to natural selection (although the precise environmental factors causing this selection remain something of a mystery, has allowed us to evolve language, a high level of tool use, the ability to plan for the future, and a wide range of other behaviors not seen in other animals.

Thus at the very least, genetic evolution both biased our ability to perceive the world and gave us the capacity to develop a vast culture. But the long-running nature-versus-nurture debate is not about sight versus smell. It is about the degree to which differences in today's human behavioral patterns from person to person, group to group, and society to society are influenced by genetic differences, that is, are traceable to differences in human genetic endowments. Do men "naturally" want to mate with as many women as possible while women "naturally" want to be more cautious in choosing their copulatory partners? Is there a "gay gene"? Are human beings "innately" aggressive? Are differences in educational achievement or income "caused" by differences in genes? And are people of all groups genetically programmed to be selfish? A critical social issue to keep in mind throughout our discussion is what the response of our society would be if we knew the answer to these questions. Two related schools of thought take the view that genetic evolution explains much of the human behavioral phenome; they are known as evolutionary psychology and behavioral genetics.

Evolutionary Psychology

Evolutionary psychology claims that many human behaviors became universally fixed as a result of natural selection acting during the environment of evolutionary adaptation, essentially the Pleistocene. A shortcoming of this argument, as emphasized by the anthropologist Robert Foley (1995–96), lies in the nonexistence of such an environment. Our ancestors lived in a wide diversity of habitats, and the impacts of the many environmental changes (e.g., glaciations) over the past million years differed geographically among their varied surroundings. Evolutionary psychologists also postulate that natural selection produced modules ("complex structures that are functionally organized for processing information") in the brain that "tell" us such things as which individuals are likely to cheat, which mates are likely to give us the best or most offspring, and how to form the best coalitions. These brain "modules," which are assumed to be biological entities fixed in humans by evolution, also have other names often bestowed on them by the same writers, such as "computational machines," "decision-making algorithms," "specialized systems," "inference engines," and "reasoning mechanisms." The research claims of evolutionary psychology have been heavily criticized by, among others, colleagues in psychology.

　　Those critics are correct. There is a general tendency for evolutionary psychologists vastly to overestimate how much of human behavior is primarily traceable to biological universals that are reflected in our genes. One reason for this overestimation is the ease with which a little evolutionary story can be invented to explain almost any observed pattern of behavior. For example, it seems logical that natural selection would result in the coding of a fear of snakes and spiders into our DNA, as the evolutionary psychologist Steven Pinker thinks. But while Pinker may have genes that make him fear snakes, as the evolutionist Jared Diamond points out, such genes are clearly lacking in New Guinea natives. As Diamond says, "If there is any single place in the world where we might expect an innate fear of snakes among native peoples, it would be in New Guinea, where one-third or more of the snake species are poisonous, and certain non-poisonous constrictor snakes are sufficiently big to be dangerous." Yet there is no sign of innate fear of snakes or spiders among the indigenous people, and children regularly "capture large spiders, singe off the legs and hairs, and eat the bodies. The people there laugh at the idea of an inborn phobia about snakes, and account for the fear in Europeans as a result of their stupidity in being unable to distinguish which snakes might be dangerous." Furthermore, there is reason to believe that fear of snakes in other primates is largely learned as well.

Another example is the set of predictions advanced by Bruce Ellis about the mating behavior that would be found in a previously unknown culture. The first five characteristics that "the average woman in this culture will seek . . . in her ideal mate," he predicts, are:

1. He will be dependable, emotionally stable and mature, and kind/considerate toward her.
2. He will be generous. He may communicate a spirit of caring through a willingness to share time and whatever commodities are valued in this culture with the woman in question.
3. He will be ambitious and perceived by the woman in question as clever or intelligent.
4. He will be genuinely interested in the woman in question, and she in him. He may express his interest through displays of concern for her well-being.
5. He will have a strong social presence and be well liked and respected by others. He will possess a strong sense of efficacy, confidence, and self-respect.

Evolutionary theory does not support such predictions, even if an "average woman" could be defined. First of all, it would be no small developmental trick genetically to program detailed, different, and *independent* reproductive strategies into modules in male and female brains. Those brains, after all are minor variants of the same incredibly complex structures, and, furthermore, the degree to which they are organized into modules is far from clear. If the women in the unknown culture actually chose mates meeting Ellis's criteria, a quite sufficient alternative evolutionary explanation would be that women (simultaneously with men) have evolved big brains, are not stupid, and respond to the norms of their cultures. Scientifically, the notion that the detailed attributes of desirable mates must be engraved in our genetic makeup is without basis, especially in light of the enormous cultural differences in sexual preferences.

For any culture, Ellis's evolutionary arguments would require that in past populations of women there were DNA-based differences that made some more likely to choose in those ways and others more likely to seek mates with other characteristics. And those that chose as Ellis predicts would have to have borne and raised more children that survived to reproduce than those with other preferences. Might, for example, a woman who married a stingy male who kept her barefoot and pregnant out-reproduce the wife of a generous and considerate mate? That is the way genetic evolution changes the characteristics of populations over time: by some genetic variants' out-reproducing others. When that happens, we say that natural selection has occurred.

But, unfortunately, there are no data that speak to whether there is (or was) genetic variation in human mate preferences—variation in, say, ability to evaluate specifically whether a potential mate is "ambitious"—upon which selection could be based. And there are no data for any population showing that women who seek those characteristics in their sexual partners are more successful reproductively—are represented by more children in the subsequent generation—than women who seek husbands with other characteristics. Ellis is simply confusing the preferences of women he knows in his society with evolutionary fitness. . . .

What Does Determine the Behavioral Phenome?

Geneticists know that a large portion of the behavioral phenome must be programmed into the brain by factors in the environment, including the internal environment in which the fetus develops and, most important, the cultural environment in which human beings spend their entire lives. Behavioral scientists know, for instance, that many dramatic personality differences *must* be traced to environmental influences. Perhaps the most important reason to doubt that genetic variation accounts for a substantial portion of observed differences in human behavior is simply that we lack an extensive enough hereditary apparatus to do the job—that we have a "gene shortage." To what extent could genes control the production of these differences?

It is important to remember that behaviors are the results of charge changes that occur in our network of neurons, the specialized cells that make up our nervous system. Behaviors are ultimately under some degree of control in the brain. Neuron networks are the locus of the memories that are also important to our behavior. That genes can control some general patterns is unquestioned; they are obviously involved in the construction of our brains. They might therefore also build in the potential for experience to affect a large part of the details involved in the neural circuitry. But they cannot be controlling our individual behavioral choices.

Human beings have only three times as many genes as have fruit flies (many of those genes appear to be duplicates of those in the flies, and the biochemistry of fly nerve cells seems quite close to ours). But in addition to having sex and eating (what flies mostly do) we get married, establish charities, build hydrogen bombs, commit genocide, compose sonatas, and publish books on evolution. It is a little hard to credit all this to the determining action of those few additional genes. Those genes are, however, likely to have contributed to the increased brain size and complexity that support the vast cultural superstructure created by the interaction of our neurons and their environments. They may also contribute to the wonderful flexibility and plasticity of human behavior—the very attributes that make our behavior less rather than more genetically determined. But to understand the development of and variation in specific human behaviors such as creating charities and cheesecakes, we must invoke culture, its evolution, and its potential interaction with biology.

It might be argued that since a relative handful of genes can control our basic body plan—one's height depends on millions of the body's cells' being stacked precisely—a handful could also determine our behavioral phe-nome. Genes initiate a process of development that might be analogized with the way a mountain stream entering a floodplain can initiate the develop-ment of a complex delta. Why, then, couldn't just a few genes have evolved to program millions of our behaviors? In theory they might have, but in that case human behavior would be very stereotyped. Consider the problem of evolving human behavioral flexibility under such circumstances of genetic determination. Changing just one behavioral pattern—say, making women more desirous of mating with affluent men—would be somewhat analogous to changing the course of one distributary (branch in the delta) without alter-ing the braided pattern of the rest of the delta. It would be difficult to do by just changing the flow of the mountain stream (equivalent to changing the genes) but easily accomplished by throwing big rocks in the distributary (changing the environment).

This partial analogy seems particularly apt in that it is apparently diffi-cult for evolution to accomplish just one thing at a time. There are two princi-pal reasons for this. The first is the complexity of interactions among alleles and phenotypic traits, especially pleiotropy and epistasis. Because there are relatively so few of them, most genes must be involved in more than one process (pleiot-ropy). Then if a mutation leads to better functioning of one process, it may not be selected for because the change might degrade the functioning of another process. And changes in one gene can modify the influence of another in very complex ways (epistasis). Second, because they are physically coupled to other genes on the same chromosome, the fates of genes are not independent. Selec-tion that increases the frequency of one allele in a population will often, because of linkage, necessarily increase the frequency of another. Selection favoring a gene that made one prefer tall mates might also result in the increase of a nearby gene that produced greater susceptibility to a childhood cancer.

The Mysteries of Environmental Control

Behavioral scientists are still, unhappily, generally unable to determine the key environmental factors that influence the behavioral phenome. For instance, in the case of the Dionne quintuplets, quite subtle environmental differences—perhaps initiated by different positions in the womb or chance interactions among young quints, their parents, and their observers—clearly led to sub-stantially different behavioral and health outcomes in five children with iden-tical genomes. As their story shows, we really know very little about what environmental factors can modify behavior. For example, some virtually undetectable differences in environments may be greatly amplified as devel-oping individuals change their own environments and those of their siblings. Equally, subtle and undetected environmental factors may put individuals with the same genetic endowments on similar life courses even if they are reared apart, perhaps explaining anecdotes about the similarities of some reunited identical twins.

We also know too little about the routes through which genes may influ-ence behavior, where again changes may be behaviorally amplified. Suppose that a study shows that identical twins, separated at birth, nonetheless show a high correlation of personality type—both members of twin pairs tend to be either introverted or extraverted. This is interpreted as a high heritability of introversion and extraversion. What really is heavily influenced by genetics, however, could be height, and tall people in that society (as in many societies) may be better treated by their peers and thus more likely to become extra-verted. Genes in this case will clearly be involved in personality type but by such an indirect route as to make talk of "genes for introversion or extraver-sion" essentially meaningless.

And, of course, scientists *do* know that what appears to be "genetic" is often simply a function of the environment. An example suggested by the philosopher Elliott Sober illustrates this. In England before the 18th century, evolutionary psychologists (had there been any) would have assumed that males had a genetic proclivity for knitting. The knitting gene would have been assumed to reside on the Y chromosome. But by the 19th century, evolution-ary psychologists would have claimed that women had that genetic proclivity, with the knitting gene on the X chromosome. With historical perspective, we can see that the change was purely culture-driven, not due to a genetic change. As it did with knitting, the environment, especially the cultural environment, seems to do a good job of fine-tuning our behavior. A major challenge for sci-ence today is to elucidate how that fine-tuning occurs.

Would Selection Generally Favor Genetic Control of Behavior?

Would we be better off if we had more than enough genes to play a con-trolling role in every one of our choices and actions and those genes could operate independently? Probably not. One could imagine a Hobbesian battle in which genes would compete with each other to improve the performance of the reproducing individuals that possessed them—genes for caution being favored in one environment one day and genes for impulsiveness in another environment the next ("Look before you leap," "He who hesitates is lost"). It is difficult to imagine how *any* organism could make the grade evolutionarily if its behavior were completely genetically determined and interactions between its genes and its environments did not exist. Even single-celled organisms respond to changes in their surroundings. Without substantial environmental inputs, evolution would not occur and life could not exist.

Biological evolution has avoided that problem by allowing our behav-ior to be deeply influenced by the environments in which genes operate. In normal human environments, genes are heavily involved in creating a basic brain with an enormous capacity for learning—taking in information from the environment and incorporating that information into the brain's structure. It is learning that proceeds after birth as an infant's brain uses inputs such as pat-terns of light from the eyes to wire up the brain so that it can see, patterns of sound that wire up the brain so that it can speak one or more languages, and so on. As the brain scientist John Allman put it, "the brain is unique among the organs of the body in requiring a great deal of feedback from experience to develop its full capacities." And the situation is not so different for height. There aren't enough genes to control a child's growth rate from day to day—adding cells rapidly in favorable (e.g., food-rich) situations and slowly or not at all under starvation. And there aren't enough genes to govern the growth of each column of cells, some to regulate those in each column on the right side of the spine, some for each in the left. Instead, all growth patterns depend on environmental feedback. . . .

Conclusions

What the recent evidence from the Human Genome Project tells us is that the interaction between genes, between the separate components of genes, and between controlling elements of these separate components must be much more complex than we ever realized. Simple additive models of gene action or of the relationship between genes and environments must be revised. They have formed the basis for our interpretation of phenotype-genotype relationships for 84 years, ever since R. A. Fisher's famous paper that for the first time related Mendelian genes to measurable phenotypes. New models and paradigms are needed to go from the genome to the phenome in any quantitative way. The simplistic approach of behavioral genetics cannot do the job. We must dig deeper into the environmental and especially cultural factors that contribute to the phenome. The ascendancy of molecular biology has, unintentionally, militated against progress in studies of cultural evolution.

Theories of culture and its evolution in the 20th century, from Boas's insistence on the particularity of cultural identities to the debates between material and cultural determinism described by Sahlins, were proudly nonquantitative. Recent discussions on the ideational or symbolic nature of the subjects of cultural evolution, while critical of attempts to construct dynamical models of cultural evolution based on individual-to-individual cultural transmission, nevertheless acknowledge the centrality of cultural evolution to human behavioral analysis. Thus, although the quantitative paradigms used in behavioral genetics do not inform evolutionary analysis, this does not mean that we cannot or should not take an evolutionary approach to the understanding and modification of human behavior. Genetically evolved features such as the dominance of our visual sense should always be kept in mind, but an evolutionary approach to changing behavior in our species must primarily focus on *cultural* evolution. In the last 40,000 years or so, the scale of that cultural evolution has produced a volume of information that dwarfs what is coded into our genes. Just consider what is now stored in human memories, libraries, photographs, films, video tapes, the Worldwide Web, blueprints, and computer data banks—in addition to what is inherent in other artifacts and human-made structures. Although there have been preliminary investigations by Cavalli-Sforza and Feldman and Boyd and Richerson, scientists have barely begun to investigate the basic processes by which that body of information changes (or remains constant for long periods)—a task that social scientists have been taking up piecemeal and largely qualitatively for a very long time.

Developing a unified quantitative theory of cultural change is one of the great challenges for evolutionary and social science in the 21st century.

Identifying the basic mechanisms by which our culture evolves will be difficult; the most recent attempts using a "meme" approach appear to be a dead end. Learning how to influence that evolution is likely to be more difficult still and fraught with pitfalls. No sensible geneticist envisions a eugenic future in which people are selected to show certain behavioral traits, and most thinking people are aware of the ethical (if not technical and social) problems of trying to change our behavior by altering our genetic endowments. Society has long been mucking around in cultural evolution, despite warnings of the potential abuses of doing so. Nazi eugenic policies and Soviet, Cambodian, Chinese, and other social engineering experiments stand as monuments to the ethical dangers that must be guarded against when trying systematically to alter either genetic or cultural evolution.

Nevertheless, we are today all involved in carrying out or (with our taxes) supporting experiments designed to change behavior. This is attested to by the advertising business, Head Start programs, and the existence of institutions such as Sing Sing Prison and Stanford University. The data used by evolutionary psychologists to infer the biological antecedents of human behavior, while not telling us anything about genetic evolution, may actually be helpful in improving our grasp of cultural evolution. What seems clear today, however, is that evolutionary psychology and behavioral genetics are promoting a vast overemphasis on the part played by genetic factors (and a serious underestimation of the role of cultural evolution) in shaping our behavioral phenomes.

Gary Marcus

→ NO

Making the Mind: Why We've Misunderstood the Nature-Nurture Debate

What do our minds owe to our nature, and what to our nurture? The question has long been vexed, in no small part because until recently we knew relatively little about the nature of nature—how genes work and what they bring to the biological structures that underlie the mind. But now, 50 years after the discovery of the molecular structure of DNA, we are for the first time in a position to understand directly DNA's contribution to the mind. And the story is vastly different from—and vastly more interesting than—anything we had anticipated.

The emerging picture of nature's role in the formation of the mind is at odds with a conventional view, recently summarized by Louis Menand. According to Menand, "every aspect of life has a biological foundation in exactly the same sense, which is that unless it was biologically possible it wouldn't exist. After that, it's up for grabs." More particularly, some scholars have taken recent research on genes and on the brain as suggesting a profoundly limited role for nature in the formation of the mind.

Their position rests on two arguments, what Stanford anthropologist Paul Ehrlich dubbed a "gene shortage" and widespread, well-documented findings of "brain plasticity." According to the gene shortage argument, genes can't be very important to the birth of the mind because the genome contains only about 30,000 genes, simply too few to account even for the brain's complexity—with its billions of cells and tens of billions of connections between neurons—much less the mind's. "Given that ratio," Ehrlich suggested, "it would be quite a trick for genes typically to control more than the most general aspects of human behavior."

According to the brain plasticity argument, genes can't be terribly important because the developing brain is so flexible. For instance, whereas adults who lose their left hemisphere are likely to lose permanently much of their ability to talk, a child who loses a left hemisphere may very well recover the ability to speak, even in the absence of a left hemisphere. Such flexibility is pervasive, down to the level of individual cells. Rather than being fixed in their fates the instant they are born, newly formed brain cells—neurons—can

From *Boston Review*, December 2003/January 2004. Copyright © 2003 by Gary Marcus. Reprinted by permission.

sometimes shift their function, depending on their context. A cell that would ordinarily help to give us a sense of touch can (in the right circumstances) be recruited into the visual system and accept signals from the eye. With that high level of brain plasticity, some imagine that genes are left on the sidelines, as scarcely relevant onlookers.

All of this is, I think, a mistake. It is certainly true that the number of genes is tiny in comparison to the number of neurons, and that the developing brain is highly plastic. Nevertheless, nature—in the form of genes—has an enormous impact on the developing brain and mind. The general outlines of how genes build the brain are finally becoming clear, and we are also starting to see how, in forming the brain, genes make room for the environment's essential role. While vast amounts of work remain to be done, it is becoming equally clear that understanding the coordination of nature and nurture will require letting go of some long-held beliefs.

How to Build a Brain

In the nine-month dash from conception to birth—the flurry of dividing, specializing, and migrating cells that scientists call embryogenesis—organs such as the heart and kidney unfold in a series of ever more mature stages. In contrast to a 17th century theory known as preformationism, the organs of the body cannot be found preformed in miniature in a fertilized egg; at the moment of conception there is neither a tiny heart nor a tiny brain. Instead, the fertilized egg contains information: the three billion nucleotides of DNA that make up the human genome. That information, copied into the nucleus of every newly formed cell, guides the gradual but powerful process of successive approximation that shapes each of the body's organs. The heart, for example, begins as a simple sheet of cell that gradually folds over to form a tube; the tube sprouts bulges, the bulges sprout further bulges, and every day the growing heart looks a bit more like an adult heart.

Even before the dawn of the modern genetic era, biologists understood that something similar was happening in the development of the brain—that the organ of thought and language was formed in much the same way as the rest of the body. The brain, too, develops in the first instance from a simple sheet of cells that gradually curls up into a tube that sprouts bulges, which over time differentiate into ever more complex shapes. Yet 2,000 years of thinking of the mind as independent from the body kept people from appreciating the significance of this seemingly obvious point.

The notion that the brain is drastically different from other physical systems has a long tradition; it can be seen as a modernized version of the ancient belief that the mind and body are wholly separate—but it is untenable. The brain is a physical system. Although the brain's function is different from that of other organs, the brain's capabilities, like those of other organs, emerge from its physical properties. We now know that strokes and gunshot wounds can interfere with language by destroying parts of the brain, and that Prozac and Ritalin can influence mood by altering the flow of neurotransmitters. The fundamental components of the brain—the neurons and the synapses that connect them—can be understood as physical systems, with chemical and electrical properties that follow from their composition.

Yet even as late as the 1990s, latter-day dualists might have thought that the brain developed by different principles. There were, of course, many hints that genes must be important for the brain: identical twins resemble each other more than nonidentical twins in personality as well as in physique; mental disorders such as schizophrenia and depression run in families and are shared even by twins reared apart; and animal breeders know that shaping the bodies of animals often leads to correlated changes in behavior. All of these observations provided clues of genetic effects on the brain.

But such clues are achingly indirect, and it was easy enough to pay them little heed. Even in the mid-1990s, despite all the discoveries that had been made in molecular biology, hardly anything specific was known about how the brain formed. By the end of that decade, however, revolutions in the methodology of molecular biology—techniques for studying and manipulating genes—were beginning to enter the study of the brain. Now, just a few years later, it has become clear that to an enormous extent the brain really is sculpted by the same processes as the rest of the body, not just at the macroscopic level (i.e., as a product of successive approximation) but also at the microscopic level, in terms of the mechanics of how genes are switched on and off, and even in terms of which genes are involved; a huge number of the genes that participate in the development of the brain play important (and often closely related) roles in the rest of the body. . . .

The . . . power of genes holds even for the most unusual yet most characteristic parts of neurons: the long axons that carry signals away from the cell, the tree-like dendrites that allow neurons to receive signals from other nerve cells, and the trillions of synapses that serve as connections between them. What your brain does is largely a function of how those synaptic connections are set up—alter those connections, and you alter the mind—and how they are set up is no small part a function of the genome. In the laboratory, mutant flies and mice with aberrant brain wiring have trouble with everything from motor control (one mutant mouse is named "reeler" for its almost drunken gait) to vision. And in humans, faulty brain wiring contributes to disorders such as schizophrenia and autism.

Proper neural wiring depends on the behavior of individual axons and dendrites. And this behavior once again depends on the content of the genome. For example, much of what axons do is governed by special wiggly, almost hand-like protuberances at the end of each axon known as growth cones. Growth cones (and the axonal wiring they trail behind them) are like little animals that swerve back and forth, maneuvering around obstacles, extending and retracting feelers known as filopodia (the "fingers" of a growth cone) as the cone hunts around in search of its destination—say in the auditory cortex. Rather than simply being launched like projectiles that blindly and helplessly follow whatever route they first set out on, growth cones constantly compensate and adjust, taking in new information as they find their way to their targets.

Growth cones don't just head in a particular direction and hope for the best. They "know" what they are looking for and can make new plans even if experimentally induced obstacles get in their way. In their efforts to find their destinations, growth cones use every trick they can, from "short-range" cues emanating from the surface of nearby cells to long-distance cues that broadcast their signals from millimeters away—miles and miles in the geography of an axon. For example, some proteins appear to serve as "radio beacons" that can diffuse across great distances and serve as guides to distant growth cones—provided that they are tuned to the right station. Which stations a growth cone picks up—and whether it finds a particular signal attractive or repellent—depends on the protein receptors it has on its surface, in turn a function of which genes are expressed within.

Researchers are now in a position where they can begin to understand and even manipulate those genes. In 2000, a team of researchers at the Salk Institute in San Diego took a group of thoracic (chest) motor neurons that normally extend their axons into several different places, such as axial muscles (midline muscles that play a role in posture), intercostal muscles (the muscles between the ribs), and sympathetic neurons (which, among other things, participate in the fast energy mobilization for fight-or-flight responses), and by changing their genetic labels persuaded virtually the entire group of thoracic neurons to abandon their usual targets in favor of the axial muscles. (The few exceptions were a tiny number that apparently couldn't fit into the newly crowded axial destinations and had to find other targets.)

What this all boils down to, from the perspective of psychology, is an astonishingly powerful system for wiring the mind. Instead of vaguely telling axons and dendrites to send and accept signals from their neighbors, thereby leaving all of the burden of mind development to experience, nature in effect lays down the cable: it supplies the brain's wires—axons and dendrites—with elaborate tools for finding their way on their own. Rather than waiting for experience, brains can use the complex menagerie of genes and proteins to create a rich, intricate starting point for the brain and mind.

The sheer overlap between the cellular and molecular processes by which the brain is built and the processes by which the rest of the body is built has meant that new techniques designed for the study of the one can often be readily imported into the study of the other. New techniques in staining, for instance, by which biologists trace the movements and fates of individual cells, can often be brought to bear on the study of the brain as soon as they are developed; even more important, new techniques for altering the genomes of experimental animals can often be almost immediately applied to studies of brain development. Our collective understanding of biology is growing by leaps and bounds because sauce for the goose is so often sauce for the gander.

Nature and Nurture Redux

This seemingly simple idea—that what's good enough for the body is good enough for the brain—has important implications for how we understand the roles of nature and nurture in the development of the mind and brain.

Beyond the Blueprint

Since the early 1960s biologists have realized that genes are neither blueprints nor dictators; instead, as I will explain in a moment, genes are better seen as *providers of opportunity*. Yet because the brain has for so long been treated as separate from the body, the notion of genes as sources of options rather than purveyors of commands has yet to really enter into our understanding of the origins of human psychology.

Biologists have long understood that all genes have two functions. First, they serve as templates for building particular proteins. The insulin gene provides a template for insulin, the hemoglobin genes give templates for building hemoglobin, and so forth. Second, each gene contains what is called a regulatory sequence, a set of conditions that guide whether or not that gene's template gets converted into protein. Although every cell contains a complete copy of the genome, most of the genes in any given cell are silent. Your lung cells, for example, contain the recipe for insulin but they don't produce any, because in those cells the insulin gene is switched off (or "repressed"); each protein is produced only in the cells in which the relevant gene is switched on. So individual genes are like lines in a computer program. Each gene has an IF and a THEN, a precondition (IF) and an action (THEN). And here is one of the most important places where the environment can enter: the IFs of genes are responsive to the environment of the cells in which they are contained. Rather than being static entities that decide the fate of each cell in advance, genes—because of the regulatory sequence—are dynamic and can guide a cell in different ways at different times, depending on the balance of molecules in their environment.

This basic logic—which was worked out in the early 1960s by two French biologists, Fran ois Jacob and Jacques Monod, in a series of painstaking studies of the diet of a simple bacterium—applies as much to humans as to bacteria, and as much for the brain as for any other part of the body. Monod and Jacob aimed to understand how *E. coli* bacteria could switch almost instantaneously from a diet of glucose (its favorite) to a diet of lactose (an emergency backup food). What they found was that this abrupt change in diet was accomplished by a process that switched genes on and off. To metabolize lactose, the bacterium needed to build a certain set of protein-based enzymes that for simplicity I'll refer to collectively as lactase, the product of a cluster of lactase genes. Every *E. coli* had those lactase genes lying in wait, but they were only expressed—switched on—when a bit of lactose could bind (attach to) a certain spot of DNA that lay near them, and this in turn could happen only if there was no glucose around to get in the way. In essence, the simple bacterium had an IF-THEN—if lactose and not glucose, then build lactase—that is very much of a piece with the billions of IF-THENs that run the world's computer software.

The essential point is that genes are IFs rather than MUSTs. So even a single environmental cue can radically reshape the course of development. In the African butterfly *Bicyclus anynana*, for example, high temperature during development (associated with the rainy season in its native tropical climate) leads the butterfly to become brightly colored; low temperature (associated with a dry fall) leads the butterfly to become a dull brown. The growing butter-fly doesn't learn (in the course of its development) how to blend in better—it will do the same thing in a lab where the temperature varies and the foliage is constant; instead it is genetically programmed to develop in two different ways in two different environments.

The lesson of the last five years of research in developmental neuroscience is that IF-THENs are as crucial and omnipresent in brain development as they are elsewhere. To take one recently worked out example: rats, mice, and other rodents devote a particular region of the cerebral cortex known as barrel fields to the problem of analyzing the stimulation of their whiskers. The exact place-ment of those barrel fields appears to be driven by a gene or set of genes whose IF region is responsive to the quantity of a particular molecule, Fibroblast Growth Factor 8 (FGF8). By altering the distribution of that molecule, research-ers were able to alter barrel development: increasing the concentration of FGF8 led to mice with barrel fields that were unusually far forward, while decreasing the concentration led to mice with barrel fields that were unusually far back. In essence, the quantity of FGF8 serves as a beacon, guiding growing cells to their fate by driving the regulatory IFs of the many genes that are presumably involved in barrel-field formation.

Other IF-THENs contribute to the function of the brain throughout life, e.g., supervising the control of neurotransmitters and participating . . . in the process of laying down memory traces. Because each gene has an IF, every aspect of the brain's development is in principle linked to some aspect of the environment; chemicals such as alcohol that are ingested during pregnancy have such enormous effects because they fool the IFs that regulate genes that guide cells into dividing too much or too little, into moving too far or not far enough, and so forth. The brain is the product of the actions of its component cells, and those actions are the products of the genes they contain within, each cell guided by 30,000 IFs paired with 30,000 THENs—as many possibilities as there are genes. (More, really, because many genes have multiple IFs, and genes can and often do work in combination.)

From Genes to Behavior

Whether we speak of the brain or other parts of the body, changes in even a single gene—leading to either a new IF or a new THEN—can have great con-sequences. Just as a single alteration to the hemoglobin gene can lead to a predisposition for sickle-cell anemia, a single change to the genes involved in the brain can lead to a language impairment or mental retardation.

And at least in animals, small differences within genomes can lead to significant differences in behavior. A Toronto team, for example, recently used genetic techniques to investigate—and ultimately modify—the foraging habits of *C. elegans* worms. Some *elegans* prefer to forage in groups, others are loners, and the Toronto group was able to tie these behavioral differences to differences in a single amino acid in the protein template (THEN) region of a particular gene known as npr-1; worms with the amino acid valine in the critical spot are "social" whereas worms with phenylalanine are loners. Armed with that knowledge and modern genetic engineering techniques, the team was able to switch a strain of loner *C. elegans* worms into social worms by altering that one gene.

Another team of researchers, at Emory University, has shown that changing the regulatory IF region of a single gene can also have a significant effect on social behavior. Building on an observation that differences in sociability in different species of voles correlated with how many vasopressin receptors they had, they transferred the regulatory IF region of sociable prairie voles' vasopressin receptor genes into the genome of a less sociable species, the mouse—and in so doing created mutant mice, more social than normal, with more vasopressin receptors. With other small genetic modifications, researchers have created strains of anxious, fearful mice, mice that progressively increase alcohol consumption under stress, mice that lack the nurturing instinct, and even mice that groom themselves constantly, pulling and tugging on their own hair to the point of baldness. Each of those studies demonstrates how behavior can be significantly changed when even a single gene is altered.

Still, complex biological structures—whether we speak of hearts or kidneys or brains—are the product of the concerted actions and interactions of many genes, not just one. A mutation in a single gene known as FOXP2 can interfere with the ability of a child to learn language; an alteration in the vasopressin gene can alter a rodent's sociability—but this doesn't mean that FOXP2 is solely responsible for language or that vasopressin is the only gene a rat needs in order to be sociable. Although individual genes can have powerful effects, no trait is the consequence of any single gene. There can no more be a single gene for language, or for the propensity for talking about the weather, than there can be for the left ventricle of a human heart. Even a single brain cell—or a single heart cell—is the product of many genes working together.

The mapping between genes and behavior is made even more complex by the fact that few if any neural circuits operate entirely autonomously. Except perhaps in the case of reflexes, most behaviors are the product of multiple interacting systems. In a complex animal like a mammal or a bird, virtually every action depends on a coming together of systems for perception, attention, motivation, and so forth. Whether or not a pigeon pecks a lever to get a pellet depends on whether it is hungry, whether it is tired, whether there is anything else more interesting around, and so forth. Furthermore, even within a single system, genes rarely participate directly "on-line," in part because they are just too slow. Genes do seem to play an active, major role in "off-line" processing, such as consolidation of long-term memory—which can even happen during sleep—but when it comes to rapid on-line decision-making, genes, which work on a time scale of seconds or minutes, turn over the reins to neurons, which act on a scale of hundredths of a second. The chief contribution of genes comes in advance, in laying down and adjusting neural circuitry, not in the moment-by-moment running of the nervous system. Genes build neural structures—not behavior.

In the assembly of the brain, as in the assembly of other organs, one of the most important ideas is that of a cascade, one gene influencing another, which influences another, which influences another, and so on. Rather than acting in absolute isolation, most genes act as parts of elaborate networks in which the expression of one gene is a precondition for the expression of the next. The THEN of one gene can satisfy the IF of another and thus induce it to turn on. Regulatory proteins are proteins (themselves the product of genes) that control the expression of other genes and thus tie the whole genetic system together. A single regulatory gene at the top of a complex network can indirectly launch a cascade of hundreds or thousands of other genes leading to, for example, the development of an eye or a limb.

In the words of Swiss biologist Walter Gehring, such genes can serve as "master control genes" and exert enormous power on a growing system. PAX6, for example, is a regulatory protein that plays a role in eye development, and Gehring has shown that artificially activating it in the right spot on a fruit fly's antenna can lead to an extra eye, right there on the antenna—thus, a simple regulatory gene leads directly and indirectly to the expression of approximately 2,500 other genes. What is true for the fly's eye is also true for its brain—and also for the human brain: by compounding and coordinating their effects, genes can exert enormous influence on biological structure.

From a Tiny Number of Genes to a Complex Brain

The cascades in turn help us to make sense of the alleged gene shortage, the idea that the discrepancy between the number of genes and the number of neurons might somehow minimize the importance of genes when it comes to constructing brain or behavior.

Reflection on the relation between brain and body immediately vitiates the gene shortage argument: if 30,000 genes weren't enough to have significant influence on the 20 billion cells in the brain, they surely wouldn't have much impact on the trillions that are found in the body as a whole. The confusion, once again, can be traced to the mistaken idea of genome as blueprint, to the misguided expectation of a one-to-one mapping from individual genes to individual neurons; in reality, genomes describe processes for building things rather than pictures of finished products: better to think of the genome as a compression scheme than a blueprint.

Computer scientists use compression schemes when they want to store and transmit information efficiently. All compression schemes rely in one way or another on ferreting out redundancy. For instance, programs that use the GIF format look for patterns of repeated pixels (the colored dots of which digital images are made). If a whole series of pixels are of exactly the same color, the software that creates GIF files will assign a code that represents the color of those pixels, followed by a number to indicate how many pixels in a row are of the same color. Instead of having to list every blue pixel individually, the GIF format saves space by storing only two numbers: the code for blue and the number of repeated blue pixels. When you "open" a GIF file, the computer converts those codes back into the appropriate strings of identical bits; in the meantime, the computer has saved a considerable amount of memory. Computer scientists have devised dozens of different compression schemes, from JPEGs for photographs to MP3s for music, each designed to exploit a different kind of redundancy. The general procedure is always the same: some end product is converted into a compact description of how to reconstruct that end product; a "decompressor" reconstructs the desired end product from that compact description.

Biology doesn't know in advance what the end product will be; there's no StuffIt Compressor to convert a human being into a genome. But the genome is very much akin to a compression scheme, a terrifically efficient description of how to build something of great complexity—perhaps more efficient than anything yet developed in the labs of computer scientists (never mind the complexities of the brain—there are trillions of cells in the rest of the body, and they are all supervised by the same 30,000-gene genome). And although nature has no counterpart to a program that stuffs a picture into a compressed encoding, it does offer a counterpart to the program that performs decompression: the cell. Genome in, organism out. Through the logic of gene expression, cells are self-regulating factories that translate genomes into biological structure.

Cascades are at the heart of this process of decompression, because the regulatory proteins that are at the top of genetic cascades serve as shorthand that can be used over and over again, like the subroutine of a software engineer. For example, the genome of a centipede probably doesn't specify separate sets of hundreds or thousands of genes for each of the centipede's legs; instead, it appears that the leg-building "subroutine"—a cascade of perhaps hundreds or thousands of genes—gets invoked many times, once for each new pair of legs. Something similar lies behind the construction of a vertebrate's ribs. And within the last few years it has become clear that the embryonic brain relies on the same sort of genetic recycling, using the same repeated motifs—such as sets of parallel connections known as topographic maps—over and over again, to supervise the development of thousands or even millions of neurons with each use of a given genetic subroutine. There's no gene shortage, because every cascade represents the shorthand for a different reuseable subroutine, a different way of creating more from less.

From Prewiring to Rewiring

In the final analysis, I think the most important question about the biological roots of the mind may not be the question that has preoccupied my colleagues and myself for a number of years—the extent to which genes prewire the brain—but a different question that until recently had never been seriously raised: the extent to which (and ways in which) genes make it possible for experience to *rewire* the brain. Efforts to address the nature-nurture question typically falter because of the false assumption that the two—prewiring and rewiring—are competing ideas. "Anti-nativists"—critics of the view that we might be born with significant mental structure prior to experience—often attempt to downplay the significance of genes by making what I earlier called "the argument from plasticity": they point to the brain's resilience to damage and its ability to modify itself in response to experience. Nativists sometimes seem to think that their position rests on downplaying (or demonstrating limits on) plasticity.

In reality, plasticity and innateness are almost logically separate. Innateness is about the extent to which the brain is prewired, plasticity about the extent to which it can be rewired. Some organisms may be good at one but not the other: chimpanzees, for example, may have intricate innate wiring yet, in comparison to humans, relatively few mechanisms for rewiring their brains. Other organisms may be lousy at both: *C. elegans* worms have limited initial structure, and relatively little in the way of techniques for rewiring their nervous system on the basis of experience. And some organisms, such as humans, are well-endowed in both respects, with enormously intricate initial architecture and fantastically powerful and flexible means for rewiring in the face of experience. . . .

CHALLENGE QUESTIONS

Does the Cultural Environment Influence Lifespan Development More than Our Genes?

- Does it make sense that the human brain would be programmed in different ways for men and women, who do, on average, show clear developmental differences?
- Do studies that show identical twins to be more alike than fraternal (nonidentical) twins provide convincing evidence of genetic dominance? Why or why not?
- Applying Darwinian principles to explain psychological aspects of behavior and development has become increasingly popular in recent years, often phrased as "evolutionary psychology." Does that popularity suggest the applications are correct, or could there be other reasons for the popularity of this approach?
- Marcus suggests that understanding genetic influences on development requires appreciating the complexity of how genes work. Is it possible that that complexity will make it too difficult to analyze?
- Much of the evidence for this debate comes from nonhuman animal research. How much can we learn about the nature and nurture of human development from experiments on other species?

Suggested Readings

S. Ceci and W. Williams, *The Nature-Nurture Debate: The Essential Readings* (Blackwell Publishers, 1999)

S. Johnson, "Sociobiology and You," *The Nation* (November 18, 2002)

G. Marcus, *The Birth of the Mind: How a Tiny Number of Genes Creates the Complexity of Human Thought* (Basic Books, 2004)

L. Menand, "What Comes Naturally," *The New Yorker* (November 25, 2002)

S. Pinker, *The Blank Slate* (Viking Adult, 2002)

S. Pinker, "Why Nature and Nurture Won't Go Away," *Daedalus* (Fall 2004)

M. Ridley, *Nature via Nurture* (Harper Collins, 2003)

ISSUE 2

Are Peers More Important than Parents during the Process of Development?

YES: Judith Rich Harris, from "How to Succeed in Childhood," *Wilson Quarterly* (Winter 1991)

NO: Howard Gardner, from "Do Parents Count?" *New York Times Book Review* (November 5, 1998)

ISSUE SUMMARY

YES: Developmental psychology writer Judith Rich Harris presents a strong and provocative argument suggesting that parents do not influence child development to any significant degree, while peers and social groups have a primary influence.

NO: Harvard psychologist Howard Gardner reviews Harris's work and suggests her argument is overstated and misleading—parents do matter.

If you ask people about their personal development—why did you turn out the way you have—most will tell you about their parents. In contrast, when you ask researchers and scholars about the role of parents in personal development their answer tends to be a little more complicated. Many years of research have focused on estimating and understanding the influence of parenting, but the results have not been as clear as you might expect.

In fact, many scholars now feel the influence of parental "socialization" (the forming of behavior and personality by parenting behaviors) may be much less than most people think. It may be that parents are simply an easy target for child rearing "experts" because most parents want to make sure they are doing the best for their children. Instead of only focusing on parents, however, researchers are devoting significant attention to at least two alternative explanations for what influences lifespan development. One explanation is based on increased attention to biological and genetic influences on behavior, finding high levels of significance for our inherited predispositions. The other explanation is based on the role of culture and society, beyond individual parents, that shapes norms and expectations for children.

That being the case, perhaps it was inevitable that someone would turn the tables on all of the parenting experts by drawing on developmental research to suggest that parents may not really matter much at all. That person turned out to be Judith Rich Harris, who had been writing textbooks about developmental psychology for years before realizing that there was very little evidence for all of the emphasis on the influence of parents in development. She eventually turned this realization into a provocative and award-winning article for psychologists and a controversial book for a popular audience. Her basic argument, stated simply as "parents don't matter nearly as much as we think, and peers matter a lot more," went against both popular wisdom and academic trends. Harris's work instigated a flurry of debate.

One of the prominent psychologists to respond was Howard Gardner, most well known for his influential theory of multiple intelligences. While appreciating Harris's ability to challenge conventional wisdom, Gardner asserts that she significantly overstates her case by massaging data. Gardner is relatively certain that parents do matter, and that the problem with research is simply that personality and character are too difficult to measure. He suggests that the lack of evidence for parents' direct influence derives from an over-reliance on crude surveys, which creates an impression of development that is not true to its complex nature.

POINT

- Most research finds a very modest correlation between parenting behaviors and developmental outcomes.

- The idea that parents matter is really a cultural myth based on invalid aspects of Freudian theory.

- Children do not want to be like their parents and other adults; children want to be like other children.

- Much of what we assume to be parenting effects is actually based on parents sharing genetic material with their children.

COUNTERPOINT

- Harris is selective in what evidence she attends to; there is more evidence than she acknowledges suggesting that parents do matter.

- While Harris claims that our ideas about how parents matter is a cultural myth, she assumes that what happens to children in American society is a true representation of development everywhere.

- It is a disservice to children to assume that they do not take direction from parents, who do most of the explicit care-giving for children.

- Most research on the influence of parents relies on methods that are too crude and general to pick up the nuances of personality development.

YES ⬅

Judith Rich Harris

How to Succeed in Childhood

Every day, tell your children that you love them. Hug them at least once every 24 hours. Never hit them. If they do something wrong, don't say, "You're bad!" Say, "What you did was bad." No, wait—even that might be too harsh. Say, instead, "What you did made me unhappy."

The people who are in the business of giving out this sort of advice are very angry at me, and with good reason. I'm the author of *The Nurture Assumption*—the book that allegedly claims that "parents don't matter." Though that's not what the book actually says, the advice givers are nonetheless justified in their anger. I don't pull punches, and I'm not impressed by their air of benevolent omniscience. Their advice is based not on scientific evidence but on prevailing cultural myths.

The advice isn't wrong; it's just ineffective. Whether parents do or don't follow it has no measurable effect on how their children turn out. There is a great deal of evidence that the differences in how parents rear their children are not responsible for the differences among the children. I've reviewed this evidence in my book; I will not do it again here.

Let me, however, bring one thing to your attention: the advice given to parents in the early part of this century was almost the mirror image of the advice that is given today. In the early part of this century, parents were not warned against damaging their children's self-esteem; they were warned against "spoiling" them. Too much attention and affection were thought to be bad for kids. In those days, spanking was considered not just the parents' right but their duty.

Partly as a result of the major retoolings in the advice industry, child-rearing styles have changed drastically over the course of this century. Although abusive parents have always existed, run-of-the-mill parents—the large majority of the population—administer more hugs and fewer spankings than they used to.

Now ask yourself this: Are children turning out better? Are they happier and better adjusted than they were in the earlier part of the century? Less aggressive? Less anxious? Nicer?

⚬◈⚬

It was Sigmund Freud who gave us the idea that parents are the be-all and end-all of the child's world. According to Freudian theory, children learn right from wrong—that is, they learn to behave in ways their parents and their society deem acceptable—by identifying with their parents. In the calm after the storm of the oedipal crisis, or the reduced-for-quick-sale female version of the oedipal crisis, the child supposedly identifies with the parent of the same sex.

Freud's name is no longer heard much in academic departments of psychology, but the theory that children learn how to behave by identifying with their parents is still accepted. Every textbook in developmental psychology (including, I confess, the one I co-authored) has its obligatory photo of a father shaving and a little boy pretending to shave. Little boys imitate their fathers, little girls imitate their mothers, and, according to the theory, that's how children learn to be grownups. It takes them a while, of course, to perfect the act.

It's a theory that could have been thought up only by a grownup. From the child's point of view, it makes no sense at all. What happens when children try to behave like grownups is that, more often than not, it gets them into trouble. Consider this story, told by Selma Fraiberg, a child psychologist whose book. *The Magic Years* was popular in the 1960s:

> Thirty-month-old Julia finds herself alone in the kitchen while her mother is on the telephone. A bowl of eggs is on the table. An urge is experienced by Julia to make scrambled eggs. . . . When Julia's mother returns to the kitchen, she finds her daughter cheerfully plopping eggs on the linoleum and scolding herself sharply for each plop, "NoNoNo. Mustn't dood it! NoNoNo. Mustn't dood it!"

Fraiberg attributed Julia's lapse to the fact that she had not yet acquired a superego, presumably because she had not yet identified with her mother. But look at what was Julia doing when her mother came back and caught her egg-handed: she was imitating her mother! And yet Mother was not pleased.

⚜

Children cannot learn how to behave appropriately by imitating their parents. Parents do all sorts of things that children are not allowed to do—I don't have to list them, do I?—and many of them look like fun to people who are not allowed to do them. Such prohibitions are found not only in our own society but everywhere, and involve not only activities such as making scrambled eggs but patterns of social behavior as well. Around the world, children who behave too much like grownups are considered impertinent.

Sure, children sometimes pretend to be adults. They also pretend to be horses and monsters and babies, but that doesn't mean they aspire to be horses or monsters or babies. Freud jumped to the wrong conclusions, and so did several generations of developmental psychologists. A child's goal is not to become an adult; a child's goal is to be a successful child.

What does it take to be a successful child? The child's first job is to learn how to get along with her parents and siblings and to do the things that are expected of her at home. This is a very important job—no question about it. But it is only the first of the child's jobs, and in the long run it is overshadowed in importance by the child's second job: to learn how to get along with the members of her own generation and to do the things that are expected of her outside the home.

Almost every psychologist, Freudian or not, believes that what the child learns (or doesn't learn) in job 1 helps her to succeed (or fail) in job 2. But this belief is based on an obsolete idea of how the child's mind works, and there is good evidence that it is wrong.

Consider the experiments of developmental psychologist Carolyn Rovee-Collier. A young baby lies on its back in a crib. A mobile with dangling doo-dads hangs overhead. A ribbon runs from the baby's right ankle to the mobile in such a way that whenever the baby kicks its right leg, the doodads jiggle. Babies are delighted to discover that they can make something happen; they quickly learn how to make the mobile move. Two weeks later, if you show them the mobile again, they will immediately start kicking that right leg.

But only if you haven't changed anything. If the doodads hanging from the mobile are blue instead of red, or if the liner surrounding the crib has a pattern of squares instead of circles, or if the crib is placed in a different room, they will gape at the mobile cluelessly, as if they've never seen such a thing in their lives.

⚜

It's not that they're stupid. Babies enter the world with a mind designed for learning and they start using it right away. But the learning device comes with a warning label: what you learn in one situation might not work in another. Babies do not assume that what they learned about the mobile with the red doodads will work for the mobile with the blue doodads. They do not assume that what worked in the bedroom will work in the den. And they do not assume that what worked with their mother will work with their father or the babysitter or their jealous big sister or the kids at the daycare center.

Fortunately, the child's mind is equipped with plenty of storage capacity. As the cognitive scientist Steven Pinker put it in his foreword to my book, "Relationships with parents, with siblings, with peers, and with strangers could not be more different, and the trillion-synapse human brain is hardly short of the computational power it would take to keep each one in a separate mental account."

That's exactly what the child does: keeps each one in a separate mental account. Studies have shown that a baby with a depressed mother behaves in a subdued fashion in the presence of its mother, but behaves normally with a caregiver who is not depressed. A toddler taught by his mother to play elaborate fantasy games does not play these games when he's with his play-mates—he and his playmates devise their own games. A preschooler who has perfected the delicate art of getting along with a bossy older sibling is no more likely than a first-born to allow her peers in nursery school to dominate her. A school-age child who says she hates her younger brother—they fight like cats and dogs, their mother complains—is as likely as any other child to have warm and serene peer relationships. Most telling, the child who follows the rules at home, even when no one is watching, may lie or cheat in the schoolroom or on the playground, and vice versa.

Children learn separately how to behave at home and how to behave outside the home, and parents can influence only the way they behave at home. Children behave differently in different social settings because different behaviors are required. Displays of emotion that are acceptable at home are not acceptable outside the home. A clever remark that would be rewarded with a laugh at home will land a child in the principal's office at school. Parents are often surprised to discover that the child they see at home is not the child the teacher sees. I imagine teachers get tired of hearing parents exclaim, "Really? Are you sure you're talking about *my* child?"

The compartmentalized world of childhood is vividly illustrated by the child of immigrant parents. When immigrants settle in a neighborhood of native-born Americans, their children become bicultural, at least for a while. At home they practice their parents' culture and language, outside the home they adopt the culture and language of their peers. But though their two worlds are separate, they are not equal. Little by little, the outside world takes precedence: the children adopt the language and culture of their peers and bring that language and culture home. Their parents go on addressing them in Russian or Korean or Portuguese, but the children reply in English. What the children of immigrants end up with is not a compromise, not a blend. They end up, pure and simple, with the language and culture of their peers. The only aspects of their parents' culture they retain are things that are carried out at home, such as cooking.

⋅◆⋅

Late-20th-century native-born Americans of European descent are as ethnocentric as the members of any other culture. They think there is only one way to raise children—the way they do it. But that is not the way children are reared in the kinds of cultures studied by anthropologists and ethologists. The German ethologist Irenäus Eibl-Eibesfeldt has described what childhood is like in the hunter-gatherer and tribal societies he spent many years observing.

In traditional cultures, the baby is coddled for two or three years—carried about by its mother and nursed whenever it whimpers. Then, when the next baby comes along, the child is sent off to play in the local play group, usually in the care of an older sibling. In his 1989 book *Human Ethology*, Eibl-Eibesfeldt describes how children are socialized in these societies:

> Three-year-old children are able to join in a play group, and it is in such play groups that children are truly raised. The older ones explain the rules of play and will admonish those who do not adhere to them, such as by taking something away from another or otherwise being aggressive. Thus the child's socialization occurs mainly within the play group. . . . By playing together in the children's group the members learn what aggravates others and which rules they must obey. This occurs in most cultures in which people live in small communities.

Once their tenure in their mothers' arms has ended, children in traditional cultures become members of a group. This is the way human children were designed to be reared. They were designed by evolution to become members of a group, because that's the way our ancestors lived for millions of years. Throughout the evolution of our species, the individual's survival depended upon the survival of his or her group, and the one who became a valued member of that group had an edge over the one who was merely tolerated.

◈

Human groups started out small: in a hunter-gatherer band, everyone knows everyone else and most are blood relatives. But once agriculture began to provide our ancestors with a more or less dependable supply of food, groups got bigger. Eventually they became large enough that not everyone in them knew everyone else. As long ago as 1500 B.C. they were sometimes that large. There is a story in the Old Testament about a conversation Joshua had with a stranger, shortly before the Battle of Jericho. They met outside the walls of the beleaguered town, and Joshua's first question to the stranger was, "Are you for us or for our adversaries?"

Are you one of *us* or one of *them*? The group had become an idea, a concept, and the concept was defined as much by what you weren't as by what you were. And the answer to the question could be a matter of life or death. When the walls came tumbling down, Joshua and his troops killed every man, woman, and child in Jericho. Even in Joshua's time, genocide was not a novelty: fighting between groups, and wholesale slaughter of the losers, had been going on for ages. According to the evolutionary biologist Jared Diamond, it is "part of our human and prehuman heritage."

Are you one of *us* or one of *them*? It was the question African Americans asked of Colin Powell. It was the question deaf people asked of a Miss America who couldn't hear very well but who preferred to communicate in a spoken language. I once saw a six-year-old go up to a 14-year-old and ask him, "Are you a kid or a grownup?"

The human mind likes to categorize. It is not deterred by the fact that nature often fails to arrange things in convenient clumps but instead provides a continuum. We have no difficulty splitting up continua. Night and day are as different as, well, night and day, even though you can't tell where one leaves off and the other begins. The mind constructs categories for people—male or female, kid or grownup, white or black, deaf or hearing—and does not hesitate to draw the lines, even if it's sometimes hard to decide whether a particular individual goes on one side or the other.

Babies only a few months old can categorize. By the time they reach their first birthday, they are capable of dividing up the members of their social world into categories based on age and sex: they distinguish between men and women, between adults and children. A preference for the members of their own social category also shows up early. One-year-olds are wary of strange adults but are attracted to other children, even ones they've never met before. By the age of two, children are beginning to show a preference for members of their own sex. This preference grows steadily stronger over the next few years. School-age girls and boys will play together in places where there aren't many children, but when they have a choice of playmates, they tend to form all-girl and all-boy groups. This is true the world around.

✤

The brain we won in the evolutionary lottery gave us the ability to categorize, and we use that skill on people as well as things. Our long evolutionary history of fighting with other groups predisposes us to identify with one social category, to like our own category best, and to feel wary of (or hostile toward) members of other categories. The emotions and motivations that were originally applied to real physical groups are now applied to groups that are only concepts: "Americans" or "Democrats" or "the class of 2001." You don't have to like the other members of your group in order to consider yourself one of them; you don't even have to know who they are. The British social psychologist Henri Tajfel asked his subjects—a bunch of Bristol schoolboys—to estimate the number of dots flashed on a screen. Then half the boys were privately told that they were "overestimators," the others that they were "underestimators." That was all it took to make them favor their own group. They didn't even know which of their schoolmates were in their group and which were in the other.

✤

The most famous experiment in social psychology is the Robber's Cave study. Muzafer Sherif and his colleagues started with 22 eleven-year-old boys, carefully selected to be as alike as possible, and divided them into two equal groups. The groups—the "Rattlers" and the "Eagles"—were separately transported to the Robber's Cave summer camp in a wilderness area of Oklahoma. For a while, neither group knew of the other's existence. But the first time the Rattlers heard the Eagles playing in the distance, they reacted with hostility. They wanted to "run them off." When the boys were brought together in games arranged by researchers disguised as camp counselors, push quickly came to shove. Before long, the two groups were raiding each other's cabins and filling socks with stones in preparation for retaliatory raids.

When people are divided (or divide themselves) into two groups, hostility is one common result. The other, which happens more reliably though it is less well known, is called the "group contrast effect." The mere division into two groups tends to make each group see the other as different from itself in an unfavorable way, and that makes its members *want* to be different from the other group. The result is that any pre-existing differences between the groups tend to widen, and if there aren't any differences to begin with, the members create them. Groups develop contrasting norms, contrasting images of themselves.

In the Robber's Cave study, it happened very quickly. Within a few days of their first encounter, the Eagles had decided that the Rattlers used too many "cuss-words" and resolved to give up cussing; they began to say a prayer before every game. The Rattlers, who saw themselves as tough and manly, continued to favor scatology over eschatology. If an Eagle turned an ankle or skinned a knee, it was all right for him to cry. A Rattler who sustained a similar injury might cuss a bit, but he would bear up stoically.

⋖◉⋗

The idea for group socialization theory came to me while I was reading an article on juvenile delinquency. The article reported that breaking the law is highly common among adolescents, even among those who were well behaved as children and who are destined to turn into law-abiding adults. This unendearing foible was attributed to the frustration teenagers experience at not being adults: they are longing for the power and privilege of adulthood.

"Wait a minute," I thought. "That's not right. If teenagers really wanted to be adults, they wouldn't be spraying graffiti on overpasses or swiping nail polish from drugstores. If they really wanted to emulate adults they would be doing boring adult things, like sorting the laundry or figuring out their taxes. Teenagers aren't trying to be like adults; they are trying to *contrast* themselves with adults! They are showing their loyalty to their own group and their disdain for adults' rules!"

I don't know what put the idea into my head; at the time, I didn't know beans about social psychology. It took eight months of reading to fill the gaps in my education. What I learned in those eight months was that there is a lot of good evidence to back up my hunch, and that it applies not only to teenagers but to young children as well.

Sociologist William Corsaro has spent many years observing nursery school children in the United States and Italy. Here is his description of four-year-olds in an Italian *scuola materna*, a government-sponsored nursery school:

> In the process of resisting adult rules, the children develop a sense of community and a group identity. [I would have put it the other way around: I think group identity leads to the resistance.] The children's resistance to adult rules can be seen as a routine because it is a daily occurrence in the nursery school and is produced in a style that is easily recognizable to members of the peer culture. Such activity is often highly exaggerated (for instance, making faces behind the teacher's back or running around) or is prefaced by "calls for the attention" of other children (such as, "look what I got" in reference to possession of a forbidden object, or "look what I'm doing" to call attention to a restricted activity).

Group contrast effects show up most clearly when "groupness"—Henri Tajfel's term—is salient. Children see adults as serious and sedentary, so when the social categories *kids* and *grownups* are salient—as they might be, for instance, when the teacher is being particularly bossy—the children become sillier and more active. They demonstrate their fealty to their own age group by making faces and running around.

This has nothing to do with whether they like their teachers personally. You can like people even if they're members of a different group and even if you don't much like that group—a conflict of interests summed up in the saying, "Some of my best friends are Jews." When groupness is salient, even young children contrast themselves with adults and collude with each other in defying them. And yet some of their best friends are grownups.

٭◉٭

Learning how to behave properly is complicated, because proper behavior depends on which social category you're in. In every society, the rules of behavior depend on whether you're a grownup or a kid, a female or a male, a prince or a peon. Children first have to figure out the social categories that are relevant in their society, and then decide which category they belong in, then tailor their behavior to the other members of their category.

That brief description seems to imply that socialization makes children more alike, and so it does, in some ways. But groups also work to create or exaggerate differences among their members—differences in personality. Even identical twins reared in the same home do not have identical personalities. When groupness is not salient—when there is no other group around to serve as a foil—a group tends to fall apart into individuals, and differences among them emerge or increase. In boys' groups, for example, there is usually a dominance hierarchy, or "pecking order." I have found evidence that dominant boys develop different personalities from those at the bottom of the ladder.

Groups also typecast their members, pinning labels on them—joker, nerd, brain—that can have lifelong repercussions. And children find out about themselves by comparing themselves with their group mates. They come to think well or poorly of themselves by judging how they compare with the other members of their own group. It doesn't matter if they don't measure up to the standards of another group. A third-grade boy can think of himself as smart if he knows more than most of his fellow third-graders. He doesn't have to know more than a fourth-grader.

٭◉٭

According to my theory, the culture acts upon children not through their parents but through the peer group. Children's groups have their own cultures, loosely based on the adult culture. They can pick and choose from the adult culture, and it's impossible to predict what they'll include. Anything that's common to the majority of the kids in the group may be incorporated into the children's culture, whether they learned it from their parents or from the television set. If most of the children learned to say "please" and "thank you" at home, they will probably continue to do so when they're with their peers. The child whose parents failed to teach her that custom will pick it up from the other children: it will be transmitted to her, via the peer group, from the parents of her peers. Similarly, if most of the children watch a particular TV show, the behaviors and attitudes depicted in the show may be incorporated into the norms of their group. The child whose parents do not permit him to watch that show will nonetheless be exposed to those behaviors and attitudes. They are transmitted to him via the peer group.

Thus, even though individual parents may have no lasting effects on their children's behavior, the larger culture does have an effect. Child-rearing practices common to most of the people in a culture, such as teaching children to say "please" and "thank you," can have an effect. And the media can have an effect.

In the hunter-gatherer or tribal society, there was no privacy: everybody knew what everybody else was doing. Nowadays children can't ordinarily watch their neighbors making love, having babies, fighting, and dying, but they can watch these things happening on the television screen. Television has become their window on society, their village square. They take what they see on the screen to be an indication of what life is like—what life is supposed to be—and they incorporate it into their children's cultures.

⋅⊙⋅

One of my goals in writing *The Nurture Assumption* was to lighten some of the burdens of modern parenthood. Back in the 1940s, when I was young, the parents of a troublesome child—my parents, for instance—got sympathy, not blame. Nowadays parents are likely to be held culpable for anything that goes wrong with their child, even if they've done their best. The evidence I've assembled in my book indicates that there is a limit to what parents can do: how their child turns out is largely out of their hands. Their major contribution occurs at the moment of conception. This doesn't mean it's mostly genetic; it means that the environment that shapes the child's personality and social behavior is outside the home.

I am not advocating irresponsibility. Parents are in charge of how their children behave at home. They can decide where their children will grow up and, at least in the early years, who their peers will be. They are the chief determiners of whether their children's life at home will be happy or miserable, and they have a moral obligation to keep it from being miserable. My theory does not grant people the license to treat children in a cruel or negligent way.

Although individual parents have little power to influence the culture of children's peer groups, larger numbers of parents acting together have a great deal of power, and so does the society as a whole. Through the prevailing methods of child rearing it fosters, and through influences—especially the media—that act directly on peer-group norms and values, a society shapes the adults of the future. Are we shaping them the way we ought to?

Do Parents Count?

1.

We all want to know how and why we got to be who we are. Parents have a special interest in answering the "how" and "why" questions with respect to their own children. In addressing the mysteries of human growth, traditional societies have invoked God, the gods, the fates, with luck sometimes thrown in. Shakespeare called our attention to the struggle between "nature and nurture."

In our own time the natural sciences and the social sciences have been supplying a bewildering variety of answers. Those with biological leanings look to heredity—the gene complexes of each parent and the ways in which their melded sets of genes express themselves in the offspring. The traits and capacities of the biological parents are seen as in large part determining the characteristics of offspring. Those with a psychological or sociological perspective point to the factors beyond the child's physiology. Psychoanalysts emphasize the pivotal role of parents, and especially the young child's relationship to his or her mother. Behaviorists look at the contingencies of reward and punishment in the child's experience; the character of the child depends on the qualities that are "reinforced," with those in control of reinforcement in early life having an especially significant influence.

Recently, three new candidates have been proposed to explain "socialization"—i.e., how children grow up within a society and absorb its norms. Impressed and alarmed by the powers of new means of communication, particularly television, students of culture like Marie Winn and Neil Postman have described a generation raised by the electronic media. The historian of science Frank Sulloway has brought new attention to the once discounted factor of "birth order": on his account, first-borns embrace the status quo, while later-borns are far more likely to support scientific, political, or religious revolutions. And now, in a much publicized new work, Judith Rich Harris suggests that all of these authorities have got it wrong. On her account, the most potent "socializers" are the child's peers, with parents having little or no effect.

Harris's work has many things going for it. For a start, she has an arresting hypothesis, one that should strike especially responsive chords in adults who feel they are inadequately involved in the formation of the post-baby boom Generation X and the generations to come. She has an appealing personal story. Kicked out of graduate school in psychology in the early 1960s and a victim of a lupus-like disease, she has hitherto led the life of a semi-invalid, making her living coauthoring textbooks in psychology. One day in 1994, after reading a scholarly article about juvenile delinquency, she was struck by the idea that the role of peers in socialization had largely been ignored while the influence of parents had been much overestimated. She succeeded in publishing a theoretical statement of her view in *Psychological Review*, the most prestigious journal of psychological theory. She soon gained recognition among scholars and, in a delicious irony, won a prestigious award named after George Miller, the very professor who had signed her letter of expulsion from Harvard almost four decades ago. Harris's book is well-written, toughly argued, filled with telling anecdotes and biting wit. It has endorsements from some of the most prestigious names in the field. Already it has been widely—and mostly favorably—reported on and reviewed in the popular press.

However, in my view, Harris's thesis is overstated, misleading, and potentially harmful. Overstated in the sense that she highlights evidence consistent with her thesis and understates evidence that undermines it. Misleading because she treats as "natural" and "universal" what, in my view, is really a characterization of contemporary American culture (and those societies influenced by America). Potentially harmful in that it may, if inadvertently, discourage parents from promoting their own beliefs and values, and from becoming models of behavior, at a time when such values and models should be clearly and continually conveyed to children.

2.

Harris begins by outlining familiar positions in psychology. On her account, Freud's view of the Oedipal period is quaint and unsupported, while the behaviorists have been widely discredited, both by the cognitivists (who put the mind back into psychology) and the biologists (who reminded us that we are as much a product of our genes as of our experiences). She then turns her keen critical skills to an attack on the branch of empirical psychology that attempts to document important contributions of parents to their children's personality and character. (Harris uses both terms.)

For over half a century, psychologists and anthropologists have observed parents and children in different settings; they have filled out checklists in which they record predominant kinds of behavior and action, and they have administered questionnaires to the parents and children themselves. These researchers, according to Harris, began with the "nurture assumption"; they presupposed that the most important force in the child's environment is the child's parents and then collected evidence to support that assumption. Moreover, while scholars themselves are often guarded in their conclusions, some "pop" psychologists have no inhibitions whatever. They stress the role of parents over all other forces, thus making parents feel guilty if they fail (according to their own criteria), and full of pride when they succeed.

As Harris shrewdly points out, there are two problems with the nurture assumption. First, when viewed with a critical eye, the empirical evidence about parental influences on their children is weak, and often equivocal. After hundreds of studies, many with individually suggestive findings, it is still diffi- cult to pinpoint the strong effects that parents have on their children. Even the effects of the most extreme experiences—divorce, adoption, and abuse—prove elusive to capture. Harris cites Eleanor Maccoby, one of the leading research- ers in the field, who concluded that "in a study of nearly four hundred fami- lies, few connections were found between parental child-rearing practices (as reported by parents in detailed interviews) and independent assessments of children's personality characteristics—so few, indeed, that virtually nothing was published relating the two sets of data.

The second problem with the nurture assumption is potentially more devastating. Harris draws heavily on recent results from behavioral genet- ics to argue that, even in those cases where children resemble their parents, the presence and actions of parents have little to do with that resemblance. The argument she makes from behavioral genetics runs as follows. Studies of siblings, fraternal twins, identical twins reared together, and identical twins reared apart all point to the same conclusion: about half of one's intellect and personality results from one's genes. That is, in any group of people drawn from a particular "population" (e.g., middle-class white youngsters living in the United States), about one half of the variations in an observed trait (for instance, IQ or aggressiveness) is owing to one's parents' genetic contribution. The other half is, of course, the result of one's environment.

For those who assume that the behavior of parents and the models they offer make up a major part of the child's environment, the results of studies in behavioral genetics are surprising. According to those studies, when we exam- ine any population of children and try to account for the nongenetic varia- tions among them, we find that remarkably few variations can be attributed to their "shared environment"—i.e., when parents treat all of their children the same way, for example, being equally punitive to each child.

In fact, according to the behavioral geneticists, nearly all of the varia- tion is due to what is called the "nonshared environment"—i.e., the variety of other influences, including instances where children are treated differently by the parents (e.g., a brother is punished more than his sister, or differently). In the case of any particular child, we simply do not know with any accuracy what makes up the nonshared environment. We can guess that it consists of siblings, printed matter, radio and television, other adults, school, luck, acci- dent, the different (as opposed to the common or "shared") ways in which each parent responds to each child, and—if Judith Rich Harris is correct—most especially, a child's peers.

⋅⟨⊙⟩⋅

So much for Harris's demolition of the importance of parents—except genetically—to the behavior and psyche of the child. Harris adduces evidence from a wide variety of sources, moreover, to stress the important contribution of peers. She goes back to the studies of nonhuman primates to indicate the importance of peer groups in child-rearing—pointing out that monkeys can be successfully reared by peers alone but not by their mothers alone. (It's not known whether this would be true in "higher" primates.) She cites observations of children in different cultures who play together as much and as early as possible, and routinely gang up on the adults (teachers, parents, masters). She searches in the experimental literature for cases where peers exert an appreciable influence upon one another—for example, adolescents who have the same friends turn out to resemble one another. And she places great emphasis on the human tendency to form groups—and particularly "in-groups" with which one strongly identifies.

Harris also provides many telling anecdotes from her own experiences, and from the press and television, about how adults are ignored and peers admired. British boys who rarely see their parents successfully absorb social values at boarding school. Secretary of Labor Robert Reich quit the Cabinet to be with his sons in Cambridge and found that they would rather hang out "in the Square." Touchingly she indicates how she and her husband tried to deal with their wayward adopted daughter but finally realized that the peers had more influence. No such problems existed with their biological daughter, who simply followed her biological destiny; the model provided by her parents was no more than an unnecessary bonus.

Harris describes recurrent situations where youngsters overlook the evident models of their parents in favor of those provided by peers. Deaf children of speaking parents ignore their parents' attempts to teach them to read lips and instead begin to invent gestural signs to communicate with other deaf children and seek opportunities to learn formal signing. The hearing children of deaf parents, Harris points out, learn to speak normally in the absence of a parental model. Analogously, children raised by parents with foreign accents soon begin to speak like their peers, without an accent; like the deaf children, they ignore the models at home and turn, as if magnetized, to the most available set of peers. Arguments like these convince Harris, and apparently many readers (both lay and professional), that young human beings are wired to attend to people of similar age, rather than to those large and obvious authority figures who give them birth and early shelter.

3.

Harris has collected an impressive set of examples and findings to fortify a position that is indeed novel in empirical investigations of "human socialization." I have sought to do justice to her arguments, though I cannot convey her passion, her missionary sense of having seen the light. Yet I do not find her "peer hypothesis" convincing, partly because I read the literature on the subject differently. My deeper reservations come from my belief that Harris has misconstrued the problem of socialization and, in doing so, has put forth a position that harbors its own dangers.

When we consider the empirical part of Harris's argument, we find it is indeed true that the research on parent-child socialization is not what we would hope for. However, this says less about parents and children and more about the state of psychological research, particularly with reference to "softer variables" such as affection and ambition. While psychologists have made genuine progress in the study of visual perception and measurable progress in the study of cognition, we do not really know what to look for or how to measure human personality traits, individual emotions, and motivations, let alone character.

Consider, as an example, the categories that the respondents must use when they describe themselves or others on the Personal Attributes Questionnaire, a test used to obtain data about a person's self-esteem and gender-linked traits. Drawing on a list reminiscent of the Boy Scout oath, those who answer the questionnaire are asked whether they would describe themselves as Gentle, Helpful, Active, Competitive, and Worldly. These terms are not easy to define and people are certainly prone to apply them favorably to their own case. Or consider the list of acts from which observers can choose to characterize children from different cultures—Offers Help, Acts Sociably, Assaults Sociably, Seeks Dominance. Even if we could agree on what kinds of physical behavior merit these labels, we don't know with any confidence what these acts mean to children, adolescents, and adults in diverse cultures—let alone to the observers from a distant university. What does a raised fist or a frown mean to a three-year-old or to the thirty-year-old who observes it? The same question could be asked about a wink or an imitated curtsy. We are not measuring chemical bonds or electrical voltage in such cases. We are seeking to quantify the most subtle human characteristics—the sentiments described so finely by Henry James. And therefore it is not surprising when studies—whether by empirical psychologists or behavioral geneticists—do not yield strong results.

I do not want to elevate psychoanalytic theory or practice over other kinds of inquiry, but at least the Freudians were grappling with the deeper aspects of human character and personality—our urgent longings, our innermost fears and anxieties, our wrenching conflicts. We might perhaps find evidence for these complex feelings—and their putative causes—through long narratives, or projective testing (where the subjects respond to ambiguous photographs or inkblots), or by analyzing a series of sessions on the couch. We won't reach them through questionnaires or checklists; yet Harris relies on many studies that use them.

As social scientists we have been frustrated by our own clumsy efforts to understand personality and character, and even relatively measurable skills, like intelligence or the capacity for problem-solving. And perhaps that is why so many talented psychologists—including the ones quoted on the jacket of *The Nurture Assumption*—have become drawn to evolutionary psychology and behavioral genetics. Here, at last, is the chance to put psychology and social science (and even squishy inquiries into personality, temperament, and character) on what seems a "real" scientific footing. Physics envy has been replaced by biological bias.

But things are not as clear-cut in the biobehavioral world as outsiders may imagine. Because of the possibility of controlled experiments, sociobiology has made genuine progress in explaining the social life of insects; but its account of human behavior remains controversial. The speculations of evolutionary psychology are just that; as commentators such as Stephen Jay Gould and Steve Jones have pointed out . . . , it is difficult to know how to disprove a hypothesis in evolutionary psychology. (For example, what evidence can help us decide whether genes, or humans, are really selfish, or really altruistic, or really both?—in which case we are back where we started.)

❧

And what of behavioral genetics? Certainly the opportunity to study twins who have been separated early in life gives us an additional advantage in understanding the heritability of various traits. And Judith Harris rightly calls attention to two enigmas: the fact that identical twins reared apart are almost as alike as those that are reared together; and the fact that identical twins still turn out to be quite different from one another.

But this subject is also dogged by difficulties. We cannot really do experiments in human behavioral genetics; we have to wait until events happen (as when twins are separated early in life) and then study the effects retrospectively. But this approach leaves too many puzzles unaddressed. First of all, for at least nine crucial months, the twins share the same environment—the womb of the birth mother—and we still know very little about the shared chemical and other effects of gestation on their neurological systems. Then, too, they may or may not have been separated right at birth. (And under what extraordinary circumstances does such separation occur?) They may or may not have been raised for a while by family members. The children are not randomly placed; in nearly all cases, they are raised within the same culture and very often in the same community, with similar social settings. Also, infants who look the same and behave the same are likely to elicit similar responses from adults, while those who are raised in the same house may try all the harder to distinguish themselves from one another. Or they may not.

When you add together the uncertainties (and I have only suggested a few of them here) of human behavioral genetics, and the imprecision of the measures used to describe personality and character, it is no wonder that we find little reliable evidence of parental influence. It would be reassuring if we did—but it is not surprising that we do not.

Which brings me to the alternative picture that Harris attempts to construct. She argues that "peers" are the real instrument of socialization. She may be right; but she does not have the evidence to show this. Her assertions depend almost entirely on what she thinks could one day be shown. Indeed, I find it extremely telling that she relies very heavily on the arguments about language—language-learning among the deaf, and the loss of foreign accents. Neither of these has to do with personality, character, or temperament, her supposed topics. In the case of accents, I assume that we are dealing with an unconscious (and presumably innate) process in which the growing child generalizes from his encounters with many of the adults and children he meets outside the home and through television, the movies, and other media. In the case of deafness, the enormous difference between child and parents forces youngsters to make use of resources outside the home—ranging from adult teachers to television and other visual media.

Indeed, despite some imaginative suggestions by Harris, it is very difficult to envision how one could test her hypothesis. For, after all, who are peers? Do they include siblings? Are they the children in the neighborhood? The children in class? The children in after-school activities or in Sunday school? The children on television? In the movies? At some remote spot on the Internet? Who decides? What happens when peers change because the family moves, or one child switches schools, or leaves (or is kicked out of) one group and then enters another? Most important, who selects peers? At least with parents, we researchers stand on fairly firm ground; and with siblings as well. But for all Ms. Harris's anecdotes, when it comes to peers, we're afloat.

Undoubtedly, psychological researchers inspired by Harris's book will seek evidence bearing on her thesis. We will learn from these studies; and some of us who have taken skeptical positions in this debate may have to acknowledge influences we hadn't sufficiently recognized. Meanwhile, I want to suggest an entirely different approach to the problem, one that might be called "the culture assumption."

4.

What is socialization about? It is about becoming a certain kind of person—gaining specific knowledge, skills, manners, attitudes, and habits. Animals have little culture; human beings revel in it. Yet what is striking in Harris's book is that the words "disciplines," "civilization," and "culture" (in the sense of civilization) are largely absent from the text and from her thinking. Socialization is reduced to having, or not having, certain personality traits—traits that are measured by rather coarsely conceived and applied tests.

The work of the much-maligned Freud remains the best point of departure for a treatment of these issues. In his *Civilization and Its Discontents*, Freud defined culture: "the sum of the achievements and institutions which differentiate our lives from those of our animal forebears, namely that of protecting humanity against nature and of regulating the relations of human beings among themselves." He concentrates particularly on "the one feature of culture which characterizes it better than any other, and that is the value that it sets upon the higher mental activities—intellectual, scientific, and aesthetic achievement." And he speculates that culture (or civilization) rests upon the human superego—the sense of guilt—which develops (or fails to develop) during the child's early interactions with his parents. Guilt keeps us from murdering our fellow citizens; guilt prompts us to delay gratification, to sublimate our primordial passions in favor of loftier pursuits.

Whether one examines the least developed preliterate culture or the most advanced technological society, the question remains the same: What structures and practices will enable children to assume their places in that culture and ultimately aid in transmitting it to the generations to come?

Children will have some say in this process, and it is to Harris's credit (and that of the authorities whom she cites) that she has called attention to this fact. But children are not born just into a family or into a peer group. They are born into an entire culture, whose assumptions begin when the parents say, happily or with a twinge of regret, "It's a girl," and continues to exert its influence in nearly every interaction and experience until the funerary rites, burial, cremation, or ascent to heaven takes place.

Earlier, I referred to Eleanor Maccoby's pessimistic conclusions about documenting parental influence, and I mentioned some of the studies of it that both Maccoby and Harris seem to have had in mind. But let me reconsider the most ambitious of these studies in a different light. In the 1950s and 1960s, John Whiting, Beatrice Whiting, and their colleagues studied childrearing in six cultures, ranging from a small New England town to agricultural settings in Kenya, India, Mexico, the Philippines, and Okinawa. What emerges from that study is that childrearing practices are distinctly different around the globe: different in treatment of infants, in parental sleeping patterns, in how children do chores, in their helping or not helping in rearing younger siblings, in initiation rites, in ways of handling aggression, and in dozens of other variables. So differently are children reared in these cultures that no one would confuse an adult New Englander with an adult Gusii of Kenya or an adult Taira of Okinawa—whether in their knowledge, skills, manners, habits, personality, or temperament.

For the social scientist, the analytic problem is to find the source of these differences. Parents behave differently in these cultures, but so do siblings, peers, other adults, and even visiting anthropologists. And of course the adult roles, natural resources, technology, and means of communication (primitive or modern) differ as well. In all probability, each of these factors makes its contribution to the child's "personality and character." But how to tell them apart? Harris chooses to minimize these other factors and zooms in on the peers, but her confident choice is not justified.

5.

Harris takes little note of a crucial fact: all but a few of the studies that she reviews, including several of the most influential behavioral genetic ones, were carried out in the United States. The United States is not a country without culture; it has many subcultures and a more general "national" culture as well. Harris and most of the authorities that she cites are not studying child-rearing in general; indeed, they are studying child-rearing largely in the white, middle-class United States during the last half-century.

From the time of Alexis de Tocqueville's visit to the United States in the early 1830s, observers have noted the relative importance in this country of peers, friends, or fellow workers of the same age, the members of one's own community. Tocqueville commented, "In America the family, in the Roman and aristocratic signification of the word, does not exist. All that remains are a few vestiges in the first years of childhood. . . ." As a sociologist might put it, America is a more horizontal, "peer-oriented" society than most others, and particularly more so than most traditional societies.

When empirical social science began in this country, these unusual cultural patterns were noted as well. Studying the America of the 1940s, the sociologist David Riesman and his coauthors called attention to the decline of tradition-centered and "inner-directed" families, where the parental models were powerful; and to the concomitant rise of the "other-directed families" that made up "the Lonely Crowd." In this increasingly common family constellation, much socialization occurred at the behest of the peer group, whether for adults or for children. Riesman wrote, "The American peer group, too, cannot be matched for power throughout the middle-class world."

Examining the America of the 1950s and 1960s, the psychologist Urie Bronfrenbrenner noted that children spend more time with peers than with parents and reached the same conclusion: "Whether in comparison to other contemporary cultures, or to itself over time, American society emerges as one that gives decreasing prominence to the family as a socializing agency. . . . We are coming to live in a society that is exaggerated not only by race and class, but also by age." Thus not only has the peer group had an important part in American society from the first; but in recent decades this trend has accelerated.

But there are many possible peer groups. To which ones are children drawn and why? Here I believe (and Harris concedes this) that parents have a decisive role—by the friendships they encourage or discourage, by the schools they select or avoid, by the after-school activities they encourage and summer camps they approve of, parents contribute substantially to the choice of possible peer groups. I would go one step further. Children themselves select—and are selected for—various peer groups according to parental predilections. The work of the social psychologist Mihaly Csikszentmihalyi on "talented teens" strongly suggests that the values exhibited at home—integrity vs. dishonesty, hard work vs. laziness, artistic interests vs. philistinism—imprint themselves on children and in turn serve as major determinants of the peer groups to which children are attracted and, not incidentally, the ones where they are welcomed or spurned.

6.

It seems that in every passing decade—perhaps in every passing selection of fall books—we are told of a new approach to bringing up children or of a new, villainous influence on family life. Certainly, we do not have the feeling of a steady scientific march toward truth. It is more as if we are on a roller-coaster, with each new hypothesis tending to invalidate the previous one.

Still, it would be defeatist simply to embrace the opposite perspective, to declare that each of the various factors—mother, father, grandparents, same-sex siblings, different-sex peers, television, etc.—is important and be done with it. As a scientific community, we can do better than this. To do so, we should be undertaking two activities.

First, even as we welcome the clarifications provided by evolution and genetics, we cannot lose sight of the different cultural settings in which research is carried out and the different meanings attached to seemingly similar traits and actions. Parents and peers have different meanings in Japan, Brazil, and the United States; what we learn from the Whitings, and from much other sociological and anthropological research, is that these "independent variables" cannot simply be equated in designing research or in interpreting findings. In fact, a father may be treated more like a sibling in one society, and an older sibling more like a father in another; parents may encourage children to associate with peers in one culture and to steer clear of them in another and, in yet another, to combat their influence in every way they can.

Second, even as we discover genes or gene clusters that appear to influence important social or psychological variables, we must not assume that we have "solved" the problem of socialization. We still don't know the physical mechanisms by which genes actually affect the brain and cause people to make one choice or another. What triggers (or fails to trigger) genes will vary across cultural settings; and how their expression is understood will also vary. Young men, for example, may have a proclivity to imitate other young men of similar size and power, but that proclivity can be manipulated, depending upon whom the child is exposed to and which rewards and punishments are contingent upon imitation or non-imitation.

Each of the numerous influences on a child's personality I have mentioned can surely have an effect, but the effect will vary among different children, families, and cultures. As science progresses, we may someday be able to predict the relative importance of each across these different factors. My reading of the research suggests that, on the average, parents and peers will turn out to have complementary roles: parents are more important when it comes to education, discipline, responsibility, orderliness, charitableness, and ways of interacting with authority figures. Peers are more important for learning cooperation, for finding the road to popularity, for inventing styles of interaction among people of the same age. Youngsters may find their peers more interesting, but they will look to their parents when contemplating their own futures.

Parental attitudes and efforts will determine to a significant extent how a child resolves the conflicting messages of the home and the wider community as well as the kind of parent the child one day becomes. I would give much weight to the hundreds of studies pointing toward parental influence and to the folk wisdom accumulated by hundreds of societies over thousands of years. And I would, accordingly, be skeptical of a perspective, such as Ms. Harris's, that relies too heavily on heritability statistics and manages to reanalyze numerous studies and practices so that they all somehow point to the peer group.

•☞•

To gain attention, an author often states a finding or hypothesis very strongly. (I've been guilty of this myself.) In Harris's case, this has led to a belittling of the roles of parents in childrearing and to a stronger endorsement of the role of peers than the current data allow. I do not question Harris's motives but I do question her judgment, which might have been better guided by the old medical oath "first, do no harm."

It is all to the good if parents do not become crushed with anxiety when they have problems with their children or when their children turn out differently than they would like. Guilt is not always productive. But to suggest, with little foundation, that parents are not important in socialization borders on the irresponsible. Perhaps, on the average, those of us who are parents are not particularly successful in encouraging the personality traits we would hope to see in our children, whether because we do not know how to get their attention, or because they are "primed" to pay attention to their peers and we are not aware of how long and how hard we must work to counter these proclivities.

But children would not—could not—grow to be members of a civilized culture if they were simply left to the examples of their peers. Indeed, parents are especially important when children's peers set strong and destructive examples. In the absence of credible parents and other adults, most children will not be able to deal effectively with life. A social science—or a layman's guide—that largely left out parents after birth would be absurd. So would a society.

Whether on the scene, or behind the scenes, parents have jointly created the institutions that train and inspire children: apprenticeships, schools, works of art and literature, religious classes, playing fields, and even forms of resistance and rebellion. These institutions, and the adults who run them, sustain civilization and provide the disciplines—however fragile they may seem—that keep our societies from reverting to barbarism.

Sad to say, these most important parts of life—which make life satisfying and fascinating—are largely absent from *The Nurture Assumption*. They are absent as well from most of the work emanating from the biotropic pole of contemporary social science. Until their importance is realized, and the biological and cultural perspectives are somehow deeply integrated with one another, scientific claims about children and family life are bound to remain barren.

CHALLENGE QUESTIONS

Are Peers More Important than Parents during the Process of Development?

- While most people automatically assume parents are the most significant influence on lifespan development, what is the tangible evidence?
- Harris never finished her PhD in developmental psychology, causing some scholars to criticize her for lacking proper academic credentials. Should that matter for her argument?
- Gardner claims that current research methods do not really give a full picture of how complex people are. Will psychology ever be able to fully describe personality and the outcomes of development in ways that are true to who we become?
- Most people concerned with lifespan development would acknowledge that many factors influence how we turn out—parents, genes, peers, the media, schools, and more. Why is it worth the effort to try and understand which of those influences matter the most and in what ways?

Suggested Readings

N. Barber, *Why Parents Matter: Parental Investment and Child Outcomes* (Greenwood Publishing Group, 2000)

W. A. Collins, E. E. Maccoby, L. Steinberg, E. M. Hetherington, and M. H. Bornstein, "Contemporary Research on Parenting: The Case for Nature and Nurture," *American Psychologist* (February 2002)

J. Rich Harris, *The Nurture Assumption: Why Children Turn Out the Way They Do* (The Free Press, 1998)

J. Rich Harris, *No Two Alike: Human Nature and Human Individuality* (W. W. Norton, 2006)

J. Rich Harris and J. Kagan, "Slate Dialogues: E-mail Debates of Newsworthy Topics—The Nature of Nurture: Parents or Peers?" available at http://slate.msn.com/id/5853/ (November 1998)

M. Spett, "Is It True That Parenting Has No Influence on Children's Adult Personalities?" *NJ-ACT Newsletter* (March 1999)

D. L. Vandell and J. R. Harris, "Genes, Parents, and Peers: An Invited Exchange of Views," *Developmental Psychology* (November 2000)

W. Williams, "Do Parents Matter? Scholars Need to Explain What Research Really Shows," *The Chronicle of Higher Education* (December 11, 1998)

ISSUE 3

Do Significant Innate Differences Influence the Career Success of Males and Females?

YES: Steven Pinker, from "The Science of Gender and Science: Pinker vs. Spelke, A Debate," *Edge: The Third Culture* (May 2005)

NO: Elizabeth Spelke, from "The Science of Gender and Science: Pinker vs. Spelke, A Debate," *Edge: The Third Culture* (May 2005)

ISSUE SUMMARY

YES: After the Harvard president controversially suggested innate gender differences may play a role in men's disproportionate representation in science careers, cognitive psychologist Steven Pinker suggested that research does find clear innate differences between men and women in some basic cognitive abilities relevant to success.

NO: Harvard psychologist Elizabeth Spelke draws on research into cognitive development to suggest that the major reasons for any differences in career success lie in social, rather than genetic, forces.

In 2004, the then-president of Harvard University Lawrence Summers stirred an energetic controversy about the origin of differences between males and females in fields such as science and math. He provocatively suggested that one of the reasons (and, it is important to note, Summers clearly identified other social forces as influential) for the differences could be innate mental capacity. Immediately after making the comments a prominent woman scientist attending the talk left the room appalled by the suggestion, and a popular uproar ensued. The comments clearly touched a nerve in a society extremely conscious of group differences in opportunity, resources, and success. The comments also spoke directly to research and scholarship addressing the development of gender differences through the lifespan.

In recent social science research and writing, it has been common to suggest that evolution designed the male and female brain for slightly different adaptive tasks. Steven Pinker, contextualizing Summers's remarks in relation to such research, has been a prominent proponent of the idea that our minds

47

have clear innate predispositions. As one of the most prodigious academic psychologists of recent decades, Pinker argues forcefully that the idea that the mind is originally a "blank slate" is highly improbable. He reviews a variety of different types of well-established gender differences and the likelihood that those differences originate with innate predispositions, referring to extensive research showing that cognitive development in areas as diverse as motivation and spatial reasoning does, on average, vary by gender.

Despite the familiarity of this argument to social science researchers, it seems a general audience displays a much more emotional response. Decontextualized, it seems Summers was simply claiming women are less able than men. We all know too many personal examples of women's achievement to believe this to be the case.

And, in fact, as Elizabeth Spelke observes in arguing against innate gender differences, the tendency to attribute male and female differences in cognitive abilities to innate biological capacities is a major part of the problem. Even though a great deal of research on infancy and early development shows significant similarities between boys and girls in basic cognitive skills, people persist in expecting differences. Spelke acknowledges that innate predispositions matter, and that gender matters, but asserts firmly that any differences in career success are much easier to explain by looking at social influences.

POINT	COUNTERPOINT
• The evidence for gender differences in cognitive abilities is too obvious to ignore.	• There is also evidence suggesting that infants come into the world with relatively equal cognitive abilities.
• Just because it is morally right to promote opportunities for women, does not mean it is empirically true that there are no innate differences.	• By focusing on gender differences we implicitly, and often unintentionally, perpetuate the social forces that lead to inequality.
• There are clear average differences (with lots of individual variation) between men and women in priorities regarding status, in the desire to work with people, in risk taking, in certain visual-spatial skills, in mathematical reasoning, and in representation at extreme ends of ability.	• Men and women may have average differences, but neither gender has a comprehensive advantage in all of the skills relevant to career success.
• Men are more variable in their abilities, so there are more who are very smart but also more who are very dumb.	• When people are at the extremes of ability, gender discrimination does not matter as much as for more average people.
• Many sex differences are universal, are present very early in life, and generally seem to not be influenced by culture.	• Gender differences in abilities are more likely to be caused by social, rather than biological, forces.

YES ↵   Steven Pinker

The Science of Gender and Science: Pinker Vs. Spelke, A Debate

For those of you who just arrived from Mars, there has been a certain amount of discussion here at Harvard on a particular datum, namely the under-representation of women among tenure-track faculty in elite universities in physical science, math, and engineering.

As with many issues in psychology, there are three broad ways to explain this phenomenon. One can imagine an extreme "nature" position: that males but not females have the talents and temperaments necessary for science. Needless to say, only a madman could take that view. The extreme nature position has no serious proponents.

There is an extreme "nurture" position: that males and females are biologically indistinguishable, and all relevant sex differences are products of socialization and bias.

Then there are various intermediate positions: that the difference is explainable by some combination of biological differences in average temperaments and talents interacting with socialization and bias.

Liz [Elizabeth Spelke] has embraced the extreme nurture position. There is an irony here, because in most discussions in cognitive science she and I are put in the same camp, namely the "innatists," when it comes to explaining the mind. But in this case Liz has said that there is "not a shred of evidence" for the biological factor, that "the evidence against there being an advantage for males in intrinsic aptitude is so overwhelming that it is hard for me to see how one can make a case at this point on the other side," and that "it seems to me as conclusive as any finding I know of in science."

Well we certainly aren't seeing the stereotypical gender difference in *confidence* here! Now, I'm a controversial guy. I've taken many controversial positions over the years, and, as a member of *Homo sapiens,* I think I am right on all of them. But I don't think that in any of them I would say there is "not a shred of evidence" for the other side, even if I think that the evidence *favors* one side. I would not say that the other side "can't even make a case" for their position, even if I think that their case is not *as good as* the one I favor. And as for saying that a position is "as conclusive as any finding in science"—well, we're talking about social science here! This statement would imply that the extreme nurture position on gender differences is more conclusive than, say the evidence that the sun is at the center of the solar system, for the laws of thermodynamics, for the theory of evolution, for plate tectonics, and so on.

These are extreme statements—especially in light of the fact that an enormous amount of research, summarized in these and many other literature reviews, in fact points to a very different conclusion. I'll quote from one of them, a book called *Sex Differences in Cognitive Ability* by Diane Halpern. She is a respected psychologist, recently elected as president of the American Psychological Association, and someone with no theoretical axe to grind. She does not subscribe to any particular theory, and has been a critic, for example, of evolutionary psychology. And here what she wrote in the preface to her book:

> "At the time I started writing this book it seemed clear to me that any between sex differences in thinking abilities were due to socialization practices, artifacts, and mistakes in the research. After reviewing a pile of journal articles that stood several feet high, and numerous books and book chapters that dwarfed the stack of journal articles, I changed my mind. The literature on sex differences in cognitive abilities is filled with inconsistent findings, contradictory theories, and emotional claims that are unsupported by the research. Yet despite all the noise in the data, clear and consistent messages could be heard. There are real and in some cases sizable sex differences with respect to some cognitive abilities. Socialization practices are undoubtedly important, but there is also good evidence that biological sex differences play a role in establishing and maintaining cognitive sex differences, a conclusion I wasn't prepared to make when I began reviewing the relevant literature."

This captures my assessment perfectly.

Again for the benefit of the Martians in this room: This isn't just any old issue in empirical psychology. There are obvious political colorings to it, and I want to begin with a confession of my own politics. I am a feminist. I believe that women have been oppressed, discriminated against, and harassed for thousands of years. I believe that the two waves of the feminist movement in the 20th century are among the proudest achievements of our species, and I am proud to have lived through one of them, including the effort to increase the representation of women in the sciences.

But it is crucial to distinguish the *moral* proposition that people should not be discriminated against on account of their sex—which I take to be the core of feminism—and the *empirical* claim that males and females are biologically indistinguishable. They are not the same thing. Indeed, distinguishing them is essential to protecting the core of feminism. Anyone who takes an honest interest in science has to be prepared for the facts on a given issue to come out either way. And that makes it essential that we not hold the ideals of feminism hostage to the latest findings from the lab or field. Otherwise, if the findings come out as showing a sex difference, one would either have to say, "I guess sex discrimination wasn't so bad after all," or else furiously suppress or distort the findings so as to preserve the ideal. The truth cannot be sexist. Whatever the facts turn out to be, they should not be taken to compromise the core of feminism.

Why study sex differences? Believe me, being the Bobby Riggs of cognitive science is not my idea of a good time. So should I care about them, especially since they are not the focus of my own research?

First, differences between the sexes are part of the human condition. We all have a mother and a father. Most of us are attracted to members of the opposite sex, and the rest of us notice the difference from those who do. And we can't help but notice the sex of our children, friends, and our colleagues, in every aspect of life.

Also, the topic of possible sex differences is of great scientific interest. Sex is a fundamental problem in biology, and sexual reproduction and sex differences go back a billion years. There's an interesting theory, which I won't have time to explain, which predicts that there should be an overall equal investment of organisms in their sons and daughters; neither sex is predicted to be superior or inferior across the board. There is also an elegant theory, namely Bob Trivers' theory of differential parental investment, which makes highly specific predictions about when you should expect sex differences and what they should look like.

The nature and source of sex differences are also of practical importance. Most of us agree that there are aspects of the world, including gender disparities, that we want to change. But if we want to *change* the world we must first *understand* it, and that includes understanding the sources of sex differences.

Let's get back to the datum to be explained. In many ways this is an *exotic* phenomenon. It involves biologically unprepared talents and temperaments: evolution certainly did not shape any part of the mind to do the work of a professor of mechanical engineering at MIT, for example. The datum has nothing to do with basic cognitive processes, or with those we use in our everyday lives, in school, or even in most college courses, where indeed there are few sex differences.

Also, we are talking about extremes of achievement. Most women are not qualified to be math professors at Harvard because most *men* aren't qualified to be math professors at Harvard. These are extremes in the population.

And we're talking about a subset of fields. Women are not underrepresented to nearly the same extent in all academic fields, and certainly not in all prestigious professions. . . .

. . . Let me begin the substance of my presentation by connecting the political issue with the scientific one. Economists who study patterns of discrimination have long argued (generally to no avail) that there is a crucial conceptual difference between *difference* and *discrimination*. A departure from a 50–50 sex ratio in any profession does not, by itself, imply that we are seeing discrimination, unless the interests and aptitudes of the two groups are equated. Let me illustrate the point with an example, involving myself.

I work in a scientific field—the study of language acquisition in children— that is in fact dominated by women. Seventy-five percent of the members the main professional association are female, as are a majority of the keynote speakers at our main conference. I'm here to tell you that it's not because men like me have been discriminated against. I decided to study language development, as opposed to, say, mechanical engineering, for many reasons. The goal of designing a better automobile transmission does not turn me on as much as the goal of figuring out how kids acquire language. And I don't think I'd be as good at designing a transmission as I am in studying child language.

Now, all we need to do to explain sex differences without invoking the discrimination or invidious sexist comparisons is to suppose that whatever traits *I* have that predispose *me* to choose (say) child language over (say) mechanical engineering are not exactly equally distributed statistically among men and women. For those of you out there—of either gender—who also are not mechanical engineers, you should understand what I'm talking about.

Okay, so what *are* the similarities and differences between the sexes? There certainly are many similarities. Men and women show no differences in general intelligence or *g*—on average, they are exactly the same, right on the money. Also, when it comes to the basic categories of cognition—how we negotiate the world and live our lives; our concept of objects, of numbers, of people, of living things, and so on—there are no differences.

Indeed, in cases where there *are* differences, there are as many instances in which women do slightly better than men as ones in which men do slightly better than women. For example, men are better at throwing, but women are more dexterous. Men are better at mentally rotating shapes; women are better at visual memory. Men are better at mathematical problem-solving; women are better at mathematical calculation. And so on.

But there are at least six differences that are relevant to the datum. we have been discussing. The literature on these differences is so enormous that I can only touch on a fraction of it. I'll restrict my discussion to a few examples in which there are enormous data sets, or there are meta-analyses that boil down a literature.

The first difference, long noted by economists studying employment practices, is that men and women differ in what they state are their priorities in life. To sum it up: men, on average, are more likely to chase status at the expense of their families; women give a more balanced weighting. Once again: Think statistics! The finding is not that women value family and don't value status. It is not that men value status and don't value family. Nor does the finding imply that every last woman has the asymmetry that women show on average or that every last man has the asymmetry that men show on average. But in large data sets, on average, an asymmetry what you find.

Just one example. In a famous long-term study of mathematically precocious youth, 1,975 youngsters were selected in 7th grade for being in the top 1% of ability in mathematics, and then followed up for more than two decades. These men and women are certainly equally talented. And if anyone has ever been encouraged in math and science, these kids were. Both genders: they are equal in their levels of achievement, and they report being equally satisfied with the course of their lives. Nonetheless there are statistical differences in what they say is important to them. There are some things in life that the females rated higher than males, such as the ability to have a part-time career for a limited time in one's life; living close to parents and relatives; having a meaningful spiritual life; and having strong friendships. And there are some things in life that the males rated higher than the females. They include having lots of money; inventing or creating something; having a full-time career; and being successful in one's line of work. It's worth noting that studies of highly successful people find that single-mindedness and competitiveness are recurring traits in geniuses (of both sexes).

Here is one other figure from this data set. As you might expect, this sample has a lot of people who like to work Herculean hours. Many people in this group say they would like to work 50, 60, even 70 hours a week. But there are also slight differences. At each one of these high numbers of hours there are slightly more men than women who want to work that much. That is, more men than women don't care about whether they have a life.

Second, interest in people versus things and abstract rule systems. There is a *staggering* amount of data on this trait, because there is an entire field that studies people's vocational interests. I bet most of the people in this room have taken a vocational interest test at some point in their lives. And this field has documented that there are consistent differences in the kinds of activities that appeal to men and women in their ideal jobs. I'll just discuss one of them: the desire to work with people versus things. There is an enormous average difference between women and men in this dimension, about one standard deviation.

And this difference in interests will tend to cause people to gravitate in slightly different directions in their choice of career. The occupation that fits best with the "people" end of the continuum is "director of a community services organization." The occupations that fit best with the "things" end are physicist, chemist, mathematician, computer programmer, and biologist.

We see this consequence not only in the choice of whether to go into science, but also in the choice which branch of science the two sexes tend to go into. Needless to say, from 1970 to 2002 there was a huge increase in the percentage of university degrees awarded to women. But the percentage still differs dramatically across fields. Among the Ph.Ds awarded in 2001, for example, in education 65% of the doctorates went to women; in the social sciences, 54%; in the life sciences, 47%; in the physical sciences, 26%; in engineering, 17%. This is completely predictable from the difference in interests between people and living things, on the one hand, and inanimate objects, on the other. And the pattern is pretty much the same in 1980 and 2001, despite the change in absolute numbers.

Third, risk. Men are by far the more reckless sex. In a large meta-analysis involving 150 studies and 100,000 participants, in 14 out of 16 categories of risk-taking, men were over-represented. The two sexes were equally represented in the other two categories, one of which was smoking, for obvious reasons. And two of the largest sex differences were in "intellectual risk taking" and "participation in a risky experiment." We see this sex difference in everyday life, in particular, in the following category: the Darwin Awards, "commemorating those individuals who ensure the long-term survival of our species by removing themselves from the gene pool in a sublimely idiotic fashion." Virtually all—perhaps all—of the winners are men.

Fourth, three-dimensional mental transformations: the ability to determine whether the drawings in each of these pairs the same 3-dimensional shape. Again I'll appeal to a meta-analysis, this one containing 286 data sets and 100,000 subjects. The authors conclude, "we have specified a number of tests that show highly significant sex differences that are stable across age, at least after puberty, and have not decreased in recent years." Now, as I mentioned, for some kinds of spatial ability, the advantage goes to women, but in "mental rotation, "spatial perception," and "spatial visualization" the advantage goes to men.

Now, does this have any relevance to scientific achievement? We don't know for sure, but there's some reason to think that it does. In psychometric studies, three-dimensional spatial visualization is correlated with mathematical problem-solving. And mental manipulation of objects in three dimensions figures prominently in the memoirs and introspections of most creative physicists and chemists, including Faraday, Maxwell, Tesla, Kéekulé, and Lawrence, all of whom claim to have hit upon their discoveries by dynamic visual imagery and only later set them down in equations. A typical introspection is the following: "The cyclical entities which seem to serve as elements in my thought are certain signs and more or less clear images which can be voluntarily reproduced and combined. This combinatory play seems to be the essential feature in productive thought before there is any connection with logical construction in words or other kinds of signs." The quote comes from this fairly well-known physicist.

Fifth, mathematical reasoning. Girls and women get better school grades in mathematics and pretty much everything else these days. And women are better at mathematical calculation. But consistently, men score better on mathematical word problems and on tests of mathematical reasoning, at least statistically. Again, here is a meta analysis, with 254 data sets and 3 million subjects. It shows no significant difference in childhood; this is a difference that emerges around puberty, like many secondary sexual characteristics. But there are sizable differences in adolescence and adulthood, especially in high-end samples. Here is an example of the average SAT mathematical scores, showing a 40-point difference in favor of men that's pretty much consistent from 1972 to 1997. In the Study of Mathematically Precocious Youth (in which 7th graders were given the SAT, which of course ordinarily is administered only to older, college-bound kids), the ratio of those scoring over 700 is 2.8 to 1 male to female. (Admittedly, and interestingly, that's down from 25 years ago, when the ratio was 13-to-1, and perhaps we can discuss some of the reasons.) At the 760 cutoff, the ratio nowadays is 7 males to 1 female.

Now why is there a discrepancy with grades? Do SATs and other tests of mathematical reasoning aptitude underpredict grades, or do grades overpredict high-end aptitude? At the Radical Forum Liz was completely explicit in which side she takes, saying that "the tests are no good," unquote. But if the tests are really so useless, why does every major graduate program in science still use them—including the very departments at Harvard and MIT in which Liz and I have selected our own graduate students.

I think the reason is that school grades are affected by homework and by the ability to solve the kinds of problems that have already been presented in lecture and textbooks. Whereas the aptitude tests are designed to test the application of mathematical knowledge to unfamiliar problems. And this, of course, is closer to the way that math is used in actually *doing* math and science.

Indeed, contrary to Liz, and the popular opinion of many intellectuals, the tests are *surprisingly* good. There is an enormous amount of data on the predictive power of the SAT. For example, people in science careers overwhelmingly scored in 90th percentile in the SAT or GRE math test. And the tests predict earnings, occupational choice, doctoral degrees, the prestige of one's degree, the probability of having a tenure-track position, and the number of patents. Moreover this predictive power is the same for men and for women. As for why there is that underprediction of grades—a slight under-prediction, one-tenth of a standard deviation—the Educational Testing Service did a study on that phenomenon, and were able to explain the mystery by a combination of the choice of major, which differs between the sexes, and the greater conscientiousness of women.

Finally there's a sex difference in variability. It's crucial here to look at the right samples. Estimates of variance depend highly on the tails of the distribution, which by definition contain smaller numbers of people. Since people at the tails of the distribution in many surveys are likely to be weeded out for various reasons, it's important to have large representative samples from national populations. In this regard the gold standard is the *Science* paper by Novell and Hedges, which reported six large stratified probability samples. They found that in 35 out of 37 tests, including all of the tests in math, space, and science, the male variance was greater than the female variance. . . .

Now the fact that these six gender differences exist does not mean that they are innate. This of course is a much more difficult issue to resolve. A necessary preamble to this discussion is that nature and nurture are not alternatives; it is possible that the explanation for a given sex difference involves some of each. The only issue is whether the contribution of biology is greater than zero. I think that there are ten kinds of evidence that the contribution of biology *is* greater than zero, though of course it is nowhere near 100 percent.

First, there are many biological mechanisms by which a sex difference *could* occur. There are large differences between males and females in levels of sex hormones, especially prenatally, in the first six months of life, and in adolescence. There are receptors for hormones all over the brain, including the cerebral cortex. There are many small differences in men's and women's brains, including the overall size of the brain (even correcting for body size), the density of cortical neurons, the degree of cortical asymmetry, the size of hypothalamic nuclei, and several others.

Second, many of the major sex differences—certainly some of them, maybe all of them, are universal. The idea that there are cultures out there somewhere in which everything is the reverse of here turns out to be an academic legend. In his survey of the anthropological literature called *Human Universals,* the anthropologist Donald Brown points out that in all cultures men and women are seen as having different natures; that there is a greater involvement of women in direct child care; more competitiveness in various measures for men than for women; and a greater spatial range traveled by men compared to by women.

In personality, we have a cross-national survey (if not a true cross-cultural one) in Feingold's meta-analysis, which noted that gender differences in personality are consistent across ages, years of data collection, educational levels, and nations. When it comes to spatial manipulation and mathematical reasoning, we have fewer relevant data, and we honestly don't have true cross-cultural surveys, but we do have cross-national surveys. David Geary and Catherine Desoto found the expected sex difference in mental rotation in ten European countries and in Ghana, Turkey, and China. Similarly, Diane Halpern, analyzing results from ten countries, said that "the majority of the findings show amazing cross-cultural consistency when comparing males and females on cognitive tests."

Third, stability over time. Surveys of life interests and personality have shown little or no change in the two generations that have come of age since the second wave of feminism. There is also, famously, *resistance* to change in communities that, for various ideological reasons, were dedicated to stamping out sex differences, and found they were unable to do so. These include the Israeli kibbutz, various American Utopian communes a century ago, and contemporary androgynous academic couples.

In tests of mental rotation, the meta-analysis by Voyer et al found no change over time. In mathematical reasoning there has been a decline in the size of the difference, although it has certainly not disappeared.

Fourth, many sex differences can be seen in other mammals. It would be an amazing coincidence if these differences just happened to be replicated in the arbitrary choices made by human cultures at the dawn of time. There are large differences between males and females in many mammals in aggression, in investment in offspring, in play aggression play versus play parenting, and in the range size, which predicts a species' sex differences in spatial ability (such as in solving mazes), at least in polygynous species, which is how the human species is classified. Many primate species even show a sex difference in their interest in physical objects versus conspecifics, a difference seen their patterns of juvenile play. Among baby vervet monkeys, the males even prefer to play with trucks and the females with other kinds of toys!

Fifth, many of these differences emerge in early childhood. It is said that there is a technical term for people who believe that little boys and little girls are born indistinguishable and are molded into their natures by parental socialization. The term is "childless."

Some sex differences seem to emerge even in the first week of life. Girls respond more to sounds of distress, and girls make more eye contact than boys. And in a study that I know Liz disputes and that I hope we'll talk about, newborn boys were shown to be more interested in looking at a physical object than a face, whereas newborn girls were shown to be more interested in looking at a face than a physical object.

A bit later in development there are vast and robust differences between boys and girls, seen all over the world. Boys far more often than girls engage in rough-and-tumble play, which involves aggression, physical activity, and competition. Girls spend a lot more often in cooperative play. Girls engage much more often in play parenting. And yes, boys the world over turn anything into a vehicle or a weapon, and girls turn anything into a doll. There are sex differences in intuitive psychology, that is, how well children can read one another's minds. For instance, several large studies show that girls are better than boys in solving the "false belief task," and in interpreting the mental states of characters in stories.

Sixth, genetic boys brought up as girls. In a famous 1970s incident called the John/Joan case, one member of a pair of identical twin boys lost his penis in a botched circumcision (I was relieved to learn that this was not done by a moyl, but by a bumbling surgeon). Following advice from the leading gender expert of the time, the parents agreed to have the boy castrated, given female-specific hormones, and brought up as a girl. All this was hidden from him throughout his childhood.

When I was an undergraduate the case was taught to me as proof of how gender roles are socially acquired. But it turned out that the facts had been suppressed. When "Joan" and her family were interviewed years later, it turned out that from the youngest ages he exhibited boy-typical patterns of aggression and rough-and-tumble play, rejected girl-typical activities, and showed a greater interest in things than in people. At age 14, suffering from depression, his father finally told him the truth. He underwent further surgery, married a woman, adopted two children, and got a job in a slaughterhouse.

This is not just a unique instance. In a condition called cloacal exstrophy, genetic boys are sometimes born without normal male genitalia. When they are castrated and brought up as girls, in 25 out of 25 documented instances they have felt that they were boys trapped in girls' bodies, and showed male-specific patterns of behavior such as rough-and-tumble play.

Seventh, a lack of differential treatment by parents and teachers. These conclusions come as a shock to many people. One comes from Lytton and Romnev's meta-analysis of sex-specific socialization involving 172 studies and 28,000 children, in which they looked both at parents' reports and at direct observations of how parents treat their sons and daughters—and found few or no differences among contemporary Americans. In particular, there was no difference in the categories "Encouraging Achievement" and "Encouraging Achievement in Mathematics."

There is a widespread myth that teachers (who of course are disproportionately female) are dupes who perpetuate gender inequities by failing to call on girls in class, and who otherwise having low expectations of girls' performance. In fact Jussim and Eccles, in a study of 100 teachers and 1,800 students, concluded that teachers seemed to be basing their perceptions of students on those students' actual performances and motivation.

Eighth, studies of prenatal sex hormones: the mechanism that makes boys boys and girls girls in the first place. There is evidence, admittedly squishy in parts, that differences in prenatal hormones make a difference in later thought and behavior even within a given sex. In the condition called congenital adrenal hyperplasia, girls in utero are subjected to an increased dose of androgens, which is neutralized postnatally. But when they grow up they have male-typical toy preferences—trucks and guns—compared to other girls, male-typical play patterns, more competitiveness, less cooperativeness, and male-typical occupational preferences. However, research on their spatial abilities is inconclusive, and I cannot honestly say that there are replicable demonstrations that CAH women have male-typical patterns of spatial cognition.

Similarly, variations in fetal testosterone, studied in various ways, show that fetal testosterone has a nonmonotic relationship to reduced eye contact and face perception at 12 months, to reduced vocabulary at 18 months, to reduced social skills and greater narrowness of interest at 48 months, and to enhanced mental rotation abilities in the school-age years.

Ninth, circulating sex hormones. . . . Though it's possible that all claims of the effects of hormones on cognition will turn out to be bogus, I suspect something will be salvaged from this somewhat contradictory literature. There are, in any case, many studies showing that testosterone levels in the low-normal male range are associated with better abilities in spatial manipulation. And in a variety of studies in which estrogens are compared or manipulated, there is evidence, admittedly disputed, for statistical changes in the strengths and weaknesses in women's cognition during the menstrual cycle, possibly a counterpart to the changes in men's abilities during their daily and seasonal cycles of testosterone.

My last kind of evidence: imprinted X chromosomes. In the past fifteen years an entirely separate genetic system capable of implementing sex differences has been discovered. In the phenomenon called genetic imprinting, studied by David Haig and others, a chromosome such as the X chromosome can be altered depending on whether it was passed on from one's mother or from one's father. This makes a difference in the condition called Turner syndrome, in which a child has just one X chromosome, but can get it either from her mother or her father. When she inherits an X that is specific to girls, on average she has a better vocabulary and better social skills, and is better at reading emotions, at reading body language, and at reading faces.

A remark on stereotypes, and then I'll finish.

Are these stereotypes? Yes, many of them are (although, I must add, not all of them—for example, women's superiority in spatial memory and mathematical calculation). There seems to be a widespread assumption that if a sex difference conforms to a stereotype, the difference must have been *caused* by the stereotype, via differential expectations for boys and for girls. But of course the causal arrow could go in either direction: stereotypes might *reflect* differences rather than cause them. In fact there's an enormous literature in cognitive psychology which says that people can be good intuitive statisticians when forming categories and that their prototypes for conceptual categories track the statistics of the natural world pretty well. For example, there is a stereotype that basketball players are taller on average than jockeys. But that does not mean that basketball players grow tall, and jockeys shrink, because we expect them to have certain heights! Likewise, Alice Eagly and Jussim and Eccles have shown that most of people's gender stereotypes are in fact pretty accurate. Indeed the error people make is in the direction of *under*predicting sex differences.

To sum up: I think there is more than "a shred of evidence" for sex differences that are relevant to statistical gender disparities in elite hard science departments. There are reliable average difference in life priorities, in an interest in people versus things, in risk-seeking, in spatial transformations, in mathematical reasoning, and in variability in these traits. And there are ten kinds of evidence that these differences are not *completely* explained by socialization and bias, although they surely are in part.

A concluding remark. None of this provides grounds for ignoring the biases and barriers that do keep women out of science, as long as we keep in mind the distinction between *fairness* on the one hand and *sameness* on the other. And I will give the final word to Gloria Steinem: "there are very few jobs that actually require a penis or a vagina, and all the other jobs should be open to both sexes."

Elizabeth Spelke → **NO**

The Science of Gender and Science: Pinker Vs. Spelke, A Debate

I want to start by talking about the points of agreement between Steve and me, and as he suggested, there are many. If we got away from the topic of sex and science, we'd be hard pressed to find issues that we disagree on. Here are a few of the points of agreement that are particularly relevant to the discussions of the last few months.

First, we agree that both our society in general and our university in particular will be healthiest if all opinions can be put on the table and debated on their merits. We also agree that claims concerning sex differences are empirical, they should be evaluated by evidence, and we'll all be happier and live longer if we can undertake that evaluation as dispassionately and rationally as possible. We agree that the mind is not a blank slate; in fact one of the deepest things that Steve and I agree on is that there is such a thing as human nature, and it is a fascinating and exhilarating experience to study it. And finally, I think we agree that the role of scientists in society is rather modest. Scientists find things out. The much more difficult questions of how to use that information, live our lives, and structure our societies are not questions that science can answer. Those are questions that everybody must consider.

So where do we disagree?

We disagree on the answer to the question, why in the world are women scarce as hens' teeth on Harvard's mathematics faculty and other similar institutions? In the current debate, two classes of factors have been said to account for this difference. In one class are social forces, including overt and covert discrimination and social influences that lead men and women to develop different skills and different priorities. In the other class are genetic differences that predispose men and women to have different capacities and to want different things.

In his book, *The Blank Slate,* and again today, Steve argued that social forces are over-rated as causes of gender differences. Intrinsic differences in aptitude are a larger factor, and intrinsic differences in motives are the biggest factor of all. Most of the examples that Steve gave concerned what he takes to be biologically based differences in motives.

My own view is different. I think the big forces causing this gap are social factors. There are no differences in overall intrinsic aptitude for science and mathematics between women and men. Notice that I am not saying the genders are indistinguishable, that men and women are alike in every way, or even that men and women have identical cognitive profiles. I'm saying that when you add up all the things that men are good at, and all the things that women are good at, there is no overall advantage for men that would put them at the top of the fields of math and science.

On the issue of motives, I think we're not in a position to know whether the different things that men and women often say they want stem only from social forces, or in part from intrinsic sex differences. I don't think we can know that now.

I want to start with the issue that's clearly the biggest source of debate between Steve and me: the issue of differences in intrinsic aptitude. This is the only issue that my own work and professional knowledge bear on. Then I will turn to the social forces, as a lay person as it were, because I think they are exerting the biggest effects. Finally, I'll consider the question of intrinsic motives, which I hope we'll come back to in our discussion.

Over the last months, we've heard three arguments that men have greater cognitive aptitude for science. The first argument is that from birth, boys are interested in objects and mechanics, and girls are interested in people and emotions. The predisposition to figure out the mechanics of the world sets boys on a path that makes them more likely to become scientists or mathematicians. The second argument assumes, as Galileo told us, that science is conducted in the language of mathematics. On the second claim, males are intrinsically better at mathematical reasoning, including spatial reasoning. The third argument is that men show greater variability than women, and as a result there are more men at the extreme upper end of the ability distribution from which scientists and mathematicians are drawn. Let me take these claims one by one.

The first claim, as Steve said, is gaining new currency from the work of Simon Baron-Cohen. It's an old idea, presented with some new language. Baron-Cohen says that males are innately predisposed to learn about objects and mechanical relationships, and this sets them on a path to becoming what he calls "systematizers." Females, on the other hand, are innately predisposed to learn about people and their emotions, and this puts them on a path to becoming "empathizers." Since systematizing is at the heart of math and science, boys are more apt to develop the knowledge and skills that lead to math and science.

To anyone as old as I am who has been following the literature on sex differences, this may seem like a surprising claim. The classic reference on the nature and development of sex differences is a book by Eleanor Maccoby and Carol Jacklin that came out in the 1970s. They reviewed evidence for all sorts of sex differences, across large numbers of studies, but they also concluded that certain ideas about differences between the genders were myths. At the top of their list of myths was the idea that males are primarily interested in objects and females are primarily interested in people. They reviewed an enormous literature, in which babies were presented with objects and people to see if they were more interested in one than the other. They concluded that there were no sex differences in these interests.

Nevertheless, this conclusion was made in the early 70s. At that time, we didn't know much about babies' understanding of objects and people, or how their understanding grows. Since Baron-Cohen's claims concern differential predispositions to learn about different kinds of things, you could argue that the claims hadn't been tested in Maccoby and Jacklin's time. What does research now show?

. . . From birth, babies perceive objects. They know where one object ends and the next one begins. They can't see objects as well as we can, but as they grow their object perception becomes richer and more differentiated.

Babies also start with rudimentary abilities to represent that an object continues to exist when it's out of view, and they hold onto those representations longer, and over more complicated kinds of changes, as they grow. Babies make basic inferences about object motion: inferences like, the force with which an object is hit determines the speed with which it moves. These inferences undergo regular developmental changes over the infancy period.

In each of these cases, there is systematic developmental change, and there's variability. Because of this variability, we can compare the abilities of male infants to females. Do we see sex differences? The research gives a clear answer to this question: We don't.

Male and female infants are equally interested in objects. Male and female infants make the same inferences about object motion, at the same time in development. They learn the same things about object mechanics at the same time.

Across large numbers of studies, occasionally a study will favor one sex over the other. For example, girls learn that the force with which something is hit influences the distance it moves a month earlier than boys do. But these differences are small and scattered. For the most part, we see high convergence across the sexes. Common paths of learning continue through the preschool years, as kids start manipulating objects to see if they can get a rectangular block into a circular hole. If you look at the rates at which boys and girls figure these things out, you don't find any differences. We see equal developmental paths.

I think this research supports an important conclusion. In discussions of sex differences, we need to ask what's common across the two sexes. One thing that's common is infants don't divide up the labor of understanding the world, with males focusing on mechanics and females focusing on emotions. Male and female infants are both interested in objects and in people, and they learn about both. The conclusions that Maccoby and Jacklin drew in the early 1970s are well supported by research since that time.

Let me turn to the second claim. People may have equal abilities to develop intuitive understanding of the physical world, but formal math and science don't build on these intuitions. Scientists use mathematics to come up with new characterizations of the world and new principles to explain its functioning. Maybe males have an edge in scientific reasoning because of their greater talent for mathematics.

As Steve said, formal mathematics is not something we have evolved to do; it's a recent accomplishment. Animals don't do formal math or science, and neither did humans back in the Pleistocene. If there is a biological basis for our mathematical reasoning abilities, it must depend on systems that evolved for other purposes, but that we've been able to harness for the new purpose of representing and manipulating numbers and geometry.

Research from the intersecting fields of cognitive neuroscience, neuropsychology, cognitive psychology, and cognitive development provide evidence for five "core systems" at the foundations of mathematical reasoning. The first is a system for representing small exact numbers of objects—the difference between *one, two,* and *three.* This system emerges in human infants at about five months of age, and it continues to be present in adults. The second is a system for discriminating large, approximate numerical magnitudes—the difference between a set of about ten things and a set of about 20 things. That system also emerges early in infancy, at four or five months, and continues to be present and functional in adults.

The third system is probably the first uniquely human foundation for numerical abilities: the system of natural number concepts that we construct as children when we learn verbal counting. That construction takes place between about the ages of two and a half and four years. The last two systems are first seen in children when they navigate. One system represents the geometry of the surrounding layout. The other system represents landmark objects.

All five systems have been studied quite extensively in large numbers of male and female infants. We can ask, are there sex differences in the development of any of these systems at the foundations of mathematical thinking? Again, the answer is no. . . .

These findings and others support two important points. First, indeed there is a biological foundation to mathematical and scientific reasoning. We are endowed with core knowledge systems that emerge prior to any formal instruction and that serve as a basis for mathematical thinking. Second, these systems develop equally in males and females. Ten years ago, the evolutionary psychologist and sex difference researcher, David Geary, reviewed the literature that was available at that time. He concluded that there were no sex differences in "primary abilities" underlying mathematics. What we've learned in the last ten years continues to support that conclusion.

Sex differences do emerge at older ages. Because they emerge later in childhood, it's hard to tease apart their biological and social sources. But before we attempt that task, let's ask what the differences are.

I think the following is a fair statement, both of the cognitive differences that Steve described and of others. When people are presented with a complex task that can be solved through multiple different strategies, males and females sometimes differ in the strategy that they prefer.

For example, if a task can only be solved by representing the geometry of the layout, we do not see a difference between men and women. But if the task can be accomplished either by representing geometry or by representing individual landmarks, girls tend to rely on the landmarks, and boys on the geometry. To take another example, when you compare the shapes of two objects of different orientations, there are two different strategies you can use. You can attempt a holistic rotation of one of the objects into registration with the other, or you can do point-by-point featural comparisons of the two objects. Men are more likely to do the first; women are more likely to do the second.

Finally, the mathematical word problems on the SAT-M very often allow multiple solutions. Both item analyses and studies of high school students engaged in the act of solving such problems suggest that when students have the choice of solving a problem by plugging in a formula or by doing Ven diagram-like spatial reasoning, girls tend to do the first and boys tend to do the second.

Because of these differences, males and females sometimes show differing cognitive profiles on timed tests. When you have to solve problems fast, some strategies will be faster than others. Thus, females perform better at some verbal, mathematical and spatial tasks, and males perform better at other verbal, mathematical, and spatial tasks. This pattern of differing profiles is not well captured by the generalization, often bandied about in the popular press, that women are "verbal" and men are "spatial." There doesn't seem to be any more evidence for that than there was for the idea that women are people-oriented and men are object-oriented. Rather the differences are more subtle.

Does one of these two profiles foster better learning of math than the other? In particular, is the male profile better suited to high-level mathematical reasoning?

At this point, we face a question that's been much discussed in the literature on mathematics education and mathematical testing. The question is, by what yardstick can we decide whether men or women are better at math?

Some people suggest that we look at performance on the SAT-M, the quantitative portion of the Scholastic Assessment Test. But this suggestion raises a problem of circularity. The SAT test is composed of many different types of items. Some of those items are solved better by females. Some are solved better by males. The people who make the test have to decide, how many items of each type to include? Depending on how they answer that question, they can create a test that makes women look like better mathematicians, or a test that makes men look like better mathematicians. What's the right solution?

Books are devoted to this question, with much debate, but there seems to be a consensus on one point: The only way to come up with a test that's fair is to develop an independent understanding of what mathematical aptitude is and how it's distributed between men and women. But in that case, we can't use performance on the SAT to give us that understanding. We've got to get that understanding in some other way. So how are we going to get it?

A second strategy is to look at job outcomes. Maybe the people who are better at mathematics are those who pursue more mathematically intensive careers. But this strategy raises two problems. First, which mathematically intensive jobs should we choose? If we choose engineering, we will conclude that men are better at math because more men become engineers. If we choose accounting, we will think that women are better at math because more women become accountants: 57% of current accountants are women. So which job are we going to pick, to decide who has more mathematical talent?

These two examples suggest a deeper problem with job outcomes as a measure of mathematical talent. Surely you've got to be good at math to land a mathematically intensive job, but talent in mathematics is only one of the factors influencing career choice. It can't be our gold standard for mathematical ability.

So what can be? I suggest the following experiment. We should take a large number of male students and a large number of female students who have equal educational backgrounds, and present them with the kinds of tasks that real mathematicians face. We should give them new mathematical material that they have not yet mastered, and allow them to learn it over an extended period of time: the kind of time scale that real mathematicians work on. We should ask, how well do the students master this material? The good news is, this experiment is done all the time. It's called high school and college.

Here's the outcome. In high school, girls and boys now take equally many math classes, including the most advanced ones, and girls get better grades. In college, women earn almost half of the bachelor's degrees in mathematics, and men and women get equal grades. Here I respectfully disagree with one thing that Steve said: men and women get equal grades, even when you only compare people within a single institution and a single math class. Equating for classes, men and women get equal grades.

The outcome of this large-scale experiment gives us every reason to conclude that men and women have equal talent for mathematics. Here, I too would like to quote Diane Halpern. Halpern reviews much evidence for sex differences, but she concludes, "differences are not deficiencies." Men and women have equal aptitude for mathematics. Yes, there are sex differences, but they don't add up to an overall advantage for one sex over the other.

Let me turn to the third claim, that men show greater variability, either in general or in quantitative abilities in particular, and so there are more men at the upper end of the ability distribution. I can go quickly here, because Steve has already talked about the work of Camilla Benbow and Julian Stanley, focusing on mathematically precocious youth who are screened at the age of 13, put in intensive accelerated programs, and then followed up to see what they achieve in mathematics and other fields.

As Steve said, students were screened at age 13 by the SAT, and there were many more boys than girls who scored at the highest levels on the SAT-M. In the 1980s, the disparity was almost 13 to 1. It is now substantially lower, but there still are more boys among the very small subset of people from this large, talented sample who scored at the very upper end. Based on these data, Benbow and Stanley concluded that there are more boys than girls in the pool from which future mathematicians will be drawn. But notice the problem with this conclusion: It's based entirely on the SAT-M. This test, and the disparity it revealed, are in need of an explanation, a firmer yardstick for assessing and understanding gender differences in this talented population.

Fortunately, Benbow, Stanley and Lubinski have collected much more data on these mathematically talented boys and girls: not just the ones with top scores on one timed test, but rather the larger sample of girls and boys who were accelerated and followed over time. Let's look at some of the key things that they found.

First, they looked at college performance by the talented sample. They found that the males and females took equally demanding math classes and majored in math in equal numbers. More girls majored in biology and more boys in physics and engineering, but equal numbers of girls and boys majored in math. And they got equal grades. The SAT-M not only under-predicts the performance of college women in general, it also under-predicted the college performance of women in the talented sample. These women and men have been shown to be equally talented by the most meaningful measure we have: their ability to assimilate new, challenging material in demanding mathematics classes at top-flight institutions. By that measure, the study does not find any difference between highly talented girls and boys.

So, what's causing the gender imbalance on faculties of math and science? Not differences in intrinsic aptitude. Let's turn to the social factors that I think are much more important. Because I'm venturing outside my own area of work, and because time is short, I won't review all of the social factors producing differential success of men and women. I will talk about just one effect: how gender stereotypes influence the ways in which males and females are perceived.

Let me start with studies of parents' perceptions of their own children. Steve said that parents report that they treat their children equally. They treat their boys and girls alike, and they encourage them to equal extents, for they want both their sons and their daughters to succeed. This is no doubt true. But how are parents perceiving their kids?

Some studies have interviewed parents just after the birth of their child, at the point where the first question that 80% of parents ask—is it a boy or a girl?—has been answered. Parents of boys describe their babies as stronger, heartier, and bigger than parents of girls. The investigators also looked at the babies' medical records and asked whether there really were differences between the boys and girls in weight, strength, or coordination. The boys and girls were indistinguishable in these respects, but the parents' descriptions were different.

At 12 months of age, girls and boys show equal abilities to walk, crawl, or clamber. But before one study, Karen Adolph, an investigator of infants' locomotor development, asked parents to predict how well their child would do on a set of crawling tasks: Would the child be able to crawl down a sloping ramp? Parents of sons were more confident that their child would make it down the ramp than parents of daughters. When Adolph tested the infants on the ramp, there was no difference whatever between the sons and daughters, but there was a difference in the parents' predictions.

My third example, moving up in age, comes from the studies of Jackie Eccles. She asked parents of boys and girls in sixth grade, how talented do you think your child is in mathematics? Parents of sons were more likely to judge that their sons had talent than parents of daughters. A panoply of objective measures, including math grades in school, performance on standardized tests, teachers' evaluations, and children's expressed interest in math, revealed no differences between the girls and boys. Still, there was a difference in parents' perception of their child's intangible talent. Other studies have shown a similar effect for science.

There's clearly a mismatch between what parents perceive in their kids and what objective measures reveal. But is it possible that the parents are seeing something that the objective measures are missing? Maybe the boy getting B's in his math class really is a mathematical genius, and his mom or dad has sensed that. To eliminate that possibility, we need to present observers with the very same baby, or child, or Ph.D. candidate, and manipulate their belief about the person's gender. Then we can ask whether their belief influences their perception.

It's hard to do these studies, but there are examples, and I will describe a few of them. A bunch of studies take the following form: you show a group of parents, or college undergraduates, video-clips of babies that they don't know personally. For half of them you give the baby a male name, and for the other half you give the baby a female name. (Male and female babies don't look very different.) The observers watch the baby and then are asked a series of questions: What is the baby doing? What is the baby feeling? How would you rate the baby on a dimension like strong-to-weak, or more intelligent to less intelligent? There are two important findings.

First, when babies do something unambiguous, reports are not affected by the baby's gender. If the baby clearly smiles, everybody says the baby is smiling or happy. Perception of children is not pure hallucination. Second, children often do things that are ambiguous, and parents face questions whose answers aren't easily readable off their child's overt behavior. In those cases, you see some interesting gender labeling effects. For example, in one study a child on a video-clip was playing with a jack-in-the-box. It suddenly popped up, and the child was startled and jumped backward. When people were asked, what's the child feeling, those who were given a female label said, "she's afraid." But the ones given a male label said, "he's angry." Same child, same reaction, different interpretation.

In other studies, children with male names were more likely to be rated as strong, intelligent, and active; those with female names were more likely to be rated as little, soft, and so forth.

I think these perceptions matter. You, as a parent, may be completely committed to treating your male and female children equally. But no sane parents would treat a fearful child the same way they treat an angry child. If knowledge of a child's gender affects adults' perception of that child, then male and female children are going to elicit different reactions from the world, different patterns of encouragement. These perceptions matter, even in parents who are committed to treating sons and daughters alike.

I will give you one last version of a gender-labeling study. This one hits particularly close to home. The subjects in the study were people like Steve and me: professors of psychology, who were sent some vitas to evaluate as applicants for a tenure track position. Two different vitas were used in the study. One was a vita of a walk-on-water candidate, best candidate you've ever seen, you would die to have this person on your faculty. The other vita was a middling, average vita among successful candidates. For half the professors, the name on the vita was male, for the other half the name was female. People were asked a series of questions: What do you think about this candidate's research productivity? What do you think about his or her teaching experience? And finally, Would you hire this candidate at your university?

For the walk-on-water candidate, there was no effect of gender labeling on these judgments. I think this finding supports Steve's view that we're dealing with little overt discrimination at universities. It's not as if professors see a female name on a vita and think, I don't want her. When the vita's great, everybody says great, let's hire.

What about the average successful vita, though: that is to say, the kind of vita that professors most often must evaluate? In that case, there were differences. The male was rated as having higher research productivity. These psychologists, Steve's and my colleagues, looked at the same number of publications and thought, "good productivity" when the name was male, and "less good productivity" when the name was female. Same thing for teaching experience. The very same list of courses was seen as good teaching experience when the name was male, and less good teaching experience when the name was female. In answer to the question would they hire the candidate, 70% said yes for the male, 45% for the female. If the decision were made by majority rule, the male would get hired and the female would not.

A couple other interesting things came out of this study. The effects were every hit as strong among the female respondents as among the male respondents. Men are not the culprits here. There were effects at the tenure level as well. At the tenure level, professors evaluated a very strong candidate, and almost everyone said this looked like a good case for tenure. But people were invited to express their reservations, and they came up with some very reasonable doubts. For example, "This person looks very strong, but before I agree to give her tenure I would need to know, was this her own work or the work of her adviser?" Now that's a perfectly reasonable question to ask. But what ought to give us pause is that those kinds of reservations were expressed *four times more often* when the name was female than when the name was male.

So there's a pervasive difference in perceptions, and I think the difference matters. Scientists' perception of the quality of a candidate will influence the likelihood that the candidate will get a fellowship, a job, resources, or a promotion. A pattern of biased evaluation therefore will occur even in people who are absolutely committed to gender equity. . . .

From the moment of birth to the moment of tenure, throughout this great developmental progression, there are unintentional but pervasive and important differences in the ways that males and females are perceived and evaluated.

I have to emphasize that perceptions are not everything. When cases are unambiguous, you don't see these effects. What's more, cognitive development is robust: boys and girls show equal capacities and achievements in educational settings, including in science and mathematics, despite the very different ways in which boys and girls are perceived and evaluated. I think it's really great news that males and females develop along common paths and gain common sets of abilities. The equal performance of males and females, despite their unequal treatment, strongly suggests that mathematical and scientific reasoning has a biological foundation, and this foundation is shared by males and females.

Finally, you do not create someone who feels like a girl or boy simply by perceiving them as male or female. That's the lesson that comes from the studies of people of one sex who are raised as the opposite sex. Biological sex differences are real and important. Sex is not a cultural construction that's imposed on people.

But the question on the table is not, Are there biological sex differences? The question is, Why are there fewer women mathematicians and scientists? The patterns of bias that I described provide four interconnected answers to that question. First, and most obviously, biased perceptions produce discrimination: When a group of equally qualified men and women are evaluated for jobs, more of the men will get those jobs if they are perceived to be more qualified. Second, if people are rational, more men than women will put themselves forward into the academic competition, because men will see that they've got a better chance for success. Academic jobs will be more attractive to men because they face better odds, will get more resources, and so forth.

Third, biased perceptions earlier in life may well deter some female students from even attempting a career in science or mathematics. If your parents feel that you don't have as much natural talent as someone else whose objective abilities are no better than yours, that may discourage you, as Eccles's work shows. Finally, there's likely to be a snowball effect. All of us have an easier time imagining ourselves in careers where there are other people like us. If the first three effects perpetuate a situation where there are few female scientists and mathematicians, young girls will be less likely to see math and science as a possible life.

So by my personal scorecard, these are the major factors. Let me end, though, by asking, could Steve also be partly right? Could biological differences in motives—motivational patterns that evolved in the Pleistocene but that apply to us today—propel more men than women towards careers in mathematics and science?

My feeling is that where we stand now, we cannot evaluate this claim. It may be true, but as long as the forces of discrimination and biased perceptions affect people so pervasively, we'll never know. I think the only way we can find out is to do one more experiment. We should allow all of the evidence that men and women have equal cognitive capacity, to permeate through society. We should allow people to evaluate children in relation to their actual capacities, rather than one's sense of what their capacities ought to be, given their gender. Then we can see, as those boys and girls grow up, whether different inner voices pull them in different directions. I don't know what the findings of that experiment will be. But I do hope that some future generation of children gets to find out.

CHALLENGE QUESTIONS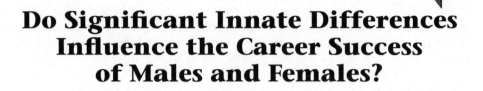

Do Significant Innate Differences Influence the Career Success of Males and Females?

- Do you agree with Pinker that part of the challenge with thinking about this issue in a reasonable way comes from the social taboo against suggesting that any differences might be innate rather than learned? Why or why not?
- Both authors agree that there are some average differences that might favor men, while others might favor women. Which of these differences seem most important for career success and other outcomes of life-span development?
- Spelke notes that we as a society tend to focus on gender from the moment children are born, when the first question is usually "boy or girl?" Given our interest in gender, is it possible to completely remove ideas about innate differences?
- Although there are still differences in career patterns for men and women, these differences have shifted greatly during recent decades. How do you think each side would explain these shifts?

Suggested Readings

B. Barres, "Does Gender Matter?" *Nature* (July 13, 2006)

L. Brizendine, *The Female Brain* (Broadway, 2006)

A. Fausto-Sterling, "Beyond Differences: A Biologist's Perspective," *Journal of Social Issues* (vol. 53, no. 2, 1997)

D. Geary, "Evolution and Developmental Sex Differences," *Current Directions in Psychological Science* (August 4, 1999)

S. Glazer, "Gender and Learning: Are There Innate Differences Between the Sexes?" *The CQ Researcher* (May 20, 2005)

C. Leaper, "The Social Construction and Socialization of Gender During Development," *Toward a Feminist Developmental Psychology* (Routledge, 2000)

R. Monastersky, "Women and Science: The Debate Goes On," *The Chronicle of Higher Education* (March 4, 2005)

A. Ripley, N. Mustafa, D. van Dyk, and U. Plon, "Who Says a Woman Can't be Einstein?" *Time* (March 7, 2005)

Internet References . . .

Safe Fetus

This Web site is an extensive reference for checking the influence of various substances on a fetus during pregnancy.

http://www.safefetus.com

The Mayo Clinic

The Mayo Clinic is a well-respected medical institution that offers a variety of articles and resources related to infant health and development.

http://www.mayoclinic.com/health/infant-and-toddler-health/MY00362

McGraw-Hill Higher Education

This site provides links to various resources related to physical, cognitive, language, and social development in infants.

http://www.mhhe.com/socscience/devel/common/infant.htm

The Centers for Disease Control and Prevention

The Centers for Disease Control and Prevention is a government agency offering information about health at all ages, including information specific to infants.

http://www.cdc.gov/ncbddd/child/infants.htm

Jean Piaget and Cognitive Development

This site provides a good overview of the work of Jean Piaget, who started the discussion of infant symbolic representation.

http://www.ship.edu/~cgboeree/genpsypiaget.html

The James S. McDonnell Foundation

The James S. McDonnell Foundation funds research related to brain development and is headed by the author of "The Myth of the First Three Years."

http://www.jsmf.org/

Zero to Three

Zero to Three is a non-profit organization working to facilitate healthy development, and their Web site contains information and resources focused on infants and their families.

http://www.zerotothree.org/

The American Pregnancy Association

The American Pregnancy Association is a non-profit organization offering educational resources related to healthy pregnancies.

http://www.americanpregnancy.org/

Prenatal Development and Infancy

*O*ur most rapid and astonishing physical changes occur during the approximately nine months prior to birth and during the first years of postnatal life. These are unique years in development because of our complete dependence on others. Being without language, a concept of self, and other complex capacities, it is easy to imagine these initial stages as a simple matter of accommodating needs and wants. There is, however, an increasing awareness that there is more to our earliest development than initially meets the eye. This section considers three issues dealing with ways that our experiences during prenatal development and infancy provide a foundation for all the complexity that follows.

- Is Drinking Alcohol While Pregnant an Unnecessary Risk to Prenatal Development?
- Is There a "Myth of the First Three Years"?
- Are There Good Reasons to Allow Infants to Consume Electronic Media, Such as Television?

ISSUE 4

Is Drinking Alcohol While Pregnant an Unnecessary Risk to Prenatal Development?

YES: Phyllida Brown, from "Drinking for Two," *New Scientist* (July 1, 2006)

NO: Julia Moskin, from "The Weighty Responsibility of Drinking for Two," *The New York Times* (November 29, 2006)

ISSUE SUMMARY

YES: Science writer Phyllida Brown reviews contemporary research about the effects of alcohol exposure during prenatal development and concludes that total abstinence from drinking is the smart option during pregnancy.

NO: Journalist Julia Moskin finds the evidence against light drinking lacking, and argues that women should be allowed to decide for themselves if an occasional alcoholic beverage is harmful.

Drinking alcohol while pregnant carries a powerful negative stigma. Public health campaigns and government warnings have effectively conveyed the message that alcohol, along with other drugs, can harm prenatal development. Most people are now familiar with Fetal Alcohol Syndrome (FAS), its symptoms, and its effects. Given that familiarity, however, it is interesting to note that FAS was only "discovered" in 1973. For generations women had drank alcohol during pregnancy. While there were certainly some negative consequences, there had significantly fewer judgments about women's choices. Has society simply become more enlightened, or have we gone too far?

Scientific research on this issue tends to devote less attention to stigma and more attention to the physical effects of prenatal exposure to alcohol and other teratogens. A teratogen is any external agent that causes malformation of organs and tissue during prenatal development. Fetal exposure to external agents, most often through the mother, is not a process of direct transmission: there are widely varying degrees of detrimental influence on prenatal development.

Further complicating matters, the relationship between teratogens and prenatal development does not necessarily correspond to popular perceptions of danger. In fact, according to ratings by the federal Food and Drug Administration, a drug such as aspirin has more established negative biological effects on a fetus than a drug such as cocaine. These biological effects, however, are often complicated by social context.

Understanding the relationship between exposure to alcohol and prenatal development is also complicated by the fact that many babies born to women who drank during pregnancy do not seem to suffer ill effects. Science writer Phyllida Brown, in arguing that it is safest to avoid all alcohol while pregnant, even acknowledges that "not all babies born to alcolohic women have FAS." So the relationship between a pregnant mother's alcohol consumption and prenatal development is imperfect and requires negotiating uncertain odds. The question then becomes about what sort of odds make drinking while pregnant worth the risk. From Brown's perspective knowing that there is some chance alcohol can harm prenatal development means the only reasonable choice is complete abstinence.

Journalist Julia Moskin argues that a pregnant women can reasonably choose to drink lightly at certain points in a pregnancy. Moskin points out that while much research has been done comparing the effects of heavy drinking during pregnancy with the effects of no drinking during pregnancy, significantly less research has considered the effects of light drinking. As such, when pressed, some doctors will acknowledge that light drinking at later points in pregnancy is not likely to have long-term effects on prenatal development. Moskin's underlying point is relevant to much of what we know about pregnancy: prenatal development is often too complicated a process to allow for simple certainties about what will or won't ensure the healthy children all parents desire.

POINT

- Many governments and researchers are becoming more stringent in recommending pregnant women should not consume any alcohol.
- Government restrictions are being overly cautious by making no distinction between heavy drinking and occasional light drinking during pregnancy.
- Fetal alcohol spectrum disorders can cause children to have a wide range of problems with both physical and mental health during later development.
- The recognition of FAS is relatively recent, and generations of women had healthy children despite drinking during pregnancy.
- Worrying about every potential minor risk to prenatal development can have a negative effect on mental health; in many world cultures, it has historically been considered normal for women to drink lightly during pregnancy.

COUNTERPOINT

- Magnetic resonance imaging studies find some changes in the brain structure of children whose mother drank during pregnancy, while animal studies suggest that exposure to alcohol during critical periods of brain development can cause neuronal cell death.
- Though the science is not yet entirely definitive, the best policy is to take no chances.

- Much of the public reaction against women drinking during pregnancy is really about not trusting women to make intelligent decisions on their own.

YES ↵

Phyllida Brown

Drinking for Two

AT FIRST, Susie's teachers thought she was a bright child. Her adoptive mother knew different. Give Susie a set of instructions and only a few seconds later she would have forgotten them. She was talkative, with a large vocabulary, but could not seem to form lasting friendships. Then, one day, Susie's adoptive mother heard a lecture that described fetal alcohol syndrome—a condition which affects some children born to heavy drinkers. "Bells went off in my head," she says. "The lecturer described eight traits, and my daughter had seven of them."

Children like Susie could well be just the tip of the iceberg. Fetal alcohol syndrome was once thought to affect only the children of heavy drinkers, such as Susie's biological mother, but a mounting body of research suggests that even a small amount of alcohol can damage a developing fetus—a single binge during pregnancy or a moderate seven small glasses of wine per week.

The new research has already prompted some governments to tighten up their advice on drinking during pregnancy. Others, however, say there is no convincing evidence that modest alcohol intake is dangerous for the fetus. With advice varying wildly from one country to another, the message for pregnant women has never been so confusing.

Last year the U.S. Surgeon General revised official advice warning pregnant women to limit their alcohol intake. Now they are told "simply not to drink" alcohol—not only in pregnancy, but as soon as they plan to try for a baby. France also advises abstinence, as does Canada. The UK's Department of Health says that pregnant women should avoid more than "one to two units, once or twice a week", but is finalising a review of the latest evidence, which it will publish within weeks. In Australia, women are advised to "consider" abstinence, but if choosing to drink should limit their intake to less than seven standard Australian drinks a week, with no more than two standard drinks on any one day.

Whichever guidelines women choose to follow, some level of drinking during pregnancy is common in many countries. The last time pregnant women in the UK were asked, in 2002, 61 percent admitted to drinking some alcohol. Even in the U.S., where abstinence is expected, and where pregnant women in some states have been arrested for drinking, 13 percent still admit to doing it.

Children with fetal alcohol syndrome (FAS) are generally smaller than average and have a range of developmental and behavioural problems such as an inability to relate to others and a tendency to be impulsive. They also have distinctive facial features such as a thin upper lip, an extra fold of skin in the inner corners of the eyes and a flattening of the groove between the nose and upper lip.

In recent years researchers investigating the effects of alcohol in pregnancy have begun to widen their definition of antenatal alcohol damage beyond the diagnosis of FAS. They now talk of fetal alcohol spectrum disorders, or FASD, an umbrella term that covers a range of physical, mental and behavioural effects which can occur without the facial features of FAS. Like children with FAS, those with FASD may have problems with arithmetic, paying attention, working memory and the planning of tasks. They may be impulsive, find it difficult to judge social situations correctly and relate badly to others, or be labelled as aggressive or defiant. In adulthood they may find it difficult to lead independent lives, be diagnosed with mental illnesses, or get into trouble with the law. Some have damage to the heart, ears or eyes.

While some children with FASD have been exposed to as much alcohol before birth as those with FAS, others may be damaged by lower levels, says Helen Barr, a statistician at the University of Washington, Seattle. Barr has spent 30 years tracking children exposed to alcohol before birth and comparing them with non-exposed children. The less alcohol, in general, says Barr, the milder the effects, such as more subtle attention problems or memory difficulties. Other factors that can affect the type of damage include the fetus's stage of development when exposed to alcohol and the mother's genetic make-up.

Although FASD is not yet an official medical diagnosis, some researchers estimate that it could be very common indeed. While FAS is thought to account for 1 in 500 live births, Ann Streissguth and her colleagues at the University of Washington believe that as many as 1 in every 100 babies born in the U.S. are affected by FASD. Others put the figure at about 1 in 300. Whichever figure is more accurate, it would still make the condition far more common than, say, Downs syndrome, which affects 1 in 800 babies born in the U.S.

Streissguth was among the first to study the long-term effects of moderate drinking in pregnancy. In 1993 she reported that a group of 7-year-olds whose mothers had drunk 7 to 14 standard drinks per week in pregnancy tended to have specific problems with arithmetic and attention. Compared with children of similar IQ whose mothers had abstained during pregnancy, they struggled to remember strings of digits or the details of stories read to them, and were unable to discriminate between two rhythmic sound patterns.

When Streissguth's team followed the alcohol-exposed children through adolescence and into their early twenties they found them significantly more likely than other individuals of similar IQ and social background to be labelled as aggressive by their teachers. According to their parents, these children were unable to consider the effects of their actions on others, and unable to take hints or understand social cues. As young adults, they were more likely to drink heavily and use drugs than their peers.

These findings were borne out by similar studies later in the 1990s by Sandra Jacobson and Joseph Jacobson, both psychologists at Wayne State University in Detroit, Michigan. To try and work out what dose of alcohol might be harmful, the Jacobsons ran a study of children born to 480 women in Detroit. In it, they compared the children born to women who, at their first antenatal appointment, said they drank seven or more standard U.S. drinks a week with the babies of women who drank less than seven, and with those whose mothers abstained altogether. The psychologists then tested the children's mental function in infancy and again at 7 years old. In the children whose mothers had seven drinks or more, the pair found significant deficits in their children's mental function in infancy, and again at age 7, mainly in arithmetic, working memory and attention (*Alcoholism: Clinical and Experimental Research,* vol 28, p 1732). Where the mother drank less than that they found no effect.

Spread it Out

Seven drinks a week may be more than many pregnant women manage, but according to the Jacobsons, what's important is when you are drinking them, whether you have eaten, and how quickly your body metabolises alcohol. In their study, only one woman of the 480 drank daily; most of the others restricted their drinking to a couple of weekend evenings. If a woman is drinking seven standard drinks on average across the week, but having them all on two nights, she must be reaching four drinks on one night. That constitutes a binge. "Women don't realise that if they save up their alcohol 'allowance' to the end of the week, they are concentrating their drinking in a way that is potentially harmful," she says. This means that even women who have fewer than seven glasses per week could potentially be putting their babies at risk if they drink them all on one night.

There is also some evidence that fewer than seven drinks a week could have measurable effects on an unborn baby. Peter Hepper at Queen's University, Belfast, UK, examined the movements of fetuses scanned on ultrasound in response to a noise stimulus. Having asked women about their drinking habits, they compared the responses of fetuses exposed to low levels of alcohol—between 1 and 6 British units per week, each containing 10 millilitres of alcohol—and those exposed to none. When tested between 20 and 35 weeks, the fetuses exposed to alcohol tended to show a "startle response" usually found only in the earlier stages of pregnancy, when the nervous system is less developed. Five months after birth, the same babies showed different responses to visual stimuli from the babies whose mothers had abstained. Hepper interprets these findings as evidence that a low dose of alcohol has some as yet unexplained effect on the developing nervous system. Whether or not these differences will translate into behaviour problems in later life is as yet unknown.

When Ed Riley and colleagues at San Diego State University in California looked at children's brains using magnetic resonance imaging, they found obvious changes in the brain structure of children whose mothers drank very heavily, but also some changes in children born to moderate drinkers. For example, there were abnormalities in the corpus callosum, the tract of fibres connecting the right and left hemispheres of the brain. The greater the abnormality, the worse the children performed on a verbal learning task.

Despite these recent studies, the link between alcohol and fetal development is far from clear. Not all babies born to alcoholic women have FAS, yet other babies appear to be damaged by their mothers indulging in just a single binge. And if 61 percent of British women drink while pregnant, how come there are not hundreds of thousands of British children with FASD? Wouldn't we notice if 1 in 100 children being born were affected?

Hepper argues that few teachers would raise an eyebrow if they had two or three children in a class of 30 with marked behaviour difficulties, and several more with milder, manageable problems. He therefore thinks it is plausible to suggest that 1 in 100 children could have alcohol-related problems of some sort.

Hepper's research is widely quoted by anti-drinking campaigners such as FAS Aware, an international organisation which advertises in the women's bathrooms of bars to encourage pregnant women not to drink. The posters warn that "drinking in pregnancy could leave you with a hangover for life" and that "everything you drink goes to your baby's head."

Critics of these tactics point out that trying to scare women into abstinence is not helpful. There are reports in North America of women rushing off for an abortion because they had one drink before they knew they were pregnant or being racked with guilt about past drinking if they have a child with a mild disability.

Researchers like the Jacobsons acknowledge that it is hard to be certain about how alcohol affects a developing fetus on the basis of epidemiological studies, especially when they measure the notoriously messy subject of human behaviour. Any effect on the developing brain would vary depending on exactly when the fetus was exposed, and since some behavioural effects may not become apparent until several years after birth, it is difficult to pin down specific disabilities to specific antenatal exposure to alcohol.

To try and get around the epidemiological problem, John Olney, a neuroscientist at Washington University in St Louis, Missouri, has examined the impact of alcohol on developing rodent brains as a model for what happens in humans. Six years ago Olney and others showed that alcohol causes neurons in the developing rat brain to undergo programmed cell death, or apoptosis (*Science,* vol 287, p 1056).

Olney found that alcohol does the most serious damage if exposure happens during synaptogenesis, a critical time in development when neurons are rapidly forming connections. In rats, this happens just after birth, but in humans it begins in the second half of pregnancy and continues for two or more years. In the *Science* study, the team found that exposure to alcohol for baby rats during this developmental stage, at levels equivalent to a binge lasting several hours, could trigger the suicide of millions of neurons, damaging the structure of the animals' forebrains. The alcohol seems to interfere with the action of receptors for two chemical signals or neurotransmitters, glutamate and GABA (gamma amino butyric acid), that must function normally for connections to form.

Lost Neurons

The changes to brain development in rodents, Olney believes, could explain some of the behavioural problems seen in children with FASD, including attention deficit, learning and memory problems. For example, in the rat study, large numbers of neurons were lost in the brain regions that comprise the extended hippocampal circuit, which is disrupted in other disorders of learning and memory (*Addiction Biology*, vol 9, p 137). Loss of cells in the thalamus, which is thought to play a role in "filtering" irrelevant stimuli, may partly explain why FASD children are easily distracted.

The timing of alcohol exposure during pregnancy dictates what type of damage will occur, Olney says: if it is early on, when facial structures are forming, the facial characteristics of FAS may be obvious. Later, when synapses are forming, mental function may be affected. This runs counter to the popular view that the fetus is only vulnerable in the first trimester; in fact, different stages may be vulnerable in different ways.

Olney has recently tried to find out exactly how much alcohol is enough to trigger apoptosis. This year he reported that, in infant mice whose brains are at the equivalent stage of development to a third-trimester fetus, some 20,000 neurons are deleted when they are exposed to only mildly raised blood alcohol levels, for periods as short as 45 minutes. In humans, he says, this is equivalent to deleting 20 million neurons with a 45-minute exposure to blood alcohol levels of just 50 milligrams per 100 millilitres of blood—which is well below the legal limit for driving, and easily achieved in "normal social" drinking (*Neurobiology of Disease*, DOI: 10.1016/j.nbd.2005.12.015). At blood alcohol levels below this, the team found no apoptosis.

Olney is quick to stress that, alarming as 20 million neurons sounds, it is "a very small amount of brain damage" in the context of the human brain, which is estimated to have trillions of neurons. He has no evidence that such small-scale damage would translate into any detectable effects on a child's cognitive abilities. "But if a mother is advised that one or two glasses of wine with dinner is OK, and if she then has two glasses with dinner three times a week, this is exposing the fetus to a little bit of damage three times a week," he says.

The bottom line is that, as yet, it's impossible to translate these findings into blanket advice for women about how many drinks they can or can't have when pregnant. A drink before food will raise blood alcohol concentrations faster than a drink with a meal; two drinks downed quickly will raise it more sharply than two drinks spread over 3 hours. Because of this uncertainty, some researchers—and some authorities—would rather take no chances. "The best possible advice I can give mothers is to totally abstain from alcohol the moment they know they are pregnant," Olney says.

Julia Moskin NO

The Weighty Responsibility of Drinking for Two

IT happens at coffee bars. It happens at cheese counters. But most of all, it happens at bars and restaurants. Pregnant women are slow-moving targets for strangers who judge what we eat—and, especially, drink.

"Nothing makes people more uncomfortable than a pregnant woman sitting at the bar," said Brianna Walker, a bartender in Los Angeles. "The other customers can't take their eyes off her."

Drinking during *pregnancy* quickly became taboo in the United States after 1981, when the Surgeon General began warning women about the dangers of alcohol. The warnings came after researchers at the *University of Washington* identified Fetal Alcohol Syndrome, a group of physical and mental birth defects caused by alcohol consumption, in 1973. In its recommendations, the government does not distinguish between heavy drinking and the occasional beer: all alcohol poses an unacceptable risk, it says.

So those of us who drink, even occasionally, during pregnancy face unanswerable questions, like why would anyone risk the health of a child for a passing pleasure like a beer?

"It comes down to this: I just don't buy it," said Holly Masur, a mother of two in Deerfield, Ill., who often had half a glass of wine with dinner during her pregnancies, based on advice from both her mother and her obstetrician. "How can a few sips of wine be dangerous when women used to drink martinis and smoke all through their pregnancies?"

Many American obstetricians, skeptical about the need for total abstinence, quietly tell their patients that an occasional beer or glass of wine—no hard liquor—is fine.

"If a patient tells me that she's drinking two or three glasses of wine a week, I am personally comfortable with that after the first trimester," said Dr. Austin Chen, an obstetrician in TriBeCa. "But technically I am sticking my neck out by saying so."

Americans' complicated relationship with food and drink—in which everything desirable is also potentially dangerous—only becomes magnified in pregnancy.

When I was pregnant with my first child in 2001 there was so much conflicting information that doubt became a reflexive response. Why was tea allowed but not coffee? How could all "soft cheeses" be forbidden if cream cheese was recommended? What were the real risks of having a glass of wine on my birthday?

Pregnant women are told that danger lurks everywhere: listeria in soft cheese, mercury in canned tuna, *salmonella* in fresh-squeezed orange juice. Our responsibility for minimizing risk through perfect behavior feels vast.

Eventually, instead of automatically following every rule, I began looking for proof.

Proof, it turns out, is hard to come by when it comes to "moderate" or "occasional" drinking during pregnancy. Standard definitions, clinical trials and long-range studies simply do not exist.

"Clinically speaking, there is no such thing as moderate drinking in pregnancy" said Dr. Ernest L. Abel, a professor at Wayne State University Medical School in Detroit, who has led many studies on pregnancy and alcohol. "The studies address only heavy drinking"—defined by the *National Institutes of Health* as five drinks or more per day—"or no drinking."

Most pregnant women in America say in surveys that they do not drink at all—although they may not be reporting with total accuracy. But others make a conscious choice not to rule out drinking altogether.

For me, the desire to drink turned out to be all tied up with the ritual of the table—sitting down in a restaurant, reading the menu, taking that first bite of bread and butter. That was the only time, I found, that sparkling water or nonalcoholic beer didn't quite do it. And so, after examining my conscience and the research available, I concluded that one drink with dinner was an acceptable risk.

My husband, frankly, is uncomfortable with it. But he recognizes that there is no way for him to put himself in my position, or to know what he would do under the same circumstances.

While occasional drinking is not a decision I take lightly, it is also a decision in which I am not (quite) alone. Lisa Felter McKenney, a teacher in Chicago whose first child is due in January, said she feels comfortable at her current level of three drinks a week, having been grudgingly cleared by her obstetrician. "Being able to look forward to a beer with my husband at the end of the day really helps me deal with the horrible parts of being pregnant," she said. "It makes me feel like myself: not the alcohol, but the ritual. Usually I just take a few sips and that's enough."

Ana Sortun, a chef in Cambridge, Mass., who gave birth last year, said that she (and the nurse practitioner who delivered her baby) both drank wine during their pregnancies. "I didn't do it every day, but I did it often," she said. "Ultimately I trusted my own instincts, and my doctor's, more than anything else. Plus, I really believe all that stuff about the European tradition."

Many women who choose to drink have pointed to the habits of European women who legendarily drink wine, eat raw-milk cheese and quaff Guinness to improve breast milk production, as justification for their own choices in pregnancy.

Of course, those countries have their own taboos. "Just try to buy unpasteurized cheese in England, or to eat salad in France when you're pregnant," wrote a friend living in York, England. (Many French obstetricians warn patients that raw vegetables are risky.) However, she said, a drink a day is taken for granted. In those cultures, wine and beer are considered akin to food, part of daily life; in ours, they are treated more like drugs.

But more European countries are adopting the American stance of abstinence. . . .

If pregnant Frenchwomen are giving up wine completely (although whether that will happen is debatable—the effects of warning labels are far from proven), where does that leave the rest of us?

"I never thought it would happen," said Jancis Robinson, a prominent wine critic in Britain, one of the few countries with government guidelines that still allow pregnant women any alcohol—one to two drinks per week. Ms. Robinson, who spent three days tasting wine for her Masters of Wine qualification in 1990 while pregnant with her second child, said that she studied the research then available and while she was inclined to be cautious, she didn't see proof that total abstinence was the only safe course.

One thing is certain: drinking is a confusing and controversial choice for pregnant women, and among the hardest areas in which to interpret the research.

Numerous long-term studies, including the original one at the University of Washington at Seattle, have established beyond doubt that heavy drinkers are taking tremendous risks with their children's health.

But for women who want to apply that research to the question of whether they must refuse a single glass of champagne on New Year's Eve or a serving of rum-soaked Christmas pudding, there is almost no information at all.

My own decision came down to a stubborn conviction that feels like common sense: a single drink—sipped slowly, with food to slow the absorption—is unlikely to have much effect.

Some clinicians agree with that instinct. Others claim that the threat at any level is real.

"Blood alcohol level is the key," said Dr. Abel, whose view, after 30 years of research, is that brain damage and other alcohol-related problems most likely result from the spikes in blood alcohol concentration that come from binge drinking—another difficult definition, since according to Dr. Abel a binge can be as few as two drinks, drunk in rapid succession, or as many as 14, depending on a woman's physiology.

Because of ethical considerations, virtually no clinical trials can be performed on pregnant women.

"Part of the research problem is that we have mostly animal studies to work with," Dr. Abel said. "And who knows what is two drinks, for a mouse?"

Little attention has been paid to pregnant women at the low end of the consumption spectrum because there isn't a clear threat to public health there, according to Janet Golden, a history professor at Rutgers who has written about Americans' changing attitudes toward drinking in pregnancy.

The research—and the public health concern—is focused on getting pregnant women who don't regulate their intake to stop completely.

And the public seems to seriously doubt whether pregnant women can be trusted to make responsible decisions on their own.

"Strangers, and courts, will intervene with a pregnant woman when they would never dream of touching anyone else," Ms. Golden said.

Ms. Walker, the bartender, agreed. "I've had customers ask me to tell them what the pregnant woman is drinking," she said. "But I don't tell them. Like with all customers, unless someone is drunk and difficult it's no one else's business—or mine."

CHALLENGE QUESTIONS

Is Drinking Alcohol While Pregnant an Unnecessary Risk to Prenatal Development?

- If science was able to offer odds as to the likelihood of drinking during pregnancy causing developmental problems, what odds would be too great to risk? Is any risk at all too much, or does the potential comfort and familiarity of light drinking matter for mothers?
- Why would government agencies be getting more conservative with their recommendations regarding drinking during pregnancy? Should mothers have the right to make informed decisions on their own, or is this really a public issue?
- How likely does it seem that a good postnatal environment could make up for significant exposure to teratogens, such as alcohol, during prenatal development?
- What would be the various advantages and disadvantages to labeling children exposed to alcohol during prenatal development as susceptible to fetal alcohol "disorders"? Is it possible such labels could themselves be a problem during development?
- What are the particular challenges of researching prenatal development, and how might those challenges complicate efforts to understand the effects of alcohol on prenatal development?

Suggested Readings

R. Gray, R.A.S. Mukherjee, and M. Rutter, "Alcohol Consumption During Pregnancy and its Effects on Neurodevelopment: What is Known and What Remains Uncertain," *Addiction* (August 2009)

E. Abel, "Fetal Alcohol Syndrome: Same Old, Same Old," *Addiction* (August 2009)

C.M. O'Leary and C. Bower, "Measurement and Clarification of Prenatal Alcohol Exposure and Child Outcomes: Time for Improvement," *Addiction* (August 2009)

C. Gavaghan, "'You Can't *Handle* the Truth'; Medical Paternalism and Prenatal Alcohol Use," *Journal of Medical Ethics*, (May 2009)

V. Nathanson, N. Jayesinghe, and G. Roycroft, "Is it All Right for Women to Drink Small Amounts of Alcohol in Pregnancy? No," *British Medical Journal* (October 2007)

P. O'Brien, "Is it All Right for Women to Drink Small Amounts of Alcohol in Pregnancy? Yes," *British Medical Journal* (October 2007)

J. Golden, *Message in a Bottle: The Making of Fetal Alcohol Syndrome*, (Harvard University Press 2006)

ISSUE 5

Is There a "Myth of the First Three Years"?

YES: Gwen J. Broude, from "Scatterbrained Child Rearing," *Reason* (December 2000)

NO: Zero to Three: National Center for Infants, Toddlers and Families, from "Zero to Three: Response to *The Myth of the First Three Years*," http://www.zerotothree.org/no-myth.html

ISSUE SUMMARY

YES: Gwen J. Broude, who teaches developmental psychology and cognitive science at Vassar College, reviews, supports, and augments John Bruer's idea that a "myth of the first three years" has falsely used neuroscience to claim that infancy is the only critical developmental period.

NO: Zero to Three, a national organization devoted to promoting healthy infant development, contradicts Bruer's idea by asserting that a great deal of diverse research supports the idea that the first three years are critical to development and success in adulthood.

Advances in technology and research methods have allowed developmental scientists to establish that there is a massive amount of complex brain activity going on during the infant years. In fact, the explosion of changing neuronal and synaptic activity (neurons being brain cells and synapses being the connections between brain cells) during infancy may be unmatched at any other point in the lifespan. After infancy it seems that much of brain development and cognitive functioning depends upon synaptic pruning—the process of shaping and organizing the way brain cells communicate with each other. The implications of these basic findings, however, are subject to much controversy.

The key question, given all the brain change during infancy, is whether that means infants need special attention and expertly enriched environments. One strain of popular wisdom suggests yes; many parents feel extremely anxious about the need to provide careful attention and stimulation to ensure that their infants develop well—buying videos, games, music, and toys that claim to be specially designed for proper brain stimulation. Most developmental scientists would agree that this extreme anxiety is unnecessary—infants for generations and across cultures have developed successfully in natural environments without scientific intervention. But does that mean that we are wrong to consider the first three years of life as special? Does that create a harmful "myth of the first three years"?

Gwen J. Broude writes that, indeed, the first three years are only crucially important to sensationalist journalism, misguided child advocates, and misinformed anxious parents. In discussing ideas from a well-publicized book titled *The Myth of the First Three Years* by John T. Bruer, Broude substantiates the idea that misinterpretations of neuroscience and developmental ideas, such as critical periods, have created the mistaken impression that infancy is a developmental stage that requires extra attention to brain development. For Broude the problem is not that we fail to provide enough attention and stimulation to infants, but that we fail to appreciate the amazing ability of a brain to develop in its own time in its own normal environment.

In contrast, Zero to Three, a national parenting organization, fears that the real danger lies in promoting the idea that the importance of the first three years is a "myth." They acknowledge that some findings related to cognitive development have been misinterpreted, but assert strongly that the first three years of life are a distinct and crucial developmental period. Thus, from this perspective, while the direct influence of brain stimulation may be overplayed by some sources, the first three years provide an essential foundation for whatever development will occur later in life.

POINT

- Neuroscience has been misinterpreted such that many parents think the more stimulation the better—something not evident in research.

- People often fail to appreciate the amazing abilities of the brain to develop within any reasonably normal circumstance.

- Most cognitive development proceeds normally, at its own pace, based on having the types of experiences most infants have every day.

- The brain is far more "plastic" than we used to think, and the idea that most learning takes place only during the first three years is obviously wrong.

COUNTERPOINT

- While some neuroscience has been misinterpreted, that does not mean infancy is any less critical.

- People need to learn about the importance of appropriate care and environments during infancy.

- While cognitive development may proceed normally at its own pace, socioemotional development depends upon healthy interactions with fully engaged caregivers.

- Although the brain and the child continue to develop throughout life, the first three years provide a critical foundation for everything that comes later.

YES ⤶

Scatterbrained Child Rearing

When it comes to raising children, there is no such thing as too much good advice. So when accounts of neuroscientific advances in our understanding of child development began to appear in the popular press a couple of years ago, it sure sounded like good news. Parents could now raise their children in line with the hard facts about the relationship between human growth and brain development.

Don't rejoice just yet. . . . Education expert John T. Bruer warn(s) us not to believe what we have been hearing about the new neuroscience of child rearing. [He points] out that the media's version of brain-based child development bears little resemblance to the real thing. Even worse, those same wrong-headed theories have landed on the desks of policy makers. The result, as Bruer describe(s) in grim detail, is policy initiatives that can be very dangerous to children.

The mangled accounts of brain science that Bruer . . . want[s] to debunk begin with the assumption that brain development is crucial to child development. So far, so good. It is the more detailed claims, or "myths," as Bruer calls them, about the relationship between brain maturation and a child's maturation that can lead to trouble. *The Myth of the First Three Years* focuses on three such myths, which will doubtless sound familiar to most readers—though most Americans would probably consider them rock-solid facts about how the brain works. Although Bruer is not himself a neuroscientist, his discussion of where and how popular brain science has gone wrong accurately reflects the current neuroscientific literature.

Bruer's three myths are that learning is limited to "windows of opportunity," or critical periods; that these windows of opportunity occur only as long as there is a significant growth of connections, or synapses, between brain cells; and that children require enriched environments for optimal learning to take place during these windows of opportunity. As there is substantial evidence of an explosion in synaptic connections during the first three years of a child's life, the conclusion from popular neuroscience is that development is basically over by the end of the third birthday.

Many recent public policy initiatives have been based on the "vital first three years" vision of brain development. For instance, the frantic push toward universal preschool from the Clinton administration follows logically from that vision, as does the loony notion from Georgia Gov. Zell Miller that state

From *Reason,* vol. 32, issue 7, December 2000. Copyright © 2000 by Reason Foundation. Reprinted by permission.

legislators should distribute CDs of classical music to newborns to give them an intellectual head start. This notion causes many parents to believe that the early experiences of their children will seal their fates forever, and to worry that a single parenting mistake will doom their youngsters for life. Bruer argues that all those ideas are based on fantasy.

The myth that learning is limited to the first years of life is based on the finding that the density of connections among brain cells increases very rapidly during the second and third years of life. After that, the number of connections begins to stabilize or to actually decrease. This is a correct description of brain maturation. But as Bruer explains, it's not correct to assume that the brain is gaining connections during the first years of life because children are cramming their skulls with learning.

The "Mythmakers" of popular neuroscience, as Bruer calls them, suppose that brain growth means that learning is happening, and that the subsequent decrease in synaptic density must mean that learning is no longer happening. While that sounds logical, no neuroscientist believes this is an accurate description of the relationship between brain maturation and development. Indeed, it would be more nearly correct to posit the opposite relationship between children's learning and what the brain is doing.

The consensus among neuroscientists is that the explosion of connections among neurons that we see in early life merely sets the stage for the acquisition of knowledge. It is as if nature is preparing the canvas on which the world subsequently paints. The decrease, or pruning, of connections is what seems to coincide with actual learning. Ironically, then, the brain is most prepared to begin learning at just the point when popular brain science says it is too late for learning to take place. After the synaptic explosion happens, children become newly capable of learning things that they could not learn before.

The idea that there are critical periods is similarly wrongheaded as a general theory of how children develop. There are certain skills that are most easily learned early in life—for instance, seeing or talking. But as Bruer points out, we are dealing here with abilities that all normal human beings acquire. Psychologists call these "experience-expectant traits" to underscore the plain fact that the kinds of experience required for their proper development are so basic that virtually no child can help but be exposed to them. It is as if the neurophysiology underlying the trait "expects" to meet up with the needed experience. And indeed, the number of children who are not exposed to language, or light, is vanishingly small. Experience-expectant traits, Bruer observes, are acquired "easily, automatically, and unconsciously."

Not all traits are experience-expectant. My brain did not expect to meet up with algebra in the environment. Nor did it expect to encounter writing. Or the piano. But the skills of math or reading or playing music are just the sorts of skills for which there are no critical periods. They are experience-dependent traits that can be learned at any point in life. These, ironically, are also the very sorts of skills on which popular versions of brain science focus when they warn us about critical periods. Children in our culture do tend to learn particular skills, such as reading or adding, at predictable ages. But "we should not confuse this kind of learning with the existence of critical periods for those skills," Bruer writes. "What is culturally normal is not biologically determined."

Bruer also debunks the idea that enriched environments are required for optimal development. This notion originates from a misunderstanding of decades-old rat studies in which the learning of rats placed in a so-called enriched environment was superior to that of rats placed in less enriched environments. From this we are to conclude that human children should be exposed to as much stimulation as possible. This is in spite of the fact that the rats in the original experiment were adults and that their enriched environments were still deprived in comparison with what any rat would experience in the wild.

Bruer assures us that all kids need for normal development is exposure to very basic experiences, like ambient light to see, a language to hear, gravity with which to interact, and so on. Thus, his advice is that parents should make sure that their children's sensory systems are in good working order—not too tough a challenge.

Indeed, there is good reason to believe that children can't make use of all the enrichment we offer them, as they tend to develop according to their own timetables regardless of our ambitions. Try to correct the grammar of a young child who is not ready to learn the lesson. Janie comes home bursting with excitement. "My teacher brought a rabbit to school and I holded it," she gushes. "You held the rabbit?" you say. "Yes, I holded it." "Did you say you held it tightly?" you ask. "No, I holded it loosely," she responds. Janie will learn about irregular verbs on her schedule, not on yours.

Contrary to the almost blatant idiocy of the "first three years" myth—clearly, most useful human learning happens long after age 3—brains are always changing, which is another way of saying that people are always learning, regardless of their age. The greatest surprises from the laboratories of neuroscientists come in the form of evidence that the brain is far more plastic than we used to think. Since the 1980s neuroscientists have demonstrated that adult brains are extremely malleable, so much so that areas of the adult primate brain originally responsible for one function can change jobs. For instance, adult primate brain cells once receiving input from the animal's arm will subsequently reorganize to receive input from the chin and jaw if connections from the arm to the brain are interrupted. If adult brains seem stable, that's only because their experiences have been stable.

This isn't just of interest to academic neuropsychologists. Bruer's Mythmakers have a message that can hurt kids: that we should try to cram all of life's lessons into the first three years of development and then call it quits. This would clearly be fatal to any child's development, as anyone familiar with how brains—or children—actually function will plainly see. If we followed the advice implied by this version of brain development, we would be trying to teach children at exactly the time in their lives when their brains are not yet ready to learn and then stop teaching them at precisely the time that their brains do become ready. Bruer tells us that public policy is in fact heading in this direction. For instance, state legislatures are already considering bills that would decrease or eliminate support for later child interventions to invest those funds in birth-to-3 programs in the belief that this is the only time during which brains are capable of learning.

. . . As Bruer tells us, children respond to the environment at their own pace. Some psychologists have begun to suggest that this allows youngsters to fine-tune basic competencies before taking up the challenge of developing more sophisticated ones. We see this self–pacing in the way that children naturally regulate the amount of stimulation to which they will respond. Babies turn their heads away if you try to get in their faces. When there is too much going on around them, infants will go to sleep on you. Basically, children tune out stimulation for which they are not ready.

. . . Bruer's robust child [is] illustrated in his example from rural Guatemala, where children spend the first 18 months of life in circumstances that we would call severely deprived. Nevertheless, these kids perform at the same cognitive level as middle-class American children by the time they reach adolescence. Neuroscientist Steve Peterson, quoted by Bruer, captures the meaning of this anecdote when he observes that "development really wants to happen. It takes very impoverished environments to interfere with development because the biological system has evolved so that the environment alone stimulates development." How does this translate into advice for parents? "Don't raise your children in a closet, starve them, or hit them in the head with a frying pan."

. . . *The Myth of the First Three Years* is a fine rebuttal to the claim that children are fragile and a vindication for those of us who have always suspected that we were still capable of growing and learning even though we were well past 3 years old.

Zero to Three: Response to *The Myth of the First Three Years*

*T*he Myth of the First Three Years, by John Bruer, is an attempt to redress some popular misconceptions about the importance to brain development of a child's earliest experiences. The book is an extension of "Education and the Brain: A Bridge Too Far," a scholarly article by Bruer that appeared in the November 1997 issue of *Educational Researcher.* Bruer, who is president of the James S. McDonnell Foundation, which awards $18 million annually for bio-medical, educational, and international projects, has no formal training in either neuroscience or child development. But his "Bridge Too Far" article provided an astute examination of the ways in which recent findings in neuro-science have been blown out of proportion and used to imply that we know how to increase the neural connections in a child's brain and ultimately, the child's intelligence. Take the so-called "Mozart effect," for example, the notion that playing classical music, especially Mozart, will boost a child's IQ. This idea was popularized in the press and capitalized on by entrepreneurs selling Mozart CDs for babies and parents, but it has no clear foundation in science.

However, in *The Myth of the First Three Years,* a book written for a popu-lar, mass audience, Bruer crosses his own bridge and then burns it, taking his correct observation that the neuroscience of early childhood is, in a sense, in its own infancy, and leaping to the extreme conclusion that what happens to a child in the early years is of little consequence to subsequent intellectual development. He also suggests that intervening in the lives of very young chil-dren at risk for poor outcomes in school and adulthood will have little or no effect. Nothing could be further from the truth.

We are particularly concerned that readers will come away from this book confused about what babies need and what parents can do to encourage development, and that policymakers will see Bruer's argument as an excuse to ignore the growing interest and demand for policies and services that support babies, toddlers, and their families.

The Myth of Boosting Baby's Brain

Zero to Three agrees with some of Bruer's assertions. He is right that science has just begun to sort out how the trillions of nerve cells in a child's brain are organized during the first three years of life to allow a child to learn to talk, read, and reason. The application of these new and exciting findings has sometimes been exaggerated, particularly by the media, or used inappropriately to make claims about what parents, educators, and policymakers should or should not be doing.

Much of the confusion centers on the notion that the first three years are a "critical period," defined as a window of opportunity for laying down circuits in a child's brain or learning a particular set of skills that closes irrevocably after a set amount of time. What we know from early research is that critical periods exist in children only for some very basic capacities, such as vision, and to a lesser extent for learning language. For example, it has been well-documented that young children can learn a second language much more easily—and often with better pronunciation and grammar—than can adolescents or adults.

We agree with Bruer that a child's brain is not even close to being completely wired when the third candle on the birthday cake has been blown out. In fact, brain research suggests the opposite conclusion: Important parts of the brain are not fully developed until well past puberty, and the brain, unlike any other organ, changes throughout life. The human brain is capable of learning and laying down new circuitry until old age. But this does not mean that the first three years are unimportant.

Why the Early Years Are So Important

While scientists have so far only confirmed a few "critical periods" in the development of the human brain, there is no doubt that the first three years of life are critical to the growth of intelligence and to later success in adulthood. We know from rigorous psychological and sociological research, and from compelling clinical experience, that early childhood is a time when infants and toddlers acquire many of the motivations and skills needed to become productive, happy adults. Curiously, Bruer turns a blind eye to the immense and crucial social and emotional development that begins during a child's first three years, which provides a foundation for continued later intellectual development. *The importance of the first three years is no myth, and parents and policymakers must not be misled by Bruer's book.*

Following are a few examples that underscore why and how a child's intellectual development rests on social and emotional skills learned in the early years:

1. Development of Trust

Every person needs to learn to trust other human beings in order to function successfully in society. It is crucial that this sense of trust begins to grow during the earliest years. While it is certainly possible to learn this later, it becomes much more difficult the older a child gets. Years of living in an interpersonal environment that is unresponsive, untrustworthy, or unreliable is difficult to undo in later relationships.

Trust grows in infancy in the everyday, ordinary interactions between the child and the significant caregivers. A baby learns to trust through the routine experiences of being fed when she is hungry, and held when she is upset or frightened. The child learns that her needs will be met, that she matters, that someone will comfort her, feed her, and keep her warm and safe. She feels good about herself and about others.

Children whose basic needs are not met in infancy and early childhood often lack that sense of trust, and have difficulty learning to believe in themselves or in others. We know this from a multitude of scientific studies, including the research of Alan Sroufe and Byron Egeland, at the University of Minnesota. In a long-term study that followed infants through toddlerhood and into adulthood, Sroufe and his colleagues found that when children were reared within relationships they could count on, they had fewer behavior problems in school, had more confidence, and were emotionally more capable of positive social relationships.

2. Development of Self-Control

From the time a child begins to walk, we can see the progress she is making in mastering an important skill: self-control. Babies do not come into the world knowing that nobody likes it when they bite and hit, or grab toys and food from them; they need help from adults to understand that these impulses are not socially acceptable. John Gottman, of the University of Washington, among others, has demonstrated that children who get no help monitoring or regulating their behavior during the early years, especially before the age of three, have a greater chance of being anxious, frightened, impulsive, and behaviorally disorganized when they reach school. Further, these children are more likely to rely on more violent or other intimidating means to resolve conflicts than their peers who have successfully begun the long process of learning self-control.

3. The Source of Motivation

Another pillar of intellectual development and success in school is motivation. Infants and toddlers develop this through day-to-day interactions with responsive caregivers. Responding to the needs of the child is a powerful process that builds confidence and an inner sense of curiosity. This motivates the child to learn and has direct effects on success in school. The more confident a child is, the more likely she is to take on new challenges with enthusiasm.

The Emotional Foundations of Learning

Trust, self-control, and motivation form the bedrock of a child's intellectual development. Intelligence and achievement in school do not depend solely on a young child's fund of factual knowledge, ability to read or recite the alphabet, or familiarity with numbers or colors. Rather, in addition to such knowledge and skills, success rests on children, of whatever background, coming to school curious, confident, and aware of what behavior is expected. Successful children are comfortable seeking assistance, able to get along with others, and interested in using their knowledge and experience to master new challenges.

Bruer is right that there is no magic bullet for making kids smart. *But by erroneously focusing exclusively on intellectual achievement, he fails to recognize that all aspects of development affect one another, and that children cannot learn or display their intelligence as well if they have not developed emotionally and socially.* The task for parents and other caregivers who want their children to succeed in school is not to force development. Rather, it is to try to ensure that the moment-to-moment events of daily life give babies and toddlers the sense of security, encouragement, and confidence that are the foundation of emotional health. It is this that will ultimately allow them to learn at home, in school and throughout life.

Dangers of the Book

We are concerned that readers will draw the wrong conclusions. Many **parents** are likely to be confused by Bruer's message, which contradicts what they may know instinctively about the importance of the first three years. The book may let other parents off the hook—particularly those parents who aren't willing or able to devote the time and attention that is needed to provide a nurturing environment for babies and toddlers.

Moreover, some parents will be offended by Bruer's assertion that "mothers who behave in acceptable American middle-class fashion tend to have securely attached children. The challenge is to get more non-complying, mostly minority and disadvantaged, mothers to act in this way." We know that there are plenty of poor, minority parents doing a marvelous job of raising their children in securely attached relationships. Whether by design or accident, Bruer stigmatizes minority racial and ethnic groups by defining them as the exception to the rule. And just what is "acceptable American middle-class" parenting? We know of no such thing as a homogeneous approach to parenting and attachment.

Policymakers may come away from Bruer's book with the misconception that efforts to help young children are a waste of money and time. Indeed, it appears that this may be Bruer's intent. For example, he attacks the very modest funding provided for such programs as Early Head Start, a desperately needed initiative that is a drop in the bucket relative to other government programs. Early Head Start was conceived on the basis of ample evidence for the value of early intervention—evidence that was gathered long before the hoopla began over neuroscience, but that Bruer conveniently omits from his book.

Pioneering work done in the 1970s by Sally Provence, at the Child Study Center at Yale University provides just one example. Over a period of several years, Provence studied two groups of families with young children who were at risk for poor outcomes in school and adulthood. One group was offered free medical care and high quality day care, which included help in learning to be more responsive parents. The other group received no assistance. Provence found that when the children of both groups reached school age, those who received help missed far less school than the others, were able to learn and retain information more easily, and were more motivated. Their families had fewer children and the births were spaced farther apart.

Efforts to help all children achieve the basic skills of trust, motivation, and self-control needed for later intellectual and emotional development should not be aimed at creating super-babies, or giving anxious parents one more thing to worry about, or overambitious parents one more reason to push their children. Our aim should be to ensure that all children reach school age with a solid foundation for learning and relating to others, and that all parents know what they can do to help their children develop. In the last decade, the United States has made important progress in recognizing the needs of young children. Businesses have made efforts to create family-friendly policies. Government has made efforts to provide services to families. Parents are increasingly interested in how best to encourage and prepare their children. Taking to heart many of the negative messages of The Myth of the First Three Years *can only set back those efforts. Our nation's youngest citizens deserve better.*

CHALLENGE QUESTIONS

Is There a "Myth of the First Three Years"?

- While some parents recognize that more extreme levels of stimulation are not necessary for healthy development, they feel that extra stimulation can do no harm. How would you respond to that feeling? Are there ways in which too much stimulation during infancy could be harmful?
- Both readings are addressing the provocative argument made by John T. Bruer in his book *The Myth of the First Three Years*. Why do you think this book was so divisive to those interested in lifespan development?
- Broude points out ways that our scientific understanding of early brain development is easily misinterpreted by a culture interested in "building better brains." Why might this be a cultural belief that is not universally shared?
- Zero to Three asserts that infancy is a special and distinct period in lifespan development. Beyond brain development, why is this the case and what really differentiates the changes of infancy from changes at other stages?
- Some developmental scientists think that the term "critical period" is a misleading term, and that a term such as "sensitive period" may be more appropriate. What difference might various labels make to how we understand infancy?

Suggested Readings

J. Bruer, "Education and the Brain: A Bridge Too Far," *Educational Researcher* (November 1997)

J. Bruer, *The Myth of the First Three Years: A New Understanding of Early Brain Development and Lifelong Learning* (Free Press, 1999)

L. Eliot, *What's Going on in There?* (Bantam Books, 2000)

S. Gerhardt, *Why Love Matters: How Affection Shapes a Baby's Brain* (Brunner-Routledge, 2004)

H. Guldberg, "The Myth of 'Infant Determinism'," www.spiked-online.com (October 2004)

K. Hirsh-Pasek and R.M. Golinkoff with D. Eyer, *Einstein Never Used Flash Cards* (Rodale, 2003)

ISSUE 6

Are There Good Reasons to Allow Infants to Consume Electronic Media, Such as Television?

YES: Victoria Rideout, Elizabeth Hamel, and the Kaiser Family Foundation, from "The Media Family: Electronic Media in the Lives of Infants, Toddlers, Preschoolers and their Parents" A Report from the Kaiser Family Foundation (May 2006)

NO: Ellen Wartella and Michael Robb, from "Young Children, New Media" *Journal of Children and Media* (Issue 1, 2007)

ISSUE SUMMARY

YES: Victoria Rideout, Elizabeth Hamel, and the Kaiser Family Foundation find that television and electronic media allow families to cope with busy schedules and are of value to parents of infants.

NO: Ellen Wartella and Michael Robb, who are scholars of children and the media, describe limitations on infant's ability to learn from electronic media and note concerns about the diminishing of direct infant to parent interactions.

In this technology age most people at all stages of the life-span consume massive amounts of electronic media, including television, computer media, music, and video games. For better or worse, the media and market forces tend to move faster than scientific efforts to understand the impact of that consumption. This fact is particularly evident in the contemporary controversy regarding electronic media and infancy. Despite a 1999 policy statement from the American Academy of Pediatricians recommending against any exposure to electronic screens during infancy, there is a growing market for DVDs, television shows, and electronic games specifically targeting very young children. The "Baby Einstein" products may be the best known, but even the Sesame Street Workshop has entered the fray with videos specifically targeting infants.

So what is the impact of this media on infants and the young mind during this developmental stage? The short answer is that no one is entirely sure. Parents and media companies hope that the impact might be positive—it seems logically possible that well-designed media could be a positive and educational influence on a developing mind. Some would argue that electronic media could not do any harm. However, many scholars are concerned that exposure to electronic media at very young ages may in fact have a negative impact on developing capacities for language, attention, and other crucial cognitive skills. Groups such as the *Campaign for a Commercial Free Childhood* have been vociferous in their opposition to electronic media marketed towards infants. At the heart of both sides is the core question for infant development: what constitutes a healthy environment for the young mind?

As Victoria Rideout, Elizabeth Hamel, and the Kaiser Family Foundation explain in their effort to understand the role of electronic media in contemporary families, many parents rely on electronic media to help create a safe environment. In surveys and interviews with diverse groups of parents, it becomes clear that parents are aware that certain types of electronic media can be problematic for infants but that there may be a thoughtful and healthy way to use other media formats to manage the challenges of raising children in contemporary society. They suggest that exposing children to electronic media is simply a realty of modern life, and that is not necessarily a bad thing.

Scholars Ellen Wartella and Michael Robb, on the other hand, focus their attention specifically on the capacity of a young mind to learn and develop in appropriate ways. They review evidence suggesting that during infancy, cognition may not allow for children to effectively learn from video, and any hopes invested in videos may actually take away from the ways that infants do learn. They are wary of the increasing amount of screen media directed toward infants, including a new cable channel named BabyFirstTV specifically targeting children younger than 3. Wartella and Robb also note that more research is needed to learn about this complex issue—with infants who have not yet acquired language, it is always a challenge to know exactly what is getting through.

POINT	COUNTER POINT
• Electronic media is an important way that parents can manage the household in the face of increasing demands on their time, and many parents are very enthusiastic about electronic media.	• The American Academy of Pediatrics recommends against children under 2 years of age watching any screen media.
• The educational value of media for infants and young children has improved.	• While some forms of video media may facilitate learning in older children, there is very little evidence for similar processes during infancy.
• The research is not very up to date—the marketplace for infant media has moved faster than the science.	• Research suggests that it is difficult for infants to learn from screen media because they are usually more attuned to physical realities and do not yet have the cognitive ability for elaborate symbolic representations.
• Children can take messages from TV and interpret them—they may pick up things they would otherwise not be exposed to (such as different languages and types of people).	• Early exposure to screen media may actually distract infants to the point where it diminishes human interaction and impairs the development of attention.

YES ⬅ Victoria Rideout, Elizabeth Hamel, and Kaiser Family Foundation

The Media Family

Introduction

Today's parents live in a world where media are an ever-changing but increasingly important part of their family's lives, including even their very youngest children. Baby videos designed for one-month-olds, computer games for 9-month-olds, and TV shows for one-year-olds are becoming commonplace. An increasing number of TV shows, videos, websites, software programs, video games, and interactive TV toys are designed specifically for babies, toddlers, and preschoolers.

One thing that hasn't changed is that parents have a tough job—in fact, maybe tougher, often with both husband and wife working and juggling complex schedules, and with a growing number of single parents. In this environment, parents often turn to media as an important tool to help them manage their household and keep their kids entertained.

And for many parents, media are much more than entertainment: from teaching children letters and numbers, to introducing them to foreign languages or how to work with computers, many parents find the educational value of media incredibly helpful.

> "My daughter is learning a lot from the different shows she watches. She's so into it. I think it's important."
>
> [Mother of a 1–3 year-old, Irvine, California]

At the same time, there is growing controversy about media use among very young children, with pediatricians recommending no screen media for babies under two, and limited screen time after that. Most child development experts believe that the stimuli children receive and the activities they engage in during the first few years of life are critical not only for their physical well-being but also for their social, emotional, and cognitive development.

But scientific research about the impact of media use on babies and toddlers has not kept pace with the marketplace. As a result, very little is known

From *The Media Family: Electronic Media in the Lives of Infants,* Toddlers, Preschoolers and their Parents, May 2006, pp. 4–7, 14–17, 21–23, 26, 32–33. Copyright © 2006 by The Henry J. Kaiser Family Foundation. This information was reprinted with permission from the Henry J. Kaiser Family Foundation. The Kaiser Family Foundation, based in Menlo Park, California, is a nonprofit, private operating foundation focusing on the major health care issues facing the nation and is not associated with Kaiser Permanente or Kaiser Industries.

for sure about what is good and bad when it comes to media exposure in early childhood.

On the positive side of the ledger, research does indicate that well-designed educational programs, such as *Sesame Street,* can help 4- and 5-year-olds read and count and that children that age also benefit from pro-social messages on TV that teach them about kindness and sharing. On the other hand, studies have also found that exposure to television violence can increase the risk of children behaving aggressively and that media use in early childhood may be related to attentional problems later in life. And while the producers of early childhood media believe their products can help children learn even at the earliest ages, other experts worry that time spent with media may detract from time children spend interacting with their parents, engaging in physical activity, using their imaginations, or exploring the world around them.

One thing this study makes clear is that for many families, media use has become part of the fabric of daily life. Parents use TV or DVDs as a "safe" activity their kids can enjoy while the grownups get dressed for work, make a meal, or do the household chores. Working parents who worry that they don't have enough time to teach their kids the basics feel relieved that educational TV shows, videos, and computer games are helping their kids count and learn the alphabet and even say a word or two in Spanish. When children are grouchy, or hyper, or fighting with their siblings, moms and dads use TV as a tool to help change their mood, calm them down, or separate squabbling brothers and sisters. Media are also used in enforcing discipline, with a TV in the bedroom or a handheld video game player offered as a powerful reward or enticement for good behavior. Everyday activities, such as eating a meal or going to sleep, are often done with television as a companion. And media are used to facilitate moments of transition in daily life: waking up slowly while groggily watching a couple of cartoons on mom and dad's bed, or calming down to a favorite video before bedtime.

> "Media makes my life easier. We're all happier. He isn't throwing tantrums. I can get some work done."

> [Mother of a 4–6 year-old, Irvine, California]

Many parents of young children are quite enthusiastic about the role media plays in their lives and the impact it has on their kids. They are grateful for what they see as higher quality, more educational choices than when they were young, and for the wider variety of options they now have available. They see their children learning from TV and imitating the positive behaviors modeled on many shows. But it appears that the primary reason many parents choose to bring media into their children's lives is not because of the educational benefits it offers kids, but because of the practical benefits it offers parents: uninterrupted time for chores, some peace and quiet, or even just an opportunity to watch their own favorite shows.

At the same time, many parents feel an underlying guilt about their children's media use: primarily a sense that they should be spending more time with their kids and that they shouldn't be feeling so relieved at not having to be responsible for teaching their children their ABCs. Some express a suspicion that they may have set in motion something they soon won't be able to control: that today's good-natured educational shows will lead to tomorrow's sassy cartoons, and to next year's violent video games. And others also bemoan the fundamental changes they see from their own childhoods when they were more likely to play outside or to use their imaginations to make up their own play activities indoors.

> "It makes life easier now, but in the long run, when they're older and starting to run into all these problems, I think I'll wish I wouldn't have let them do it when they were five."
>
> [Mother of a 4–6 year-old in Columbus, Ohio]

Parents' beliefs about media—and their own media habits—are strongly related to how much time their children spend with media, the patterns of their children's use, and the types of content their children are exposed to. Two- and four-year-olds watching *CSI* and *ER* with their moms don't seem to be as rare as one might think. Parents who are big TV fans and hate the interruptions from their little ones are more likely to get a TV for their child's bedroom. Dads who play a lot of video games use that activity as a way to bond with their sons. And parents who think TV mostly hurts children's learning are more likely to limit their children's viewing and less likely to leave the TV on during the day. In short, children's media use is as much or more about parents as it is about children.

This report presents the results of a national study to document how much time infants, toddlers, and preschoolers are spending with media, what types of media they're using, and what role media are playing in their environments. The study has two parts: a nationally representative telephone survey of parents about their children's media use; and a series of focus groups with parents, for a more in-depth discussion of issues raised in the survey. All statistical findings in this report are from the national survey; all quotes are from the focus groups.

The study concerns children ages 6 months to 6 years old. It focuses primarily on the role of electronic screen media in young people's lives, including television, videos or DVDs, computers, and video games. Occasional references to "children 6 years and under" or "children six and under" are made as shorthand and refer to children ages 6 months to 6 years old. References to children "under two" refer to children 6–23 months old. . . .

One thing this study makes clear is that even the youngest children in our society have a substantial amount of experience with electronic media. Perhaps not surprisingly, almost all children ages 6 months to 6 years old have watched television (94%) and videos or DVDs (87%). But use of "new" media among this age group also abounds. More than four in ten (43%) have used a computer, about three in ten (29%) have played console video games, and just under one in five (18%) have played handheld video games.

Figure 1

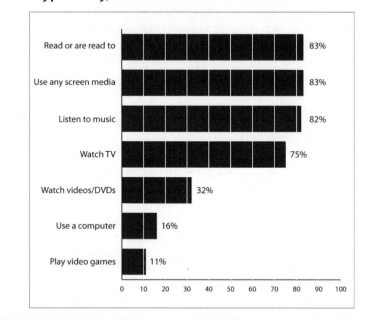

In a Typical Day, Percent of Children 6 and Under Who . . .

Note: Screen media includes TV, videos/DVDs, video games, or computers.

In a typical day, 83% of children ages 6 months to 6 years use some form of screen media, including 75% who watch television, 32% who watch videos or DVDs[1], 16% who use a computer, and 11% who play either console or handheld video games. The percent of children who watch TV in a typical day is somewhat smaller than the share who spend any time reading or being read to (83%) and listening to music (82%).

Kids who watch television and those who watch videos or DVDs spend an average of about one and a quarter hours on each (1:19 for TV and 1:18 for videos/DVDs), while those who play video games and use computers spend an average of just under an hour on each (0:55 for video games and 0:50 for computers). On the whole, the 83% of children who use screen media in a typical day spend an average of just under 2 hours (1:57) doing so. . . .

> "For our little guy, TV time is all of us on the couch together. The cat comes and sits with us. We'll talk about what's going on. If it's *Blues Clues*, we'll answer back. We only do 20 minutes a night."
>
> [Mother of a 1–3 year-old, Irvine, California]

Parents' Attitudes about Children's Media Use

Why Parents Want Their Kids to Use Media

Focus groups indicate that many parents are encouraging their children to spend time with media because they think it's good for their kids, and because it gives them a chance to get things done without their children underfoot. Indeed, in focus groups parents speak about "getting" their kids to watch certain videos or TV shows, or about DVDs being better than TV because they're longer and afford a longer chunk of time in which to get things done.

> "They wake up and get to watch TV while I shower and get dressed. It keeps them in my sight line."
>
> [Mother of a 4–6 year-old, Denver, Colorado]

Many parents speak of the numerous demands on their time and of their strong need to keep their kids occupied while they get chores done. As a mom from Denver said about her 1–3 year-old, "If he is watching TV, I can get other things done. I don't have to constantly watch him." Some parents spoke about the fact that they simply can't let their kids play outdoors unsupervised. Others pointed out how much trouble their children could cause inside the house if they are left unmonitored: "If the TV isn't on, he's putting the 'Orange Glo' all over my daughter's bedspread. That makes more work for me."

> "He's a good little boy. He won't bother anything. He won't get into stuff. He's glued to the TV."
>
> [Mother of a 4–6 year-old from Columbus, Ohio]

Many parents also talked about how important it is for them to have "me" time, which often means getting their kids set up with a TV show or a DVD. The mother of a 4–6 year-old from the Denver area pointed out that: "Being an adult is hard. There are times when my interacting with my children is best served by me having an opportunity to allow them to do something alone so I can regroup. When I got laid off a couple of weeks ago, I didn't know it was coming. I got blindsided. I couldn't have interacted with my children that night. I couldn't have done it. 'Let's watch *Finding Nemo*, kids. Here are some chicken strips, here are sippy cups—I'll see you in about an hour and a half'."

The Educational Value of Television

In the national survey, parents are fairly evenly split on whether, in general, TV mostly helps (38%) or mostly hurts (31%) children's learning (22% say it doesn't have much effect either way). But in focus groups, many parents cited "learning" as one of the positive things about television, and indicated that they thought their children were learning from TV. Several mothers mentioned being surprised by their children saying a word in Spanish or being able to count. The mother of a 4–6 year-old from Denver said, "My daughter started saying something to me in Spanish—I don't know a word of Spanish. [TV is] definitely educational." Another Denver-area mom said, "My 2-year-old can count to 10. I haven't really practiced that much with her. She did it. Where else would she have possibly learned it?"

> "Out of the blue one day my son counted to five in Spanish. I knew immediately that he got that from *Dora.*"
>
> [Mother of a 1–3 year-old, Columbus, Ohio]

Mothers are also enthusiastic about the different experiences children are exposed to through television and videos. "[My son] has developed a passion about the ocean and angler fish because of Nemo," said one Denver mom. "He fell in love with that character. That door wouldn't have even been open if it wasn't for *Finding Nemo.*" Another Denver mother said her 4–6 year-old son was "always telling me what is right and wrong from the things he sees on TV. It has opened doors in being able to talk to him." Several mothers mentioned the "diversity" TV brings their young children. As one mom from Columbus said, "I think they are exposed to a little bit more diversity. I think that it's good for them to be comfortable with that. . . . to know that it's okay for everyone to be different."

> "My daughter knows . . . her letters from *Sesame Street.* I haven't had to work with her on them at all."
>
> [Mother of a 1–3 year-old, Columbus, Ohio]

> "It shows them a world that they aren't familiar with. We live in the suburbs. She watches *Dora* and learns a little bit of Spanish."
>
> [Mother of a 4–6 year-old, Columbus, Ohio]

Some parents feel they need media to help them with their child's education. As one mother from Irvine, California, said, "I think they (media) are in a way necessary. So much more is expected of kids these days. . . . When you go to kindergarten now, you can't just go and play with toys. You have to know how to write your name and spell. It's all about what you know." Most parents seemed to think their children would learn what they needed to know just fine without media, but they would be under a lot more pressure to do the teaching themselves. As the mother of a 1–3 year-old from Denver said, "I don't think it's important to use it as a learning tool, but for me to use it to keep them occupied."

The national survey indicates that there is a relationship between parents' attitudes about the educational value of television and how much time their children spend watching TV. Children whose parents think TV mostly

Table 1

Relationship of Parental Attitudes to Children's Media Use

Child's Media Use	Parent Attitude Towards TV		
	Mostly helps	No effect	Mostly hurts
Percent who watch TV on typical day	84%‡~	75%~	64%
Mean hours watching TV for kids who watched	1:27~	1:16	1:12
Mean hours watching TV for all kids	1:12‡~	0:57~	0:45
Percent who watch TV daily	76%~	71%~	48%

‡Significantly higher than "No effect"; ~Significantly higher than "Mostly hurts."

hurts learning are *less likely* to watch than those whose parents say it mostly helps or doesn't have much effect one way or the other. For example, 48% of children whose parents say TV mostly hurts learning watch every day, compared to 76% of those whose parents believe TV mostly helps children's learning. Likewise, children whose parents say TV mostly hurts learning spend an average of 27 minutes less per day watching than children whose parents think TV mostly helps.

It is not possible to tell from this survey whether parents who think TV hurts learning are more likely to restrict their children's viewing, or whether parents whose children spend more time watching TV develop a higher opinion of television's role in learning, or whether some other factor is influencing this relationship.

> "I just don't have time to sit on the computer with him to try and teach him all this other stuff. . . . I'm not going to put him on it if I have to teach him how to use the mouse or something else. . . . I am like—play it at your dad's and break *his* computer."

> [Mother of a 1–3 year-old, Denver, Colorado]

Educational Value of Computers

When it comes to using computers, most parents think this activity helps rather than hurts learning (69% vs. 8%, with 15% saying it doesn't have much effect).

Many parents feel that since their children are going to have to use computers later in life, getting familiar with them at an early age is a benefit in and of itself, regardless of what they're doing on the computer. One mother from Irvine said, "Anything they are doing on the computer I think is learn-ing." Another mom from Columbus said, "I think they get more skills from the computer. Our world is so computer-oriented. I certainly didn't know how to use a computer when I was 3. . . . If I had a choice of the computer or TV, I would definitely choose the computer."

> "They'll survive without the video games and TV. . . . I don't think they'll survive without the computer. When they're older, they aren't going to have a cashier to check them out at Kroger."
>
> [Mother of a 4–6 year-old, Columbus, Ohio]

Other focus group mothers pointed to certain features of the computer that they found beneficial, such as interactivity or the parent being able to control the content through specific software. The mother of a young child from Irvine said, "The computer is far more interactive than TV. His mind is more active when he is using the computer. It's more of an analysis and figur-ing things out." A Denver-area mom (of a 4–6 year-old) said, "I think you have more control over the computer. If they're watching TV, you don't know what the lesson is going to be. With the computer you can put in specific software or go to a specific website."

> "I don't spend nearly as much time with my son as I need to. He has learned huge amounts through the video and computer games that we have. . . . I'm very grateful for the computer games. My kid learned his colors and letters from the computer. It's been very beneficial to us."
>
> [Mother of a 1–3 year-old, Irvine, California]

Another mother from Denver (of a 1–3 year-old) described one of the CD-ROMs she and her daughter enjoy using: "They have a 5-a-day vegetable game. My daughter doesn't like to eat, so we show her all the different foods that are good for her. We make things on the computer, and then we will go downstairs and make them to eat. She seems to eat better after we play the food game."

Despite the advantages some focus group mothers pointed to, many oth-ers expressed a lot of concerns about having their kids use the family compu-ter. There was a sense that most of what children can learn from a computer they can also learn from TV or videos—without as much parental oversight and without as much risk to expensive equipment. As one mom from Irvine said, "If they're on the Internet, I have to be right there with them. That can be annoying because I don't always have the time to sit there while my 3- and 6-year-old go on the Internet. It isn't that fun for me to watch the same *Dora* clip 20,000 times. I would rather do other things." Some pointed to the safety of the Nickelodeon TV channel over the Nick Jr. website: one mom said, "If I leave my son on Nick Jr. for just a minute, he will click on every possible ad or whatever, and there will be a thousand things open," while another noted, "If they're watching Nickelodeon, you know they aren't going to have any porn sites popping up."

Educational Value of Video Games

According to the national survey, most parents think playing video games hurts rather than helps learning (49% vs. 17%, with 22% saying not much effect). In the focus groups, parents didn't indicate having as much experience using educational video games as they did with TV, computers, or videos and DVDs. One mother of a 4–6 year-old from Columbus did have experience with an educational video game: "My daughter and I played a Mickey Mouse (video) game where you had to . . . move the cursor around to find different things. If you find the remote, you can go back to the TV, and it will show a clip. It's like thinking."

Focus group parents also felt that video games tended to be more violent, especially those for the older kids. Some worried about the types of games young children see their older siblings play: "My older kids play . . . a lot of the violent stuff. They let [my younger son] play one time, and the poor child was traumatized. . . . He couldn't even sleep that night. He kept telling us about it all night."

Many parents noted that their younger children tried to mimic either their dads or their older siblings by playing with game controllers, but just got frustrated because they couldn't do it properly.

Figure 2

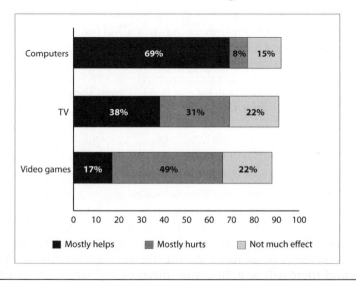

Percent of Parents Who Say Each Medium Mostly Helps or Hurts Children's Learning:

Conversations with Pediatricians

Relatively few parents (15%) say that their pediatrician has ever discussed their child's media use with them. Parents with higher income and more formal education are more likely to say their pediatrician has discussed this with them (for example, 22% of college graduates, vs. 11% of those with a high school education or less). There is no indication from these data that children whose parents have discussed media use with their pediatrician are less likely to watch TV or that the household media environment is different for these children than for those whose parents haven't had those discussions. Even the youngest children are growing up in homes where media are an integral part of the environment—with multiple TVs, VCRs, computers, and video game players in the home; TVs left on much of the time (many with large screens and surround sound), whether anyone is watching or not; TVs in children's bedrooms; and portable DVD players and handheld video game players ready for children on the go.

Television

Nearly all children ages 6 months to 6 years (99%) live in a home with at least one television. Eighty-four percent live in a home with two or more televisions, and nearly a quarter (24%) live in homes with four or more TVs.

A large majority (80%) of these children live in homes that have cable or satellite TV, and about half (53%) live in homes where the largest TV is 30 inches or larger (25% have TVs 40 inches or larger). Four in ten (40%) have a television with surround sound, and two in ten (20%) have TiVo or some other type of digital video recorder. The presence ofTiVo in the home was not related to either the amount or type of shows children watched.

VCRs and DVD Players

Nearly all (93%) children ages 6 months to 6 years have a VCR or DVD player in the home, and a third (33%) have a portable DVD player. In addition, nearly one in five (18%) have a television or DVD player in their car.

> "While my daughter has her princess movie in, my son can be upstairs playing his *Blues Clues* CD-ROM. . . . It gives them their own space and their own quality time to be apart."
>
> [Mother of a 1–3 year-old, Denver, Colorado]

Video Games

Half (50%) of children 6 years and under have a console video game player in the home, and nearly three in ten (28%) have a handheld video game player. Children ages 4–6 are more likely than children ages 0–3 to live in homes with a console video game player (54% vs. 46%), and with a handheld video game player (34% vs. 22%).

"I told my kids we weren't going to get an Xbox. . . . because we have the computer. To me it's just one more thing that I would have to fight over with them. I'm big on entertaining yourself—go play. Don't just sit here vegetating."

[Mother of a 1–3 year-old, Columbus, Ohio]

Computers

More than three-quarters (78%) of children 6 years and under live in a household with a computer, and about three in ten (29%) live in a household with two or more computers. Nearly seven in ten (69%) have Internet access in the household, including 42% who have high-speed Internet access (26% have dial-up access). . . .

Calming Children Down or Pumping Them Up

Just over half (53%) of parents say that TV tends to calm their child down, while only about one in six (17%) say that TV gets their child excited. The rest of parents either say: TV calms and excites their child equally (9%); it depends on what the child is watching (8%) or on the child's mood or time of day (3%);

Figure 3

Percent of Children Age 6 and Under Who Live in a Home with . . .

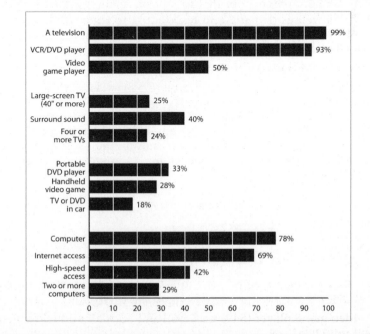

or they don't know (10%). Television's effect on children does not vary reliably with the child's age or gender. Children who watch mostly entertainment shows are more likely to be calmed by TV than are those who watch mostly educational shows (72% vs. 50%).

> "When he watched the *Buzz Lightyear of Star Command* video from the library, he was a monster child. The very next week I got *Teletubbies,* and it was completely opposite. He was very mellow."
>
> [Mother of a 1–3 year-old, Columbus, Ohio]

In focus groups, parents describe a range of responses their children have to TV. A number of parents talked about how TV can calm their children down. The mother of a 4–6 year-old from Irvine said, "My son is really hyper. That's a time when I can get him to actually calm down and watch a little TV. . . . He will slow down and that helps change his mood. . . . It's much better for him and for me."

> "She plays along with what she's watching most of the time. She's dancing. She's not being a couch potato . . ."
>
> [Mother of a 4–6 year-old, Columbus, Ohio]

But another mother, from Columbus, said, "My 2-year-old is so rambunctious you cannot turn your back for a second. With TV I notice that his temperament changes. He gets more wild and hyper when he is watching the stuff that he likes." Many parents pointed to a positive energy their kids get from watching TV as well as dancing and responding to the screen. "My kids will stand in front of the TV and hop and clap," a mother of a 1–3 year-old from Columbus said. Others describe kids who "zone out"or appear hypnotized by the TV. "The TV kind of turns their brain off, that's what I don't like," said one Denver mother.

> "I think [TV] builds confidence and self-esteem. My daughter was very introverted until she was about three and a half. She was very shy. . . . By her acting out with her imaginary friends on the TV or *Dora,* it just really brought her out. It really opened her up in preschool and she is really doing well."
>
> [Mother of a 4–6 year-old, Irvine, California]

Imitating Behavior from TV

Nearly seven in ten parents (68%) say they have seen their child imitate some type of behavior from TV. Far more parents say their child imitates positive behavior, such as sharing or helping (66%), than say their child imitates aggressive behavior, like hitting or kicking (23%). Parents of children ages 4–6 years

(83%) and of children ages 2–3 years (77%) are more likely than parents of children under 2 years (27%) to say their child imitates any type of behavior.

> "She was going around kissing everyone with her mouth open. She wanted to be like Ariel and Eric."(From Disney's *The Little Mermaid*.)

> [Mother of a 1–3 year-old, Columbus, Ohio]

Boys in both age ranges (2–3 and 4–6) are more likely than girls to imitate aggressive behavior (nearly half—45%—of parents of boys ages 4–6 say their child imitates aggressive behavior). Children who primarily watch kids' educational programming are more likely than those who primarily watch kids' entertainment shows to imitate positive behavior (76% vs. 59%).

> "My daughter just sits in the beanbag chair watching TV. If it's something that she's really into, she just sits there with her mouth hanging open."

> [Mother of a 4–6 year-old, Columbus, Ohio]

Response to Commercials

In focus groups, when asked to list the positives and negatives of TV for their children, many parents mentioned commercials as a negative. But when asked how many commercials their children were exposed to in a typical day, most parents seemed at a loss to guess, and estimates ranged from 5 to 100. Many parents indicated that their children liked commercials and were influenced by them. "She pays attention to the commercials more than the shows," said the mother of one 1–3 year-old from Columbus. "That's what gets her attention." Several talked about their children memorizing things from commercials. A

Table 2

Imitating Positive or Aggressive Behavior from TV

	Ages 2–3 Years			Ages 4–6 Years		
Percent whose parents say they . . .	All	Boys	Girls	All	Boys	Girls
Imitate positive behavior	75%	75%	75%	80%	79%	82%
Imitate aggressive behavior	24%	31%[†]	17%	33%[*]	45%[†]	21%
Imitate neither	23%[^]	20%	25%	17%	17%	17%

[*]Significantly higher than ages 2–3, [^]Significantly higher than ages 4–6; [†]Significantly higher than girls in this age range.

Denver mom (of a 4–6 year-old) said, "My kids are—'I want that, I want that, I want that'. They commit things to memory for months." But one mother said she thought the commercials just went right past her kids: "I don't think they watch them. . . . I don't think they're paying attention."

"I want this, I want that, I want chocolate cereal."

[Mother of a 1–3 year-old, Denver, Colorado]

At the same time, a couple of parents mentioned that ads give them gift ideas, and they're grateful for them. The mother of one 1–3 year-old girl from Columbus said, "My daughter's birthday is next week. She saw a commercial for a Strawberry Shortcake doll toy. She said she wanted it for her birthday. If she hadn't seen the commercial, she wouldn't have known about it. I was glad that I was in the room and she could tell me that."

"I would be at a total loss if it wasn't for commercials at Christmas time. I wouldn't know what to get my kids. They know what they like when they see it on TV."

[Mother of a 4–6 year-old, Denver, Colorado]

Among parents whose children watch TV at least several times a month, the vast majority (83%) say their child watches mostly shows specifically for

Figure 4

Percent of Children Who Watch . . .

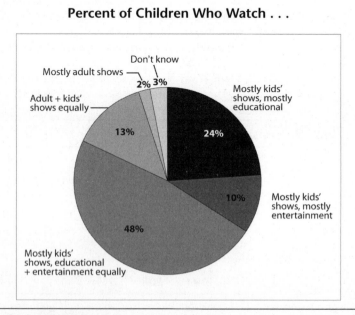

Note: Among those who watch TV at least several times a month.

kids around his or her age (2% say the child watches mostly shows for all ages, including adults; and 13% say the child watches both types of shows about equally). More parents say their child watches mostly educational shows (24%) than say their child watches mostly entertainment shows (10%), but a plurality (48%) say their child watches both types of shows about equally.

> "A show can seem fine one minute, and in the next minute Tom pulls a gun on Jerry."
>
> [Mother of a 4–6 year-old, Denver, Colorado]

In focus groups, a number of parents indicated that their young children watch mature content and that both the child and the parent seem fine with that. For example, the mother of one 4-year-old from Denver said, "*The Punisher,* my son loves that movie. He's more mature." Another said she "goes by her child's personality" in deciding what he can or can't watch. "Not a lot of people would be comfortable with a 4-year-old watching medical shows where they show people coming in and bleeding and crying," she said. "Obviously it is a tragedy. But he really loves the human body." Another mom from Irvine said, "I try not to really shelter my daughter. . . . She's two. She wants to watch *Jurassic Park.* . . . There's a dinosaur [that] ate a guy—that's what dinosaurs do—they eat people and animals. She understands that. She doesn't getfreaked about it. She even watched *Chuckie* the other day. She thought it was funny."

> "I've found that my kids are usually about a year ahead of what the games or movies say. My son is two so I look at ones for 3–4 year-olds. I always pick one that is above their level to help them learn."
>
> [Mother of a 1–3 year-old, Denver, Colorado]

Many parents in focus groups say they are guided by brands in choosing what their kids can or can't watch. One Denver mom said that children's TV shows are "all pretty much educational now. They help teach the kids how to help each other and how to love one another. Everything on Nick is like that." Another had a similar feeling about PBS: "I like my kids to watch PBS because it's more of a learning thing instead of the cartoons. I have no problem with them watching PBS for two hours straight. They have all those good learning shows." But one mother of a 4–6 year-old from Columbus said she made a mistake thinking she could go by the brand alone: "I thought you could trust Cartoon Network because of the name. I just recently paid attention to what he was watching and saw it. I said, 'What the *heck!*' I couldn't believe it."

> "Because of the rules that I have set forth he doesn't ask to watch things that he can't watch."
>
> [Mother of a 4–6 year-old, Denver, Colorado]

A number of parents in focus groups talked about the influence of their older siblings on what their younger kids see on TV or videos. The mother of one 1–3 year-old from Denver told about a time when her young son watched the movie *Alien vs. Predator:* "He liked it. . . . When I saw it I couldn't believe my older son let him watch it. I thought he would be up all night, but it didn't bother him at all." . . .

Children Under Age Two

Many experts consider the first two years of life especially critical for children's development and are particularly interested in monitoring media use patterns during this period. For example, the American Academy of Pediatrics has recommended no screen media use at all for children under two.

In fact, this study indicates that children under age 2 have quite different media habits than children 2 years and older, although it also indicates that they live media-rich lives. Almost all babies 6–23 months old have listened to music (98%), or been read to (94%). Nearly eight in ten (79%) have watched TV, and two-thirds (65%) have watched videos or DVDs. Only a very few have ever used a computer (5%) or played any kind of video game (3%).

More than four in ten (43%) children this age watch TV *every* day, while another 17% watch several times a week. Nearly one in five (18%) watch videos or DVDs every day, while another 26% watch at least several times a week. In a typical day, 61% of children this age watch TV, a video, or a DVD, for an average of one hour and nineteen minutes. Most parents say they are in the same room with their child while they're watching TV either all or most of the time (88% of those whose children this age watch TV in a typical day).

Around four in ten children under two can turn on the TV by themselves (38%) and change channels with the remote (40%). Almost one in five (19%) have a TV in their bedroom. A quarter (26%) of parents report that their children this age have already imitated a positive behavior from a TV show, like sharing or helping. Among the 63% of children this age who watch at least several times a month or more, 35% watch mostly kids' educational shows, 40% watch a mix of kids' educational and entertainment shows, and 19% watch a mix of programming for both children and adults.

In addition to watching their own shows, babies this age are also exposed to "background" television. A third (33%) live in homes where the TV is on most or all of the time, whether anyone is watching or not. Seventy percent of parents with children under two say they watch their own TV shows in a typical day, for an average of an hour and forty-three minutes, including 32% who say their child was in the room with them all or most of the time, 17% who say half or less of the time, and 20% who say none of the time.

More than half (58%) of children under two are read to every day, with another 25% being read to several times a week. In any given day, 77% are read to, for an average of 44 minutes. . . .

Figure 5

Percent of Children Under Age Two Who Watch TV . . .

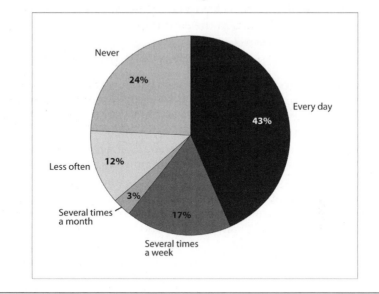

Summary and Conclusions

The Role of Parents

In the public debate about children and media, people on all sides of the issue often end up pointing to the role of parents in monitoring their children's media use, encouraging them to push the "off" button. This study provides important documentation of just how powerful a role parents have in shaping their children's media habits. A third of children live in homes where parents simply leave the TV on most of the day, whether anyone is watching or not—and, not surprisingly, those children end up watching significantly more than other kids do. Many parents spend a fair amount of time watching TV or on the computer themselves, and again, children of those parents also spend more time watching a screen each day. And a third of children 6 years and under have been allowed to have a TV in their bedroom—mostly to avoid conflicts with parents'or other family members' viewing—and again, those children spend more time watching TV.

Why Parents Are Drawn to Media

Many parents find media a tremendous benefit in parenting and can't imagine how they'd get through the day without it (especially TV, videos, and DVDs). Media allow parents a chance to get their chores done, quiet their kids down, or just have some "me" time, knowing that their kids are "safe"—not playing outside, and less likely to be making trouble around the house. Multiple

TV sets, DVD players, and computers help solve sibling quarrels and also let parents get their own screen time uninterrupted. While fewer than four in ten (38%) parents say they think TV mostly helps children's learning, parents are relieved that they can make use of media in these ways with less guilt, because of what they see as real advances in the educational quality of media content.

The Educational Value of Children's Television

While parents in the survey seem pretty evenly split on whether TV in general is mostly helpful (38%) or harmful (31%) to children's learning, in the focus groups almost all parents pointed to "learning" as one of the big positives of TV for their kids, and many made comments about observing their children learning things from TV shows. In general, parents in the focus groups seemed well satisfied with the quality of programming available to their kids. Most felt their children would learn just as well *without* TV, but didn't want the extra burden that that would place on them as parents. The reigning sentiment seemed to be that there is simply no way they can live their lives and get everything done without TV and videos, and that the educational content and positive lessons in much of the programming lessens their guilt at not spending more time with their kids. And while parents in the survey indicate that they think the computer is more educational than is TV, the focus groups revealed that many parents greatly prefer TV or videos because they require less supervision (and because they're worried about their kids hurting the computer).

A Big Role for Media

Media, especially television, are clearly playing a key role in children's lives, starting at an early age. In a typical day, more than eight in ten (83%) children ages 6 months to 6 years old use screen media, averaging about two hours each (1:57). As mentioned above, a third live in homes where the TV is left on most or all of the time, whether anyone is watching or not, and a similar proportion (30%) have the TV on during most or all of their meals. Homes with multiple TV sets and portable media allow kids to watch in the privacy of their rooms, or when they're on the go—a third (33%) have a portable DVD player, and a third (33%) have a TV in their bedroom. About one in eight (12%) are put to bed with the TV on at least half the time.

Less Time with TV and DVDs

While there haven't been any major changes in children's daily media habits since a similar survey was conducted in 2003—they aren't more likely to use computers or video games, or less likely to watch TV—when children *do* watch TV or videos, they are spending less time doing so (10 minutes less watching TV, and 7 minutes less watching videos or DVDs). It's possible that this change follows on the slight—but statistically significant—drop in the proportion of parents nationally who say they leave the TV on all or most of time (from 37% to 32%) or who say they usually eat meals in front of the TV (from 35% to

30%). It is also possible that the shift comes from a greater number of parents thinking TV mostly *hurts* children's learning (up from 27% to 31%). However, it is also possible that it is an artifact of a shift in the time of year the survey was conducted, from April and May to September, October, and November. Slight decreases in time spent with computers and playing video games were not statistically significant. We will continue to track these data over time.

American Academy of Pediatrics Recommendations

A substantial number of children are using media in excess of the amounts recommended by the American Academy of Pediatrics (AAP). In a typical day, nearly two-thirds (61%) of babies under two years old use screen media, and 43% of children this age watch TV *every* day (the AAP recommends no screen time for babies under two). And while the AAP recommends no more than 1–2 hours per day of screen media for children two and older, in a typical day 41% of 2–3 year-olds and 43% of 4–6 year-olds use screen media for 2 hours or more. Few parents report having spoken with their doctor about their child's media use. . . .

Electronic media have clearly become a central focus of many young children's lives, a key component in family routines such as working up, eating, relaxing, and falling asleep. Not only do children—starting when they are just babies—spend hours a day using media, but they are also learning to use the media by themselves, often watching their own TVs, DVD players or hand-held devices, many times in the privacy of their own rooms. As much as media have become a part of the fabric of family life, they are often consumed separately, used as much or more to keep the peace than to bring family members together.

It is hoped that the data in this report will be used to help families assess their own media habits; to spur the development of media products that are beneficial to children and families; to inform policy debates about public broadcasting, digital media, and children's commercial exposure; and to provide the data to help inform future research about the impact of various media on young children. To date, there has been very little research about the impact of media on the youngest children, especially those 2 years and under. Given how much a part of children's lives these media are, it seems important to explore in greater depth the impact media may be having on their development.

Note

1. The percent of parents who report that their children watched videos or DVDs may be an underestimate due to the way the question was worded. The question read "Did your child spend anytime watching videos or DVDs, including while riding in the car?" In a previous survey, the question was asked without the phrase "including while riding in a car," and a far greater proportion of parents reported that their children had watched videos or DVDs (46%, compared to 32% in the current survey). Many respondents in the current survey may have misunderstood the question and answered "yes" *only* if their child watched videos or DVDs while riding in the car.

**Ellen Wartella and
Michael Robb**

NO

Young Children, New Media

In May 2006 a new cable channel entered American television; BabyFirstTV became the first 24 hour cable and satellite network to offer programming aimed at viewers between 6 months and 3 years old. Earlier in the spring, Sesame Workshop released a DVD series, "Sesame Beginnings," designed for children 6 months to 2 years old to compete with the well known "Baby Einstein" series of infant videos. These media directed at the very young are only the latest of a trend to both program for and attract very young children to audio-visual media. In addition to cable networks and DVDs, interactive toys, cell phones, websites, and other content are now directed at the very young child as well. . . . Data from two Kaiser Family Foundation surveys of the parents of children 6 months to 6 years over the past 4 years . . . provide evidence that electronic media are an increasingly important part of the lives of the very young. This paper will examine the use of electronic media by children under three and will examine what impact such early viewing might have on children's development.

The past decade in American media life has demonstrated the presence of screen media—television, videos, DVDs, computers, videogames—in the lives of very young children. Both the 2003 and 2006 national surveys of media use by children under six conducted by the Kaiser Family Foundation have provided evidence that American children are more likely today to spend time with screen media than print media or free play. All of this is occurring at a time when media directed at young children is facing criticism: for instance, since 1999 the American Academy of Pediatrics recommends discouraging children under two from watching any screen media and limiting older children to 2 hours or less per day. . . . There are questions regarding the impact of such early media use on children's cognitive and social development, including questions regarding just how and when children do learn from screen media. . . . Moreover, more than 35 years of experience with preschoolers using *Sesame Street* has demonstrated that 4- to 6-year-olds can learn important skills such as their numbers and letters, as well as pre-reading skills that can have a positive effect on them as they enter elementary school . . .; however, the impact of these educational shows on younger children is less clear. . . . There is no clear cut evidence regarding young children's learning from screen media. In fact, what is most surprising is the dearth of studies on the very young (those under three) including examination of the likely consequences of their early screen media on development.

Young Children's Media Use

The Kaiser Family Foundation has conducted two national studies in the US on very young children's media use: the Zero To Six study . . . and The Media Family. . . . In addition, a January 2005 issue of the *American Behavioral Scientist* reported on several subsequent analyses of the Kaiser Family Foundation . . . data set. The two national surveys are consistent on the large role of electronic media in the lives of very young children, those from 6 months to 3 years. According to the 2006 study (based on a representative sample of parents of children ages 0–6, $N = 1051$), American children under six almost universally live in homes with television (98.4 percent), with a vast majority having computers as well (80 percent) and nearly half having videogame consoles. A fairly large proportion of these very young children have television sets in their bedrooms (18 percent of those 0–2 years old, 39 percent of 3–4 year olds, and 37 percent of 4–6 year olds). These data are comparable to data collected on a similar national sample of parents of young children 0–6 conducted in 2003. . . .

As Anderson and Pempek note . . . , when compared to data from the 1980s and 1990s, data from Kaiser's studies show a dramatic increase in the number of very young children now attending to TV on an average day. Anderson and Pempek compared Kaiser data from 2003 to data analyzed by Certain and Kahn . . . from studies conducted in the early to mid-1990s and note that non-viewers of television on a typical day dropped between the 1990s and early 2000s such that for children younger than 1 year of age, the non-viewers dropped from 83 percent to 43 percent 10 years later; for 1-year-olds the non-viewers dropped from 52 to 40 percent. As Anderson and Pempek remark, it is the very young children who are now likely to watch television and videos and this is different from earlier years. . . .

What is clear from these surveys is that the very young child in the US is now exposed to unprecedented levels of screen media. Screen media use is a dominant activity of childhood. Such use is occurring against the backdrop of public concern about the consequences of such early exposure. This appears to be a trend that has arisen in the past decade of American life. It would appear that the majority of American parents of children under two are not following the AAP guidelines recommending no screen time for children under two. And considering that young children under two spend much of a 24 hour period sleeping—typically 12 or more hours a day—then media use is occupying a large part of their waking hours. In the next section we will discuss potential consequences of such early screen media use.

Consequences of Screen Viewing by Young Children

It is worth noting that over the course of the past several years there has been a heightened emphasis among child development specialists on the importance of the very early years of life, especially the first three years, on children's development. In particular the publication in 2000 of *From Neurons to Neighborhoods* by the National Research Council and Institute of Medicine . . . in the US sig-naled a major summary statement of the research literature on the importance of developmental growth in the first 3 years of life. How media use might influence such early development is increasingly the subject of academic spec-ulation and public policy concerns.

There are several questions that need to be addressed regarding the very young child's use of screen media: first, can children three and younger learn from screen media? If so, how well can they learn from screen media? Finally, are there any benefits and/or risks to children's development from early screen media use? Each of these questions will be considered in turn.

Can Children Under Three Learn from Screen Media?

The success of baby videos is clearly based on parental observations of babies watching and apparently enjoying such videos; of course, almost all of this is based on anecdotal evidence. At least two studies have examined infants' attention to these specially designed baby videos: Rachel Barr and her col-leagues . . . observed infants from 12 to 15 months watching baby videos in their home and found that the infant's attention varied from 48 to 74 percent of the time watching the screen with greater attention to familiar videos. Anderson and Pempek . . . report "high levels" of looking at *Teletubbies*—a program designed for 1-year-olds—when infants are placed on their parents laps in front of a screen in a laboratory setting and have a table of toys to play with in front of them. These studies would appear to confirm the anecdotal reports of parents of the success of baby videos and television programs in elic-iting infants' attention to screen programming. Furthermore, Anderson and Pempek review a few studies that suggest that children as young as 18 months show more attention to televised content created especially for them, such as *Teletubbies,* than to adult content and show a sensitivity to the comprehensi-bility of the program (as indicated by distorting shot sequences or language distortion), both of which suggests that by 18 months children's attention to television is more than a primitive orienting response to visual and auditory elements on the screen (the formal features of the content) and may be guided by higher level cognitive skills such as the comprehensibility of the program. This would suggest that when a program is designed especially for infants they might be able to learn from that program. Indeed, this is the claim of the mar-keters of infant videos.

What evidence do we have that young infants can and do learn from screen images? What are the cognitive developmental skills necessary for babies to learn from screen media? What we might expect is that the ability of infants to make sense of screen images should follow the developmental achievement of infants' ability to learn to internally represent their environment, men-tally encoding information across a wide spectrum of experience. . . . In doing so, they become able to use their representations to make sense of the world and more fully interact with it—from a Piagetian theoretical perspective such symbolic functioning occurs during the last stage of the sensorimotor period or somewhere between 18 and 24 months of age. Until this point, children are thought to not be able to represent information mentally or internally, but only through physical actions. For example, when faced with a problem, such as putting a toy block through a hole, an infant younger than 18 months would be unable to solve the problem internally through a mental representation, but rather would use physical action such as trying out different blocks until finding the right block that fits in the hole. By 24 months, development has proceeded so that children mentally represent objects (through language, symbolic play, and mental imagery) so that they can solve such problems without having to physically manipulate the object.

Media representations may be particularly difficult for infants to make sense of because they are more demanding than physical reality, offering images that manipulate time and space. Infants who already have difficulty understanding some of the basic properties of reality, such as the solid nature of objects and the continuity of objects over time (i.e., that objects cannot just disappear), may be even more confused when faced with object manipulations on television. In short, basic developmental achievements, such as understanding object permanence, may be necessary before infants learn much, if anything at all, from television or screen images.

What Evidence Do we Have That Children Can Learn from a Screen Image—and at What Age?

There is some evidence that infants under two may be more competent than Piaget suggests. Two sorts of studies are relevant here: studies that demonstrate deferred imitation of a televised model, or the ability to observe a model, mentally represent the observed behavior and then reproduce that behavior at a later time; and studies that demonstrate dual representation, or the ability to simultaneously represent an object as the object itself and as a representation of something else.

With respect to the first question, at what age do we have evidence that children can model what they see on television at some later time? There are a few, somewhat contradictory experimental studies of infant learning from televised models. Meltzoff . . . demonstrated deferred imitation from a video presentation in infants as young as 14 months. Meltzoff showed infants 14–24 months' old a simple task of pulling apart a dumbbell-shaped object on video; a control condition saw an experimenter place the dumbbell on a table, but not perform the designated action. Results showed that when children were allowed to play with the object after a 24 hour delay, the infants who had seen the target act were more likely to produce the action than the control group and that the 24-month-old infants were more successful than 14-month-old infants, although there was some evidence of imitation of this very simple action by the 14-month-olds.

However, when infants' ability to imitate a video action is compared to imitation of a live model, infants perform less well in the video condition— leading to a video deficit hypothesis. . . . For instance, Barr and Hayne . . . found that infants at 12, 15, and 18 months could imitate a behavior live, but that there were significant age-related and task-related differences in their abilities to demonstrate a behavior from a video. As in the Melztoff . . . experiment, infants were tested after a 24 hour delay but the behavior involved multiple steps. Infants observed an experimenter holding a puppet, removing a mitten from the puppet's hand, shaking a bell inside the mitten, and then putting the mitten back on the puppet's hand. In order for a child to successfully imitate this behavior, the behavior had to be mentally represented, encoded and expressed after a delay. The children had difficulty performing this behavior. Even in a second experiment eliminating the delay between the observed behavior and the imitation tests, the 12- and 15-month-olds generally did not imitate the video demonstration. The task appeared to strain the cognitive abilities of these young children.

However, in another study designed in a manner more similar to the research of Meltzoff, Barr and Hayne . . . found that when the task was made very simple (in this case demonstrating taking a mitten off) and children were tested immediately following the demonstration, even 15-month-old infants performed equally well in live and video demonstration conditions. Subsequent research also tested whether multiple exposures to a video task improved imitation. Muentener, Price, Garcia, and Barr . . . found that it took six repetitions of the more complex task to yield imitation effects as strong as one real life presentation for infants as young as 6 months and as old as 30 months. Under some conditions, infants younger than two can be shown to imitate a video as well as a live model. There is also some evidence for the potential of television for early learning from observational studies of babies in their home environment, including deferred imitation of behaviors . . . and language learning. . . .

A subsequent question is whether and when infants understand that a video of an object is not the same thing as an object, that it is a representation of that object. To perform this task, children must have acquired the cognitive ability of dual representation, the ability to represent an object simultaneously as the object itself and as a representation of something else. . . . This cognitive ability is thought to develop around 2 ½ years, or the late sensori-motor period. Again, screen presentations of objects may confuse even children who have acquired the ability of dual representation since most of what children see on television is distinctly different from reality. Not only do children deal with the two dimensionality of the presentation, but they are also viewing things that have been scaled down in size to fit inside the television monitor.

In a study by Pierroutsakos and Troseth . . . , the researchers examined infants' manual investigation of a video screen. On video, the experimenters displayed a toy, tapped it on a table to get the child's attention, and then left the frame, leaving the toy on the table. They observed 9-month-olds' evidencing behavior that suggested they did not understand the dual nature of the image and tried to manipulate the objects they were seeing on video. Over the presentation of ten toys, the 9-month-olds displayed on average 1.4 manual behaviors per toy trying to grasp, hit, or rub the toys observed. By 19 months, the infants appeared to grasp the distinction between the video representation and a real object. Further support for this distinction comes from an observational study by Lemish . . . in which very young children were observed to "pet" animals on the television screen. This behavior disappeared during the second year of life, suggesting children had acquired the ability to distinguish between television and reality, a hallmark of dual representation.

Aside from the ability to distinguish between an object and its representation, can young children use a video representation to guide their own behavior? In several studies, researchers have presented children with an object retrieval task in a video or live action condition to see whether children can find a hidden object. This task typically involves showing children a toy being hidden in a room while watching the event on television or while looking through a window at a live presentation. The children are then sent into the same room as seen in the video or through the window and asked to find the toy. Troseth and DeLoache . . . hypothesized that if the children in the video condition could find the hidden object, this would be evidence that they understood the representational nature of television. They found that 2½-year-olds were able to successfully find the toy almost 80 percent of the time, whereas 2-year-olds only found it 44 percent of the time, supporting the achievement of dual representation (and learning from video) for older but not the younger infants. By contrast when the children watched the toy being hidden live through a window of the same size, both the 2- and 2½-year-olds were able to find it.

Schmitt and Anderson . . . conducted a related experiment testing 2- to 3-year-olds' ability to use video to guide their behavior. Utilizing an object retrieval task similar to Troseth and DeLoache . . ., their findings were quite consistent with the earlier study: 2-year-olds did poorly on the object retrieval test in the video condition, completing the task only 23 percent of the time, compared to 2½-year-olds who were successful 56 percent of the time in the video condition and the 3-year-olds who performed equally well in the televised and live model conditions.

A reasonable hypothesis might be that the 2-year-old children need the perceptually richer 3-D representation of real world space in order to complete the task. . . . Television only allows for a 2-D representation, which might impair their ability to use it to guide their behavior. This possibility was tested by Troseth and DeLoache . . . using the same hidden object test but placing the television set behind a window and obscuring the body of the monitor, thus making it appear as though the children were looking through a window into the room and not at a television. They hypothesized that if the degraded 2-D quality of the video image hampered children's ability to complete the task, then children still would not be able to find the hidden toy when they entered the room themselves. However, if they believed they were seeing the actual room rather than a television image of the room, then they would be able to find the toy as accurately as they did in the real window condition. This is in fact what occurred, indicating that perceptual factors were not the reason for their failure in the hidden toy task. Since the television image was no longer a symbol of reality, but rather reality itself (or so it seemed), dual representation was not necessary.

Taken together these studies suggest that until about 2½ years of age, children's learning from video presentations may be limited. While 9-month-olds show little evidence of grasping the representational nature of very simple video images, there is some evidence that children as young as 14 months can imitate simple actions from a televised model . . .; however, learning more complex actions tends to occur around 2½ to 3 years of age. Up until this age, television is inferior to learning in live interactive situations, especially when the behavior being taught is complex. It has been shown to take up to six repetitions for children younger than two to complete a toy finding task that children of the same age can complete after one exposure to a live model.

Secondly, there is evidence of a developmental shift between 24 and 30 months, close to what Piaget calls the last sub-stage of sensori-motor development and the acquisition of mental representation of cognitive tasks. This developmental achievement is evidenced in learning from televised images. Schmitt and Anderson . . . theorize that part of the problem may also lie with information processing difficulties, such that connecting television's smaller images with real world objects may pose cognitive demands on young children that interfere with successful encoding of the televised objects. By 2½ to 3 years, maturational development has improved infants' limited cognitive capacity, allowing them to deal simultaneously with the perceptual differences and the dual nature of the video images. . . . Thus, a confluence of symbolic and representational limitations coupled with processing difficulties may preclude infants from understanding the nature of television and video and without this understanding learning from the medium proves extremely difficult for children younger than 30 months. This is consistent with evidence of a video deficit in children's ability to learn from video versus live models before this age.

What Are the Potential Benefits and/or Risks to Early Screen Viewing?

In any discussion of the potential benefits or potential risks from early screen viewing, it is easy for academics to stress the risks over the benefits and for television and video producers to do the opposite. It is quite clear that baby targeted videos with titles like "Baby Galileo" and "Baby Mozart" in the *Baby Einstein* series are all intended to give the impression that educational media that engages infants can make them smarter or at least give them early and successful preparation for schooling. Data from the Kaiser Family Foundation . . . surveys of parents of 6-month- to 6-year-olds suggests that parents believe that educational television can teach their child language, pre-reading, and other skills that will help them have a step up once they start school. Moreover, the research evidence of *Sesame Street* and other planned educational programs' positive impact on 4- and 5-year-olds' learning of the televised curriculum and even performance in elementary school . . . is more widely known today by American parents of young children. As well, there may be other benefits of early media use such as increased visual and spatial ability or earlier academic achievement or an increased ability to multitask in a world demanding such abilities. We can only speculate in the absence of empirical evidence and longer term studies.

There is additional speculation and concern about the likely risks such early screen use might engender. It has now become well known that when the American Academy of Pediatrics in 1999 recommended that children under two not use screen media and that even older children should be limited to only 2 hours a day of screen media use, they did so in the absence of research evidence on the impact of early screen media use, but with an understanding that for healthy development children need caring adults and creative environments with objects that allow for engaged interaction.

DeLoache . . . has observed that there are several risks that might be associated with infants use of screen media such as (1) interference with the acquisition of crucial developmental skills that are engendered by playing with toys and enriching objects; (2) deprivation of social interaction with caring adults; and (3) interference with learning about real objects and reality per se, such as the fact of object permanence. Others, such as Christakis . . . have speculated on whether such early television use may be related to attention deficit disorder or other impaired brain development.

While these are all speculations, there is some empirical evidence that television as background to daily life may impair infants' ability to concentrate on tasks and consequently impact their development. Anderson and Pempek . . . are engaged in research examining how the presence of adult television programming (especially in heavy television households) as a background to the daily life of infants and toddlers might influence children's play activities and their ability to engage in sustained and concentrated attention to an object. They have argued that children's play is a necessary aspect of cognitive development in infancy and that the complexity of children's play is increased with parental involvement. However, such involvement may be diminished when parents and infants share a living room or other space while parents are watching television. Anderson and his colleagues have conducted research in a laboratory setting observing 12-, 24-, and 36-month-old children's toy play with and without an adult television program playing in the background . . . and noted that such background television reduces both the length of infants' play episodes and their apparent concentration during play. This seeming interference in children's concentration during play is coupled with decreased interaction between parents and children in the presence of background television—the parents are attending to the television and not their infants. Thus, Anderson argues that one risk of the presence of adult television (and not specially designed baby videos) on infants' development is that the presence of background television can interfere directly with children's play concentration at a time when play is important for their cognitive development and may also indirectly diminish parent–child interaction important for infant development.

Conclusions

Very young children's media use has increased steadily over the last few decades. While research in infant DVDs and television programs is still sparse, the evidence thus far suggests a developmental framework is needed to understand potential impact. While questions should certainly be asked about the appropriateness of screen media for children this age and potential outcomes, research should also be asking developmental questions about infants' cognitive abilities in relation to their exposure to screen media. Although it appears that infants can mentally represent and imitate very simple behaviors from video, there is strong evidence of a significant learning deficit when compared to live infant-adult interaction. The research thus far suggests that there may be too many representational and perceptual limitations on children under two for television and videos/DVDs to be of substantial educational or instructional value, although this eases somewhat between 30 and 36 months. Additionally, early screen media use may come at the cost of critical parent–child interaction time, as well as interfering with infants' play at a time when play is important to normal cognitive development. . . .

CHALLENGE QUESTIONS

Are There Good Reasons to Allow Infants to Consume Electronic Media, Such as Television?

- Both sides in this controversy agree that more research needs to be done to fully understand the impact of electronic media on infants. What types of research would be most convincing to you? What are the key questions that we really need to understand?
- If you were talking to the parents of an infant, what would you say? Do the potential benefits of electronic media outweigh the potential risks?
- Rideout, Hamel, and the Kaiser Family Foundation rely entirely on parents' perspectives, without contrasting those to what research finds. Is this a case of parents know best, or do parents' perspectives need to be contrasted with scientific research?
- Wartella and Robb do not consider the usefulness of electronic media in allowing parents to manage family life. Does that matter? Is it possible that by making parenting a more manageable task, electronic media may actually create a more healthy general environment for infants even if causing some immediate cognitive deficits?

Suggested Readings

American Academy of Pediatrics, "Media Education," *Pediatrics*, (August 1999)

D. Anderson and M. Evans, "Peril and Potential of Media for Infants and Toddlers," *Zero to Three* (2001)

J. Golin, "Breaking Free from Baby TV," *Mothering.com* (July 2006)

D. Christakis, F. Zimmerman, D. DiGiuseppe, and C. McCarty, "Early Television Exposure and Subsequent Attentional Problems in Children," *Pediatrics* (April 2004)

S. Fisch and R. Truglio, (Eds.) *"G" is for "growing": Thirty years of research on children and Sesame Street* (Lawrence Erlbaum 2001)

A. Poussaint, S. Linn, and J. Golin, "Zero to Three and Sesame Beginnings: The Consequences of Selling Out Babies." *CommonDreams* (April 19, 2006)

Zero to Three, "Statement from ZERO TO THREE on Partnership with Sesame Workshop on *Sesame Beginnings* DVDs," . . .

E. Wartella, A. Caplovitz, and J. Lee "From Baby Einstein to Leapfrog, From Doom to Sims, From Instant Messaging to Internet Chat Rooms: Public

Interest in the Role of Interactive Media in Children's Lives." *Society for Research in Child Development Social Policy Report* (2004)

M.L. Courage and A. Setliff, "Debating the Impact of Television and Video Material on Very Young Children: Attention, Learning, and the Developing Brain." *Child Development Perspectives* (2009)

D.R. Anderson and T.A. Pempek, "Television and Very Young Children." *The American Behavioral Scientist* (2005)

Internet References . . .

Public Broadcast System

The non-profit public broadcasting system offers a year-by-year guide to the developmental milestones of the first eight years.

http://www.pbs.org/parents/childdevelopmenttracker/

Child Trends

Child Trends is a non-profit research center that provides data and information related to research on child development.

http://www.childtrends.org/

The Children's Defense Fund

The Children's Defense Fund is a non-profit child advocacy organization that provides research publications related to public policy and providing children equal opportunities.

http://www.childrensdefense.org/child-research-data-publications/

National Association for the Education of Young Children

Official site for the National Association for the Education of Young Children, an organization focused on pre-school and other forms of early childhood education.

http://www.naeyc.org/

The Character and Education Partnership

The Character and Education Partnership is a coalition trying to promote character education as a way of shaping children to be good citizens.

http://www.character.org/

Attention Deficit Disorder Association

Official site for the Attention Deficit Disorder Association, which is one of the largest international clearinghouses of information about AD/HD.

http://www.add.org/

Mayo Clinic Health Center

Information about childhood obesity from the Mayo Clinic Health Center:

http://www.mayoclinic.com/health/childhood-obesity/DS00698

Early Childhood and Middle Childhood

*E*arly childhood *(sometimes referred to as toddlerhood) generally encompasses the years between 2 and 6, while middle childhood generally refers to early school years prior to puberty. These ages comprise a gradual transition into the physical, social, and psychological ways of being that orient any lifespan. As such, scholars of development take particular interest in trying to ensure that these ways of being are healthy, hoping to give all children the chance to succeed in an increasingly complex world. The issues in this section focus on three topics that underlie healthy physical, social, and psychological development: our bodies, our schools, and our mental health.*

- Is Advertising Responsible for Childhood Obesity?
- Does Emphasizing Academic Skills Help At-Risk Preschool Children?
- Is Attention Deficit Disorder (ADD/ADHD) a Legitimate Medical Condition That Affects Childhood Behavior?

ISSUE 7

Is Advertising Responsible for Childhood Obesity?

YES: The Kaiser Family Foundation, from "The Role of Media in Childhood Obesity," *Issue Brief* (February 2004)

NO: The Federal Trade Commission Bureau of Economics Staff, from "Children's Exposure to Television Advertising in 1977 and 2004: Information for the Obesity Debate," *Federal Trade Commission Bureau of Economics Staff Report* (June 1, 2007)

ISSUE SUMMARY

YES: In a review of research on media exposure and childhood obesity, the Kaiser Family Foundation concludes that exposure to advertising, more than inactivity, best explains the increasing rates of childhood obesity.

NO: In contrast, the Federal Trade Commission Bureau of Economics Staff specifically evaluated television advertising to children and found that increasing rates of childhood obesity do not correspond with increasing exposure to food advertising.

Groups from the World Health Organization to the United States Centers for Disease Control have spent considerable effort in recent years warning us about an "epidemic" of obesity. According to the Kaiser Family Foundation report, since 1980 the proportion of overweight children in the United States has doubled, and for adolescents it has tripled. They estimate that 20% of 2–5-year-olds and 30% of 6–19-year-olds are at least "at risk" for being significantly overweight. Although the epidemic is certainly not limited to children, children are a primary focus of scholarly investigation because they represent the future of our public health.

The developmental norms that are relevant to obesity are a complex mix of biological, psychological, and social factors. From a biological perspective, there does seem to be a genetic component to obesity—but that component depends heavily upon an interaction with environmental factors. For example, children today are simply less physically active than in the past and thus are more prone to put on weight. From a psychological perspective, it is clear that attitudes toward both physical activity and food contribute significantly to obesity and other weight issues. As such, much attention is devoted to facilitating the development of healthy attitudes toward food and exercise. That attention, however, is only part of broader social influences that shape eating and exercise patterns. The availability and popularity of fast food, for example, is a relatively new social phenomenon that is a part of most childhoods.

While there is not one clear culprit in the childhood obesity epidemic, the influence of advertising and electronic media is a popular target for blame because it relates in various ways to the biological, psychological, and social issues at hand. The popularity of advertising and media may lead children to be less physically active because the attitudes toward food and physical activity are often guided by advertising, and the social world is saturated with a commercial and somewhat sedentary food culture.

In their report, the Kaiser Family Foundation presents data suggesting that advertising and electronic media do indeed play a significant role in the obesity epidemic. They note that media consumption correlates with being overweight, and that food advertising commonly encourages children to make unhealthy diet choices. Thus, while the Kaiser Family Foundation acknowledges that other factors play a significant role in childhood obesity, their data seem to suggest that advertising plays an important role and should be regulated.

The United States Government's Federal Trade Commission, on the other hand, in an analysis of food-related advertising on television, finds no reason to assume it plays any causal role in childhood obesity. They think that the usual estimates about children's exposure to food marketing are too high, and find that advertising exposure has not really gone up significantly during the last 30 years. Yet, this 30-year period is exactly when the obesity epidemic came into being. The Federal Trade Commission notes that regulating food advertising to children has the potential to merely exacerbate the problem since children would be likely to see much more advertising for sedentary activities and entertainments.

POINT

- The exposure of children to food advertising is likely one of several factors contributing to increased rates of obesity.
- Children who consume more electronic media generally are more likely to be overweight.
- Food advertising tends to encourage children toward unwise food choices.

- Limiting advertising directed at children could help to reduce obesity.

COUNTERPOINT

- The estimates of the amount of ads children view are likely significantly too high.
- Most ads that children see are for non-food products.
- Children in 2004 saw fewer ads than children in 1977, thus the rise in obesity has not corresponded with a rise in advertising.
- Restricting food advertising might just lead to more ads for other products that contribute to obesity.

YES    The Kaiser Family Foundation

The Role of Media in Childhood Obesity

Introduction

In recent years, health officials have become increasingly alarmed by the rapid increase in obesity among American children. According to the Centers for Disease Control and Prevention (CDC), since 1980 the proportion of overweight children ages 6–11 has more than doubled, and the rate for adolescents has tripled. Today about 10% of 2- to 5-year-olds and 15% of 6- to 19-year-olds are overweight. Taking into consideration the proportion who are "at risk" of being overweight, the current percentages double to 20% for children ages 2–5 and 30% for kids ages 6–19. Among children of color, the rates are even higher: 4 in 10 Mexican American and African American youth ages 6–19 are considered overweight or at risk of being overweight.

According to the American Academy of Pediatrics, the increase in childhood obesity represents an "unprecedented burden" on children's health. Medical complications common in overweight children include hypertension, type 2 diabetes, respiratory ailments, orthopedic problems, trouble sleeping, and depression. The Surgeon General has predicted that preventable morbidity and mortality associated with obesity may exceed those associated with cigarette smoking. Given that an estimated 80% of overweight adolescents continue to be obese in adulthood, the implications of childhood obesity on the nation's health—and on health care costs—are huge. Indeed, the American Academy of Pediatrics has called the potential costs associated with childhood obesity "staggering."

In an effort to seek the causes of this disturbing trend, experts have pointed to a range of important potential contributors to the rise in childhood obesity that are unrelated to media: a reduction in physical education classes and after-school athletic programs, an increase in the availability of sodas and snacks in public schools, the growth in the number of fast-food outlets across the country, the trend toward "super-sizing" food portions in restaurants, and the increasing number of highly processed high-calorie and high-fat grocery products.

From *Issue Brief #7030*, February 2004. Copyright © 2004 by The Henry J. Kaiser Family Foundation. This information was reprinted with permission from the Henry J. Kaiser Family Foundation. The Kaiser Family Foundation, based in Menlo Park, California, is a nonprofit, independent national health care philanthropy and is not associated with Kaiser Permanente or Kaiser Industries.

Figure 1

Proportion of Overweight Children in the United States

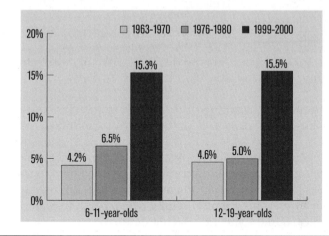

Source: Centers for Disease Control and Prevention, National Center for Health Statistics, Health, United States, 2009, Table 69.

The purpose of this issue brief is to explore one other potential contributor to the rising rates of childhood obesity: children's use of media.

During the same period in which childhood obesity has increased so dramatically, there has also been an explosion in media targeted to children: TV shows and videos, specialized cable networks, video games, computer activities and Internet Web sites. Children today spend an average of five-and-a-half hours a day using media, the equivalent of a full time job, and more time than they spend doing anything else besides sleeping. Even the very youngest children, preschoolers ages six and under, spend as much time with screen media (TV, videos, video games and computers) as they do playing outside. Much of the media targeted to children is laden with elaborate advertising campaigns, many of which promote foods such as candy, soda, and snacks. Indeed, it is estimated that the typical child sees about 40,000 ads a year on TV alone.

For the first time, this report pulls together the best available research, going behind the headlines to explore the realities of what researchers do and do not know about the role media plays in childhood obesity. In addition, the report lays out media-related policy options that have been proposed to help address childhood obesity, and outlines ways media could play a positive role in helping to address this important public health problem.

Pediatricians, child development experts, and media researchers have theorized that media may contribute to childhood obesity in one or more of the following ways:

- The time children spend using media displaces time they could spend in physical activities;
- The food advertisements children are exposed to on TV influence them to make unhealthy food choices;

- The cross-promotions between food products and popular TV and movie characters are encouraging children to buy and eat more high-calorie foods;
- Children snack excessively while using media, and they eat less healthy meals when eating in front of the TV;
- Watching TV and videos lowers children's metabolic rates below what they would be even if they were sleeping;
- Depictions of nutrition and body weight in entertainment media encourage children to develop less healthy diets.

The research to date has examined these issues from a variety of perspectives ranging from health sciences and public health, to child development and family relations, to advertising and mass communications. These investigations have been methodologically diverse, and the results have often been mixed. As with any research, caution must be used when comparing the outcomes of studies because of variations in the methods and measures used. For example, some studies are regional, while others use large, nationally representative samples. Some focus on specific demographic subsets, such as 6th-grade girls, while others are broader. Some studies rely on detailed data sets, others on fairly simplistic measures. For example, television use may be measured through self-reports, parental reports, or detailed diaries. Likewise, body fat may be assessed through multiple clinical measures or by self-reports of height and weight.

The following section of this report reviews the major research that has been conducted on the key issues concerning media and childhood obesity, and summarizes the major findings.

Defining Childhood Obesity

The phrases "obese," "overweight," and "at risk for being overweight" are commonly used in the public health community. With regard to children, the terms "obese" and "overweight" are generally used interchangeably in the medical literature. The Body Mass Index (BMI), which measures the ratio of weight to height, is a standard tool used to define these terms. BMI definitions for children and adolescents are age- and gender-specific in order to accommodate growth patterns. The Centers for Disease Control and Prevention (CDC) classify children as "overweight" if they are above the 95th percentile for their age and sex, and "at risk of being overweight" if they are between the 85th and 95th percentile.

Research on Media and Childhood Obesity

Do major studies find a relationship between childhood obesity and the time children spend using media?   The first major evidence that children's media consumption may be related to their body weight came in a 1985 article by William Dietz and Stephen Gortmaker in the journal *Pediatrics*, and it was dramatic. An analysis of data from a large national study of more than 13,000 children, the National Health Examination Survey (NHES), found significant associations between the amount of time children spent watching television and the prevalence of obesity. The authors concluded that, among 12- to 17 year-olds, the prevalence of obesity increased by 2% for each additional hour of television viewed, even after controlling for other variables such as prior obesity, race, and socio-economic status. Indeed, according to the authors, "only prior obesity had a larger independent effect than television on the prevalence of obesity." In a commentary published in 1993, the authors went on to note that another interpretation of their findings is that "29% of the cases of obesity could be prevented by reducing television viewing to 0 to 1 hours per week."

Since then, several more studies have found a statistically significant relationship between media use and rates of obesity, while others have found either a weak relationship or no relationship at all. In addition to the Dietz and Gortmaker study, other large-scale national studies have found a correlation between media use and body weight:

- Analysis of data from a nationally representative survey of more than 700 kids ages 10–15, conducted in the late 1980s, concluded that "the odds of being overweight were 4.6 times greater for youth watching more than 5 hours of television per day compared with those watching for 0–1 hours," even when controlling for prior overweight, maternal overweight, race, and socio-economic status. The authors concluded, "Estimates of attributable risk indicate that more [than] 60% of overweight incidence in this population can be linked to excess television viewing time."
- Data from the 1988–1994 waves of the National Health and Nutrition Examination Surveys (NHANES) were analyzed to explore the relationship between TV watching and obesity among 8- to 16-year-olds. The study concluded that "television watching was positively associated with obesity among girls, even after controlling for age, race/ethnicity, family income, weekly physical activity, and energy intake." The study did not find a correlation for boys.
- Another analysis of the 1988–1994 NHANES data found that among 8- to 16-year-olds, both boys and girls "who watched the most television had more body fat and greater BMIs than those who watched less than 2 hours a day."
- A study based on the CDC's 1999 Youth Risk Behavior Survey which sampled more than 12,000 high school students nationwide, found that watching television more than 2 hours a day was related to being overweight; these findings were consistent for the entire student population, controlling for race, ethnicity, and gender.
- A later study found a link between television viewing and obesity using a different methodology. The Framingham Children's Study was a longitudinal study in which slightly more than 100 children were enrolled as preschoolers and followed into early adolescence. In this study, published in 2003, the authors found that "television watching was

an independent predictor of the change in the child's BMI" and other measures of body fatness. They noted that the effect of TV viewing was "only slightly attenuated" by controlling for factors such as the child's body-fat measures at the time they were enrolled in the study, and their parents' BMI or education. The authors concluded that "television watching is a risk factor for change in body fat, not simply reflective of more obese children tending to watch more television as a consequence of their obesity making it difficult to exercise."

Other studies—one from a nationally representative cross-sectional sample and the others from specific regions or communities—have not found a relationship between television viewing and childhood obesity:

- A recent analysis of data from a national study of more than 2,800 children ages 12 and under, which relied on detailed time-use diaries, found a "striking" lack of relationship between time spent watching television and children's weight status. On the other hand, this study did find a relationship between obesity and time spent playing video games, although that relationship was not linear: Children with higher weight played moderate amounts of games, while those with low weight played electronic games either very little or a lot.
- A 1993 study of 6th- and 7th-grade girls in Northern California found that over a two-year period "baseline hours of after-school television viewing was not significantly associated with either baseline or longitudinal change in BMI." The authors argued that their study "refutes previous suggestions that . . . television viewing is causally related to obesity."
- A study of nearly 200 preschoolers in Texas observed the children for several hours on each of four different days a year, over the course of three years, recording the amount of TV the children watched and their physical activities. This study found that although television watching was weakly negatively correlated with physical activity levels, it was not associated with body composition.

In evaluating this research, it is important to note that some of these studies are cross-sectional rather than longitudinal—that is, they take a specific point in time and look at whether TV viewing is associated with obesity. One problem with this approach is that while a study may indicate a relationship between TV viewing and being overweight, it does not prove that the TV viewing *caused* the increased weight. Controlling for other risk factors such as socio-economic status and parental body weight (as many studies do) can help clarify the results. Another problem with the cross-sectional approach is that the causal relationship could run in the opposite direction: that is, being obese may cause children to engage in more sedentary (and isolated) activities, including watching more television.

Longitudinal studies can help address the causality issue; however, the results of these studies have varied. As noted above, the two-year longitudinal study of adolescent girls in Northern California did not find a causal relationship between children's weight and the time they spent with media. On the other hand, the Framingham Children's Study, which tracked preschoolers through early adolescence, did find such a relationship. The authors of the latter study have theorized that the effects of media use on body weight may emerge slowly over time, and hence were not revealed in the two-year study in Northern California. It has also been argued that the lack of effect in that study may be due to factors specific to the sample of 6th- and 7th-grade girls in Northern California. Additionally, the study of 700 10- to 15-year-olds referenced above used height and weight data from 1986 and compared it to TV viewing and BMI measures in 1990. These authors concluded that "no evidence was found for a selective effect of overweight; i.e., children who were overweight in 1986 were unlikely to watch more television in 1990 than were children who were not overweight."

Others argue that the only way to truly demonstrate a causal relationship is through an experimental trial; for example, reduce TV viewing and see whether that affects children's weight when compared to a control group. Several interventions of this nature have been found to have a positive impact in reducing children's body weight.

Do experimental interventions that reduce children's media time result in weight loss? Experimental trials are considered the best way of determining whether there is a causal relationship between television viewing and childhood obesity. Some experiments have incorporated reductions in media time as part of a more comprehensive program involving diet and increased physical activity as well. Another experiment used reduced media time as the only intervention, yet still found an impact on children's weight and body fatness.

- During the 1996–97 school year, Stanford University researchers conducted a randomized controlled trial in which they reduced the amount of time a group of about 100 3rd- and 4th-graders in Northern California spent with TV, videos, and video games. Two matched elementary schools were selected to participate, one of which served as the control group. The intervention involved a "turnoff" period of no screen time for 10 days followed by limiting TV time to 7 hours per week, as well as learning media literacy skills to teach selective viewing. At the end of a 6-month, 18-lesson classroom curriculum, students who received the intervention achieved statistically significant reductions in their television viewing and meals eaten in front of the TV set, as well as decreases in BMI, triceps skinfold thickness, waist circumference, and waist-to-hip ratio. While these changes were not accompanied by reduced high-fat food intake or increased physical activity, the findings do appear to demonstrate the feasibility of decreasing body weight by reducing time spent with screen media.
- Another school-based intervention found improved diet, increased physical activity, and decreased television time to be effective. The study, which measured prevalence, incidence, and remission of obesity among ethnically diverse middle-school boys and girls, involved a randomized controlled field trial with five intervention and five control schools. Classroom teachers in math, science, language arts, social

studies, and physical education incorporated lessons within the existing curricula over two years. The lessons focused on decreasing television viewing to 2 hours per day, increasing physical activity, reducing consumption of high-fat food, and increasing servings of fruits and vegetables. For each hour television viewing was reduced, the prevalence of obesity was reduced among girls in the intervention schools compared with the control schools; no similar effect was found for boys. The program also resulted in an increase in girls' consumption of fruits and vegetables.

- A family-based weight-control program found that decreasing sedentary behaviors (such as screen media use) is a viable alternative to increasing physical activity in treating childhood obesity. Families with obese children ages 8–12 were randomly assigned to one of four groups that included dietary and behavior change information, but differed in whether they tried to decrease sedentary activities or increase physical activity. Results indicated that significant decreases in percent of overweight and body fat were associated with decreasing sedentary behaviors such as watching TV or videos, or playing video or computer games.

These interventions indicate that reducing the time children spend with media may indeed be an effective way to address childhood obesity. Researchers, health professionals, and advocates have theorized several ways media may contribute to childhood obesity. The following sections summarize some of the major scientific studies in order to provide an understanding of media's potential influence on the incidence of overweight among children and adolescents in the United States.

Does the time children spend using media displace time spent in more physical activities?   From toddlers to teens, American youth are spending a substantial part of every day of their lives using media. But the time children spend using media does not necessarily mean a decrease in time spent in physical activities. Surprisingly, few studies have examined this relationship, and results have been mixed. Some studies have found a weak but statistically significant relationship between hours of television viewing and levels of physical activity, while others have found no relationship between the two.

- A study of 6th- and 7th-grade adolescent girls in four Northern California middle schools found that the number of hours they spent watching TV after school was negatively associated with their level of physical activity; however, the relationship accounted for less than 1% of the variance and there was no connection with body weight.
- A study of a small sample of preschool children in Texas, conducted in a naturalistic setting, found a weak but statistically significant relationship between TV viewing and physical activity, although it did not find a relationship between viewing and body weight.
- A recent national telephone survey of parents of children ages 4–6 found that children who spent more than two hours watching TV the previous day spent an average of a half-hour less playing outside that day than did other children their age.

- A review of data from the 1999 National Youth Risk Behavior Study, which includes a nationally representative sample of more than 15,000 high school students, found that among white female students only, time spent watching TV was associated with being sedentary.
- A survey of close to 2,000 9th-graders in Northern California found a weak but statistically significant relationship between TV viewing and physical activity for white males only.
- A study of national data from the 1988–1994 NHANES found no relationship between TV viewing and the number of bouts of vigorous physical activity, although it did find a statistically significant relationship between TV viewing and body weight.

While logic suggests that extensive television viewing is part of a more sedentary lifestyle, the evidence for this relationship has been surprisingly weak to date. In order for this relationship to be true, as one study noted, children who watch less TV would have to be choosing physically vigorous activities instead of TV, rather than some other relatively sedentary pastime such as reading books, talking on the phone, or playing board games.

Another possibility is that the act of watching TV itself actually reduces children's metabolic rate, contributing to weight gain. One study of 8- to 12 year-olds found that TV viewing decreased metabolic rates even more than resting or sleeping, but several other studies found no such effect.

The fact that most studies have failed to find a substantial relationship between the time children spend watching TV and the time they spend in physical activity may suggest that the *nature* of television viewing—that is, how children watch and what they watch—may be as or more important than the number of hours they watch.

Do the food ads children are exposed to on TV influence them to make unhealthy food choices?   Many researchers suspect that the food advertising children are exposed to through the media may contribute to unhealthy food choices and weight gain. Over the same period in which childhood obesity has increased so dramatically, research indicates that the number of ads children view has increased as well. In the late 1970s, researchers estimated that children viewed an average of about 20,000 TV commercials a year; in the late 80s, that estimate grew to more than 30,000 a year. As the number of cable channels exploded in the 1990s, opportunities to advertise directly to children expanded as well. The most recent estimates are that children now see an average of more than 40,000 TV ads a year.

The majority of ads targeted to children are for food: primarily candy (32% of all children's ads), cereal (31%), and fast food (9%). One study documented approximately 11 food commercials per hour during children's Saturday morning television programming, estimating that the average child viewer may be exposed to one food commercial every 5 minutes. According to another study, even the two minutes of daily advertising targeted to students in their classrooms through Channel One expose them to fast foods, candy, soft drinks, and snack chips in 7 out of 10 commercial breaks.

A review of the foods targeted to children in commercials on Saturday morning television indicates that the nutritional value has remained consistently low over the past quarter-century. Over the years, the most prevalent foods advertised have been breakfast cereals. Up until the 1990s, the next most-advertised products were foods high in sugar, such as cookies, candy, and other snacks. By the mid-1990s, canned desserts, frozen dinners, and fast foods overtook ads for snack foods. The data indicate that ads for these high-fat and high-sodium convenience foods have more than doubled since the 1980s. While studies vary as to the exact percentages, the same pattern emerges: a predominance of ads for high-sugar cereals, fast food restaurants, and candy, and an absence of ads for fruit or vegetables.

The Effect of Food Advertising on Children

The vast majority of the studies about children's consumer behavior have been conducted by marketing research rms and have not been made publicly available. Clearly, the conclusion advertisers have drawn is that TV ads can influence children's purchases—and those of their families. Fast food outlets alone spend $3 billion in television ads targeted to children. Recent years have seen the development of marketing firms, newsletters, and ad agencies specializing in the children's market. The New York Times has noted that "the courtship of children is no surprise, since increasingly that is where the money is," and added that marketing executives anticipate that children under 12 will spend $35 billion of their own money and influence $200 billion in household spending in 2004. The enthusiasm of marketers can be felt in the Februray 2004 edition of Harris Interactive's "Trends and Tudes" newsletter, which notes that "This generation has become a huge consumer group that is worthy of attention from many businesses seeking to maximize their potential. Kids, teens and young adults spend significant amounts of their own money, and they influence the shopping behavior of their parents, their siblings, their relatives, and other adults in their lives."

Scientific studies that are available in the public realm back up these marketing industry assessments of the effectiveness of advertising directed at children. Studies have demonstrated that from a very young age, children influence their parents' consumer behavior. As many parents can attest after a trip down the grocery aisle with their children, television viewing has also been found to impact children's attempts to influence their parents' purchases at the supermarket. For example, several studies have found that the amount of time children had spent watching TV was a significant predictor of how often they requested products at the grocery store, and that as many as three out of four requests were for products seen in TV ads. These studies have also found that children's supermarket requests do indeed have a fairly high rate of success.

One study found that among children as young as 3, the amount of weekly television viewing was significantly related to their caloric intake as well as their requests and parent purchases of specific foods they saw advertised on television. Another study manipulated advertising shown to 5- to

8-year-olds at summer camp, with some viewing ads for fruit and juice, and others ads for candy and Kool-Aid. This study found that children's food choices were significantly impacted by which ads they saw.

Experimental studies have demonstrated that even a brief exposure to food commercials can influence children's preferences. In one study, researchers designed a randomized controlled trial in which one group of 2- to 6-year-olds from a Head Start program saw a popular children's cartoon with embedded commercials, and the other group saw the same cartoon without commercials. Asked to identify their preferences from pairs of similar products, children who saw the commercials were significantly more likely to choose the advertised products. Preference differences between the treatment and control group were greatest for products that were advertised twice during the cartoon rather than only once.

Researchers are beginning to document a link between viewing television and children's consumption of fast foods and soda, a possible result of exposure to food advertising. A recent study found that students in grades 7–12 who frequently ate fast food tended to watch more television than other students. Another study found that middle-school children who watched more television tended to consume more soft drinks.

Other evidence of television's potential impact on children's dietary habits indicates a negative relationship between viewing television and consuming fruits and vegetables. The USDA's Dietary Guidelines recommend that youth eat three to five daily servings of fruits and vegetables, yet only 1 in 5 children meet the guideline, and one-quarter of the vegetables consumed reportedly are french fries. In a recent study, more than 500 middle school students from ethnically diverse backgrounds were studied over a 19-month period to determine whether daily television and video viewing predicted fruit and vegetable consumption. Using a linear regression analysis, researchers found that for each additional hour of television viewed per day, daily servings of fruits and vegetables decreased among adolescents. The researchers who conducted the study conclude that this relationship may be a result of television advertising.

Some researchers believe that TV ads may also contribute to children's misconceptions about the relative health benefits of certain foods. One of the earlier studies found that 70% of 6- to 8-year-olds believed that fast foods were more nutritious than home-cooked foods. Another study showed a group of 4th- and 5th-graders a series of paired food items and asked them to choose the healthier item from each pair (for example, corn flakes or frosted flakes). Children who watched more television were more likely to indicate that the less healthy food choice was the healthier one. These results replicated the results of an earlier study conducted with children of the same age.

Do cross-promotions between food products and popular TV and movie characters encourage children to buy and eat more high-calorie foods?
Recent years have seen what appears to be a tremendous increase in the number of food products being marketed to children through cross-promotions with popular TV and movie characters. From SpongeBob Cheez-Its to Hulk pizzas and Scooby-Doo marshmallow cereals, today's grocery aisles are filled

with scores of products using kids' favorite characters to sell them food. Fast food outlets also make frequent use of cross-promotions with children's media characters.

A recent article in the New York Times business section noted that "aiming at children through licensing is hardly new. What has changed is the scope and intensity of the blitz as today's youth become unwitting marketing targets at ever younger ages through more exposure to television, movies, videos and the Internet." One food industry executive was quoted as saying that licensing "is a way to . . . infuse the emotion and popularity of a current kids' hit into a product."

Some promotions involve toys based on media characters that are included in the food packages or offered in conjunction with fast food meals. McDonald's and Disney have an exclusive agreement under which Happy Meals include toys from top Disney movies. In the past, Happy Meals have reportedly also included toys based on the Teletubbies TV series, which is aimed at pre-verbal babies. Burger King has also featured Teletubbies tie-ins, along with Rugrats, Shrek, Pokemon and SpongeBob. More than a decade ago, researchers were finding that the typical "kid's meal" advertised to children consisted of a cheeseburger, french fries, soda, and a toy. One study found that about 1 in 6 (16.9%) food commercials aimed at children promise a free toy. In addition to the use of toys as an incentive in marketing food to children, many commercials use cartoon characters to sell products, which research has shown to be particularly effective in aiding children's slogan recall and ability to identify the product.

A recent example of the effectiveness of this technique is the growth in the dried fruit snack market. Almost half (45%) of fruit snacks had licensing agreements in 2003 compared to 10% in 1996. Sales have increased substantially every year since 1999: 5.6% in 2000, 8.7% in 2001, 3.2% in 2002, and 5.5% in 2003. Marketing experts attribute the sales growth to children's influence on their parents' purchasing decisions and parental beliefs that dried fruit snacks are healthier than other sweets. . . .

Reduce or regulate food ads targeted to children   For decades, policymakers, child advocates, pediatricians, and others have advocated for policy measures to protect children from advertising, including ads for unhealthy food. In light of the rapid increase in childhood obesity, food ads aimed at children have come under increasing scrutiny. Policy suggestions to reduce or regulate food advertising targeted to children take a wide array of forms, from voluntary action taken by media companies or the food industry to government regulation. [See box on next page.]

Most researchers agree that children do not understand commercials in the same way adults do. Most children under age 6 cannot distinguish between program content and commercials, and most children under age 8 do not understand that the purpose of advertising is to sell a product. Even children ages 8–10 who have the cognitive ability to understand the nature of advertising may not always discern the persuasive intent or understand the wording of a disclaimer. The American Academy of Pediatrics reviewed the publicly available research about children and advertising and concluded that "advertising directed toward children is inherently deceptive and exploits children under 8 years of age."

Children's advertising guidelines are currently regulated by the Federal Communications Commission (FCC), which requires compliance before renewing a station's license. One guideline requires that a clear distinction between program content and commercial messages be maintained by using separation devices known as "bumpers" to signal the beginning and end of a commercial break. Others prohibit ads with character endorsements from running during or immediately adjacent to that character's show. The Children's Television Act, passed by Congress in 1990, also mandates advertising limits during programming aired primarily for children under age 12 to 10.5 minutes per hour on weekends and 12 minutes per hour on weekdays.

Children's advertising is also subject to self-regulatory policies adopted under the Children's Advertising Review Unit (CARU). The Grocery Manufacturers Association has pointed out that CARU guidelines suggest that advertising should: not mislead children about the nutritional benefits of products; depict appropriate amounts of a product for the situation portrayed; depict food products "with a view toward development of good nutritional practices"; refrain from portraying snacks as substitutes for meals; and show mealtime products in the context of a balanced diet. The latter policy, for example, is illustrated in cereal ads that show a bowl of cereal with milk and juice, and a voice-over noting that cereal should be part of a balanced, healthy breakfast.

Among the Options That Have Been Suggested Are:

- A ban on any advertising to preschoolers
- A ban on advertising of "junk" food to very young children
- An FTC investigation into marketing of "junk" food to children
- A prohibition on food product placement in children's programming
- The provision of "equal time" for messages on nutrition or fitness, to counteract food ads in children's shows
- Parental "warnings" about the nutritional value of advertised foods
- A repeal of the tax deduction for company expenses associated with advertising "junk" food products to children
- A prohibition on food advertising in school-based TV programs such as Channel One
- Explicit announcement of food-related product placement deals in popular TV shows or movies seen by large numbers of children
- Eliminating or limiting cross-promotions between popular children's media characters and unhealthy food products
- Increasing the use of popular media characters and celebrities to promote healthy food alternatives

In December 2003, while on the campaign trail, Senator Joseph Lieberman called for a Federal Trade Commission (FTC) investigation into the marketing practices of companies that target unhealthy foods to children. Just recently a coalition of obesity experts, health professionals, and child advocates asked Sesame Workshop not to air sponsorship messages for McDonald's before or after "Sesame Street." In response, children's TV producers note that banning food advertising or underwriting would remove one of the most lucrative sources of funding for children's television, particularly given the lack of public funds available in this country for that purpose.

Several industrialized democracies have adopted policies designed to protect children from excessive marketing practices. Sweden, Norway, and Finland, for instance, do not permit commercial sponsorship of children's programs. Sweden also does not permit any television advertising directed to children under age 12. Belgium imposes restrictions on commercials five minutes before and after as well as during children's programming. The BBC decided to prohibit use of its cartoon characters in fast food ads, and England is pushing for stricter guidelines for advertising aimed at children. . . .

Conclusion

The rising rates of childhood obesity present one of the most significant public health challenges we face. While there are many factors that contribute to the problem, this review of the major studies indicates that children's use of media is an important piece of the puzzle. Fortunately, there are an array of options for policymakers, food companies, media companies and parents to consider that may help minimize any negative effect media may be having and maximize the positive role media can play in addressing the problem.

Most large national cross-sectional studies and several longitudinal studies indicate that children who spend more time with media are more likely to be overweight than children who don't. While several regional studies have come to different conclusions, experimental interventions clearly indicate that there is an opportunity to reduce children's body weight by curbing the time they spend with media.

Exactly *how* media may contribute to childhood obesity has not been conclusively documented. Contrary to common assumptions, most studies have found only limited evidence for the theory that the time children spend with media displaces time they would otherwise spend in more vigorous physical activities. There may be limitations to the measures used in these studies, and more research needs to be done in this area.

But in the absence of such research at this time, it appears likely that the main mechanism by which media use contributes to childhood obesity may well be through children's exposure to billions of dollars worth of food advertising and cross-promotional marketing year after year, starting at the very youngest ages, with children's favorite media characters often enlisted in the sales pitch. Research indicates that children's food choices—and parents' food purchases—are significantly impacted by the advertising they see. The number of ads children see on TV has doubled from 20,000 to 40,000 since the 1970s, and the majority of ads targeted to kids are for candy, cereal, and fast food. More research, perhaps removing ads from children's media while not reducing their overall time spent with media, could help clarify this issue.

While the magnitude of the impact of media's effects on childhood obesity is not clear, the body of evidence indicates there is a role for media-related policies to play in a comprehensive effort to prevent and reduce childhood obesity. While this report does not endorse any specific policies, it does lay out a variety of possibilities for consideration, from reducing the time children spend with media, to reducing their exposure to food advertising, to increasing the number of media messages promoting fitness and sound nutrition.

The Federal Trade Commission  **NO**

Children's Exposure to TV Advertising in 1977 and 2004: *Information for the Obesity Debate*

Executive Summary

Obesity has become a major health concern in the U.S. and other countries as overweight and obesity rates have increased markedly since the early 1980s. The rise in children's obesity is a particular concern, because overweight children are more likely to become overweight adults, and because obese children are likely to suffer from associated medical problems earlier in life.

Food marketing is among the postulated contributors to the rise in obesity rates. Food marketing to children has come under particular scrutiny because children may be more susceptible to marketing and because early eating habits may persist. Some researchers report that children's exposure to television advertising has been increasing along with the rise in children's obesity rates.

This report presents a comprehensive analysis of the exposure of children, ages 2–11, to television advertising based on copyrighted Nielsen Monitor-Plus/ Nielsen Media Research audience data from the 2004 television programming season. The detailed data covers the individual advertisements shown during four weeks of national and local ad-supported programming and includes paid commercials, public service announcements, and promotions for television programming. These data are projected to annual estimates.

Thirty years ago similar assessments of children's television advertising were done for the Federal Trade Commission's 1978 Children's Advertising Rulemaking. Since these research reports were done before the rise in children's obesity, they provide a baseline to measure changes in children's exposure to television advertising.

Since the late 1970s, other marketing has likely changed and new forms of marketing have emerged, including Internet-based advertising techniques. This report does not cover these marketing activities, but the FTC is in the process of conducting another study to attempt to gauge the extent of all forms of marketing to children.[1]

Federal Trade Commission Bureau of Economics Staff Report, June 1, 2007, pp. ES-1–ES-9.

This report can also be used to measure future changes in children's exposure to television advertising as industry, parents, and children react to these health concerns.

Summary of Major Findings for 2004

Children's Exposure to Television Advertising   In 2004 we estimate that children ages 2–11 saw about 25,600 television advertisements. In this study, advertisements include paid ads, promotions for other programming, and public service announcements. Of these 25,600 ads, approximately 18,300 were paid ads and most of the remaining 7,300 ads were promotions for other programming. The average ad seen by children was about 25 seconds long. Thus, children saw about 10,700 minutes of TV advertising in 2004. For comparison, adults saw approximately 52,500 ads and 22,300 minutes of advertising.

Our estimates differ from other published estimates of children's exposure to television advertising; one widely cited estimate, that children see around 40,000 ads per year, is more than 50 percent higher than ours. Our estimates are based on very detailed data not available to most researchers. Most published estimates are based on aggregate estimates of the amount of time children watch television, combined with counts of ads aired per hour on selected samples of TV programming. This approach can be accurate as long as the component estimates are accurate representations of children's viewing habits. But our results indicate, for instance, that ad-supported television accounts for only 70 percent of children's TV viewing in 2004, and children get much of their advertising exposure from prime time and other nonchildren's programming. These and related issues must be reflected in the component estimates for such aggregate estimates to be accurate.

Amount of Time Children Spend Viewing Ad-Supported Television   We estimate that in 2004 children 2–11 watched about two and one-quarter hours of ad-supported television per day, for a total of 16 hours per week, about 70 percent of their total television viewing time, about 23 hours per week. Teens, ages 12–17, watched about two and one-half hours of ad-supported television daily. Adults watched nearly four and one-quarter hours daily, almost twice as much as children, and this accounts for most of adults' greater ad exposure.

When Children Are Exposed to Ads   We find considerable dispersion in when children accumulated their ad exposure. Saturday morning between 8 AM and noon was an important contributor to children's ad exposure, but was only 4.3 percent of the total. Sunday morning contributed 2.5 percent. Evenings between 8 PM and 12 AM contributed nearly 29 percent of children's total ad exposure. The time between 4 PM and 8 PM contributed another 26 percent of the total. Prime-time viewing peaked around 8 PM and was the primary time when ad exposure from broadcast programming exceeded that from cable programming. These patterns of ad exposure have important implications for studies that sample children's programming in an effort to produce broad

Figure 1

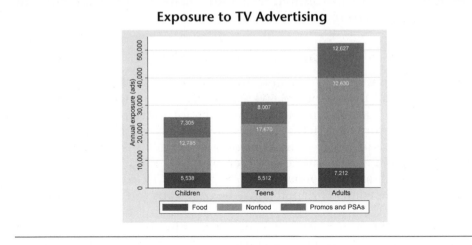

estimates of children's ad exposure, and they help to explain some of the differing results found in the research literature.

Children's Exposure to Food Advertising   Children 2–11 saw approximately 5,500 food ads in 2004, 22 percent of all ads viewed. The leading categories of food advertising seen by children include Restaurant and Fast Food (5.3 percent of total ad exposure); Cereal (3.9 percent; Highly Sugared Cereals are 85 percent of this category); Desserts and Sweets (3.5 percent); Snacks (1.9 percent); Sweetened Drinks (1.7 percent); Dairy (1.4 percent); and Prepared Entrees (0.9 percent). All other food categories combined are 3.1 percent of ad exposure.

We also group shows according to whether the children's share of the audience is at least 20 percent (family shows) or at least 50 percent (children's shows). Food advertising is a larger share of children's advertising exposure as child share increases—from 22 percent of ad exposures on all shows to 32 percent on children's shows. The proportion of children's ad exposure is higher on children's shows for all of the food categories listed above, except for Restaurant and Fast Food ads. Children get nearly 80 percent of their Cereal ad exposure on children's shows and about one-third of their Sweetened Drink and Restaurant and Fast Food advertising there. The other food categories are between these extremes.

Sedentary Entertainment Dominates Other Ads Seen by Children   Seventy-eight percent of the ads children saw in 2004 were for nonfood products. The top three nonfood product categories were Promotions for television programming (28 percent), Screen/Audio Entertainment (7.8 percent), and Games, Toys and Hobbies (7.5 percent). Together these three categories of sedentary entertainment products amounted to 43 percent of children's ad exposure, approximately double the number of food ads seen by children.

Children got approximately 85 percent of their Games, Toys and Hobbies ad exposure on children's shows, as well as 44 percent of their

Screen/Audio Entertainment exposure, and 33 percent of their Promotions exposure. Together these three categories constituted 85 percent of children's nonfood ad exposure from children's shows.

Children's TV Viewing Is Concentrated on Cable   Cable programming was a major source of children's television viewing and ad exposure in 2004. Sixty-one percent of children's ad exposure and 72 percent of their food ad exposure was from cable programming. For children's programming, the concentration was even higher; 96.5 percent of all children's ad exposure from children's shows and 97.6 percent of their food ad exposure from children's shows was from cable programming.

Changes in Children's Exposure to Advertising Between 1977 and 2004

Children's Exposure to Paid Advertising Has Fallen; Overall Ad Exposure Is Up   Studies from the FTC's Children's Advertising Rulemaking indicate that children 2–11 saw about 19,700 paid ads and 21,900 ads overall in 1977. When compared to our estimates of 18,300 paid ads and 25,600 ads in 2004, we find that children's exposure to paid advertising fell by about 7 percent and exposure to all advertising rose by about 17 percent since 1977. This difference reflects the substantial increase in children's exposure to promotional ads for television programming over this time period. Children saw approximately 2 percent fewer minutes of advertising and 19 percent fewer minutes of paid advertising in 2004 than in 1977. These reductions reflect the combined impact of the reduced amount of time children spend watching ad-supported television in 2004 compared to 1977 and ads that are shorter on average.

Children's Exposure to Food Advertising Has Not Risen   The 1977 studies do not give a complete estimate of children's exposure to food ads, but using other data from the period we find that food ad exposure has not risen and is likely to have fallen modestly. In our primary scenario, we estimate that children saw 6,100 food ads in 1977. This suggests that children saw about 9 percent fewer food ads in 2004 than in 1977.

In 1977 ads for Cereals and for Desserts and Sweets dominated children's food ad exposure, with the Restaurant and Fast Food and the Sweetened Drinks categories also among the top categories. As seen above, in 2004 these categories were still among the top categories of food ads children saw, though Cereals and Desserts and Sweets no longer dominated. Restaurant and Fast Food ads had an increased presence, and were joined by Snacks, Dairy and Prepared Entrees as substantial sources of children's food ad exposure. Thus, the mix of food ads seen by children in 2004 is somewhat more evenly spread across these food categories than in 1977.

Children's Exposure to Ads for Sedentary Entertainment Has Grown   The reduction in food advertisements seen by children has been more than compensated for by substantially increased Promotions for television programming

Figure 2

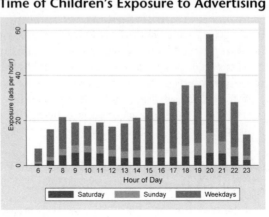

Time of Children's Exposure to Advertising

and increased advertising for Screen and Audio Entertainment. These two categories are both larger than any food category in 2004 and exceed Games, Toys and Hobbies, which had been the top nonfood category in 1977.

Children's Ad Exposure Is More Concentrated on Children's Cable Programming in 2004   Children get approximately half of their food advertising and about one-third of their total advertising exposure from programs in which children are at least 50 percent of the audience in 2004, compared to about one quarter in 1977. Ads for some food categories and for toys appear to be targeted to children.[2] Virtually all of this 2004 ad exposure on children's programming is from cable shows; in 1977, when cable programming was in its infancy, children's shows came from national broadcast and local sources.

Discussion of Empirical Findings and Obesity

Evidence on TV Advertising's Relation to Obesity   Many commentators have suggested that marketing to children may be a significant factor in the growth of obesity in U.S. children. This hypothesis is well beyond anything we could test formally with the television advertising data analyzed here. Nonetheless, our data can shed light on aspects of this hypothesized link.

First, our data do not support the view that children are exposed to more television food advertising today. Our best estimates indicate that children's exposure to food advertising on television has fallen by about 9 percent between 1977 and 2004. Children's exposure to all paid television advertising has fallen as well.

Second, our data do not support the view that children are seeing more advertising for low nutrition foods. In both years the advertised foods are concentrated in the snacking, breakfast, and restaurant product areas. While the foods advertised on children's programming in 2004 do not constitute a balanced diet, this was the case as well in 1977, before the rise in obesity.

Evidence Related to Ad Restrictions on Children's Programming   Some have called for various restrictions on advertising to children, including a complete ban on advertising to younger children and further restrictions on the number of minutes of advertising on children's television programming. Others have called for self-regulation or legislation that would limit advertising on children's programming to foods that meet specified nutrition characteristics. Some industry members have proposed voluntary commitments along these lines. This report does not provide a basis to assess the likely effects of any of these approaches, or the substantial legal issues that would have to be addressed for regulation, but it does have several findings that relate to this discussion.

First, children today do get half of their food advertising from shows where children are at least 50 percent of the audience. Thus, changes to the mix of ads on children's shows could potentially have an effect on the mix and number of food advertisements that children see. This effect would be considerably larger than would have been the case in 1977, when programming was not as specialized and children did not get much of their advertising exposure from children's programs. That said, children also get half of their food advertising exposure from nonchildren's shows and food ads on those shows might increase if restrictions were placed on children's programming.

Second, our study does provide some insight on another issue that has received little attention in the public discussion: what type of advertising would likely replace the restricted food advertising, if it is replaced? The hope is that advertising for better food might increase. Beyond that, the best guidance on this question is found by looking at the other products currently advertised on children's programs, since these are the products most likely to increase their advertising if food advertising is reduced. Currently, advertisements for sedentary entertainment products outnumber food advertisements by two to one and constitute most of the other advertising on children's programming. Presumably these products would expand their advertising further, if food advertising is reduced. Whether such a shift in advertising seen by children would affect obesity in U.S. children—either positively or negatively—is an open question which has received little attention.

Finally, it is worth noting that a restriction on advertising on children's programming would not fall evenly on industry participants. In 2004 broadcast networks had very few programs where children were more than 50 percent of the audience. Successful children's programming is now largely on children's cable networks. In fact, over 97 percent of food advertisements children see on children's shows are from cable programming.

Final Notes

Our study is limited to advertising on television. Television is still the medium where food advertisers spend most of their advertising dollars. In 2004 approximately 75 percent of all food advertising spending on measured media was spent on television, down from 83 percent in 1977. Many producers are exploring other advertising media and methods as television audiences become more expensive to reach. This is true for advertising to children as well. Advergaming, child-oriented producer-sponsored websites, product placements and other tie-ins with movies and television programming are all part of the marketing landscape, and research to quantify these efforts is only beginning.[3]

This study was conducted to provide a comprehensive assessment of the amount and type of television advertising seen by children in 2004. It has been nearly 30 years since the last evaluation of children's television ad exposure using detailed viewing data. Advertising seen by children has received considerable attention in recent years as a possible contributor to rising obesity in American children, and as a possible vehicle to help reverse that trend. Hopefully, this report will provide useful information to guide discussion of the issues. The report also provides a baseline against which to measure future changes in children's exposure to television advertising as parents, firms and children react to obesity concerns.

Notes

1. **Federal Register** / Vol. 72, No. 74 / Wednesday, April 18, 2007 / Notices. See also Moore (2006) on advergaming.

2. See Gantz et al. (2007) for a recent content analysis of television advertising on children's and general interest programming. Neither this report nor Gantz et al. (2007) considers whether children may respond differently to the types of ads aired on children's programs.

3. The FTC is beginning a study to attempt to guage the extent of these other forms of marketting to children. **Federal Register** / Vol. 72, No. 74 / Wednesday, April 18, 2007 / Notices.

CHALLENGE QUESTIONS

Is Advertising Responsible for Childhood Obesity?

- Both sides acknowledge that advertising alone is not responsible for increasing rates of child obesity. Of the other factors, is it possible that some interact with the influence of the media to create weight problems?
- While the Federal Trade Commission focuses on direct food advertising, the Kaiser Family Foundation also considers the cross-marketing of food with media figures. What seems most likely to influence the eating choices of children?
- One of the arguments for limiting any advertising directed at children is that at young ages they have not yet developed the ability to take a critical perspective on information. Based on what you know about childhood as a developmental stage, how would you expect children to respond to advertising?
- The Federal Trade Commission offers a comparison of advertising between 1977 and 2004 partially because 1977 was before the rise in obesity. What other influences on children's health and diet choices may have differed significantly in 1977?

Suggested Readings

Dateline NBC Special Report: Food Fight . . .

C. Ebbeling, D. Pawlak, and D. Ludwig, "Childhood Obesity: Public-Health Crisis, Common Sense Cure," *The Lancet* (August 10, 2002)

M. Gard and J. Wright, *The Obesity Epidemic: Science, Morality and Ideology* (2005)

W. Gibbs, "Obesity: An Overblown Epidemic?" *Scientific American* (June 2005)

C. Hawkes, "Marketing Food to Children: Changes in the Global Regulatory Environment 2004–2006," (The World Health Organization)

J. Hersey and A. Jordan, "Reducing Children's TV Time to Reduce the Risk of Childhood Overweight: The Children's Media Use Study Highlights Report," Prepared for the Centers for Disease Control and Prevention Nutrition and Physical Activity Communication Team (2007)

Institute of Medicine, *Food Marketing to Children and Youth: Threat or Opportunity?* (2006)

J. Krishnamoorthy, C. Hart, and E. Jelalian, "The Epidemic of Childhood Obesity: Review of Research and Implications for Public Policy," *Society for Research in Child Development Social Policy Report* (2006)

D. Kulick and A. Meneley, *Fat: The Anthropology of an Obsession* (2005)

ISSUE 8

Does Emphasizing Academic Skills Help At-Risk Preschool Children?

YES: U.S. Department of Health and Human Services, from *Strengthening Head Start: What the Evidence Shows* (June 2003)

NO: C. Cybele Raver and Edward F. Zigler, from "Another Step Back? Assessing Readiness in Head Start," *Young Children* (January 2004)

ISSUE SUMMARY

YES: The U.S. Department of Health and Human Services argues that preschool programs can help young children most by emphasizing academic and cognitive skills.

NO: Professors C. Cybele Raver and Edward F. Zigler argue that overemphasizing academic and cognitive skills at the expense of social, emotional, and physical well-being is a mistake dependent on misguided efforts to make the entire educational system focused on concrete assessment.

A hallmark of early childhood is the start of educational experiences outside the home. For many children this means formal preschool. Many people take for granted that a quality preschool experience is essential to future success. You may have heard about exclusive preschools that are as competitive for admission as Ivy League colleges, and as expensive to match. On the other side of the spectrum, many children raised by families mired in poverty lack the opportunity for quality preschool. These children often start primary school behind their more well-off peers, and have difficulty breaking the cycle of poverty. As preschool became more common during the twentieth century, scholars of development became more aware that breaking the grip of poverty required early intervention.

The most famous and intensive North American effort to facilitate early childhood development for children from poor families is the Head Start program. Started in the 1960s as part of President Lyndon Johnson's "War on Poverty," Head Start was a collaborative effort between the government and scholars to provide an educational environment that would allow children living in poverty to succeed. One of the foundational ideas upon which Head

Start was built is that early childhood development progresses as an integration of distinct components of children's well-being. Thus, rather than focusing exclusively on academic skills, Head Start has attempted to provide diverse services that attend to academic, social, emotional, cognitive, and physical aspects of development.

Longitudinal research following children years after Head Start has shown mixed results. Research on IQ, for example, shows that Head Start does provide an early bump in IQ scores that lasts several years. The positive impact, however, dissipates over time until Head Start children end up returning to IQ levels consistent with other poor individuals who did not experience Head Start. Other evidence, however, suggests that Head Start children are less likely to be held back later in school, less likely to be labeled with learning disabilities, and more likely to continue their education.

Both sides of this debate agree that Head Start has not done enough to eliminate the gaps between the success of children from poor and rich families. The controversy is about what needs to change. And this question ultimately gets at a fundamental issue in development: Can we separate out the different aspects of development or do they all work in integrated ways?

The U.S. Government's Department of Health and Human Services under the George W. Bush administration declares that to break the cycle of poverty, the most important developmental aspect of early childhood is cognitive skills. They assert that Head Start needs to focus more on cognitive and academic skills such as pre-math and pre-literacy. The idea is to test these specific cognitive capacities and hold teachers and administrators accountable.

C. Cybele Raver and Edward F. Zigler point out that focusing exclusively on cognitive skills runs counter to the way most developmental scholars understand the importance of early childhood. These authors offer a convincing historical perspective, partially because Zigler was involved in the founding of Head Start. He notes that children from poor families do not simply have a cognitive disadvantage, but they have an integrated set of developmental needs.

POINT	COUNTERPOINT
• Head Start has not been successful enough in improving IQ and core cognitive abilities.	• Cognitive development cannot be separated out from social and emotional development.
• Skills, such as pre-literacy, will give children the best chance to succeed in school and escape poverty.	• Poverty is more complex than just doing well or poorly academically.
• The reason Head Start has failed is because it does not focus enough on academic skills.	• Head Start has not received sufficient resources, and is only part of the puzzle required to address poverty.
• Testing can ensure that children are learning the specific skills they need to succeed in school.	• Testing will serve to distract from inequalities such as access to resources and well-qualified teachers.

YES ⬅

U.S. Department of Health and Human Services

Strengthening Head Start: What the Evidence Shows

Introduction

The period from birth through age 5 is a critical time for children to develop the physical, emotional, social, and cognitive skills they will need to be successful in school and the rest of their lives. Children from poor families, on average, enter school behind children from more privileged families. Targeting preschoolers in low-income families, the Head Start program was created in 1965 to promote school readiness to enable each child to develop to his or her fullest potential. Research shows that acquiring specific pre-reading, language, and social skills strongly predict future success in school.

As our knowledge about the importance of high quality early education has advanced dramatically since 1965, so have data on the outcomes for children and families served by Head Start. The knowledge and skill levels of low-income children are far below national averages upon entering the program. When the school readiness of the nation's poor children is assessed, it becomes clear that Head Start is not eliminating the gap in educational skills and knowledge needed for school. Head Start is not fully achieving its stated purpose of "promot[ing] school readiness by enhancing the social and cognitive development of low-income children." Head Start children show some progress in cognitive skills and social and emotional development. However, these low-income children continue to perform significantly below their more advantaged peers once they enter school in areas essential to school readiness, such as reading and mathematics.

States and the federal government fund a wide variety of programs that are either intended to enhance children's educational development or that could, with some adjustments, do a better job of preparing children for school. Head Start is one of many federal and state programs that together provide approximately $23 billion in funding for child-care and preschool education. Because these programs have developed independently, they are not easily coordinated to best serve the children and families who need them. In programs other than Head Start, states have the responsibility and the authority through planning, training, and the regulatory process to have a substantial impact on the type and quality of services provided, and are held accountable

From U.S Department of Health and Human Services, June 2003.

for the delivery of high quality programs. However, Head Start funding goes directly from the federal level to local organizations, and thus states do not have the authority to integrate or align Head Start programs with other early childhood programs provided by the states.

The single most important goal of the Head Start reauthorization should be to improve Head Start and other preschool programs to ensure children are prepared to succeed in school. This paper describes the limited educational progress for children in Head Start and the problems resulting from a fragmented approach to early childhood programs and services. The paper also presents evidence from early childhood research and documents state efforts that have successfully addressed these problems. Finally, the paper explains the President's proposal for Head Start reauthorization, which builds on the evidence to strengthen the program and, through coordination, improve preschool programs in general to help ensure that children are prepared to succeed in school.

Children in Head Start Are Not Getting What They Need to Succeed in School

Certain knowledge, skills, and experiences are strong markers of school readiness. For example, we know that children who recognize their letters, who are read to at least three times a week, who recognize basic numbers and shapes, and who demonstrate an understanding of the mathematical concept of relative size as they entered kindergarten have significantly higher reading skills in the spring of first grade than children who do not have this background. In fact, the difference between children who do and do not have this knowledge upon entering kindergarten is approximately one year's worth of reading development at the end of first grade. This is true regardless of family income and race or ethnicity.

Head Start is a comprehensive early childhood development program designed to provide education, health, and social services to low-income children, ages 3 to 5, and their families. Federal grants to operate Head Start programs are awarded directly to the local organizations that implement the program, including public agencies, private non-profit and for-profit organizations, Indian Tribes, and school systems. Since it began in 1965, Head Start has enrolled over 20 million children.

However, while making some progress, Head Start is not doing enough to enhance the language, pre-reading, and pre-mathematics knowledge and skills that we know are important for school readiness. The knowledge and skill levels of young children entering Head Start are far below national averages. Children graduating from Head Start remain far behind the typical U.S. child. We know also that all disadvantaged children who need high quality early educational instruction are not in Head Start. Some are in pre-kindergarten programs, others are in child-care settings, and still others are at home with parents.

Most Children Enter and Leave Head Start with Below-Average Skill and Knowledge Levels

Currently, the primary source of information on outcomes for children and families served by Head Start comes from the Family and Child Experiences Survey (FACES). . . . These data are from the class of children who entered the program in 1997. The percentile scores show how Head Start children perform compared with the average performer. On a percentile scale, an average performer would be at the 50th percentile, meaning that half of children who take the test score above the average performer and half score below the 50% mark. Head Start children as a group fall far below the 50th percentile in all areas of achievement. Though children are making some progress, clearly few children perform as poorly as children who enter and leave the Head Start program. . . .

Both higher achieving and lower achieving Head Start children have low scores overall and show limited progress. Children who were in the upper 25% of their Head Start class when they entered Head Start in 1997 showed no gains on any measure of cognitive ability over the course of the Head Start program year, and actually experienced losses on some measures in comparison to national norms. Gains over the Head Start year were limited to children who were in the bottom 25% of their class. However, even these gains fell far short of bringing children to levels of skill necessary for school success. For example, children in the bottom 25% of their Head Start class left Head Start with language skill scores at the 5th percentile, meaning that only 5% of all children who take the test score lower than these Head Start children do. Findings for mathematics showed a similar pattern.

The more recent 2000 FACES data show modest improvement in results for children, but overall progress is still too limited. Children continue to lag behind national norms when they exit Head Start. Data from Head Start FACES 2000 shows that:

- The level of children's achievement in **letter-recognition** for the 2000 Head Start year is far below the majority of U.S. children who know all letters of the alphabet upon entering kindergarten, according to the Early Childhood Longitudinal Study of the Kindergarten class of 1998.

    Spanish-speaking children in Head Start did not gain at all in **letter recognition** skills in 2000.
- Although **writing** scores increased 2 points during the 2000 Head Start year, this was a drop from children who entered Head Start in 1997 who increased 3.8 points in writing during the 1997 Head Start year.
- Children entered Head Start in 2000 with scores at about the 16th percentile in **vocabulary,** or about 34 percentile points below the average. Children entering Head Start scored at about the 31st percentile in **letter recognition** and at about the 21st percentile in early **mathematics.**
- Children who entered Head Start in 2000 made progress in early **mathematics** during the Head Start year that was statistically significant; however the difference was small (from 87.9 to 89.0 on a scale for

which 100 is the average). [This] 1.2-point difference is not a substantial gain toward national averages. Moreover, this amount of progress was no greater than that found for children who attended Head Start from Fall to Spring in 1997.

- Children who entered the program in 2000 with overall lower levels of knowledge and skill showed larger gains during the program year compared to children who entered with higher levels of knowledge. However, they still lagged far behind national averages.
- Head Start children did not start kindergarten with the same social skill levels as their more socio-economically advantaged peers, and they continued to have more emotional and conduct problems.
- A follow-up study of children enrolled in Head Start in 1997 showed that children who attend Head Start make less progress than the average kindergartener. Thirty-four percent of Head Start children showed proficiency in knowing the ending sounds of words, 53% in knowing the beginning sounds of words, and 83% in letter recognition. Data from a nationally representative sample of all first-time kindergartners shows that fifty-two percent demonstrated proficiency in knowing the ending sounds of words, 72% in knowing the beginning sounds of words, and 94% in letter recognition.

. . . Head Start children have made some progress in some areas. A more detailed look shows that:

- In 2000, the mean standard score for vocabulary increased 3.8 points, from 85.3 to 89.1 on a scale for which the average is 100. This result is similar to the data for 1997 that showed Head Start children scored about 85 at the beginning of the year and gained about 4 points by the end of the year.
- In 2000, the mean standard score for writing increased by 2 points, from 85.1 to 87.1.
- In 2000, children showed gains in book knowledge and print conventions (that is, they can show an adult the front of a storybook and open it to where the adult should start reading). This progress is statistically greater than for the 1997 Head Start year during which no progress was made in this area.
- In 2000, Spanish-speaking children in Head Start showed significant gains in English vocabulary skills without declines in their Spanish vocabulary.
- In 2000, children showed growth in social skills and reduction in hyperactive behavior during the Head Start year. Even children with the highest levels (scoring in the top quarter) of shy, aggressive, or hyperactive behavior showed significant reductions in these problem behaviors. Teachers rated children's classroom behavior as more cooperative at the end of the Head Start year than when children first entered the program.
- In 2000, children who received higher cooperative behavior ratings and lower problem behavior ratings from Head Start teachers scored better on cognitive assessments at the end of kindergarten, even after controlling for their scores on cognitive tests taken while in Head Start.
- Children who entered Head Start in 1997 showed significant gains in their social skills, such as following directions, joining in activities, and

waiting turns in games, and gains in cooperative behaviors, according to ratings by teachers and parents. The quality of children's social relationships, including relating to peers and social problem solving, also improved.

Head Start program and teacher characteristics show some positive relationships to educational and social outcomes for children. Examples include:

- Teachers' educational credentials are linked to greater gains in early writing skills. Children taught by Head Start teachers with bachelors' degrees or associates' degrees showed gains toward national averages in an assessment of early writing skills, whereas children taught by teachers with lesser credentials merely held their own against national norms.
- Provision of preschool services for a longer period each day is linked to greater cognitive gains. Children in full-day classes in Head Start showed larger fall to spring gains in letter recognition and early writing skills than did children in part-day classes.

Head Start has other positive qualities:

- In 1997, the program received very high ratings of satisfaction from parents, and for the roughly 16% of children in Head Start with a suspected or diagnosed disability, 80% of parents reported that Head Start had helped them obtain special needs resources for the child.
- A follow up study of children who attended Head Start in 1997 showed that children were capable of making some progress during their kindergarten year in vocabulary, writing, and early mathematics, though performance remained significantly below national norms.

How do eligible children fare when they do not receive Head Start services? The FACES study is not designed to answer this question; there is no control group. Eligible children who do not receive services could be falling further behind or could be making gains similar to or greater than those for children in the program. The national Head Start Impact Study was launched in 2002 and is using a randomized design to answer this question. Additional experimental studies are being conducted to assess the effectiveness of specific quality improvement strategies.

A national study of Early Head Start, which is part of the Head Start program serving low-income pregnant women and children from birth through three, was recently conducted using a randomized experimental design. Results show that children receiving Early Head Start have scores that are statistically higher than their peers who did not receive Early Head Start on measures of cognitive, language, and social and emotional competency. Fewer Early Head Start children scored in the "at-risk" range of functioning in both language and cognitive functioning. However, Early Head Start children continue to perform below the national average.

In summary, there is more work to do. Despite the positive qualities of Head Start programs, children in Head Start are making only very modest progress in only some areas of knowledge and skill, and children in Head Start are leaving the program far behind their peers. More progress must be made and can be made to put Head Start children on par with others by the time they enter kindergarten.

Disadvantaged Children Lag Behind Throughout the School Years

Effective early childhood intervention is important because disadvantaged children are at great risk for poor educational outcomes throughout the school years. Data from the National Center for Education Statistics' (NCES) Early Childhood Longitudinal Study—Kindergarten Cohort (ECLS-K) and National Assessment of Educational Progress (NAEP) are reviewed below.

Children with Multiple Risks Suffer the Greatest Educational Disadvantage

Achievement differences in school are greatest for children who suffer the greatest disadvantage, in particular for children whose families have **multiple risk factors** or **receive welfare.** While many of the children we are trying to reach in early childhood are in Head Start and federal and state pre-kindergarten programs, others are in child-care and home-settings.

A key set of **risk factors** has been repeatedly associated with educational outcomes, such as low achievement test scores, grade repetition, suspension or expulsion, and dropping out of high school. These risk factors include: (a) having parents who have not completed high school, (b) coming from a low-income or welfare-dependent family, (c) living in a single-parent family, and (d) having parents who speak a language other than English in the home. Children who have one or more of these characteristics are more likely to be educationally disadvantaged or have difficulty in school.

These same risk factors are linked to achievement disparities in reading and mathematics skills at the point of kindergarten entry. Research emphasizes that achievement difficulties children experience in school "cannot be attributed solely to bad schools; many children are already behind when they open the classroom door."

- Children with **two or more risk factors** are about three times as likely as those with no risk factors to score in the bottom 25% in reading.
- Children from families with **3 or more risk factors** typically do not know their letters and cannot count to 20. Fifty-six percent could not identify letters of the alphabet compared with 25% in the no risk group. They are about one-third as likely to be able to associate letters with sounds at the end of words.
- Children with even **one risk factor** are twice as likely to have reading scores that fall into the lowest 25% of children studied compared to children with no risk factors. They are half as likely to be able to associate letters with sounds at the ends of words. Some children with one risk factor have good reading scores, but far too few. They are half as likely to score in the top quartile as children with no risk factors (16% vs. 33%).

- In mathematics, 38% of the multiple risk group could count beyond 10 or make judgments of relative length compared with 68% in the no risk group. They were one-third as likely to be able to recognize 2-digit numerals or identify the ordinal position of an object in a series.
- Forty-four percent of children with multiple risk factors rarely paid attention, compared to 28% of children with no risk factors.

Children are at risk for poor educational outcomes when their families receive **welfare** (defined as receiving welfare or having received welfare in the past). These children were significantly less competent in reading, mathematics, and social skills compared to children who had never received welfare.

- In reading, children of welfare recipients are less likely to show pre-reading competencies that include letter recognition, recognition of beginning and ending sounds, and print familiarity. Forty-nine percent of these children scored in the lowest quartile, compared to 22% of children whose families were not welfare recipients.
- In mathematics, half of children whose families received welfare scored in the lowest quartile for mathematics, compared to 22% of children whose families had never received welfare. Twenty-three percent of children of welfare recipients scored in the top half for reading, compared to 53% of children whose families had never received welfare.
- Children from welfare families also are under-represented in the higher performing category: Fifty-three percent of children who had never received welfare scored in the top half for reading, compared to only 24% of children whose families were welfare recipients.
- Children of welfare recipients are also at risk for poor social skills. Kindergarten teachers rated these children as having more difficulty with forming friendships and interacting with peers compared to children whose families were not welfare recipients.

The Achievement Gap for Disadvantaged
Children Widens During Kindergarten

Children who start behind are likely to stay behind and get further behind. Research shows that the achievement gap between advantaged and disadvantaged groups of children widens from Fall to Spring. Global reading and mathematics scores show gains for all children in reading and mathematics scores during the kindergarten year. But a closer look shows that achievement disparities between disadvantaged and more advantaged children depend on the particular knowledge and skills assessed.

By Spring, children from homes with at least one risk factor begin to close gaps in basic skills, such as recognizing letters, counting beyond 10, or comparing the size of objects. But because their more advantaged classmates move on to acquire more complex skills, these children are even further behind by Spring in reading and mathematics skills, such as reading words or solving simple addition and subtraction problems. Moreover, despite improvements in basic reading and mathematics skills during the kindergarten year, the disparity between advantaged and disadvantaged children was not eliminated.

The Achievement Gap Persists into Elementary and High School
Poor children eligible for the National School Lunch Program do not perform as well as more advantaged children who are ineligible for the program. Average scores for reading, mathematics and writing achievement are statistically lower for children who are eligible for the school lunch program compared to ineligible children. This achievement gap continues throughout the school years. . . .

Research Evidence Shows We Can Do Better in Helping Children Achieve

Research Has Identified What Children Need to Succeed in School

Before children can read, write or calculate, research shows that children must acquire foundational knowledge, skills, and behaviors that are stepping stones toward mastery of more advanced and complex skills.

Children Are Better Off If They Enter Kindergarten with Cognitive Resources
Children who bring certain knowledge and skills with them to kindergarten are likely to be at an advantage in classroom learning compared to their peers who do not possess these resources. A Department of Education report described the predictive power of having specific cognitive and health "resources" on children's reading and mathematics achievement. These resources included:

- possessing specific basic literacy knowledge and skills;
- being read to at least three times a week at kindergarten entry;
- being proficient in recognizing numbers and shapes at kindergarten entry;
- showing productive approaches to learning, such as an eagerness to learn, task persistence and ability to pay attention; and
- possessing good to excellent health.

Each of these was a key predictor of children's reading and mathematics achievement in the Spring of kindergarten and in first grade, even after controlling for children's race, ethnicity and poverty status. These data confirm that we must ensure that *all* children, regardless of background, are physically healthy *and* have the same basic literacy, mathematics, and cognitive experiences and skills needed to succeed in school.

Child Development Research Shows Which Areas of Competency to Target
Research experts and practitioners in fields relating to early childhood recommend that children make progress in each of the following areas to help ensure they are developing school readiness knowledge and skills.

- In the area of **pre-reading**, children should develop: phonological processing skills (hearing and playing with sounds in words, for example, through rhyming games), letter knowledge (knowing the names and sounds of letters), print awareness (knowing how to hold a book, that we read in English from left to right and usages of print), writing, and interest in and appreciation of books, reading, and writing.
- In the area of **language**, children should develop receptive and expressive vocabulary skills (ability to name things and use words to describe things and actions); narrative understanding (ability to understand and produce simple and complex stories, descriptions of events, and instructions); phonology (ability to distinguish and produce the different sounds of language); syntactic or grammatical knowledge (knowing how to put words together in order to communicate with meaning); and oral communication and conversational skills (knowing how to use words in appropriate contexts for a variety of purposes, such as knowing when and how to ask a teacher for more information, or understanding how to take turns in a conversation).
- Children should develop **pre-mathematics** knowledge and skills that include number concepts (recognizing written numerals, counting with an understanding of quantity, knowing quantitative relationships such as "more" and "less"), number operations (such as adding and subtracting); geometry concepts (such as recognizing shapes); space, patterns, and measurement concepts and skills (such as measuring length using their hands or measuring using conventional units such as inches).
- Children should develop **cognitive skills** that include the ability to plan and problem-solve, the ability to pay attention and persist on challenging tasks, intellectual curiosity and task engagement, and achievement motivation and mastery.
- Children need **social and emotional competencies** important for school success and a constructive learning environment. These include the ability to relate to teachers and peers in positive ways, the ability to manage feelings of anger, frustration and distress in age-appropriate ways, and the ability to inhibit negative behaviors with teachers and peers, for example, aggression, impulsiveness, noncompliance, and constant attention-seeking.

The Right Programs and Training Can Improve Children's School Readiness

Research, though limited, clearly demonstrates the value of providing comprehensive interventions with strong language and pre-academic components that develop the knowledge and skills necessary for kindergarten and the early grades and for closing the achievement gap. Though more research is needed, a few approaches that have been evaluated using rigorous designs show that comprehensive and language and literacy-rich early childhood programs can reduce achievement gaps for disadvantaged children. Here are highlights of major studies.

The Chicago Child-Parent Center (CPC) Program
This program for low-income minority children in high-poverty neighborhoods in innercity Chicago, funded in part by the Department of Education, includes

half-day preschool for one or two years, full or part-day kindergarten, continuing support services in linked elementary schools, and a parent education program. The Chicago CPC program provides educational and health and nutrition services, such as hearing screening, speech therapy and nursing services, to children ages 3 to 9 years. The intervention emphasizes the acquisition of basic knowledge and skills in language arts and mathematics through relatively structured but diverse learning experiences. An intensive parent program includes volunteering in the classroom, attending school events and field trips, and completing high school. Teachers are required to have bachelor's degrees, are paid at the level of teachers in public school, and participate in regular staff development activities. Child-to-staff ratios are low (17:2).

A longitudinal study funded by the National Institutes of Health and other funders compared participant children to a non-experimental comparison group of children with similar demographics. Findings include:

Reading and mathematics achievement.   At the end of the program in third grade, CPC graduates surpassed their comparison group counterparts by 4 to 6 points in reading and mathematics achievement, as measured by the Iowa Test of Basic Skills.

Preschool participation.   One or two years of CPC preschool participation was associated with statistically significant advantages of 5.5 and 4.2 points in standard scores for reading achievements for ages 14 and 15. This corresponds to about a 4- to 5-month change. Likewise, preschool participation was significantly associated with a 4.4-point increase in standard scores in math achievement at age 14 and a 3.3-point advantage at age 15, above and beyond gender, environmental risk factors, and participation in follow-on interventions. This translates into a 3- to 4-month performance advantage over the comparison group. These effect sizes are considered moderate; however the effects persist up to 10 years after children leave the program, which is unique among early interventions and almost all social programs.

Follow-on participation.   Because the early childhood program is linked to the kindergarten and elementary schools, children may participate in the program from 1 to 6 years. Each year of participation was associated with an increase of 1.3 to 1.6 points in the standard score for reading. Years in the follow-on intervention were significantly associated with reading achievement at ages 14 and 15 and went beyond that attributable to preschool participation. The most dramatic effect occurring after 4 years of intervention: Five or six years of participation resulted in the best performance, with children performing at or above the Chicago averages in reading and mathematics. (Even 6 years of participation, however, did not elevate the performance of the maximum intervention group to the national average.) A similar pattern occurred for mathematics achievement, though the size of the effect was smaller. The findings showed that the relationship between years of participation and school achievement is not strictly linear—greater advantages accrue as the length of the intervention increases.

Other outcomes.   Preschool participation was associated with lower rates of grade retention (23% vs. 38.4%) and special education placement (14.4% vs. 24.6%). Preschoolers who participated in the intervention spent an average of 0.7 years in special education compared with 1.4 years for non-participants. Children who participated in the preschool intervention for 1 or 2 years had a higher rate of high school completion (49.7% vs. 38.5%), more years of completed education (10.6 vs. 10.2), and lower rates of juvenile arrests (16.9% vs. 25.1%). Boys benefited from preschool participation more than girls, especially in reducing the school dropout rate.

Cost-benefit analyses.   With an average cost per child of $6,692 for 1.5 years of participation, the preschool program generates a total return to society at large of $47,759 per participant. These benefits are the result of participants' increased earnings capacity due to educational attainment, criminal justice system savings, reduced school remedial services, and averted tangible costs to crime victims. Benefits realized in each of these areas exceed the cost of just one year of the preschool program, which is $4,400. Overall, every dollar invested in the preschool program returns $7.14 in individual, educational, social welfare and socioeconomic benefits.

The Abecedarian Project

The Abecedarian Project was a carefully controlled study in which 57 infants from low-income families living in a small North Carolina town were randomly assigned to receive early intervention in a high quality child-care setting and 54 were in a non-treated control group. The treated children received full-time educational intervention in a high quality child-care setting from infancy through age five, which included cognitive development activities with a particular emphasis on language, and activities focusing on social and emotional development. Teachers were required to have bachelor's degrees and were paid at the level of teachers in public school.

Starting at age 18 months, and through follow-ups at ages 12 and 15, the treatment children had significantly higher scores on cognitive assessments. Treated children scored significantly higher on tests of reading and math from the primary grades through age 21 (though scores did not reach national averages).

At age 21, those in the treatment group were significantly more likely to still be in school and more likely to have attended a four-year college. Employment rates were higher for the treatment group than for the control group, although the trend was not statistically significant.

The Perry Preschool Study

This pioneering study begun in the 1960s was one of the first to identify lasting effects of high quality preschool programs on children's outcomes. One hundred twenty-three poor African American 3- and 4-year-olds were randomly assigned either to attend a high quality preschool program or to no preschool. The two groups began the study with equivalent IQ scores and socioeconomic status. Children attended 2½ hour classes and teachers conducted weekly 1.5-hour home-visits.

Results showed positive impacts on several intellectual and language tests prior to school entry and up to age 7, showing that the program enhanced children's school readiness. At age 14, participants outperformed non-participants on a school achievement test in reading, language, and mathematics. At age 19, participants' general literacy skills were better than non-participants. At age 27, participants had higher earnings and economic status, higher education and achievement levels in adolescence and young adulthood, as well as fewer arrests.

Benefit-cost analyses show that by the time participants were 27 years old, the program showed a sound economic investment, with significant savings from settlement costs for victims of crimes never committed, reduced justice system costs, increased taxes paid due to higher earnings, reduced need for special education services, and reduced welfare costs. . . .

Conclusions

Research shows that children in Head Start are falling behind and too often are not ready for school. In particular, those children who are the poorest and have the most risk factors do not enter kindergarten with the intellectual resources they need to succeed. Some of these children are being served by Head Start, but others are in state pre-kindergarten, child-care, and home-settings. From basic science on learning and development and from intervention studies we know a great deal about how to narrow the achievement gap for Head Start and other disadvantaged children before they enter kindergarten. Research tells us the knowledge and skills children need in language, pre-reading, and pre-mathematics, and the social and emotional competencies they must have to succeed in school. The President believes that the Head Start program must be strengthened and provide more emphasis on pre-reading, language, pre-mathematics and other cognitive skills, while continuing to promote children's health and social and emotional competence as part of school readiness. Research tells us that early childhood education implemented with qualified and well-trained teachers can make a significant and meaningful impact on the development of children's knowledge and skills, their achievement in school, and success in life. . . .

C. Cybele Raver and
Edward F. Zigler

NO

Another Step Back? Assessing Readiness in Head Start

Since its founding in 1965, Head Start's goal has been to help children who live in poverty prepare for school. Over the last three and a half decades, Head Start has maintained a staunch commitment to the provision of genuinely comprehensive services. While impressive in its breadth, this wide range of services has made it difficult for researchers to benchmark children's progress in the program. One solution has been to rely on strictly cognitive measures as a means to assess the benefits of Head Start. We criticized this approach in an earlier paper entitled "Three Steps Forward, Two Steps Back." In that article, we pointed out that sole reliance on children's cognitive outcomes was neither in keeping with the goals of Head Start nor with many definitions of what it means to be ready to succeed in early elementary school.

Recently Head Start has been subjected to major policy changes at the federal administrative and legislative levels. In particular, the Bush Administration instituted a new set of accountability measures that will be used to test Head Start children twice a year on language, literacy, and pre-math skills. This policy is swiftly being put into place with full implementation plans announced in both April and June 2003. The assessment system, under the National Reporting System that is part of the current law but left to the Secretary to determine, has been controversial. The measures were quickly developed by Westat, Inc., and the national assessment process is now underway. This fall, all four- and five-year-old children in Head Start (who are eligible to enroll in kindergarten next year) will undergo the first of two annual assessments. This quick pace of change proceeded despite a letter to administrators signed by some 300 professionals questioning the psychometric properties of the measures.

⌘

The spring of 2003 was also the time Congress began work on reauthorizing Head Start's funding. The House version of the reauthorization bill (HR 2210) proposed substantial changes to the 38-year-old program. Most controversial was a plan to devolve Head Start to the states, but the bill also raised the issue of assessment. The bill (as introduced) emphasized children's knowledge and skills in the areas of language, literacy, and pre-math and deleted the current law's references to children's social competence, emotional development, and cultural diversity. Why did the Bush Administration move so sharply away from Head Start's emphasis on school readiness in broadly defined terms, and toward a narrow emphasis on cognitive development as the critical factor in preparing for school?

⤝◉⤞

Perhaps these moves are driven by well-meaning intentions on the part of policy makers to improve the educational chances of our nation's most disadvantaged young children. The evidence shows that while Head Start children make significant gains in preschool, they still score well below the national average on vocabulary, pre-reading, writing, and early math skills. Secretary of Health and Human Services Tommy Thompson argues that poor children deserve a better start to their educational trajectories. Lawmakers on both sides of the political spectrum began to focus the debate on what it means to close the achievement gap of Head Start children with their middle-class peers. However, their pathways to that goal were quite different, as were their expectations of closing that gap merely by adding a stronger focus on literacy and math skills.

On the face of it, there is some logic to the idea that if children are less knowledgeable regarding early academics like letters and numbers, strengthening these skills should help them when they begin school. And perhaps lawmakers were persuaded by a small number of studies that suggest that some programs (but not others) have shown limited short-term improvements in older children's educational achievement when "high-stakes" achievement tests are used to increase school monitoring and accountability. In our view, however, these intentions are misguided. As we will argue, the application of a strictly cognitive focus to assessments of school readiness runs counter to what the best developmental research tells us and what past policy experience has shown. A narrow focus on benchmarking Head Start's programmatic success on early cognitive gains to the exclusion of children's emotional and social development has been tried in the past and has backfired. In this article, we briefly review these past rounds of policy debate, and consider scientific evidence regarding what disadvantaged preschoolers need to be ready for school. We then offer three concrete policy recommendations for alternatives to the steps that are in the works for Head Start accountability.

What Does Past Policy Experience Tell Us?

This is not the first time that policy makers and research scientists have tried to peg evidence of Head Start's success to children's cognitive gains. During Head Start's early years, evaluators commonly found substantial gains in children's IQ scores after even brief periods of intervention. These gains were publicized as striking evidence that the programs worked. However, when the IQ benefits were found apparently to dissipate as children progressed through elementary school, intervention efforts were quickly deemed a failure not worthy of public support.

·◦·

When Head Start and other early interventions failed to show permanent gains in children's cognitive scores (as assessed by IQ), policy makers had two choices: either to capitulate to the skeptical view that early intervention is not effective, or to question whether IQ gains were the appropriate metric to have used in the first place and whether the programs were improperly evaluated. Workers in a variety of disciplines eventually convinced policy makers that intelligence alone does not guarantee academic success—that even a very bright child will do poorly in school if he or she suffers physical health or emotional problems, has trouble staying motivated, or does not interact well with teachers or peers. Consequently, researchers, policy professionals, and practitioners in the field of early childhood education seemingly resolved this issue by establishing that Head Start must continue to encompass a broader mission of school readiness that includes physical and mental health, social and emotional needs, and academic skills. This emphasis on both cognitive and social-emotional development was validated by specific language in the 1998 Head Start reauthorization act. Further verifying policy makers' acceptance, data on children's social and emotional development (though in limited form) began to be collected in large-scale national surveys including the Family and Child Experiences Survey (FACES, Department of Health and Human Services), the Early Childhood Longitudinal Study (ECLS-K, Department of Education), and the Head Start National Impact Study (U.S. Department of Health and Human Services). Suddenly, however, the current administration decided to reverse course.

In part, we suspect that this reversal is due to consensus that there is an unacceptably large "achievement gap" between economically disadvantaged children and their more advantaged counterparts, and that it is our responsibility as a nation to do something to reduce that gap. Yet there is major disagreement regarding the best remedies to take. Similar to ongoing debate in educational research and policy, one view is that early interventions such as Head Start are not doing a good job teaching disadvantaged preschoolers. From an economic and partisan perspective, the argument is that Head Start programs (like public schools) are monopolies that are inefficient and have few incentives to improve because of the lack of competition. More strictly defined standards of child performance are seen as a way to impose accountability. Literacy and math skills can be tested, and test scores can yield information about school performance to consumers (e.g., parents, government funding agencies, etc.). The hope is that market-based systems will weed out bad performers and reward higher performers, that providers will strive to improve, and that children will benefit.

The opposing view, held by many early childhood educators and advocates, sees this emphasis on accountability as a way for fiscally conservative policy makers to avoid paying for the relatively expensive solutions that are needed to enact real gains in poor children's educational attainment. This group contends that high-quality early education and care can advance disadvantaged children's learning but that it is not cheap to provide. Advocates and educators in early childhood suggest that if policy makers really wanted to close the education gap, they would make the kind of fiscal investments that are needed to provide children with the things that we know work: comprehensive, full-day services with highly trained, well-paid staff, with fewer children in each classroom, and with more time and resources to devote to learning, literacy, and social and emotional development. They further argue that changes at the preschool level will not be enough. For Head Start children to maintain the gains they make in preschool, fiscal resources will be needed to improve the elementary schools they attend and—even more daunting—to alleviate home and community stressors that are likely to impede their future academic performance.

                                   ⟨◉⟩

Our point is not to take one side of this debate or the other, but to suggest that a strictly cognitive approach to early education and assessment is likely to backfire, regardless of the position taken on best remedies for the "achievement gap" between affluent and poor preschoolers. For the sake of argument, let us consider the highly touted Texas prekindergarten program that Secretary of Health and Human Services Thompson uses as a model of success and as a purportedly strong contrast to Head Start. Using a nonexperimental research design (where investigators can inflate program effects by assigning better-performing schools to the treatment group), the evaluation of the program revealed moderate impacts on children's language scores for *less than half* of the participating sites. At best, this translates to modest success in narrowing the educational gap between low-income Texas preschoolers and their more affluent counterparts. But, even if we believe that the Texas program included the strongest of teaching efforts tied to the best curricular choices, it could just as easily be argued that the program did not meaningfully close the gap between poor and wealthier children. Using such narrow, cognitively oriented definitions of success, not only will programs be viewed as failures but poor children will be viewed as impervious to help.

                                   ⟨◉⟩

To avoid this likely scenario, policy makers must understand that vocabulary, pre-reading, and pre-math tests only provide a rough approximation of where preschoolers stand in relation to their agemates, or where they stand relative to their own prior performance. But these tests do not capture the value of a program in supporting the multiple facets of development and learning that are undoubtedly taking place, both in those Texas classrooms and in Head Start classrooms across the country. For example, while IQ gains children make in preschool arguably fade out, graduates of quality intervention programs (including Head Start) are less likely to be retained in grade or placed in special education than similar children without good preschool experience. Clearly a wealth of learning experiences and benefits were accrued during intervention and carried through later schooling, but these were not tapped by cognitive measures. Thus a focus on cognitive outcomes without an understanding of the multiple processes that lead to school success runs the risk of disenfranchising children from learning, disenfranchising good teachers from teaching disadvantaged preschoolers, and disenfranchising voters from the view that investments in young children pay off.

What Does Early Educational Research Tell Us?

Policy makers must also understand that sole reliance on cognitively oriented measures is unsupported by the best scientific evidence we have about ways to support early learning. There is a bounty of scientific literature indicating that children's social and emotional skills are predictive of early achievement, with children's thinking skills *and* self-regulation likely to play important roles in early learning.

One might ask: What does self-regulation have to do with learning the basics such as preliteracy and early math? Children must be able to handle their emotions when sharing instructional materials, taking turns holding or choosing a book for story time, or getting in line. They must be able to focus their attention away from distracting sights and sounds outside the classroom window and toward the task at hand. They must be able to organize their activities and listen to and heed teachers' instructions. Emotionally supportive preschool classrooms foster children's motivation, their development of enthusiasm about school as a good place to be, and positive views of themselves as learners capable of tackling new problems and challenges. Children who are less distractible and more emotionally positive are viewed by teachers as more "teachable." In fact, a majority of teachers surveyed suggested that curiosity, enthusiasm, and ability to follow directions play a potent role in their judgment of children's "readiness" to learn.

꿏

Recent research in both areas of cognitive and emotional development has highlighted the ways in which children differ from each other in terms of "executive functioning" or "behavioral self-control." That is, while some children are good at planning, staying organized and focused when given a difficult task, and remaining attentive and calm in a classroom setting, other children have problems regulating their emotions and their attention. Decades of research suggest that (1) Children with emotional and behavioral difficulties are at greater risk for long-term academic problems, and (2) poverty-related stressors impose additional psychological strain on young children that may interfere with their ability to concentrate, pay attention, and control their feelings of sadness and frustration. Prevalence estimates suggest that between 7 percent and 25 percent of low-income children enrolled in early educational settings exhibit elevated behavioral problems. Children exposed to high levels of community and family violence also are more likely to be sad and withdrawn, with symptoms of inattentiveness and difficulty interacting prosocially with teachers and peers. In short, these problems are likely to have serious ramifications for learning. Low-income preschoolers' acquisition of preliteracy and other cognitive skills is likely to be *suppressed* unless the social and emotional domains of learning and development are recognized and supported.

In addition, research suggests that preschool-age children learn more and are more motivated when they are in emotionally supportive, "child-centered" classrooms, as compared to classrooms that emphasize drills, worksheets, seat-work, and "basic skills." In the recent U.S. Department of Health and Human Services report critiquing Head Start, the authors recognize the importance of teaching pre-academic content "without compromising social and emotional development." In the model Texas program that the report endorses, the evaluation included assessments of children's readiness in both cognitive and socioemotional domains. It is therefore baffling that some leaders want to eradicate social and emotional assessments from Head Start's planned evaluation efforts.

⋘☙⋙

Plans to abandon assessment of children's social and emotional competencies in Head Start represent a grave loss of opportunity for social scientists and educators. With the emotional and behavioral data from the FACES and Head Start Impact Study, we can address questions of how changes in particular noncognitive domains are associated with changes in learning. Without the data that these assessments will provide, researchers will be unable to test the very hypotheses that may lead to teaching and curricula innovations. Finally, if measures of social and emotional development are struck from national evaluations, policy makers will be making a statement that these features are unrelated to learning and are therefore unimportant. A slew of developmental evidence, and a modicum of common sense, should tell them otherwise.

Cautions and Recommendations

What will the impact of national testing of Head Start's preschoolers be? We can imagine a range of scenarios that might result from the plan to use cognitively oriented tests to assess Head Start children. One benefit might be that training and technical assistance could be targeted to centers that need the help the most. On the other hand, classrooms in areas with high levels of community and family violence are likely to have children who are less able to weather the behavioral challenges involved in test-taking, so programs serving our nation's most vulnerable families will receive the greatest share of blame and the least amount of help for children's compromised performance.

In short, we may repeat past policy mistakes, with Head Start and poor children blamed for their supposed educational failures rather than rewarded and supported for their successes in the face of substantial income and educational inequality. Without being able to predict the outcome, and without being able to forestall the implementation of cognitively oriented assessments, we offer a set of cautions and recommendations.

1. First, we remind readers that there is no single cognitive "magic bullet" to the problems of poverty or to the achievement gap between economically disadvantaged children and their more affluent classmates. Good curriculum and hard work on the part of teachers may partially remedy that gap, and programs, teachers, parents, and children themselves are to be lauded when such successes are achieved. Certainly, comprehensive services that address families' economic self-sufficiency, housing, health, and welfare are also needed, and we know that those services are expensive. If policy makers genuinely wish to see Head Start and low-income children succeed, they must match their interest in cognitive assessment with a substantially increased investment in families, programs, and teachers so that desired gains can be realized.

2. Second, we caution readers that there is not clear consensus of the predictive value of cognitive assessments in guaranteeing later school performance. School success likely rests on an integrated foundation, with physical health, cognitive features, and behavioral/emotional adjustment all playing key facilitative roles in children developing positive orientations toward learning. Children's beliefs in themselves as capable learners, their skills in working with teachers and peers in prosocial ways, their ability to stay focused and on task, and their capacity to maintain emotional and behavioral self-control may offer important advantages in learning. We will not know the relative importance of these abilities if we do not collect the data. Thus, we urge that the twin foci on both learning and socioemotional outcomes be maintained in all Head Start evaluation and research efforts.

3. Third, we recommend that current teacher-rated assessments of emotional and social development be continued. But we also recommend that better methods and measures be used to provide more direct assessments. The task is possible. Emotionally and behaviorally oriented direct assessments were developed and successfully implemented in the national evaluation of Early Head Start that included thousands of toddlers. Researchers have adequate empirical background on which to develop a comprehensive battery, through "consensus conference" on what measures provide most specificity and predictive validity on measurable change in children's emotional and behavioral adjustment. In short, researchers could standardize and validate a short set of age-appropriate measures that could be included in future years of Head Start assessments. Without such direct measurements, children's emotional and behavioral development will always be more vaguely defined and less vigorously measured than their cognitive development.

CHALLENGE QUESTIONS

Does Emphasizing Academic Skills Help At-Risk Preschool Children?

- Ultimately, identifying the developmental needs of children in poverty is the central issue for this controversy. What do young children in poverty-stricken communities need from schools and society in order to develop well?
- Raver and Zigler suggest that part of the academic problem with Head Start is simply not having enough qualified teachers and staff. Do you agree with their suspicion that the exclusive emphasis on cognitive skills and testing is more of a way to impose market values on preschool rather than really thinking about the developmental needs of children?
- While providing better access to early childhood education is a popular intervention against poverty, some people argue that it is not enough to solve inequality. What do young children need beyond quality education to ensure they have equal opportunities?
- Some people have suggested that the problem with Head Start is that it does not start early enough. From a developmental perspective, how effective would it be to put younger children in formal schooling?
- In addition to the larger developmental question about early intervention, this issue revolves around a question about the interaction of various developmental domains: the cognitive, the social, the emotional, the physical, and so on. Is development best facilitated by considering these diverse domains as they relate to each other?
- Is it reasonable to expect that simple intervention during early childhood will produce a lifetime of change?

Suggested Readings

S. Barnett and J. Huestedt, "Head Start's Lasting Benefits," *Infants & Young Children* (January–March 2005)

C. Bordignon and T. Lam, "The Early Assessment Conundrum: Lessons from the Past, Implications for the Future," *Psychology in the Schools* (September 2004)

R. Fewell, "Assessment of Young Children with Special Needs: Foundations for Tomorrow," *Topics in Early Childhood Special Education* (2000)

K. Kafer, "A Head Start for Poor Children?" *Backgrounder* (May 4, 2004)

S. Meisels, "Testing Culture Invades Lives of Young Children," *FairTest Examiner* (Spring 2005)

J. Neisworth and S. Bagnato, "The Case Against Intelligence Testing in Early Intervention," *Topics in Early Childhood Special Education* (Spring 1992)

J. Neisworth and S. Bagnato, "The MisMeasure of Young Children: The Authentic Assessment Alternative," *Infants and Young Children* (2004)

S. Olfman, "All Work and No Play: How Educational Reforms Are Hurting Our Preschoolers," *Rethinking Schools Online* (Winter 2004/2005)

A. Papero, "Is Early, High-Quality Daycare an Asset for the Children of Low-Income, Depressed Mothers?," *Developmental Review* (2005)

R. Stahlman, "Standardized Tests: A Teacher's Perspective," *Childhood Education* (Summer 2005)

P. Williamson, E. Bondy, L. Langley, and D. Mayne, "Meeting the Challenge of High-Stakes Testing While Remaining Child-Centered," *Childhood Education* (Summer 2005)

ISSUE 9

Is Attention Deficit Disorder (ADD/ADHD) a Legitimate Medical Condition That Affects Childhood Behavior?

YES: Michael Fumento, from "Trick Question" *The New Republic* (February 2003)

NO: Rogers H. Wright, from "Attention Deficit Hyperactivity Disorder: What It Is and What It Is Not," in Rogers H. Wright and Nicholas A. Cummings, eds., *Destructive Trends in Mental Health: The Well-Intentioned Path to Harm* (Routledge, 2005)

ISSUE SUMMARY

YES: Science journalist and writer Michael Fumento suggests that despite the extensive political controversy, it is clear that ADHD is a legitimate medical condition disrupting childhood.

NO: Psychologist Rogers Wright argues that ADHD is a transitory condition and fad diagnosis rather than an enduring disease.

Middle childhood is often a period of changing behavior. As children move from primarily spending time with their parents and family to primarily spending time with peers and at school, they often establish new habits and attitudes. While most children adapt to the changes well, there are inevitably some children who struggle. In these cases, many children can be disruptive, hyperactive, and deviant. Their behavior is no longer just a family issue, but it is an issue for the school and community in which they interact. The controversial question, is whether extreme behavior constitutes a medical disorder requiring medication or a radical variation on normal childhood created by social forces.

Part of the controversy is due to the success of drugs such as Ritalin in modifying the behavior of children. Individuals who were previously out of control and unable to concentrate have used Ritalin and related drugs to control their attention and behavior. These drugs allowed parents to manage unruly children and schools to educate difficult students. Does applying a medical model and medication to extreme behavior prove that ADHD is a legitimate medical condition?

Ritalin, like any psychoactive drug, alters brain chemistry: our concentration, mood, attention, excitement, energy, and so on. As such, a drug that alters brain chemistry has the potential to both rectify disordered behavior and manage normal behavior. While some scholars argue that the efficacy of Ritalin and similar drugs proves the reality of ADHD, others argue that these drugs could have socially redeeming effects on anyone—including college students who have learned that Ritalin (and related drugs) will help their concentration and attention span.

Beyond the fact that Ritalin works to influence children's brains, statistics about ADHD serve to stir further controversy. First, ADHD is a relatively recent disorder—the diagnosis did not exist by that name until the last few decades. To some this suggests that ADHD is not an organic, or biological, disorder but an artifact of changing social norms. To others this demonstrates the advances made in medical science. Second, the overwhelming majority of cases of ADHD are diagnosed in North America. To some this suggests that ADHD reflects part of our culture that refuses to accept responsibility for the challenges of middle childhood. To others this shows the advanced progress of our system for managing children with serious problems. Third, ADHD is much more commonly diagnosed in boys than in girls. To some this means that ADHD is linked to male biology. To others this suggests that the tendency of boys to be more aggressive and assertive is more than contemporary parents and teachers can handle.

Michael Fumento asserts that any argument against the reality of ADHD is misguided. He points out that the efficacy of Ritalin in changing behavior should be considered positive, rather than negative. Children diagnosed with ADHD are different, and it is not just because of parenting. Ritalin helps them function effectively but it does not, contrary to popular opinion, create zombies.

Psychologist Rogers Wright takes a clinical perspective and suggests that biomedical approaches to ADHD have gone too far. He notes that ADHD is an easy way to explain extreme behavior, but that medication can often do more harm than good. He also notes that behavioral interventions—efforts to systematically shape children's behavior through environmental changes—are a more effective primary option for dealing with disruptive children than medication.

POINT	COUNTERPOINT
• Mostly, the diagnosis of ADHD is based on clear and dramatic behavioral differences—similar to many other medical conditions.	• The frequency of diagnosing ADHD among children is a "fad" rather than a representation of a true medical condition.
• The behavioral problems that mark ADHD are extreme disruptions in functioning.	• ADHD is more of a "behavioral aberration" than a real disease, similar to Social Anxiety Disorder.
• The effectiveness of drugs such as Ritalin and the problems caused by ADHD clearly demonstrate that it is a neurological problem.	• There is a difference between being hyperactive and having a neurological disorder that originates in dysfunction.
• Medications often help children and families to have the opportunity for normal developmental experiences.	• Research suggests that behavioral interventions are more effective than medication—we are often too quick to medicate.

YES ↵

Michael Fumento

Trick Question

It's both right-wing and vast, but it's not a conspiracy. Actually, it's more of an anti-conspiracy. The subject is Attention Deficit Disorder (ADD) and Attention Deficit Hyperactivity Disorder (ADHD), closely related ailments (henceforth referred to in this article simply as ADHD). Rush Limbaugh declares it "may all be a hoax." Francis Fukuyama devotes much of one chapter in his latest book, *Our Posthuman Future*, to attacking Ritalin, the top-selling drug used to treat ADHD. Columnist Thomas Sowell writes, "The motto used to be: 'Boys will be boys.' Today, the motto seems to be: 'Boys will be medicated.' " And Phyllis Schlafly explains, "The old excuse of 'my dog ate my homework' has been replaced by 'I got an ADHD diagnosis.' " A March 2002 article in *The Weekly Standard* summed up the conservative line on ADHD with this rhetorical question: "Are we really prepared to redefine childhood as an ailment, and medicate it until it goes away?"

Many conservative writers, myself included, have criticized the growing tendency to pathologize every undesirable behavior—especially where children are concerned. But, when it comes to ADHD, this skepticism is misplaced. As even a cursory examination of the existing literature or, for that matter, simply talking to the parents and teachers of children with ADHD reveals, the condition is real, and it is treatable. And, if you don't believe me, you can ask conservatives who've come face to face with it themselves.

Myth: ADHD Isn't a Real Disorder

The most common argument against ADHD on the right is also the simplest: It doesn't exist. Conservative columnist Jonah Goldberg thus reduces ADHD to "ants in the pants." Sowell equates it with "being bored and restless." Fukuyama protests, "No one has been able to identify a cause of ADD/ADHD. It is a pathology recognized only by its symptoms." And a conservative columnist approvingly quotes Thomas Armstrong, Ritalin opponent and author, when he declares, "ADD is a disorder that cannot be authoritatively identified in the same way as polio, heart disease or other legitimate illnesses."

The Armstrong and Fukuyama observations are as correct as they are worthless. "Half of all medical disorders are diagnosed without benefit of a lab

From *The New Republic*, Vol. 228, no. 4, February 3, 2003, pp. 18–21. Copyright © 2003 by New Republic. Reprinted by permission.

procedure," notes Dr. Russell Barkley, professor of psychology at the College of Health Professionals at the Medical University of South Carolina. "Where are the lab tests for headaches and multiple sclerosis and Alzheimer's?" he asks. "Such a standard would virtually eliminate all mental disorders."

Often the best diagnostic test for an ailment is how it responds to treatment. And, by that standard, it doesn't get much more real than ADHD. The beneficial effects of administering stimulants to treat the disorder were first reported in 1937. And today medication for the disorder is reported to be 75 to 90 percent successful. "In our trials it was close to ninety percent," says Dr. Judith Rapoport, director of the National Institute of Mental Health's Child Psychiatry Branch, who has published about 100 papers on ADHD. "This means there was a significant difference in the children's ability to function in the classroom or at home."

Additionally, epidemiological evidence indicates that ADHD has a powerful genetic component. University of Colorado researchers have found that a child whose identical twin has the disorder is between eleven and 18 times more likely to also have it than is a non-twin sibling. For these reasons, the American Psychiatric Association (APA), American Medical Association, American Academy of Pediatrics, American Academy of Child Adolescent Psychiatry, the surgeon general's office, and other major medical bodies all acknowledge ADHD as both real and treatable.

Myth: ADHD Is Part of a Feminist Conspiracy to Make Little Boys More Like Little Girls

Many conservatives observe that boys receive ADHD diagnoses in much higher numbers than girls and find in this evidence of a feminist conspiracy. (This, despite the fact that genetic diseases are often heavily weighted more toward one gender or the other.) Sowell refers to "a growing tendency to treat boyhood as a pathological condition that requires a new three R's— repression, re-education and Ritalin." Fukuyama claims Prozac is being used to give women "more of the alpha-male feeling," while Ritalin is making boys act more like girls. "Together, the two sexes are gently nudged toward that androgynous median personality . . . that is the current politically correct outcome in American society." George Will, while acknowledging that Ritalin can be helpful, nonetheless writes of the "androgyny agenda" of "drugging children because they are behaving like children, especially boy children." Anti-Ritalin conservatives frequently invoke Christina Hoff Sommers's best-selling 2000 book, *The War Against Boys*. You'd never know that the drug isn't mentioned in her book—or why.

"Originally I was going to have a chapter on it," Sommers tells me. "It seemed to fit the thesis." What stopped her was both her survey of the medical literature and her own empirical findings. Of one child she personally came to know she says, "He was utterly miserable, as was everybody around him. The drugs saved his life."

Myth: ADHD Is Part of the Public School System's Efforts to Warehouse Kids Rather Than to Discipline and Teach Them

"No doubt life is easier for teachers when everyone sits around quietly," writes Sowell. Use of ADHD drugs is "in the school's interest to deal with behavioral and discipline problems [because] it's so easy to use Ritalin to make kids compliant: to get them to sit down, shut up, and do what they're told," declares Schlafly. The word "zombies" to describe children under the effects of Ritalin is tossed around more than in a B-grade voodoo movie.

Kerri Houston, national field director for the American Conservative Union and the mother of two ADHD children on medication, agrees with much of the criticism of public schools. "But don't blame ADHD on crummy curricula and lazy teachers," she says. "If you've worked with these children, you know they have a serious neurological problem." In any case, Ritalin, when taken as prescribed, hardly stupefies children. To the extent the medicine works, it simply turns ADHD children into normal children. "ADHD is like having thirty televisions on at one time, and the medicine turns off twenty-nine so you can concentrate on the one," Houston describes. "This zombie stuff drives me nuts! My kids are both as lively and as fun as can be."

Myth: Parents Who Give Their Kids Anti-ADHD Drugs Are Merely Doping Up Problem Children

Limbaugh calls ADHD "the perfect way to explain the inattention, incompetence, and inability of adults to control their kids." Addressing parents directly, he lectures, "It helped you mask your own failings by doping up your children to calm them down."

Such charges blast the parents of ADHD kids into high orbit. That includes my Hudson Institute colleague (and fellow conservative) Mona Charen, the mother of an eleven-year-old with the disorder. "I have two non-ADHD children, so it's not a matter of parenting technique," says Charen. "People without such children have no idea what it's like. I can tell the difference between boyish high spirits and pathological hyperactivity. . . . These kids bounce off the walls. Their lives are chaos; their rooms are chaos. And nothing replaces the drugs."

Barkley and Rapoport say research backs her up. Randomized, controlled studies in both the United States and Sweden have tried combining medication with behavioral interventions and then dropped either one or the other. For those trying to go on without medicine, "the behavioral interventions maintained nothing," Barkley says. Rapoport concurs: "Unfortunately, behavior modification doesn't seem to help with ADHD." (Both doctors are quick to add that ADHD is often accompanied by other disorders that are treatable through behavior modification in tandem with medicine.)

Myth: Ritalin Is "Kiddie Cocaine"

One of the paradoxes of conservative attacks on Ritalin is that the drug is alternately accused of turning children into brain-dead zombies and of making them Mach-speed cocaine junkies. Indeed, Ritalin is widely disparaged as "kiddie cocaine." Writers who have sought to lump the two drugs together include Schlafly, talk-show host and columnist Armstrong Williams, and others whom I hesitate to name because of my long-standing personal relationships with them.

Mary Eberstadt wrote the "authoritative" Ritalin-cocaine piece for the April 1999 issue of *Policy Review,* then owned by the Heritage Foundation. The article, "Why Ritalin Rules," employs the word "cocaine" no fewer than twelve times. Eberstadt quotes from a 1995 Drug Enforcement Agency (DEA) background paper declaring methylphenidate, the active ingredient in Ritalin, "a central nervous system (CNS) stimulant [that] shares many of the pharmacological effects of amphetamine, methamphetamine, and cocaine." Further, it "produces behavioral, psychological, subjective, and reinforcing effects similar to those of d-amphetamine including increases in rating of euphoria, drug liking and activity, and decreases in sedation." Add to this the fact that the Controlled Substances Act lists it as a Schedule II drug, imposing on it the same tight prescription controls as morphine, and Ritalin starts to sound spooky indeed.

What Eberstadt fails to tell readers is that the DEA description concerns methylphenidate *abuse.* It's tautological to say abuse is harmful. According to the DEA, the drugs in question are comparable when "administered the same way at comparable does." But ADHD stimulants, when taken as prescribed, are neither administered in the same way as cocaine nor at comparable doses. "What really counts," says Barkley, "is the speed with which the drugs enter and clear the brain. With cocaine, because it's snorted, this happens tremendously quickly, giving users the characteristic addictive high." (Ever seen anyone pop a cocaine tablet?) Further, he says, "There's no evidence anywhere in literature of [Ritalin's] addictiveness when taken as prescribed." As to the Schedule II listing, again this is because of the potential for it to fall into the hands of abusers, not because of its effects on persons for whom it is prescribed. Ritalin and the other anti-ADHD drugs, says Barkley, "are the safest drugs in all of psychiatry." (And they may be getting even safer: A new medicine just released called Strattera represents the first true non-stimulant ADHD treatment.)

Indeed, a study just released in the journal *Pediatrics* found that children who take Ritalin or other stimulants to control ADHD cut their risk of future substance abuse by 50 percent compared with untreated ADHD children. The lead author speculated that "by treating ADHD you're reducing the demoralization that accompanies this disorder, and you're improving the academic functioning and well-being of adolescents and young adults during the critical times when substance abuse starts."

Myth: Ritalin Is Overprescribed Across the Country

Some call it "the Ritalin craze." In *The Weekly Standard,* Melana Zyla Vickers informs us that "Ritalin use has exploded," while Eberstadt writes that "Ritalin use more than doubled in the first half of the decade alone, [and] the number of schoolchildren taking the drug may now, by some estimates, be approaching the *4 million mark.*"

A report in the January 2003 issue of *Archives of Pediatrics and Adolescent Medicine* did find a large increase in the use of ADHD medicines from 1987 to 1996, an increase that doesn't appear to be slowing. Yet nobody thinks it's a problem that routine screening for high blood pressure has produced a big increase in the use of hypertension medicine. "Today, children suffering from ADHD are simply less likely to slip through the cracks," says Dr. Sally Satel, a psychiatrist, AEI fellow, and author of *PC, M.D.: How Political Correctness Is Corrupting Medicine.*

Satel agrees that some community studies, by the standards laid down in the APA's *Diagnostic and Statistical Manual of Mental Disorders (DSM),* indicate that ADHD may often be over-diagnosed. On the other hand, she says, additional evidence shows that in some communities ADHD is *under*-diagnosed and *under*-treated. "I'm quite concerned with children who need the medication and aren't getting it," she says.

There *are* tremendous disparities in the percentage of children taking ADHD drugs when comparing small geographical areas. Psychologist Gretchen LeFever, for example, has compared the number of prescriptions in mostly white Virginia Beach, Virginia, with other, more heavily African American areas in the southeastern part of the state. Conservatives have latched onto her higher numbers—20 percent of white fifth-grade boys in Virginia Beach are being treated for ADHD—as evidence that something is horribly wrong. But others, such as Barkley, worry about the lower numbers. According to LeFever's study, black children are only half as likely to get medication as white children. "Black people don't get the care of white people; children of well-off parents get far better care than those of poorer parents," says Barkley.

Myth: States Should Pass Laws That Restrict Schools from Recommending Ritalin

Conservative writers have expressed delight that several states, led by Connecticut, have passed or are considering laws ostensibly protecting students from schools that allegedly pass out Ritalin like candy. Representative Lenny Winkler, lead sponsor of the Connecticut measure, told *Reuters Health,* "If the diagnosis is made, and it's an appropriate diagnosis that Ritalin be used, that's fine. But I have also heard of many families approached by the school system [who are told] that their child cannot attend school if they're not put on Ritalin."

Two attorneys I interviewed who specialize in child-disability issues, including one from the liberal Bazelon Center for Mental Health Law in Washington,

D.C., acknowledge that school personnel have in some cases stepped over the line. But legislation can go too far in the other direction by declaring, as Connecticut's law does, that "any school personnel [shall be prohibited] from recommending the use of psychotropic drugs for any child." The law appears to offer an exemption by declaring, "The provisions of this section shall not prohibit *school medical staff* from recommending that a child be evaluated by an appropriate medical practitioner, or prohibit school personnel from consulting with such practitioner, with the consent of the parent or guardian of such child." [Emphasis added.] But of course many, if not most schools have perhaps one nurse on regular "staff." That nurse will have limited contact with children in the classroom situations where ADHD is likely to be most evident. And, given the wording of the statute, a teacher who believed a student was suffering from ADHD would arguably be prohibited from referring that student to the nurse. Such ambiguity is sure to have a chilling effect on any form of intervention or recommendation by school personnel. Moreover, 20-year special-education veteran Sandra Rief said in an interview with the National Education Association that "recommending medical intervention for a student's behavior could lead to personal liability issues." Teachers, in other words, could be forced to choose between what they think is best for the health of their students and the possible risk of losing not only their jobs but their personal assets as well.

"Certainly it's not within the purview of a school to say kids can't attend if they don't take drugs," says Houston. "On the other hand, certainly teachers should be able to advise parents as to problems and potential solutions. . . . [T]hey may see things parents don't. My own son is an angel at home but was a demon at school."

If the real worry is "take the medicine or take a hike" ultimatums, legislation can be narrowly tailored to prevent them; broad-based gag orders, such as Connecticut's, are a solution that's worse than the problem.

The Conservative Case for ADHD Drugs

There are kernels of truth to every conservative suspicion about ADHD. Who among us has not had lapses of attention? And isn't hyperactivity a normal condition of childhood when compared with deskbound adults? Certainly there are lazy teachers, warehousing schools, androgyny-pushing feminists, and far too many parents unwilling or unable to expend the time and effort to raise their children properly, even by their own standards. Where conservatives go wrong is in making ADHD a scapegoat for frustration over what we perceive as a breakdown in the order of society and family. In a column in *The Boston Herald,* Boston University Chancellor John Silber rails that Ritalin is "a classic example of a cheap fix: low-cost, simple and purely superficial."

Exactly. Like most headaches, ADHD is a neurological problem that can usually be successfully treated with a chemical. Those who recommend or prescribe ADHD medicines do not, as *The Weekly Standard* put it, see them as "discipline in pill-form." They see them as pills.

In fact, it can be argued that the use of those pills, far from being liable for or symptomatic of the Decline of the West, reflects and reinforces conservative values. For one thing, they increase personal responsibility by removing an excuse that children (and their parents) can fall back on to explain misbehavior and poor performance. "Too many psychologists and psychiatrists focus on allowing patients to justify to themselves their troubling behavior," says Satel. "But something like Ritalin actually encourages greater autonomy because you're treating a compulsion to behave in a certain way. Also, by treating ADHD, you remove an opportunity to explain away bad behavior."

Moreover, unlike liberals, who tend to downplay differences between the sexes, conservatives are inclined to believe that there are substantial physiological differences—differences such as boys' greater tendency to suffer ADHD. "Conservatives celebrate the physiological differences between boys and girls and eschew the radical-feminist notion that gender differences are created by societal pressures," says Houston regarding the fuss over the boy-girl disparity among ADHD diagnoses. "ADHD is no exception."

But, however compatible conservatism may be with taking ADHD seriously, the truth is that most conservatives remain skeptics. "I'm sure I would have been one of those smug conservatives saying it's a made-up disease," admits Charen, "if I hadn't found out the hard way." Here's hoping other conservatives find an easier route to accepting the truth.

Rogers H. Wright   → **NO**

Attention Deficit Hyperactivity Disorder: What It Is and What It Is Not

It is almost axiomatic in the mental health field that fads will occur in the "diagnosis" and treatment of various types of behavioral aberrations, some of which border on being mere discomforts. Although the same faddism exists to some degree in physical medicine, its appearance is not nearly as blatant, perhaps in part because physical medicine is more soundly grounded in the physical sciences than are diagnoses in the mental health field. These fads spill over into the general culture, where direct marketing often takes place. One has to spend only a brief period in front of a television set during prime time to discover ADHD (Attention Deficit Hyperactivity Disorder), SAD (Social Anxiety Disorder), or IBS (Irritable Bowl Syndrome). Even when purporting to be informational, these are more or less disguised commercials, inasmuch as they posit a cure that varies with the drug manufacturer sponsoring the television ad.

The other certainty is that these "diagnoses" will fall from usage as other fads emerge, as was the case a decade or so ago with the disappearance of a once-common designation for what is now sometimes called ADHD. That passing fad was known as minimal brain syndrome (MBS) and/or food disorder (ostensibly from red dye or other food additives). From this author's perspective, these fad "diagnoses" don't really exist. Other writers in this volume have commented on the slipperiness of these "diagnoses"—that is, the elevation of a symptom and/or its description to the level of a disorder or syndrome—and the concomitant tendency to overmedicate for these nonexistent maladies.

Children and ADHD

Certainly, there are deficiencies of attention and hyperactivity, but such behavioral aberrancies are most often indicative of a transitory state or condition within the organism. They are not in and of themselves indicative of a "disorder." Every parent has noticed, particularly with younger children, that toward the end of an especially exciting and fatiguing day children are literally "ricocheting off the walls." Although this behavior may in the broadest sense be classifiable as hyperactivity, it is generally pathognomonic

From *Destructive Trends in Mental Health: The Well Intentioned Path to Harm*, 2005, pp. 129–141. Copyright © 2005 by Taylor & Francis Books, Inc. Reprinted by permission.

of nothing more than excessive fatigue, for which the treatment of choice is a good night's sleep. Distractibility (attention deficit) is a frequent concomitant of excessive fatigue, particularly with children under five years of age, and can even be seen in adults if fatigue levels are extreme or if stress is prolonged. However, such "symptoms" in these contexts do not rise to the level of a treatable disorder.

Conversely, when distractibility and/or hyperactivity characterize the child's everyday (especially if accompanied by factors such as delayed development, learning difficulties, impaired motor skills, and impaired judgement), they may be indicative of either a neurological disorder or of developing emotional difficulties. However, after nearly fifty years of diagnosing and treating several thousand such problems, it is my considered judgement that the distractibility and hyperactivity seen in such children is not the same as the distractibility and hyperactivity in children currently diagnosed as having ADHD. Furthermore, the hyperactivity/distractibility seen in the non-ADHD children described above is qualitatively and quantitatively different, depending on whether it is caused by incipient emotional maldevelopment (functional; i.e., nonorganic) or whether it is due to neurological involvement.

It is also notable that most children whose distractibility and/or hyperactivity is occasioned by emotional distress do not show either the kind or degree of learning disability, delayed genetic development, poor judgement, and impaired motor skills that are seen in children whose "distractibility/hyperactivity" is occasioned by neurological involvement. Only in children with the severest forms of emotional disturbance does one see the kind of developmental delays and impaired behavioral controls that are more reflective of neurological involvement (or what was known as MBS until the ADHD fad took hold). Differentiating the child with actual neurological involvement from the child that has emotionally based distractibility is neither simple nor easy to do, especially if the behavioral (as opposed to neurological) involvement is severe.

A major and profound disservice occasioned by the current fad of elevating nonspecific symptoms such as anxiety and hyperactivity to the level of a syndrome or disorder and then diagnosing ADD/ADHD is that we lump together individuals with very different needs and very different problems. We then attempt to treat the problem(s) with a single entity, resulting in a one-pill-fits-all response. It is also unfortunately the case that many mental health providers (e.g., child psychiatrists, child psychologists, child social workers), as well as many general care practitioners (e.g., pediatricians and internists), are not competent to make such discriminations alone. Therefore, it follows that such practitioners are not trained and equipped to provide ongoing care, even when an appropriate diagnosis has been made.

To add to an already complicated situation, the symptom picture in children tends to change with time and maturation. Children with neurological involvement typically tend to improve spontaneously over time, so that the symptoms of distractibility and hyperactivity often represent diminished components in the clinical picture. Conversely, children whose distractibility and hyperactivity are emotionally determined typically have symptoms that tend to intensify or be accompanied/replaced by even more dramatic indices of emotional distress.

Management of Children Exhibiting "ADHD" According to Etiology

It is apparent that somewhat superficially similar presenting complaints (i.e., distractibility and hyperactivity) may reflect two very different causative factors, and that the successful treatment and management of the complaint should vary according to the underlying causation. Neurological damage can stem from a number of causative factors during pregnancy or the birth process, and a successful remedial program may require the combined knowledge of the child's pediatrician, a neuropsychologist specializing in the diagnosis and treatment of children, and a child neurologist. In these cases approptiate medication for the child is often very helpful.

Psychotherapy for the child (particularly younger children) is, in this writer's experience, largely a waste of time. On the other hand, remedial training in visual perception, motor activities, visual–motor integration, spatial relations, numerical skills, and reading and writing may be crucial in alleviating or at least diminishing the impact of symptoms. Deficits in these skills can be major contributors to the hyperactivity and distractibility so frequently identified with such children. Counseling and psychotherapeutic work with the parents is very important and should always be a part of an integrated therapeutic program. Such children need to be followed by an attending pediatrician, a child neurologist, a child neuropsychologist, and an educational therapist, bearing in mind that treatment needs change throughout the span of remediation. For example, medication levels and regimens may need to be adjusted, and training programs will constantly need to be revised or elaborated.

It is also noteworthy that so-called tranquilizing medication with these children typically produces an adverse effect. This writer remembers a situation that occurred early in his practice, a case he has used repeatedly to alert fledgling clinicians to the importance of a comprehensive initial evaluation and ongoing supervision in the development of neurologically involved children.

John, a two-and-a-half-year-old boy, was referred by his pediatrician for evaluation of extreme hyperactivity, distractibility, and mild developmental delay. The psychological evaluation elicited evidence of visual perceptual impairment in a context of impaired visual motor integration, a finding suggestive of an irritative focus in the parietal-occipital areas of the brain. This finding was later corroborated by a child neurologist, and John was placed on dilantin and Phenobarbital. A developmental training program was instituted, and the parents began participation in a group specifically designed for the parents of brain-injured children. Over the next couple of years, the patient's progress was excellent, and his development and learning difficulties were singularly diminished. The parents were comfortable with John's progress and with their ability to manage it, so they decided to have a long-wanted additional child. In the meantime, the father's work necessitated moving to another location, leading to a change of obstetrician and pediatrician.

The second pregnancy proceeded uneventfully and eventuated in the birth of a second boy. Shortly after the mother returned home with the new infant, John began to regress, exhibiting a number of prior symptoms such as hyperactivity and distractibility, as well as problems in behavioral control. The new pediatrician referred the family to a child psychiatrist, who promptly placed John on a tranquilizer. Shortly thereafter, John's academic performance began to deteriorate dramatically, and his school counseled the parents about the possibility that he had been promoted too rapidly and "could not handle work at this grade level."

At this point, the parents again contacted this writer, primarily out of concern for John's diminished academic performance. Because it had been more than two years since John had been formally evaluated, I advised the parents that another comprehensive evaluation was indicated. The parents agreed, and a full diagnostic battery was administered to John, the results of which were then compared to his prior performance. It immediately became apparent that he was not functioning at grade level, and that the overall level of his functioning had deteriorated dramatically.

In his initial evaluation, John's functional level had been in the Bright Normal range (i.e., overall IQ of 110 to 119), whereas his current functioning placed him at the Borderline Mentally Retarded level (IQ below 60). The history revealed nothing of significance other than the behavioral regression after the birth of the sibling and the introduction of the new medication. I advised the parents that I thought the child was being erroneously medicated, with consequent diminution of his intellectual efficiency, and that the supposition could be tested by asking the attending child psychiatrist to diminish John's medication to see if the child's performance improved.

The attending child psychiatrist was quite upset by the recommendations and the implications thereof and threatened to sue me for "practicing medicine without a license." I informed the physician that I was not practicing medicine but rather neuropsychology, along with deductive reasoning known as "common sense," which we could test by appropriately reducing John's dosage level for a month and then retesting him. Faced with the alternative of a legal action for slander or libel for having accused this neuropsychologist of a felony, the child psychiatrist agreed.

Upon retesting a month later, the child's performance level had returned to Bright Normal, and his academic performance and behavior in school had improved dramatically. By this time approximately six to eight months had elapsed since the birth of the sibling, and John had become accustomed to his new brother. All concerned agreed that the medication had not been helpful and that the child should continue for another three to six months without medication. Subsequent contact with the parents some six months later indicated that John was doing well at school. The parents were quite comfortable with the behavioral management skills they had learned, which enabled them to handle a child with an underlying neurological handicap.

As noted earlier, the marked distractibility and/or hyperactivity in children with neurological involvement tends to diminish through adolescence, especially after puberty, as do many of the other symptoms. As a consequence, these children present a very different clinical picture in adolescence and adulthood. Typically, they are characterized by impulsivity, at times poor judgement, and excessive fatigability. It is generally only under the circumstances of extreme fatigue (or other stress) that one will see fairly dramatic degreees of distractibility and hyperactivity. Thus an appropriate diagnosis leading to productive intervention is difficult to make.

Conversely, children who exhibit the symptoms of distractibility and hyperactivity on an emotional basis typically do not show the diminution of symptomatology with increasing age. In fact, the symptoms may intensify and/or be replaced by even more dramatic symptoms, especially during puberty and adolescence. It should also be emphasized that the kind of distractibility and hyperactivity exhibited by the emotionally disturbed youngster is very different in quality and quantity from that of a youngster whose hyperactivity and distracibility has a neurological basis. Unfortunately, it is also frequently the case that a youngster with a neurological handicap may have significant emotional problems overlaying the basic neurological problems, making diagnosis even more complicated. But the overriding problem confronting parents today is the misdiagnosis of emotionally-based symptoms that brings the recommendation of unwarranted medication.

In the largest study of its kind, Cummings and Wiggins retrospectively examined the records of 168,113 children and adolescents who had been referred and treated over a four-year period in a national behavioral health provider operating in thirty-nine states. Before beginning treatment, sixty-one percent of the males and twenty-three percent of the females were taking psychotropic medication for ADD/ADHD by a psychiatrist, a pediatrician, or a primary care physician. Most of them lived in a single parent home, and lacked an effective father figure or were subjected to negative and frequently abusive male role models. Behavioral interventions included a compassionate but firm male therapist and the introduction of positive male role models (e.g., fathers, Big Brothers, coaches, Sunday school teachers, etc.) into the child's life. Counseling focused on helping parents understand what constitutes the behavior of a normal boy.

After an average of nearly eleven treatments with the parent and approximately six with the child, the percentage of boys on medication was reduced from sixty-one percent to eleven percent, and the percentage of girls on medication went from twenty-three percent to two percent. These dramatic results occurred despite very strict requirements for discontinuing the medication, which seems to point to an alarming overdiagnosis and overmedication of ADD/ADHD and greater efficacy of behavioral interventions than is generally believed to be the case by the mental health community. . . .

Summary

When hyperactivity and/or distractibility is truly one of the presenting symptoms, it is indicative of a complex situation that warrants extensive and thoughtful evaluation, and, more often than not, complex and comprehensive treatment planning from the perspective of a variety of specialists. In situations where the attention deficit and/or hyperactivity reflects problems in parenting, chemotherapeutic intervention for the child is likely to be, at best, no more than palliative and, at worse, may succeed in considerably complicating the situation. In this writer's experience, chemotherapeutic intervention for emotionally disturbed children is a last resort and of minimal value in addressing the overall problem. Psychotherapeutic intervention with the parents, which may or may not include the child, is more often than not the treatment of choice. This is a judgment that is best made only after exhaustive study by pediatrics, psychology, neurology, and perhaps, last of all, psychiatry, which so often seems all too eager to overmedicate (see chapter 6).

Where the presenting complaints of hyperactivity and distractibility are in a context of delayed development, excessive fatigability, learning deficits, and other such signs, the complexity of the diagnostic problem is substantially increased. In such circumstances, it is absolutely not in the child's best interest to limit the diagnostic evaluation to a single specialty. With the increasing evidence that neurological involvement can follow any number of prenatal and postnatal exposures, wise and caring parents will insist on a comprehensive evaluation by specialists in pediatrics, child neurology, and child neuropsychology. More often than not, if medication is indicated, it will be of a type quite different than what is used in the management of so-called ADHD.

Furthermore, treatment intervention and case management will likely involve skilled educational training of the specialized type developed for use with the brain-injured child. In the case of a friendly pediatrician, a concerned psychologist, or a caring child psychiatrist, any or all attempting unilaterally to diagnose and/or manage the treatment regimen, the concerned and caring parent is well advised to promptly seek additional opinions. . . .

CHALLENGE QUESTIONS

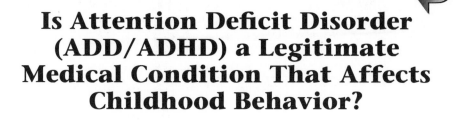

Is Attention Deficit Disorder (ADD/ADHD) a Legitimate Medical Condition That Affects Childhood Behavior?

- One piece of evidence commonly used to question the trend toward diagnosing ADHD for disruptive children is to note that the diagnosis occurs much more frequently in North America and among boys. If ADHD is a standard medical condition, how would you confront that evidence?
- There is no conclusive medical test for ADHD; instead it is diagnosed by the clinical judgment that sufficient criteria for the disorder are met. How might the lack of a clear diagnostic test influence this controversy?
- Are children who deviate from obedient and compliant behavioral expectations troubled or simply challenging? How much can parents, communities, teachers, and schools change the behavior of difficult children? Can people really change just by making enough effort?
- While drugs such as Ritalin do not always work, both authors would likely acknowledge that these drugs can produce dramatic behavioral changes in children. What seem to be the relative risks and benefits to using medication to modify childhood behavior?

Suggested Readings

American Academy of Pediatrics, "Clinical Practice Guideline: Treatment of the School-Aged Child with Attention-Deficit/Hyperactivity Disorder," *Pediatrics* (October 2001).

"An Update on Attention Deficit Disorder," *Harvard Medical Health Letter* (May, 2004). Also at: . . .

R. A. Barkley, "Psychosocial Treatments for Attention-Deficit/Hyperactivity Disorder in Children," *Journal of Clinical Psychiatry* (vol. 63, suppl. 12, pp. 36–43, 2002).

A. Bowd, "'Curing' ADHD," *Skeptical Inquirer* (May/June 2006)

D. Cohen and J. Leo, "An Update on ADHD Neuroimaging Research," *The Journal of Mind and Behavior* (Spring 2004)

L. Diller, "Defusing the Explosive Child," *Salon* (August 18, 2001)

D. Matthews, *Attention Deficit Disorder Sourcebook* (Omnigraphics, 2002)

M. Olfson, et al., "National Trends in the Treatment of Attention Deficit Hyperactivity Disorder," *American Journal of Psychiatry* (June 2003)

B. Seitler, "On the Implications and Consequences of a Neurobiochemical Etiology of Attention Deficit Hyperactive Disorder (ADHD)," *Ethical Human Psychology and Psychiatry* (Fall/Winter 2006)

Internet References . . .

The Society for Research on Adolescence

The Society for Research on Adolescence provides information for academics, clinicians and students.

http://www.s-r-a.org/

About Our Kids

This Web site is sponsored by a center at New York University focused on mental health in childhood and adolescence.

http://aboutourkids.org/

The National Clearinghouse on Families & Youth

The National Clearinghouse on Families & Youth (NCFY) offers free information related to teens, youth, and families, and offers relevant links at their Web site.

http://www.ncfy.com/links/

After-school Programs

This site presents "promising practices in afterschool" programs, and is managed by the Academy for Educational Development's Center for Youth Development and Policy Research.

http://www.afterschool.org/

Public/Private Ventures

Public/Private Ventures is a research group that has information about out-of-school time and adolescent development available on their Web site.

http://www.ppv.org/ppv/outofschooltime.asp

The MacArthur Foundation Research Network

This site offers research reports related to adolescence and delinquency.

http://www.adjj.org/content/index.php

Psychology Central

This site provides articles summarizing research about mental health as related to adolescent development.

http://psychcentral.com/blog/archives/category/children-teens/

The Society for Neuroscience

This Web site offers information and links to contemporary brain science research.

http://www.sfn.org/

Youth Today

Youth Today is an independent newspaper and network that focuses on youth work.

http://www.youthtoday.org/

Adolescence

*A*dolescence is a distinctive stage in the life-span because it is marked by a clear biological change: puberty. Developing adolescents cope with dramatic physical changes that often seem to combine a mature body with an immature mind. Further, because adolescence is associated with increasing independence and responsibility, adolescents seem both powerful and vulnerable. Society is compelled to provide adolescents care and opportunity, while simultaneously fearing that they will rebel. The issues in this section deal with the nature of success and failure in adolescence by asking two questions about the range of adolescent experiences.

- Should Contemporary Adolescents Be Engaged in More Structured Activities?
- Does the Adolescent Brain Make Risk Taking Inevitable?

ISSUE 10

Should Contemporary Adolescents Be Engaged in More Structured Activities?

YES: Joseph L. Mahoney, Angel L. Harris, and Jacquelynne S. Eccles, from "Organized Activity Participation, Positive Youth Development, and the Over-Scheduling Hypothesis," *Social Policy Report* (August 2006)

NO: Alvin Rosenfeld, from "Comments on 'Organized Activity Participation, Positive Youth Development, and the Over-Scheduling Hypothesis'," . . . .

ISSUE SUMMARY

YES: Psychologist Joseph Mahoney and colleagues recognize the concern about "over-scheduling" but present research suggesting that the benefits to structured activities outweigh any costs.

NO: Child psychiatrist Alvin Rosenfeld asserts that all of the data suggest that most youth and adolescents need less structured activity and more balance.

$\mathbf{S}$tructured activities, including sports, music, academics, drama productions, and more, have become a standard part of many adolescent experiences. These activities, with their promise of a safe environment for enriching experiences, are popular with diverse constituencies from parents and educators to policymakers and scholars. From a developmental perspective, however, the phenomenon of a highly structured youth brings both opportunities and risks. While structured activities and youth organizations provide many rich opportunities for adolescents, structured time also has the potential to put stress on youth and families while taking away the joy and creativity that can come from free leisure.

Because of these two potential outcomes, the growing availability of structured activities has been accompanied by a growing concern that some children are over-scheduled. News outlets are reporting on youth and families that spend so much time with structured activities that the teens end up deprived of sleep and the families end up without any significant time together. Scholars have also been pointing out concerns in books such as *The Hurried*

Child and *The Power of Play* by developmental psychologist David Elkind and *Unequal Childhoods* by sociologist Annette Lareau. This work describes fatigued and overwhelmed youth whom child psychiatrist Alvin Rosenfield and journalist Nicole Wise categorized in a 2000 book as *The Over-Scheduled Child*.

While the image of the over-scheduled child may seem familiar from the media, developmental psychologists Joseph Mahoney et al. realized that there was little direct research investigating broad issues related to the scheduling of today's youth. They thus compiled a review of new and existing research addressing specific issues related to structured activity participation, and empirically tested what they phrase "the over-scheduling hypothesis." In the selection, which is excerpted from their work, they find that overall, youth seem more likely to be under-scheduled than over-scheduled.

Mahoney and colleagues frame their work in relation to the emerging scholarly field of "positive youth development," which focuses on how to create environments for successful development. The general consensus is that structured activities are part of such environments, and few would disagree that activities can be a beneficial part of anyone's childhood years. But that does not necessarily mean the more the better.

Perhaps we are at a point where the quantity of structured activities has become too much of a good thing? This is the position articulated by child psychiatrist Alvin Rosenfeld in response to Mahoney and his colleagues. Rosenfeld thinks that Mahoney et al. have over-simplified the issue by comparing youth who participate in activities with youth who participate in no activities. Rosenfeld notes that structured activities are such a common part of growing up today that the children who do not participate at all are the exception. From Rosenfeld's perspective, the important thing is to balance reasonable amounts of structured activity participation with free leisure and family life.

POINT

- Most children participate in activities because they enjoy them, and do not experience undue pressure.
- On average, American youth actually spend very little time directly participating in structured activities.

- There is a consistently positive relationship between activity participation and healthy developmental outcomes.

- By claiming that children are over-scheduled there may be an impetus to cut much-needed funding for positive youth development programs.

COUNTERPOINT

- The effects are not just on youth, but also on stressed parents and family life in general.
- The real goal is a balance of activities and free time. It is unreasonable to compare youth who are participating in no activities because the contemporary norm is to participate in some.
- Data suggest that moderation is best regarding structured activity participation, and there have been notable declines in family life during recent decades.
- Identifying over-scheduling does not seem to lead to cuts in funds for activity programs.

YES ↵ Joseph L. Mahoney, Angel L. Harris, and Jacquelynne S. Eccles

Organized Activity Participation, Positive Youth Development, and the Over-Scheduling Hypothesis

School-aged children in the U.S. and other Western nations average 40–50% of their waking hours in discretionary activities outside of school. There has been increasing awareness that how young people use this time has consequences for their development. As a result, research on the risks and benefits of a variety of after-school activities has been expanding rapidly and considerable attention has been devoted to school-age children's (ages 5–11) and adolescents' (ages 12–18) involvement in organized activities. Organized activities occur outside of the school day and are characterized by structure, adult-supervision, and an emphasis on skill-building. Common activities include school-based extracurricular activities (e.g., sports, clubs, and fine arts), after-school (i.e., programs, often targeted to youth between the ages 5–14, that provide participants with adult supervision during the afternoon hours while many parents are working and offer opportunities for academic assistance, recreation, and/or enrichment learning) and community-based programs and youth organizations (e.g., 4-H, Boys & Girls Clubs of America, and Girls, Inc). Organized activities can be contrasted with alternative ways that young people spend their discretionary time such as educational activities, household chores, watching television, playing games, hanging out, and employment.

Participation in organized activities is a common developmental experience for young people. For example, the 1999 National Survey of America's Families (NSAF) reported that 81% of 6- to 11-year-olds and 83% of 12- to 17-year-olds participated in one or more sports, lessons, or clubs during the past year. Approximately 7 million children are enrolled in after-school programs. Millions more participate in community-based programs and youth organizations such as 4-H, Boys & Girls Clubs of America, and Girls Inc. Moreover, national studies show that participation in some organized activities such as sports and before/after-school programs has increased significantly in recent years.

The growth of organized activities has resulted from several factors. First, there has been an expansion of local, state, and Federal expenditures to support organized activities. A well–known example is the increase in Federal support for 21st-Century Community Learning Center grants that support after-school programs. This funding grew exponentially from $40 million in

From *Social Policy Report*, vol. XX, no. IV, 2006. Copyright © 2006 by Society for Research in Child Development. Reprinted by permission. Reference omitted.

1998 to $1 billion in 2002. Second, the historic rise in maternal employment has resulted in a gap between the school day of children and work day of their parents. This fact, coupled with research pointing to dangers for children who are unsupervised during the after-school hours, has called attention to organized activities as a means to provide safety and supervision for children with working parents. Finally, on balance, the bulk of research on organized activities has shown positive consequences of participation for academic, educational, social, civic, and physical development.

In combination, these factors have increased awareness that organized activities represent a valuable resource for promoting positive youth development. This in evident in the out-of-school initiatives of major research intuitions (e.g., Chapin Hall Center for Children, Harvard Family Research Project), granting institutions and foundations (e.g., C. S. Mott Foundation, W. T. Grant Foundation), advocacy and lobbying groups (e.g., Afterschool Alliance, Fight Crime Invest in Kids, National Institute on Out-of-School Time, National School-Aged Care Alliance), as well as the initiation of a bipartisan Congressional After-school Caucus in March 2005.

The Over-Scheduling Hypothesis

At the same time that initiatives to expand opportunities for organized activity participation have been increasing, concern exists that some youth are participating in too many organized activities. Written and televised media reports and popular parenting books suggest that the lives of many young people are now replete with hurry, stress, and pressure brought on, in part, because of their involvement in too many organized activities. These articles maintain that an over-scheduling of organized activity participation may undermine family functioning and youth well-being.

With respect to organized activities, the over-scheduling hypothesis is based on three interrelated propositions. First, the motivation for participation in organized activities is viewed as extrinsic. Youth are seen as taking part in a variety of activities because of the perceived pressure from parents or other adults to achieve and attain long-term educational and career goals (e.g., a college scholarship). Second, the time commitment required of children and parents to participate in organized activities is believed to be so extensive that traditional family activities—dinnertime, family outings, and even simple discussions between parents and children—are sacrificed. Finally, owing to the assumed pressures from parents, coupled with the extensive time commitment and disruption of family functioning, youth devoting high amounts of time to organized activity participation are thought to be at risk for developing adjustment problems and poor relationships with parents.

Although the basis for these propositions has been seldom anchored by empirical research, scientific evidence has been used to advance the notion that some youth (particularly middle class and affluent youth) are over-scheduled in some cases and that such over-scheduling can be detrimental to the optimal development of young people and their families. This evidence draws on qualitative studies of how organized activity participation affects family life and quantitative studies suggesting that perceived pressure from parents and other adults (e.g., coaches, teachers) may lead to poor adjustment particularly for affluent youth (i.e., families whose annual household earnings are at least twice as high the medium annual income for families in the US). As far as we know, the argument has not been directed to poor or working-class youth and there have been no studies of this issue focused on less advantaged populations.

Whether youth participate in organized activities depends, in part, on the behavior of their parents. Studies of children and adolescents suggest that they are more likely to become involved and to stay involved in organized activities when parents value and encourage their participation, provide the necessary material resources, and are participants themselves. However, a recent ethnographic study conducted with children (ages 9–10) from 12 diverse families suggests that organized activity schedules can determine the pace of life for all family members. The findings from Lareau's study show that the time budgeting and schedule commitments required of parents to support their children's activity participation can be challenging—particularly for working parents with several children. The qualitative accounts also suggest that participation in many organized activities can limit children's down time and constrain the nature parent-child interactions. While her study has been used to justify the inference that such scheduling might be problematic, Lareau did not actually investigate the children's well-being. Moreover, a systematic evaluation of how time spent in organized activities may affect discretionary time or parent-child interactions was not a goal of this study. Finally, although provocative, the findings are based on a small number of families and this raises concern about whether the results can be generalized beyond the study sample.

Quantitative studies suggesting possible risks for affluent adolescents have also been cited in support of the over-scheduling hypothesis. For example, in one of a few relevant studies, Luthar and her colleagues concluded, first, that adolescents (6th and 7th graders) from affluent homes can be at greater risk for substance use, depression, and anxiety as they enter adolescence than children living in less affluent homes, and, second, that excessive achievement pressures and isolation from parents may help to explain these associated risks. However, this research did not assess the association between time spent participating in organized activities and achievement pressures or adolescent adjustment. Accordingly, these studies neither intended to nor do they provide evidence that adolescents (affluent or otherwise) perceive pressure to participate in organized activities from their parents or are at-risk for adjustment problems as a result of their participation.

Our interest in conducting an evaluation of the scientific underpinnings of these propositions is twofold: First, these propositions suggest negative consequences resulting from too much organized activity participation. This has the potential to undermine recent efforts to support and expand opportunities for youth to participate in organized activities. Because policy decisions concerning children and families will be made with or without the use of scientific knowledge, this concern holds despite the limited evidence on which the over-scheduling hypothesis is based.

Indeed, the response to findings from the national evaluation of 21st-Century Community Learning Centers show that substantial reductions in funding for organized activities can be proposed on the basis of a single study with controversial findings.

Second, despite research available to inform propositions of the over-scheduling hypothesis, the scientific community has been relatively silent on this issue. As the value and worth of psychological research depends increasingly on an appropriate and timely integration of science with policy, it is essential that the existing research informing this matter be communicated. To that end, one of our major goals is to evaluate the scientific basis of the over-scheduling hypothesis. Our second major goal is to evaluate the evidence for the alternative positive youth development perspective; namely, that participation in organized activities facilitates positive development and that more participation is associated with more positive development. . . .

Discussion

In this paper, we have explored two perspectives regarding the relation of organized activity participation and development: the positive youth development perspective and the over-scheduling perspective. On the one hand, advocates of positive youth development have argued that participation in organized activities facilitate optimal development and therefore policymakers should provide more opportunities for American youth to be involved in such activities. On the other hand, some writers have suggested that participating in organized activities has become excessive for some young people, owing, in part, to achievement pressures from parents and other adults. These authors maintain that external pressures, along with the activity-related time commitment, can contribute to poor psychosocial adjustment for youth and to undermine relationships with parents. If this is the case, then attention from scientists, practitioners, and policymakers are warranted. Our goal was to bring scientific evidence to bear on both of these perspectives.

The available research base provides far more support for the positive youth perspective than for the over-scheduling perspective. To begin, the belief that organized activity participation is often motivated by parental pressure to achieve or attain long-term educational and career goals is not supported by the limited available empirical data. Overwhelmingly, the primary reasons adolescents give for participating in organized activities are intrinsic and focus on the here and now. This holds for the few studies that sampled affluent and suburban youth with relatively high levels of involvement in organized activities. However, there is a paucity of information on whether the reasons for participation vary according to either the amount or type of organized activity participation, or the age and other demographic characteristics of the participants and their families. We need to know much more about the relation between the participants' and their parents' motivations, goals, values, and expectations and the choices children/adolescents make about their discretionary time, in general, and the amount of time they devote to various types of organized activities, more specifically.

On the basis of time alone, very few American youth devote enough time to organized activities to be classified as "over-scheduled." For example, youth in the PSID-CDS—the only nationally representative sample of American youth with time use data—averaged about 5 hours/week in organized activities on any given week during the school year; furthermore, roughly 40% of the PSID-CDS youth did not participate in any organized activities and those who did typically spent fewer than 10 hours/week doing so. Comparable estimates emerged in the other studies we reviewed. These findings suggest that organized activities do not dominate the vast majority of American youth's free time. Instead, the majority of their time is consumed by other leisure pursuits such as watching television, educational activities, playing games, hanging out, and personal care. In other words, given the considerable amount of discretion time typically available to young Americans, most appear able to balance their organized activity participation effectively with school-related tasks, family time, informal socializing with peers, and relaxing. Nevertheless, there was evidence in some of the studies reviewed as well as in the PSID-CDS analyses reported in this paper, of a subgroup of youth (3% of children and 6% of adolescents) who spend a very high amount of time (20 or more hours/week) participating in organized activities. Are these youth poorly adjusted as a result of their high levels of participation in organized activities? By and large the evidence suggests not. Like their slightly less involved peers, they appear to be functioning better than non-involved youth. We discuss this more later.

In general, youth who participate in organized activities score better on a variety of indicators of healthy development than youth who do not participate. For example, those PSID-CDS youth who participated in organized activities for fewer than 20 hours/week scored better than the youth who did not participate in any activities on all of the indicators of well-being. This finding was true for all of the studies we reviewed and is consistent with the evidence summarized by Eccles and Gootman in their 2002 report for the National Research Council and the Institute of Medicine on the Community Based Programs for Youth. Thus, reliable support for the benefits of participation in organized activities emerged across studies and these benefits, by and large, become stronger with increased participation. Although the scheduling of responsibilities surrounding organized activities can sometimes be challenging for families, the associated benefits of participation are apparent nonetheless.

What about those youth who participate a great deal? Once again the findings across studies provide very limited support for the hypothesis that too much participation can be harmful. Many of the existing studies find a linear increase in the psychological, social, and academic well-being of youth as the number of organized activities or weekly hours of participation increases. Other studies report a curvilinear trend such that the well-being of youth with very extreme levels of involvement may level off or decline somewhat; however, these studies do not provide evidence that even very high amounts participation confers risk. The findings regarding the well-being of the extreme 6% of PSID-CDS youth who participated in organized activities 20 or more hours/week are generally consistent with these other studies. Clearly, the White youth who participated for 20 or more hours/week were better off than those White youth who did not participate in any activities on all but one of the indicators assessed: They reported higher levels of self-esteem and psychological and emotional well-being; lower alcohol, marijuana, and cigarette use; and ate meals with their parents and engaged in discussion with them more frequently. The only potentially negative finding for these White youth was that shared activities with their parents occurred less frequently. The findings for PSID-CDS Black youth were less consistent. On the one hand, the Black youth who participated in organized activities for 20 or more hours/week had higher reading achievement; reported higher emotional well-being; lower alcohol, marijuana, and cigarette use; and ate meals together with their parents more frequently than their Black peers who did not participate in any organized activities. On the other hand, these Black youth also reported less frequent parent-adolescent discussions and lower self-esteem and psychological well-being than their Black peers who did not participate.

The reasons for few the negative findings from the PSID-CDS and other studies need to be investigated before policy implications can be drawn. They may or may not be indicators of a negative impact of over-scheduling on adolescent development. For example, in the PSID-CDS, the fact that older adolescents may spend somewhat less time with their parents is not necessarily an indication of problems. Instead it could reflect normative increases in autonomy among competent young people. Thus, more needs to be known about the causes and consequences of this association before drawing any conclusions about whether they imply a developmental risk in these adolescents' lives. Likewise, the finding by Luthar et al. that a very small group of early adolescent females from affluent families demonstrated high internalizing symptoms and poor school adjustment when they were both highly involved in academic activities and perceived their parents as critical and overly achievement-oriented requires additional study before conclusions concerning over-scheduling can be made. One possibility is that a high amount of activity participation is associated with adjustment problems primarily for youth who do not receive positive support from their parents. This is consistent with research showing that activity-related support and encouragement from parents plays an important role in youths' enrollment and continued participation in organized activities. Parent-adolescent relations may also help to explain why the PSID-CDS findings showed that a very high amount of organized activity participation was associated with lower self-esteem and psychological well-being for Black adolescents; these same youth also reported a low frequency of parent-adolescent discussions. However, other studies have found have found a positive, linear association between the amount of organized activity participation and self-esteem during adolescence. Thus, to understand better what underlies these associations, process-oriented longitudinal research is needed. Moreover, given the many associated benefits of participation for other areas of their adjustment, follow-up studies are required to assess whether these highly involved adolescents are at risk for poor adjustment in the long term.

Despite these few possible risks of very high levels of activity participation, we do not believe efforts to limit adolescents' participation in organized activities are warranted for several reasons. First, across all studies reviewed, those few youth with very high levels of organized activity participation did not show negative adjustment in most of the indicators assessed and they demonstrated significantly healthier functioning than non-participants on many indicators of well-being. Furthermore, there is evidence that greater amounts of participation are positively associated with civic engagement, high school graduation, and college attendance, and are negatively related to antisocial behaviors and criminal offending. Therefore, even if a causal relation exists between very high amounts of participation and some negative outcomes, it is not clear that the cumulative effect of limiting participation for this extreme subgroup would be positive or negative.

Second, none of the studies reviewed in this report focused on stability and change in the amount of organized activity participation over time. Therefore, they tell us nothing about whether the very high amounts of participation that characterizes a small subgroup of youth is stable or transient across adolescence. It is possible that some youth extend their time commitment in organized activities to a very high level for a limited time. During this time, certain indicators of well-being may decline somewhat. However, this does not imply that such youth maintain a very high level of participation across all of adolescence or that their long-term well-being is compromised as a result. To evaluate whether this is the cause, longitudinal data measuring adolescents' time use and well-being over time are required.

Third, the existing research concerning amount of organized activity participation and youth adjustment has only begun to examine whether findings vary according to individual characteristics or features of the activity context. For example, studies of high-risk youth show that a lack of organized activity participation predicts poor academic adjustment and high rates of obesity, school dropout, and crime. For these youth, even a very high amount of organized activity participation may be better than spending time in arrangements that lack adult supervision or do not provide opportunities to build competencies. Likewise, the consequences of high amounts of participation are certain to depend on the features of the activity considered. Participation in high-quality organized activities is likely to be associated with positive youth development across the full range of hours considered in this report. In contrast, participation in activities that are poorly designed is predictive of relatively poor adjustment. Thus, attention to person and program features is needed before making decisions concerning the small proportion of youth who demonstrate very high amounts of organized activity participation.

Fourth, attention to person and program features is also relevant when interpreting the somewhat small effect sizes reported in some studies reviewed in this report. For example, results from Marsh's study indicate that, across the multiple significant and positive outcomes, the well-being of youth who were highly involved in organized activities youth was, on average, .22 *SD* (range .05–.58) above that of youth who did not participate. Results from the PSID-CDS showed that the time spent in organized activities explained an average of 8.8% of variance in the adolescent outcomes considered. Because youth typically spend much less time in organized activities than in other contexts (e.g., school and family), the associated impact of participation in any one area of adjustment should ordinarily be modest. However, in regard to the positive youth development perspective, such effects sizes are reported consistently across a broad array of outcomes and, therefore, are large enough to be of practical importance. In addition, research suggests that the magnitude of activity-related benefits may be greatest for: 1) youth who show stable participation over time; 2) those at the highest risk for poor developmental outcomes; 3) when long-term indicators of well-being are considered; and 4) when the quality of the program is high. Thus, there are likely to be many youth for whom participating in organized activities has a very large and positive effect. Similarly, to the extent that some youth participate in low-quality organized activities, the average effect sizes reported may have been diminished. Given the positive associations identified in the PSID-CDS and the other studies reviewed, one conclusion that is possible is that we need to provide America's youth with more, rather than less, opportunities to participate in high-quality, organized activities.

Finally, we note some parallels between the findings connected to organized activity participation and those pertaining adolescent participation in the paid labor force. Both become normative developmental experiences during adolescence, show variability according the family earnings and race, are viewed as a source of preparation for adult roles and responsibilities, and call attention to a small proportion of youth with very high levels of involvement— the consequences of which appear mixed. In the youth employment literature, research on working conditions and quality, reasons that motivate long hours of work, and long-term follow-ups have helped to clarify the pros/cons of young people who work extended hours. These types of studies suggest next steps for research aimed at understanding better the consequences of very high amounts of organized activity participation.

Our overall conclusion is that there is scant support for the over-scheduling hypothesis and considerable support for the positive youth development perspective. As such, we recommend that recent efforts to expand opportunities for organized activity participation should stay the course. For the vast majority of young people, participation in organized activities is positively associated with indicators of well-being. Of greater concern than the over-scheduling of youth in organized activities is the fact that many youth do not participate at all. The well-being of youth who do not participate in organized activities is reliably less positive compared to youth who do participate.

Alvin Rosenfeld

→ **NO**

"Organized Activity Participation, Positive Youth Development, and the Over-Scheduling Hypothesis," by Mahoney, Harris, and Eccles

Testing sociological hypotheses is difficult, so Mahoney, Harris, and Eccles should be commended for trying to approach a very complex child rearing question in a scientific fashion. Although these authors follow many well-accepted standards for empirical research, their study is based, in part, on an inaccurate account of Wise and my work and a questionable interpretation of their own data. The authors' conclusions are overly broad and their recommendations may misinform readers, persuading ambitious parents that over-scheduling their children is a scientifically validated way to raise emotionally well, academically successful children. In my opinion, that could have very unfortunate consequences.

Mahoney, Harris, and Eccles' paper contains serious shortcomings. I will name those I consider most important:

1. *Mahoney, Harris, and Eccles misrepresent our work:* Mahoney, Harris, and Eccles' paper tests "the overscheduling hypothesis," attributed in part to *The Over-Scheduled Child* (Griffin/St. Martin's, 2001) by Rosenfeld and Wise. Unfortunately, this "over-scheduling hypothesis" is a creation of their own that bears only scant resemblance to our work. For instance, Mahoney, Harris, and Eccles write that "the overscheduling hypothesis predicts that youth with very high amounts of organized activity participation will demonstrate poor adjustment relative to both those *with little or no participation* [italics added] and those with moderate amounts of participation." In their opinion, testing that contention will test the validity of what Wise, I, and others have said. Wise and I have never suggested that children do better if they participate in no activities nor have we posited that children who are in numerous organized activities do worse than *those who do none*. In fact, we repeatedly call for balance in families, where activities, education, family time, and down time all get sufficient attention. We write that up to a point, enrichment activities can benefit children. When asked, we have responded that

young children who participate in no activities should be urged—even forced—to try some out. We also write that the contemporary pressure to fill every moment with activities can frazzle children *and parents,* diminish the amount of quiet time families spend together, make parents and children resentful and critical, and de-emphasize the importance of creativity and character development.

2. *After creating an inaccurate, simplistic version of Wise and my work and labeling it "the overscheduling hypothesis," the authors design a study—using existing time-use survey data collected for other purposes—to test it:* After grossly misrepresenting our work, Mahoney, Harris, and Eccles compare children who participate in many activities to those in a "no activity" group, arguing—erroneously—that we say the "no activity" group should be doing better. In addition to misrepresenting our position, this comparison is highly flawed. Likely, the "no activity" group is quite diverse; some percentage of it probably does no activities because they are drop-outs, acting out, have failed at school subjects and so are not allowed to participate, etc. Comparing these kids to almost any other group—other than perhaps to foster children and incarcerated youth—would prove the second group, however composed, to be doing better. Mahoney, Harris, and Eccles have selected a well-known marker of poor adjustment—as indicated by the children's partaking in no activities that are normative for their age—and used it as a normative comparison group. They then reverse cause and effect, saying that these children are doing less well because they are not in activities.

3. *Some of Mahoney, Harris, and Eccles' findings support our actual position:* What does Mahoney, Harris, and Eccles' data actually show? In some ways, rather than contradicting our ideas, it supports the position that we put forth, suggesting that balance is best. In published reports, Mahoney maintains that "the more activities they do, the better kids stack up on measures of educational achievement and psychological adjustment" (Newsweek). However, some of Mahoney, Harris, and Eccles' own data suggests the opposite: Black youth spending over 20 hours a week in organized activities had self-esteem lower even than those who participated in no organized activities and far lower than those who participate in a moderate number. Adolescents in 15 or more hours of scheduled activities drink more alcohol than those with 5–15 hours. White youth with 20 or more hours of organized activities report fewer shared activities with parents and doing fewer favorite activities with parents than did youth with 5–15 hours of activities. Black youth with more than 15 hours of organized activities reported fewer shared activities with parents than did those with 5–15 hours of activities; those with more than 20 hours of scheduled activities spent less time with parent-child favorite activities than did those with 10–20 hours of scheduled activities. Black youth with more than 20 hours of activities had fewer parent-adolescent discussions than did any other group, even those with no activities. Reading achievement for black youth doing over 15 hours of organized activities is significantly below those of adolescents doing 5–15 hours. Reading achievement for white youths doing over 20 hours a week of organized activities is almost identical

to those doing *no* organized activities and substantially below those doing moderate activity (though the authors' state that this did not reach statistical significance.) To us, this data seems to support our contention that a balanced number of activities is best rather than the idea that the more the better.

4. *The Mahoney, Harris, and Eccles study lacks observational data and does not include travel time:* The study analyzes data based on self-reports. As such, the data is subject to all the well known difficulties non-observational studies are prone to. It relies on time diaries asking people to put down everything they did in a 24 hour period. However, these diaries are written up to three days after a weekday set of activities and up to a week after a weekend day. It is highly questionable that a week after the events, people can accurately remember their activities and how much time they spent on each for an entire 24 hour period which may explain why Mahoney, Harris, and Eccles' study cannot account for how 13–14% of the time is spent. Furthermore, the study does not include travel time. Mahoney, Harris, and Eccles overlook the reality that many families have several children. A parent with three children each with three activities may spend four hours a day driving between activities. In our experience, this driving schedule creates substantial irritation, particularly among highly educated mothers; they love their kids but resent feeling they have become chauffeurs. It also leads to some siblings becoming "car potatoes."

5. *Mahoney, Harris, and Eccles approach the subject simply from the active child's perspective, discounting the effects on other family members:* The omission of travel time is part of Mahoney, Harris, and Eccles' general discounting of parental stress. Their study states, "although the scheduling of responsibilities surrounding organized activities can sometimes be challenging for families (Lareau, 2003), the associated benefits of participation are apparent nonetheless." It seems that they regard a child or adolescent seeming to be doing well by questionnaire report as a sufficient outcome marker. This runs diametrically against observational data, including our own clinical observations. Our books stress the importance of the whole family's needs being taken into account, *including the parents'*. Mahoney, Harris, and Eccles seem to contend that no matter how much the parents sacrifice and no matter how resentful they may feel, their kids do well in the long run if they have more activities. Much of the literature about over-scheduled children speaks of the ways the parents *feel* about leading stressed, overscheduled, and often frenzied lives. Mahoney, Harris, and Eccles do not take these into account.

In contrast, our books, and my talks since the book was published, speak of the need for parents to be sure that they are enjoying their lives because in my clinical experience parents who are satisfied with their situation—rather than feeling frenzied much of the time—have kids who do better. We repeatedly argue against one-size-fits-all solutions and speak of how in arriving at the number and types of activities that are suitable for the family as a whole, each family needs to balance the child's temperament and desires with the number of children in the family and the parents' abilities, capacity, needs, and schedules. We have said that some children—in our experience, often ambitious first born children—want to do everything and need to be reined in a bit. Other children are "couch potatoes" and need to be encouraged, even forced, to partake in organized activities.

6. *Mahoney, Harris, and Eccles discount a large body of data to the contrary and feel that results from their single, flawed study are sufficiently robust to conclude that the more scheduled activities children have, the better:* The conclusions Mahoney, Harris, and Eccles draw from this study seem to run contrary to what numerous experienced observers have noted. We will note just a few: Studies show that in just the past 20 years household conversations have become far less frequent and family dinners have declined 33%. Numerous observers have spoken of sleep deprivation among high achieving adolescents. This study does not even acknowledge that sleep deprivation may be a significant issue among over-scheduled children, nor does it note that as children's sports have become professionalized, orthopedic surgeons have reported an alarming increase of stress related sports and overuse injuries among 5–14 year olds. They ignore work that shows that homework among middles schoolers has grown dramatically and that some scholars feel that the high amount spent could actually harm children. They report but discount the findings, including their own, of higher levels of alcohol use among adolescents with many activities. We have noted that resumes are being shaped for what elite colleges supposedly expect; we and others have commented that community service no longer is a sign of a good heart but a box that must be checked. Speaking of over-scheduled youth, Harvard University's admissions director said that admitted freshman, and we paraphrase, look like the dazed survivors of a life long boot camp. MIT's admissions director has concurred. Parents and adolescents we speak to seem well aware of the pressure they are under. Mahoney, Harris, and Eccles acknowledge none of this as valid.

7. *Mahoney, Harris, and Eccles raise a concern that "the over-scheduling hypothesis," attributed in part to us, could lead to programs for the underprivileged being cut. In almost seven years since our book was first published, this has not happened even once:* Mahoney, Harris, and Eccles state, "These propositions [the "over-scheduling hypothesis"] suggest negative consequences resulting from too much organized activity participation. This has the potential to undermine recent efforts to support and expand opportunities for youth to participate in organized activities" (P 10 draft) particularly for the underprivileged.

   A. We agree with the authors' contention that one of the cases in which activity-related benefits may be greatest is for "those at the highest risk for poor development," and when the program's quality is high (35). As a child advocate who has worked with—and written extensively about—indigent and high risk populations, I am quite sensitive to the needs of people in these situations.

Whenever Wise and I have been asked about underprivileged populations, we have said that they needed *more—not fewer—* organized activities.

B. Several months back, I wrote a letter to Dr. Mahoney after reading the final draft of this paper: "I would appreciate knowing where and when I—or my work—has been used *in any way* in opposition to these initiatives. In the almost seven years since our book was first published, *I have not once received a single contact or communication from any group or individual asking that my ideas, writings, or speeches be used as support for decreasing activity programs or funding* [italics added]. If such an attempt has ever occurred, I would be grateful if you could inform me of it." To date, I have not received a reply.

In summary, Mahoney, Harris, and Eccles take complex, nuanced ideas and try to make them one-dimensional caricatures. Our books have subtle ideas and a social commentary about the way American families are living their lives and the pressures they are responding to. To name just a few, our books speak of "hyper-parenting," a cultural pressure to involve children in increasing activities so that they turn out "winners" not "losers." We speak of how, from birth on, media play on parents' uncertainty, and how marketers use the idea that the more "enrichment" the better to sell unnecessary products to new parents. We note how individual families and children differ, how what benefits one may be counter-productive for another. Some families thrive on endless activities and sports while others prefer quiet down time. *We suggest that each individual family needs to assess what suits it; when activities are getting parents or the children frenetic, we suggest that they try cutting back 5–10%, hardly a notion that scheduled activities be eliminated.* We speak of needing down time to develop imagination, and of how focusing on activities and accomplishments often de-emphasizes relationships, character, and play which we consider critical to a good life. Our books have recommendations, such as trusting yourself, rather than relying on the experts who don't know you or your family. We suggest that parents do not rely on the most recent "scientific" study whose recommendations may change tomorrow. Mahoney, Harris, and Eccles take all this and create a one-dimensional "over-scheduling hypothesis" which attributes to us the idea that simply counting the number of activities a child participates in accurately and inversely reflects their mental health and life success.

We could discuss many other serious limitations in Mahoney, Harris, and Eccles' paper, but that would serve little purpose. As I wrote to Dr. Mahoney: "It is excellent that you are trying to do reliable, valid scientific work that criticizes my position and refutes my contentions. That keeps the academic process vigorous. If I turn out to have been mistaken, I will shamefacedly admit that I was in error. Nothing I see in my daily observation in our communities makes me think that I am. However, I would appreciate it if in trying to test a hypothesis you ascribe to me, you at the very least represent my positions accurately."

If competitive, affluent parents take to heart Dr. Mahoney's assertion that the more activities kids do the better—as they are wont to do with "expert, scientific" advice from a professor at an elite university—they may be following a path that leads them to more resentment, criticism of their children, and ultimately to damaging them. That would truly be a very unfortunate outcome.

CHALLENGE QUESTIONS

Should Contemporary Adolescents Be Engaged in More Structured Activities?

- Some commentators have noted that much of this issue seems to depend upon socioeconomic status—with wealthier children being at risk of having too much structured activity and children from other families being at risk of having too little. How do you think socioeconomic status may influence one's position on this controversial issue?
- Mahoney, Harris, and Eccles suggest that only a very small portion of youth participate in significant weekly hours of structured activities. Does that seem to be true among your friends and neighbors? Why or why not?
- What do you make of Rosenfeld's claim that structured activities influence the whole family, not just the involved youth? Why do you think Mahoney and colleagues did not test effects on family life more generally?
- If you were giving advice to parents about activity participation, what would you say? What does the research allow you to conclude?
- What might be the benefits of not having structured activities as part of adolescence? What might be the costs?

Suggested Readings

D. Brooks, "The Organization Kid," *The Atlantic Monthly* (April 2001)

D. Elkind, *The Power of Play* (Da Capo Books, 2007)

K. Ginsburg and the Committee on Communications and the Committee on Psychosocial Aspects of Child and Family Health, from "The Importance of Play in Promoting Healthy Child Development and Maintaining Strong Parent-Child Bonds," *Pediatrics* (January 2007)

R. Larson, "The Tip of an Iceberg?" *Society for Research in Child Development Social Policy Report* (2006)

S. Luthar, "Over-Scheduling Versus Other Stressors: Challenges of High Socioeconomic Status Families," *Society for Research in Child Development Social Policy Report* (2006)

J. Mahoney, R. Larson, and J. Eccles (Eds.), *Organized Activities as Contexts of Development: Extracurricular Activities, After-school and Community Programs* (Lawrence Erlbaum & Associates, 2005)

A. Rosenfeld and N. Wise, *The Over-scheduled Child: Avoiding the Hyperparenting Trap* (St. Martin's Griffin, 2000)

J. Roth, "Next Steps: Considering Patterns of Participation," *Society for Research in Child Development Social Policy Report* (2006)

ISSUE 11

Does the Adolescent Brain Make Risk Taking Inevitable?

YES: Laurence Steinberg, from "Risk Taking in Adolescence: New Perspectives From Brain and Behavioral Science," *Current Directions in Psychological Science* (April 2007)

NO: Michael Males, from "Does the Adolescent Brain Make Risk Taking Inevitable?: A Skeptical Appraisal," *Journal of Adolescent Research* (January 2009)

ISSUE SUMMARY

YES: Although adolescent risk-taking has proved difficult to study and explain, psychology professor Laurence Steinberg claims brain science is now demonstrating that basic biological changes explain much about the issue.

NO: Sociologist Michael Males rejects "biodeterminism" as an over-simplification that exaggerates the effects of brain age and ignores the realities of social and economic differences.

One of the most common stereotypes of adolescents is that they are prone to take risks without adequately accounting for consequences. Much attention has been directed toward influencing adolescents to be more careful and safe. But despite all the attention, the stereotypes persist. Which raises the interesting developmental question of whether the stereotypes are true to begin with.

The idea of adolescence as a tumultuous period that inevitably results in "storm and strain" has long been a controversial issue for developmental research. It has also long been popular to attribute whatever tumult research finds to biological changes—most often to "raging hormones." In fact, adolescence is the rare stage in the life-span with a clear biological marker: puberty. And because puberty does produce dramatic physical changes, it is not hard to imagine that psychological changes would follow.

Advances in technology and brain science seem to have only perpetuated debates about the nature of adolescent behavior. There are ways in which the adolescent brain seems, on average, to function differently than the brain at other ages. Unfortunately, while those differences are often interpreted as indicating biological inevitabilities, patterns of brain activity alone tell us very little about the causes of behavior: social experiences activate the brain just as do genetic programs. Brain activity is both a cause and an effect of behavior. So one of the great challenges that comes with technological advancement is the art and science of interpretation.

Laurence Steinberg explains, the brain's ability to reason and logically think through problems matures more consistently than its ability to manage social and emotional stimulation. Steinberg thinks this difference helps explain a paradox of adolescent risk-taking: despite effective educational efforts to help teens logically understand the consequences of risk-taking, they often act as if they do not care. From his perspective, the maturation of function in the teen brain makes risk-taking nearly inevitable.

Another interpretation is that the facts of biological change distract our attention from the social realities of teenage life. Thus, as Michael Males explains, there are many ways in which adolescents take less risks than adults—particularly when it comes to risk outcomes such as accidental deaths and drug overdoses. In fact, Males argues, there is much more variation in risk-taking *within* the stage of adolescence than there is *between* adolescents and adults. Males is particularly concerned that artificially inflating the importance of the brain, which does change with experiences, puts too much emphasis on biology and not enough emphasis on the types of socioeconomic disadvantage that really influence risky adolescent behavior.

However we interpret the findings of modern brain research, it is clear that new technologies raise as many questions as they answer. And some of those questions may allow us to re-evaluate stereotypes about adolescence.

POINT	COUNTERPOINT
• There has been much study of adolescent risk-taking, but no satisfactory explanation until recent advances in brain science.	• Claims of adolescent risk-taking are regularly exaggerated, often in service of other social or political agendas.
• Adolescents are able to engage in mature logical reasoning, but their psychosocial capacities often remain more immature.	• Focusing on the adolescent brain as the cause of risk-taking is a type of "biodeterminism" that over-simplifies complicated issues; brain science is still not advanced enough to really make clear links between biology and behavior.
• Puberty seems to accelerate socioemotional networks associated with risk-taking, overwhelming cognitive-controls—particularly in group contexts.	• Teenagers have lower rates of risk compared to adults for suicide, drug overdoses, and accidents—yet those statistics are often ignored when making claims about adolescent risk.
• Increases in risk-taking are closely associated with the biological changes of puberty regardless of chronological age.	• Researchers such as Steinberg fail to control for the most important cause of risk-taking: socioeconomic differences predict risk-taking better than age.
• Educational interventions to minimize adolescent risk-taking have been largely ineffective, suggesting it is not about rational thinking.	

YES ⤶

Laurence Steinberg

Risk Taking in Adolescence: New Perspectives From Brain and Behavioral Science

. . . Adolescents and college-age individuals take more risks than children or adults do, as indicated by statistics on automobile crashes, binge drinking, contraceptive use, and crime; but trying to understand why risk taking is more common during adolescence than during other periods of development has challenged psychologists for decades. . . . Numerous theories to account for adolescents' greater involvement in risky behavior have been advanced, but few have withstood empirical scrutiny. . . .

False Leads in Risk-Taking Research

Systematic research does not support the stereotype of adolescents as irrational individuals who believe they are invulnerable and who are unaware, inattentive to, or unconcerned about the potential harms of risky behavior. In fact, the logical-reasoning abilities of 15-year-olds are comparable to those of adults, adolescents are no worse than adults at perceiving risk or estimating their vulnerability to it . . ., and increasing the salience of the risks associated with making a potentially dangerous decision has comparable effects on adolescents and adults. . . . Most studies find few age differences in individuals' evaluations of the risks inherent in a wide range of dangerous behaviors, in judgments about the seriousness of the consequences that might result from risky behavior, or in the ways that the relative costs and benefits of risky activities are evaluated. . . .

Because adolescents and adults reason about risk in similar ways, many researchers have posited that age differences in actual risk taking are due to differences in the information that adolescents and adults use when making decisions. Attempts to reduce adolescent risk taking through interventions designed to alter knowledge, attitudes, or beliefs have proven remarkably disappointing, however. . . . Efforts to provide adolescents with information about the risks of substance use, reckless driving, and unprotected sex typically result in improvements in young people's thinking about these phenomena but seldom change their actual behavior. Generally speaking, reductions in adolescents' health-compromising behavior are more strongly linked to changes in

From *Current Directions in Psychological Science*, April 2007, pp. 55–59. Copyright © 2007 by the Association for Psychological Science. Reprinted by permission of Wiley-Blackwell.

the contexts in which those risks are taken (e.g., increases in the price of cigarettes, enforcement of graduated licensing programs, more vigorously implemented policies to interdict drugs, or condom distribution programs) than to changes in what adolescents know or believe.

The failure to account for age differences in risk taking through studies of reasoning and knowledge stymied researchers for some time. Health educators, however, have been undaunted, and they have continued to design and offer interventions of unproven effectiveness, such as Drug Abuse Resistance Education (DARE), driver's education, or abstinence-only sex education.

A New Perspective on Risk Taking

In recent years, owing to advances in the developmental neuroscience of adolescence and the recognition that the conventional decision-making framework may not be the best way to think about adolescent risk taking, a new perspective on the subject has emerged. . . . This new view begins from the premise that risk taking in the real world is the product of both logical reasoning and psychosocial factors. However, unlike logical-reasoning abilities, which appear to be more or less fully developed by age 15, psychosocial capacities that improve decision making and moderate risk taking—such as impulse control, emotion regulation, delay of gratification, and resistance to peer influence—continue to mature well into young adulthood. . . . Accordingly, psychosocial immaturity in these respects during adolescence may undermine what otherwise might be competent decision making. The conclusion drawn by many researchers, that adolescents are as competent decision makers as adults are, may hold true only under conditions where the influence of psychosocial factors is minimized.

Evidence From Developmental Neuroscience

Advances in developmental neuroscience provide support for this new way of thinking about adolescent decision making. It appears that heightened risk taking in adolescence is the product of the interaction between two brain networks. The first is a socioemotional network that is especially sensitive to social and emotional stimuli, that is particularly important for reward processing, and that is remodeled in early adolescence by the hormonal changes of puberty. It is localized in limbic and paralimbic areas of the brain, an interior region that includes the amygdala, ventral striatum, orbitofrontal cortex, medial pre-frontal cortex, and superior temporal sulcus. The second network is a cognitive-control network that subserves executive functions such as planning, thinking ahead, and self-regulation, and that matures gradually over the course of adolescence and young adulthood largely independently of puberty. . . . The cognitive-control network mainly consists of outer regions of the brain, including the lateral prefrontal and parietal cortices and those parts of the anterior cingulate cortex to which they are connected.

In many respects, risk taking is the product of a competition between the socioemotional and cognitive-control networks . . . , and adolescence is a period in which the former abruptly becomes more assertive (i.e., at puberty) while the latter gains strength only gradually, over a longer period of time. The socioemotional network is not in a state of constantly high activation during adolescence, though. Indeed, when the socioemotional network is not highly activated (for example, when individuals are not emotionally excited or are alone), the cognitive-control network is strong enough to impose regulatory control over impulsive and risky behavior, even in early adolescence. In the presence of peers or under conditions of emotional arousal, however, the socioemotional network becomes sufficiently activated to diminish the regulatory effectiveness of the cognitive-control network. Over the course of adolescence, the cognitive-control network matures, so that by adulthood, even under conditions of heightened arousal in the socioemotional network, inclinations toward risk taking can be modulated.

It is important to note that mechanisms underlying the processing of emotional information, social information, and reward are closely interconnected. Among adolescents, the regions that are activated during exposure to social and emotional stimuli overlap considerably with regions also shown to be sensitive to variations in reward magnitude. . . . This finding may be relevant to understanding why so much adolescent risk taking—like drinking, reckless driving, or delinquency—occurs in groups. . . . Risk taking may be heightened in adolescence because teenagers spend so much time with their peers, and the mere presence of peers makes the rewarding aspects of risky situations more salient by activating the same circuitry that is activated by exposure to nonsocial rewards when individuals are alone.

The competitive interaction between the socioemotional and cognitive-control networks has been implicated in a wide range of decision-making contexts, including drug use, social-decision processing, moral judgments, and the valuation of alternative rewards/costs. . . . In all of these contexts, risk taking is associated with relatively greater activation of the socioemotional network. For example, individuals' preference for smaller immediate rewards over larger delayed rewards is associated with relatively increased activation of the ventral striatum, orbitofrontal cortex, and medial prefrontal cortex—all regions linked to the socioemotional network—presumably because immediate rewards are especially emotionally arousing (consider the difference between how you might feel if a crisp $100 bill were held in front of you versus being told that you will receive $150 in 2 months). In contrast, regions implicated in cognitive control are engaged equivalently across decision conditions. . . . Similarly, studies show that increased activity in regions of the socioemotional network is associated with the selection of comparatively risky (but potentially highly rewarding) choices over more conservative ones. . . .

Evidence From Behavioral Science

Three lines of behavioral evidence are consistent with this account. First, studies of susceptibility to antisocial peer influence show that vulnerability to peer pressure increases between preadolescence and mid-adolescence, peaks in mid-adolescence—presumably when the imbalance between the sensitivity to socioemotional arousal (which has increased at puberty) and capacity for cognitive control (which is still immature) is greatest—and gradually declines thereafter. . . . Second, as noted earlier, studies of decision making generally show no age differences in risk processing between older adolescents and adults when decision making is assessed under conditions likely associated with relatively lower activation of brain systems responsible for emotion, reward, and social processing (e.g., the presentation of hypothetical decision-making dilemmas to individuals tested alone under conditions of low emotional arousal. . . . Third, the presence of peers increases risk taking substantially among teenagers, moderately among college-age individuals, and not at all among adults, consistent with the notion that the development of the cognitive-control network is gradual and extends beyond the teen years. In one of our lab's studies, for instance, the presence of peers more than doubled the number of risks teenagers took in a video driving game and increased risk taking by 50% among college undergraduates but had no effect at all among adults. . . . In adolescence, then, not only is more merrier—it is also riskier.

What Changes During Adolescence?

Studies of rodents indicate an especially significant increase in reward salience (i.e., how much attention individuals pay to the magnitude of potential rewards) around the time of puberty . . ., consistent with human studies showing that increases in sensation seeking occur relatively early in adolescence and are correlated with pubertal maturation but not chronological age. . . . Given behavioral findings indicating relatively greater reward salience among adolescents than adults in decision-making tasks, there is reason to speculate that, when presented with risky situations that have both potential rewards and potential costs, adolescents may be more sensitive than adults to variation in rewards but comparably sensitive (or perhaps even less sensitive) to variation in costs. . . .

It thus appears that the brain system that regulates the processing of rewards, social information, and emotions is becoming more sensitive and more easily aroused around the time of puberty. What about its sibling, the cognitive-control system? Regions making up the cognitive-control network, especially prefrontal regions, continue to exhibit gradual changes in structure and function during adolescence and early adulthood. . . . Much publicity has been given to the finding that synaptic pruning (the selective elimination of seldom-used synapses) and myelination (the development of the fatty sheaths that "insulate" neuronal circuitry)—both of which increase the efficiency of information processing—continue to occur in the prefrontal cortex well into the early 20s. But frontal regions also become more integrated with other brain regions during adolescence and early adulthood, leading to gradual improvements in many aspects of cognitive control such as response inhibition; this integration may be an even more important change than changes within the frontal region itself. Imaging studies using tasks in which individuals are asked to inhibit a "prepotent" response–like trying to look away from, rather than toward, a point of light—have shown that adolescents tend to recruit the cognitive-control network less broadly than do adults, perhaps overtaxing the capacity of the more limited number of regions they activate. . . .

In essence, one of the reasons the cognitive-control system of adults is more effective than that of adolescents is that adults' brains distribute its regulatory responsibilities across a wider network of linked components. This lack of cross-talk across brain regions in adolescence results not only in individuals acting on gut feelings without fully thinking (the stereotypic portrayal of teenagers) but also in thinking too much when gut feelings ought to be attended to (which teenagers also do from time to time). In one recent study, when asked whether some obviously dangerous activities (e.g., setting one's hair on fire) were "good ideas," adolescents took significantly longer than adults to respond to the questions and activated a less narrowly distributed set of cognitive-control regions. . . . This was not the case when the queried activities were not dangerous ones, however (e.g., eating salad).

The fact that maturation of the socioemotional network appears to be driven by puberty, whereas the maturation of the cognitive-control network does not, raises interesting questions about the impact—at the individual and at the societal levels—of early pubertal maturation on risk-taking. We know that there is wide variability among individuals in the timing of puberty, due to both genetic and environmental factors. We also know that there has been a significant drop in the age of pubertal maturation over the past 200 years. To the extent that the temporal disjunction between the maturation of the socioemotional system and that of the cognitive-control system contributes to adolescent risk taking, we would expect to see higher rates of risk taking among early maturers and a drop over time in the age of initial experimentation with risky behaviors such as sexual intercourse or drug use. There is evidence for both of these patterns. . . .

Implications for Prevention

What does this mean for the prevention of unhealthy risk taking in adolescence? Given extant research suggesting that it is not the way adolescents think or what they don't know or understand that is the problem, a more profitable strategy than attempting to change how adolescents view risky activities might be to focus on limiting opportunities for immature judgment to have harmful consequences. More than 90% of all American high-school students have had sex, drug, and driver education in their schools, yet large proportions of them still have unsafe sex, binge drink, smoke cigarettes, and drive recklessly (often more than one of these at the same time . . .). Strategies such as raising the price of cigarettes, more vigilantly enforcing laws governing the sale of alcohol, expanding adolescents' access to mental-health and contraceptive services, and raising the driving age would likely be more effective in limiting adolescent smoking, substance abuse, pregnancy, and automobile fatalities than strategies aimed at making adolescents wiser, less impulsive, or less shortsighted. Some things just take time to develop, and, like it or not, mature judgment is probably one of them.

The research reviewed here suggests that heightened risk taking during adolescence is likely to be normative, biologically driven, and, to some extent, inevitable. There is probably very little that can or ought to be done to either attenuate or delay the shift in reward sensitivity that takes place at puberty. It may be possible to accelerate the maturation of self-regulatory competence, but no research has examined whether this is possible. In light of studies showing familial influences on psychosocial maturity in adolescence, understanding how contextual factors influence the development of self-regulation and knowing the neural underpinnings of these processes should be a high priority for those interested in the well-being of young people.

Michael Males ➔ **NO**

Does the Adolescent Brain Make Risk Taking Inevitable?: A Skeptical Appraisal

. . . If grown-ups are paragons of mature restraint, our discussion of teenagers and the "teenage brain" must be an exception. A survey of stories in the popular press on the teenage brain and risk taking found reporters and commentators, including experts, lambasting teens as "reckless," "stupid," "irrational," "callous," "lazy," "violent;" even "alien". . . . Psychologist Michael Bradley's . . . *Yes! Your Teen Is Crazy!* brands teens "stupid," "crazy," and "brain damaged" on virtually every page, wildly exaggerates the tolls of teens killed by guns (by 200%) and drunken driving (by 600% . . .), and still wins endorsement from psychologist Jay Giedd of the august National Institutes of Health. University of California public health professors Martha Campbell and Malcolm Potts . . . blame global violence on young men's aggressive natures, as if political and military leaders played no part. The March 2008 *Developmental Review*'s special issue contains eight articles on "risk and decision making;" six of these entirely concern adolescents and the remaining two mostly so, and all adopt the framework of developmental theory. . . . The National Research Council . . . held a forum on the "emerging . . . science of adolescence" led by physician Ronald Dahl warning of "the tinderbox of the teenage brain."

Adolescence, this new science holds . . . is a mélange of biohazard, a frightening mistake of nature. Temple University psychologist Laurence Steinberg . . . declares, "Heightened risk-taking during adolescence is likely to be normative, biologically driven, and, to some extent, inevitable." . . . The age range designated as biologically inferior is expanding rapidly. From minimum-subject experiments maximally interpreted, Steinberg . . . has suggested no one less than the age of 25 years should be allowed to drive, Giedd . . . has questioned the rights of persons under that age to drive or vote, and Harvard School of Public Health assistant professor Deborah Yurgelun-Todd suggests even older teens should not be allowed to hold licenses or employment in such areas as lifeguard or military service. . . . Lobbies across the spectrum find the idea of biodetermined teenage incompetence useful to promote varied agendas, including imposing sweeping curfews on young people, requiring parental consent for adolescents' abortions, abolishing the death penalty for juveniles, and soliciting funding for youth management industries.

From *Journal of Adolescent Research,* January 2009, pp. 3–20 excerpted. Copyright © 2009 by Sage Publications. Reprinted by permission via Rightslink.

This article will argue that this new biodeterminist "science of adolescence" . . . now cascading through American media and political forums incorporates major violations of scholarly ethics, research fundamentals, critical scientific debate, and the right of young people to objective and accurate treatment. A future Stephen Jay Gould applying a science historian's skepticism is likely to find ample reason for alarm in the way brain research has proven "vulnerable to over-simplification, over-interpretation, and the confirmation of prior prejudices." . . .

Is "Adolescent Risk Taking" Scientifically Founded?

Claims about the "teenage brain" depend on the theory of "adolescent risk taking:" that "adolescents, on average, engage in more reckless behavior than do individuals of other ages." . . . If adolescent behaviors are not generally riskier than those of adults when relevant factors are controlled, then interpreting teenage biologies as provoking riskier behavior would be a torturous exercise indeed.

"If kids are as smart as adults, why do they do such dumb things?" Steinberg asks . . ., presaging a biodeterminist explanation:

> The temporal gap between puberty, which impels adolescents toward thrill-seeking, and the slow maturation of the cognitive control system, which regulates these impulses, makes adolescence a time of heightened vulnerability for risky behavior . . . Risk-taking is the product of a competition between the socio-emotional and cognitive control networks . . . and adolescence is a period in which the former abruptly becomes more assertive at puberty while latter gains strength only gradually, over a longer period of time. . . .

Theorists then link risk-prone teenage brain biology to enhanced social hazard:

> Studies of susceptibility to antisocial peer influence show that vulnerability to peer pressure increases between preadolescence and mid-adolescence, peaks in mid-adolescence, presumably when the imbalance between the sensitivity to socio-emotional arousal (which has increased at puberty) and capacity for cognitive control (which is still immature) is greatest, and gradually declines thereafter." . . .

However, the biodeterminist views presented by Steinberg . . . and others as scientific consensus are disputed. Eminent researchers caution that we know too little about brain biology to make sweeping claims, Asked, "How much do we know about the relationship between the anatomy or biology of the brain and behavior?" Kurt W. Fischer, Professor of Education and Human Development and director of the Mind, Brain, & Education Program at the Harvard Graduate School of Education replied,

> We do not know very much! . . . Most of the recent advances in brain science have involved knowledge of the biology of single neurons and synapses, not knowledge of patterns of connection and other aspects of the brain as a system . . . but we have a very long way to go . . . People naturally want to use brain science to inform policy and practice, but our limited knowledge of the brain places extreme limits on that effort. . . .

Daniel Siegel of the University of California, Los Angeles's (UCLA) School of Medicine, coinvestigator at UCLA's Center for Culture, Brain, and Development, and director of the Center for Human Development, agreed: "We are just beginning to identify how systems in the brain work together in an integrated fashion to create complex mental processes." . . . Richard Lerner, director of Tufts University's Institute for Applied Research in Youth Development, likewise points out that brain research is "in its infancy" and "it's way too premature to make those specific links" between biology and behavior. . . .

In addition to being premature, biological risk theories fail fundamental tests. What objective evidence shows that "adolescent risk taking" exists at all? What, in fact, is an "adolescent"?

Here arises the first major contradiction: True "adolescents" whose puberty-impelled risk taking would be highest and cognitive control systems the least developed according to biodeterminist theory, do not display inordinately high risks. Puberty now occurs from around the age of 10 to 13 years for girls and 12 to 15 years for boys. Thus, developmental, cognitive, and social influences should combine to render "mid-adolescence a time of heightened vulnerability to risky and reckless behavior." . . . Second, modern "teenagers spend so much time with their peers." . . . If the theory of greater thrill seeking driven by immature cognitive control, more peer association, and increasing independence from adults is correct, we would expect that adolescents would account for an increasing share of society's risks.

However, few of the results we would expect from this "adolescent risk" theory turn out to be true either in cross section or longitudinally. Modern, presumably peer-socialized adolescents are not acting riskier than their parent-socialized counterparts of the past; the highest rates for most teenage ills occurred 30 to 40 years ago. Today, the parent generation seems more at risk. The latest statistics for rates of violent death—those from accidents, suicides, homicides, and those of undetermined intent—reveal that teens aged 15 to 19 years (49.7 deaths per 100,000 population in 2005) have lower rates than every adult age group. The worst rates are for ages 20 to 24 years (73.8 deaths per 100,000 population), followed closely by what had been assumed the safest grown-up ages: 45 to 49 years (70.1) 40 to 44 years (67.6), and 50 to 54 years (65.0). . . . For unintentional deaths (accidents) thought to be the scourge of reckless youth, age 45 to 49 years (44.6 deaths per 100,000 population) is the worst, followed by age 20 to 24, 50 to 54, and 40 to 44 years; age range 15 to 19 years (31.4) is safer than every adult age group. Even for the risk for which teenagers show the most excessive rate, motor vehicle fatality, travel survey, and accident reports show a 16-year-old would have to drive from Boston to Los Angeles and back 1,000 times to run even odds of being in a fatal traffic crash. . . .

More than 99.5% of all 16-year-olds live to be 17—a higher annual survival rate than for any single year of adult age to the next even if only violent deaths are considered. Indeed, the safest ages from accidental death for ages from 16 to 64 years are 16, followed by 17, and 35; middle-age now is riskier even than age 18. Yet authorities have failed to mention these trends and continue to insist that "statistics" prove adolescence is the time of greatest risk. . . .

That there are very few areas in which even the riskiest adolescent ages, 16 and 17 years, suffer the worst risk outcomes clearly is not due to adults' effective control. Such large majorities of high schoolers report alcohol, cigarettes, firearms, sex, and other risk enhancers are easy to obtain and/or frequently indulged that those who abstain must be doing so voluntarily. If self-reports such as Monitoring the Future's . . . indicating adolescents experience widespread opportunities to take risks are creditable, then, it's hard to attribute the day-to-day safety of the overwhelming majority of teenagers to anything other than self-restraint. The argument that legal protections and supervision shield adolescents from the opportunities to engage in risky behaviors does not explain why, as noted later, teenagers do commit crimes and get in car wrecks at higher rates than adults do but experience lower rates of other risks.

Because adolescents of the ages that developmentalists and biodeterminists predict would be suffering the highest risks actually display relatively safe behavior, theorists have extended the definition of "adolescence" into the 18 to 25 age range when, paradoxically, risk outcomes are worse even though puberty is long past and cognitive controls more advanced. Indeed, Giedd . . . has questioned the rights of young people to vote before the age of 25 years and both Giedd and Steinberg . . . have questioned the rights of young people to drive before that age, though neither has produced research findings justifying such radical assertions. In any case, the peculiar reality is that "adolescent risk taking" now is driven by emerging adults, not adolescents. Adding in statistics of age group 18 to 25 years or 20 to 24 years to artificially boost adolescent and teenage risk numbers should no longer be tolerated in the literature.

What Behaviors Define "Risk Taking?"

Beyond the extension of adolescence well into adulthood, the second troubling question involves why only certain risk behaviors, and only when adolescents engage in them, are considered evidence for biodeterminist theories. If the prevalence of certain risk behaviors demonstrates teenagers' developmental and/or cognitive immaturity, then how do we explain the similar or greater prevalence of these same or equally perilous behaviors in adult populations? For example, teenagers display lower risks than do adults for outcomes such as suicide, drug overdose, and accidents in general. . . . Why not use these measures as indexes of "risk taking?" We might then term teenagers' relative safety *adolescent prudence* and credit the cautionary influence of the amygdala.

Even when assessing the same behavior, characterizations of teenage and adult risks often seem inconsistent. For example, claims that teenagers' greater tendency than adults to commit crimes in groups demonstrates the developmental dangers of youthful peer associations become dubious when applied to similar variations by race. The National Crime Victimization Survey . . . , considered our best measure of crime, shows that victims report that around one fourth of the violent offenses perceived as involving offenders less than the age of 21 years were perpetrated by groups, triple the proportion for perceived older offenders. However, in addition to showing massive declines in group offending by teens in recent decades, the same survey shows an even larger proportion (one third) of violent offenses by perceived African American offenders of all ages involved groups. The most logical inference is that group offending is a feature not of age or race, but of conditions common to both Blacks and young people, such as high rates of poverty.

In a particularly strange assertion, Steinberg . . . argues that adolescents' low rates of suicide do not imply low risks; rather, the fact that "the rate of attempted suicide is higher among teenagers than adults" . . . means "adolescents take more risks; adults are merely more competent, so to speak—consistent with the brain science." . . . True, teens in the age group of 15 to 19 years perpetrate around 40 self-inflicted injuries requiring medical attention for every actual suicide, compared with a 10:1 ratio for adults aged from 25 to 64 years. . . . But the NCIPC also reports 33 suicide "attempts" per completion for women of all ages versus 6 for men. If we accept Steinberg's logic that greater success in committing suicide reflects greater cognitive competence, then male brains are far more competent at every age than females'; teenage boys are more competent than women in their 30s and 40s; Whites' brains are more competent than those of Blacks; and Black females of all ages (averaging over 60 attempts for every suicide) are the least biologically competent of all. Alternatively, we could look at "suicide attempts" not as evidence of cognitive incompetence but as stemming from motives other than to die, as research on survivors finds. . . .

Similarly, a small study (widely cited in media stories) reported that adolescents perceived a wider variety of emotions in pictured "fearful faces" than adults did, yielding researchers' assertion that teenagers' reliance on the brain's "primitive" amygdala leads them to misjudge basic social cues such as fear. . . . However, similar picture-image studies have found that economically disadvantaged subjects also are more prone to interpret facial expressions as communicating aggressiveness . . . , suggesting that reactions to facial expressions stem more from differing social environments than differing brains. Likewise, video-game simulation experiments supposedly showing that teenagers react in more reckless, peer-pressured, unempathic, lazy, or otherwise objectionable ways compared with adults . . . may "have nothing to do with the process of emotions and everything to do with a difference in the way teenagers process *simulations*" stemming from "generational differences in the experience teenagers and adults have" with visual media. . . . Notably, even large racial differences in risk taking found in these studies . . . are not similarly attributed to brain differences.

Still another contradiction involves positing teenage behavior as "risky" if it fails to meet absolute standards of perfection.

More than 90% of all American high school students have had sex, drug, and driver education in their schools, yet large proportions of them still have unsafe sex, binge drink, smoke cigarettes, and drive recklessly (some all at the same time). . . .

Antidrunken driving, antidrug, safe sex, and similar messages have also been directed at grown-ups, yet tens of millions of adults engage in risky behaviors now extending well into middle age. It seems peculiar to brand "incompetent" adolescents as reckless for failing to meet standards stricter than those expected of "competent" grown-ups.

Ignoring Socioeconomic Context

Teenage brain and adolescent risk-taking theories seem to have been developed with a disregard for alternative explanations. "Brain research needs to be pulled alongside other established cognitive and sociological research, rather than common prejudice," Sercombe . . . contends. Risk outcomes must be assessed not as absolutes but in the context of risk exposure—that is, the social factors governing teens' and adults' risk opportunities. Yet when behavior contexts are incorporated into the analysis, the entire "adolescent risk taking" construct becomes shaky indeed. Researchers who assert unique adolescent risk, whether blaming it on biology, peer pressure, developmental singularities, or some combination have failed to control even for the most rudimentary socioeconomic conditions.

Let us examine the two major behaviors cited by Steinberg and widely considered gold standards of adolescent risk: crime and automobile crashes. Compared straight across, older adolescents and emerging adults aged from 16 and 19 years do indeed display worse rates than do older adults for these behaviors. But even if we accept criminal arrest and traffic crashes as seminal indexes of risk, how do we know older adolescents' worse outcomes result from their teen age and not some other covariate? After all, males, African Americans, and urban dwellers of all ages display high arrest rates and males, Southerners, and Native Americans suffer excess traffic fatality, yet very few scientists (any longer) blame these on inferior biologies. Compelling warning signs loom that teenagers' higher rates of criminal arrest and traffic accidents are not "adolescent" at all. Here, I will cite California's statistics, which are similar in magnitude and provided in greater demographic detail compared with those nationally.

If adolescents were generically miswired, we would expect teenagers from varied backgrounds to act more like each other and less like adults—in mathematical terms, the within-group risk variation for separate adolescent populations should be significantly less than the between-group risk variations for adolescent versus adult populations. Yet the opposite is the case. At the microlevel, teenagers from unstable, violent, drug- and alcohol-abusing, tobacco-using, mentally troubled families and communities are many times more likely to display corresponding problems than teenagers from nurturing, peaceful, healthy, nonsmoking homes, and communities. . . .

These parallels also show up in macrostatistics. The state-by-state correlations between teenage and adult rates of drinking, binge drinking, smoking, marijuana use, unwed births, drunken-driving deaths, firearms deaths, homicide, suicide, criminal arrest, and a host of other major risks are powerful, ranging from 0.70 to 0.95. . . . If teenage and adult brains reason so fundamentally differently, we would not expect teenage behaviors to be better predicted by the behaviors of adults around them than by those of teenagers elsewhere.

If there is a consensus of literature and statistics, it is that teenage troubles are not randomly distributed, but highly concentrated. Most serious risks track socioeconomic inequalities more closely than age. For example,

- California's Black adolescents suffer felony arrest rates five times higher, including murder arrest rates 14 times higher, than do White non-Hispanic adolescents. The felony arrest rate for older African Americans (ages 30 to 69 years) is double that of older White teens, including homicide arrest rates four times higher. . . .
- Firearms homicide death rates are 25 times higher among California teens in areas in which adolescent poverty rates exceed 30% than among teenagers in areas in which their poverty levels are below 5%. African Americans in their 50s and 60s suffer gun murder rates five times higher than even the riskiest ages of White teens and emerging adults, while White teens have lower firearms mortality rates than every age group of White adults. . . .
- Teen drivers aged between 16 to 19 years in California's poorest major counties suffer fatal traffic crash rates averaging six times higher per mile driven (the best measure of risk exposure) than teens in the richest counties. Middle-aged adults in poorer counties suffer fatal crash rates averaging three times higher per mile driven than do teenagers in wealthier counties. . . .

Such wide variations in behavior within all ages along socioeconomic lines should raise a red flag to those asserting unique adolescent risk. . . .

Socioeconomic status predicts risk outcome more consistently than age. When poverty rates are held constant for California's major counties, adolescents and emerging adults even at the riskiest ages generally are less prone to risk taking than are middle-aged adults, with adults aged from 25 and 39 years, in between. For many serious risks—including, murder, rape, and assault arrest; homicide and motor vehicle death; and external injury—adolescents' and middle-aged adults' rates become startlingly similar under equalized levels of poverty. Some adolescent and emerging adult excesses do remain; robbery arrest, property crime arrest, and firearms injury (but not death) rates remain higher for older adolescents than for middle-agers. However, these teenage risks are dwarfed by middle-agers' much higher rates of risk outcome across a broad spectrum: violent death, accidental death, suicide, drug overdose, and firearms death as well as white-collar crimes that cost society far more than street crime. If "the cognitive control system of adults is more effective than that of adolescents" and "some things just take time to develop, and, like it or not, mature judgment is probably one of them" . . ., why do adults do such dumb things?

The best generalization seems to be that most risks are tied to external conditions, and each age level displays its own particular hazards. In short, "adolescent risk" disappears on a level playing field. Unfortunately, the field is far from level. More than any other Western society, American grown-ups render youth a time of poverty and middle age a time of wealth, a political choice exposing our young to greater dangers. This suggests that claims of innate "adolescent risk" and "teenage brain" flaws not only reflect "a bias in interpretation that privileges the age, class, and culture position of the researcher" . . . but serve to defend older age groups' economic privileges as well.

The Danger of New "Adolescent Science"

Theories affirming innate adolescent risk-taking benefit adults in many ways. "By emphasizing the irrationality and disturbance of young people we affirm our own basic rationality, peacefulness, conformity, and decency." . . . Biodeterminist claims about adolescents shift attention away from social inequalities that form the genuine bases for the risky behaviors now mislabeled "adolescent risk," including the large and widening gap between the economic fortunes of young versus middle-aged Americans. They allow the dismissal of unsettling youthful complaints against adults as merely the products of faulty teenage thinking. . . . They obscure the troubling eruptions in drug abuse, criminal arrest, imprisonment, HIV, family breakup, and related difficulties among middle-aged Americans over the last 25 to 35 years.

Ever-more restrictive policies against young people are being proposed and rationalized by claims that "new scientific discoveries" show teenagers and even emerging adults must be custodialized like children rather than afforded adult rights. The United States has instituted an unprecedented barrage of youth-control measures that are increasing in prevalence and intensity even as long-term research finds them ineffective or even harmful. Raising drinking ages to 21 years was initially associated with reduced traffic crashes among 18- to 20-year-olds, but later study associated it with even greater increases among 21- to 24-year-olds. . . . Graduated driver licensing laws were followed by fewer traffic deaths among 16-year-olds, but 18-year-old driver fatalities rose even more sharply. . . . Mandatory drug testing of public school students not only has proven ineffective, it may foster greater use of harder, less detectible drugs. . . . Research consistently finds curfews neither improve youth safety nor reduce crime. . . . School uniforms and zero tolerance policies are associated with negative effects on school participation and academics and no demonstrable benefits. . . . Policies banning teenagers and emerging adults from legally acquiring lodging, transportation, and an increasing array of products, services, and medications pose distinct threats to their well-being.

Far from justifying antiprecocity measures, emerging brain science, viewed in social contexts, indicates the dangers of efforts to restrict youth and to banish them from adult behaviors and public spaces. Preliminary analyses of brain physiology suggest that "taking risks is precisely the experience that develops the pre frontal cortex . . . you don't learn what you need for adulthood by being excluded from it until you can demonstrate that you have got the right circuits." . . . Viewed as a system, American social and health policies built on age-segregating measures may well be contributors to the extraordinarily high-risk behaviors prevailing among American youths and adults well into middle age compared with their counterparts in peer nations.

There may be a price to pay in the adaptability of larger society as well. If brain science is to be credited with biodeterminist findings, neuroscannings and cognitive tests reveal developments in the middle-aged brain that make worry over teenage brains look silly. Significant losses in key memory and learning genes . . ., mental fluidity . . ., and measurable losses in IQ show up in middle age and accelerate in senior years. Although some research indicates that myelinization (the pruning and selection of certain cerebral nerve fibers for myelin sheathing) aids adult brains in handling familiar situations more efficiently, it also renders them less able to address new challenges than more flexibly circuited younger brains. Adults' difficulty in changing unhealthy behaviors as they age could be seen as a brain-based developmental stage promoting greater risk taking.

That young people's "brains are different because the experience of young people is different" than that of older adults . . . confers distinct advantages in a changing, diversifying society. In the face of aging adults "managing clumsily and often unsuccessfully the tasks imposed on them by the new conditions" argued Mead . . ., changing societies must learn to share leadership with the more flexible young informed by "experiential knowledge." Unfortunately, both young people's well-being and the adaptive value to a changing society of integrating the diverse capacities of older and younger thinking are threatened by today's resurgence of biological determinism that, like its discredited predecessors, reveals more popular prejudice than scientific rigor. . . .

CHALLENGE QUESTIONS

Does the Adolescent Brain Make Risk Taking Inevitable?

- Is the debate about the adolescent brain just another version of the old debate about whether teens are at the mercy of "raging hormones?"
- Steinberg focuses on age differences in risk-taking, where Males focuses on socioeconomic differences; what are the relative advantages for understanding development of each approach?
- Males argues that claims of adolescent risk-taking are exaggerated because many researchers include young adults in their calculations. How do the teenage years seem meaningfully different from young adulthood in regard to risk-taking, and is that enough to explain this controversy?
- What qualifies as "risk-taking" in adolescence? Why does Males think researchers often manipulate categories of risk to suggest adolescents take more risks?
- Both authors discuss the public policy implications of their perspectives; what are the important public policies that might change depending on how we come to understand adolescent risk-taking?

Suggested Readings

J. Bessant, "Hard Wired for Risk: Neurological Science, 'the Adolescent Brain' and Developmental Theory," *Journal of Youth Studies* (June 2008)

R. Epstein, "The Myth of the Teen Brain," *Scientific American Mind* (April 2007)

J.N. Giedd, "The Teen Brain: Insights from Neuroimaging," *Journal of Adolescent Health*, (April 2008)

D. Yurgelun-Todd, "Emotional and Cognitive Changes during Adolescence," *Current Opinion in Neurobiology* (April 2007)

M. Payne, "'Teen Brain' Science and the Contemporary Storying of Psychological (Im)maturity," *inter-disiplinary.net* (July 2009)

D. Offer and K.A. Schonert-Reichl, "Debunking the Myths of Adolescence: Findings from Recent Research," *Journal of the American Academy of Child and Adolescent Psychiatry* (November 1992)

L Steinberg, "A Social Neuroscience Perspective on Adolescent Risk-taking," *Developmental Review* (March 2008)

M. Gardner and L. Steinberg, "Peer influence on risk-taking, risk preference, and risky decision-making in adolescence and adulthood: An experimental study," *Developmental Psychology* (July 2005)

R. Restak, *The secret life of the brain* (Joseph Henry 2001)

J.J. Arnett, "Adolescent storm and stress, reconsidered," *American Psychologist* (May 1999)

Internet References . . .

The Forum for Youth Investment

The Forum for Youth Investment uses research to promote the idea that all young people should be "Ready by 21" and offers a variety of related information on their Web site.

http://www.forumforyouthinvestment.org/

The Network on Transitions to Adulthood

The Network on Transitions to Adulthood is a scholarly effort sponsored by the MacArthur Foundation and offers data and resources at their Web site.

http://www.transad.pop.upenn.edu/

The Narcissism Epidemic

The Web site for the book *The Narcissism Epidemic* by Jean Twenge and W. Keith Campbell offers information about related research.

http://www.narcissismepidemic.com/

All Kinds of Minds Organization

A page on the Web site of Dr. Mel Levine's "All Kinds of Minds" organization, this is a summary of his book about "work-life unreadiness."

http://www.allkindsofminds.org/product/Summary_ReadyOrNot.aspx

Jeffrey Arnett on Emerging Adulthood

A list of useful references related to "emerging adulthood" by the originator of the concept, Jeffrey Jensen Arnett.

http://www.jeffreyarnett.com/articles.htm

The Society for the Study of Emerging Adulthood

This Web site is the home for a relatively new scholarly group named the Society for the Study of Emerging Adulthood.

http://www.ssea.org/

Emerging Adulthood Blog

An academic's blog about emerging adulthood as a life-span stage between adolescence and adulthood.

http://emergingadulthood.blogspot.com/

Transition to Adulthood

This site is the homepage for an academic network studying changes in the transition to adulthood.

http://www.transad.pop.upenn.edu/

Youth and Emerging Adulthood

*W*hile we often talk about "youth" in everyday conversation, it is an ill-defined concept as a stage of the life-span. Generally, "youth" refers to a period when a person is developing the characteristics of adulthood but does not yet have adult responsibilities (such as a career and marriage) nor the full psychological sense of responsibility. In many contemporary societies this period of life seems longer and more intense because of increasing educational expectations, later average ages for starting a family, and more time allocated to self-exploration. Thus, youth and early adulthood are primarily times where people gradually make the transition to fully adult roles. That transition involves both psychological and practical challenges, several of which are dealt with in the issues covered in this section.

- Is There a "Narcissism Epidemic" Among Contemporary Young Adults?
- Are College Graduates Unprepared for Adulthood and the World of Work?
- Is There Such a Thing as "Emerging Adulthood"?

ISSUE 12

Is There a "Narcissism Epidemic" Among Contemporary Young Adults?

YES: Jean M. Twenge and Joshua D. Foster, from "Mapping the scale of the narcissism epidemic: Increases in narcissism 2002–2007 within ethnic groups." *Journal of Research in Personality* (December 2008)

NO: M. Brent Donnellan, Kali H. Trzesniewski, and Richard W. Robins, from "An emerging epidemic of narcissism or much ado about nothing?" *Journal of Research in Personality* (June 2009)

ISSUE SUMMARY

YES: Jean M. Twenge and Joshua D. Foster present evidence from surveys of college students that reinforces their claim of a "narcissism epidemic."

NO: Research psychologists M. Brent Donnellan, Kali H. Trzesniewski, and Richard W. Robins take the evidence used by Twenge and colleagues and draw different conclusions, arguing claims of an epidemic are greatly exaggerated.

In the hit 2004 Disney movie *The Incredibles,* Dash, the boy child in a family of superheroes, finds himself frustrated by his mother's insistence that he not use his super-speed to beat other children in running races—despite his father telling him his powers make him "special." His mother explains to Dash that beating the other children would make them feel bad, and that "everyone's special." "Which," according to Dash, "is another way of saying that nobody is." Though the movie was imaginary, it touches on a very real issue for contemporary children and youth: emphasizing the idea that "everyone is special" may create a culture where young people believe they are extraordinary regardless of their actual accomplishments or aptitudes.

Many scholars attribute the contemporary emphasis on ways that "everyone is special" to the prominence of the self-esteem movement and to the importance of individualism in Western cultures. Although the value of individual rights have long been emphasized, there is a sense that the priority on individualism in contemporary society is new and extreme. Self-reflection, self-awareness, and self-esteem are now considered basic needs. Jean Twenge points out in her 2006 book *Generation Me*, in the 1950's only 12 percent of teenagers agreed with the statement "I am an important person," but thirty years later 80 percent of teenagers agreed with the same statement.

Twenge thinks our contemporary emphasis on self-esteem and individualism has created an entire group characterized by self-absorption: a phenomena leading her, along with psychologist W. Keith Campbell, to title their 2009 book *The Narcissism Epidemic*. Narcissism, according the book's Web site, "is a positive, inflated and grandiose sense of self . . . Along with this inflated sense of self is a lack of warm, emotionally intimate or caring relationships with others. This does not mean a lack of social relationships—often the opposite is the case—but a lack of emotionally deep relationships." Psychologists also have a technical classification for "Narcissistic Personality Disorder" that highlights the traits associated with narcissism as problematic for normal functioning.

M. Brent Donnellan, Kali H. Trzesniewski, and Richard W. Robins, think that claims of a narcissism epidemic are an exaggeration. They have engaged in an ongoing empirical debate with Twenge and colleagues, consistently taking similar data and drawing very different conclusions. While Donnellan and colleagues acknowledge there may be some small generational differences for a few specific groups in scores on narcissism inventories, they question whether those differences are meaningful enough to warrant claims of an epidemic that describes an entire generation.

The broader issue here relates to other controversial questions in the study of life-span development. The fact that there may be significant differences in narcissism between ethnic groups, for example, raises questions about the influence of cultural differences in child rearing. In addition, the question of whether the term "generation me" is accurate relates to questions about how to characterize age groups at any point in the life-span. And finally, the broad question of self-esteem has been the subject of much debate. Scholars have realized that while emphasizing self-esteem for children is popular, that emphasis produces mixed results.

POINT

- National data suggests that college students' scores on the Narcissistic Personality Inventory have risen significantly between 1982 and 2006.

- Other data suggesting few cohort changes in narcissism have not adequately accounted for differences between ethnic groups.

- Though Asian-American students score lower overall on narcissism than other ethnic groups, within ethnic groups narcissism scores have increased significantly even if only considering the years between 2002 and 2007.

COUNTERPOINT

- The evidence of a "narcissism epidemic" is mixed, depending on who has analyzed the data.

- Claims of generational changes would not fit with differences between 2002 and 2007—since those young adults would essentially be of the same generation.

- When looking at changes in scores on sub-scales of the Narcissistic Personality Inventory, there seem to be no significant differences in "entitlement"—which would likely be the most harmful characteristic of narcissism.

YES ↵ Jean M. Twenge, Joshua D. Foster

Mapping the Scale of the Narcissism Epidemic: Increases in Narcissism 2002–2007 within Ethnic Groups

1. Introduction

Several authors have argued that American culture has become more individualistic over the past few decades. . . . Perhaps as a result, young people's self-views have grown more positive and agentic over the generations. . . . But has young Americans' increasing individualism recently crossed the line into narcissism?

Two recent papers reported conflicting findings on whether narcissism has increased among American college students during the past 25 years. Twenge, Konrath, Foster, Campbell, and Bushman . . . found that Narcissistic Personality Inventory (NPI) scores rose by 0.33 standard deviations between 1982 and 2006 among 16,475 students attending 31 colleges throughout the United States. However, Trzesniewski, Donnellan, and Robins . . . found that NPI scores remained unchanged between 1982 and 2007 in samples of 26,887 college students from the University of California (primarily UC Davis). Trzesniewski et al.'s paper received widespread media attention, including stories in *The New York Times* and *USA Today,* with the *Times* declaring that "young Americans are not more self-absorbed than earlier generations, according to new research challenging the prevailing wisdom".

In our reply to their set of results . . . , we argued that Trzesniewski et al. . . . failed to find an increase in narcissism because Asian-American enrollment at the UC campuses nearly doubled over the time of their investigation, and Asians typically score lower on individualistic traits . . . , including narcissism. . . . For example, among college age (18–23) participants in Foster et al.'s . . . data, Asian-Americans scored 0.21 SDs lower on the NPI than White Americans. Thus as proportionally more Asian-American students entered the samples used by Trzesniewski et al., NPI means would appear to remain constant (or go down) even if scores within ethnic groups actually increased.

Unfortunately, Trzesniewski et al. did not report their data broken down by ethnic group. Trzesniewski et al. did report that the interaction between

From *Journal of Research in Personality,* Vol. 42, 2008, pp. 1619–1622. Copyright © 2008 by Elsevier Ltd. Reprinted by permission.

ethnicity and time was not significant. However, that is a different question: If NPI means increased similarly within each ethnic group, there would indeed be no interaction between time and ethnicity. Examining the pattern of change within ethnic groups, however, eliminates the possible confound of samples changing in ethnic composition over time (e.g., the percentage of Asian-Americans in the samples rising over time). Both generational differences and ethnic group membership reflect the impact of culture on the individual. . . . These effects can be additive (or, in this case, subtractive), so if both change over time, generational effects might not appear. Because ethnicity data were only available for the 2002–2007 samples, we examined change in NPI scores over only this 5-year period, another difference from Trzesniewski et al., who concentrated on the change between 1982 and 2007.

2. Method

Trzesniewski et al. graciously provided the NPI means for their UC Davis samples separated into four ethnic groups: Whites, Blacks, Hispanics, and Asians. Respondents who did not answer the ethnicity question or who chose "other" are not included in this analysis. Trzesniewski et al. noted that means broken down by ethnic group were only available for the 2002–2007 samples; thus the 1996 and 1979–1985 datapoints from their paper are not included here. The 1979–1985 datapoint is from Raskin and Terry . . . , also the first datapoint in the Twenge et al. . . . analysis, and Raskin and Terry did not report means by ethnic group nor the percentage of their sample from each ethnic group. The participants in the present analysis, collected every year 2002–2007 in introductory psychology classes at UC Davis, were 48.3% Asian-American, 37.6% White, 11.4% Hispanic, and 2.7% Black.

3. Results and Discussion

We examine two questions critical to our theory: (1) Did Asian-Americans score lower on the NPI than other ethnic groups in Trzesniewski et al. . . . samples of UC Davis undergraduates? And, more importantly, (2) did narcissism increase over time among UC Davis undergraduates when examined within ethnic group?

The answers to both questions were unambiguous. First, using all of the data from 2002 to 2007, Asian-American undergraduates at UC Davis ($M = 13.75$, SD = 6.85, $n = 9969$) scored significantly lower in narcissism than Whites ($M = 15.77$, SD = 6.82, $n = 7747$), $t(17,715) = 19.50$, $p < .001$, $d = 0.30$, and lower than Whites, Hispanics, and Blacks combined ($M = 15.97$, SD = 6.78, $n = 10,658$), $t(20,626) = 23.40$, $p < .001$, $d = 0.33$.

Second, when the data were separated by ethnicity, the UC Davis samples showed a significant increase in narcissism between 2002 and 2007. White students' NPI scores increased significantly between 2002 ($M = 15.30$, SD = 6.59) and 2007 ($M = 16.42$, SD = 7.05), $t(1916) = 3.57$, $p < .001$, $d = 0.17$. Fifty-nine percent of White students in 2007 scored higher on narcissism than the average White student in 2002. Because this change occurred over only 5 years—compared to 24 years in the Twenge et al. . . . meta-analysis—this modest d represents a large yearly increase of $d = .034$, more than twice the yearly increase in narcissism found in the Twenge et al. . . . meta-analysis ($d = .014$, which totals 0.33 over 24 years). If the 5-year change in the Davis samples continued for 24 years, it would result in an increase of $d = 0.82$ (about 5 points on the NPI), or 81% of White students in 2007 scoring higher than the 1980s average. For comparison, this rate of change is three times larger than the increase in Americans' body mass index over the same time period, often referred to as the "obesity epidemic" ($d = 0.31$ . . .).

A regression equation for the 6 yearly means weighted by sample size also showed a significant effect for year among Whites, Beta $= .96$, $p < .002$; using the individual-level SD, the $d = 0.14$. These results are consistent with Twenge et al. . . . , which found that the rise in narcissism was apparently accelerating in recent years, with an increase of $d = 0.18$ between 2000 and 2006 (a year-by-year change of $d = 0.03$, vs. $d = 0.014$ for 1982–2006).

Asian-Americans' narcissism scores also increased significantly from 2002 ($M = 13.26$, SD $= 6.67$) to 2007 ($M = 14.04$, SD $= 6.93$), $t(2416) = 2.81$, $p < .01$, $d = 0.12$, with 57% of Asian students in 2007 scoring higher than the average Asian student in 2002 (extrapolated for 24 years, $d = 0.58$, or 74% of Asian 2007 students scoring higher than the average Asian student in the 1980s). The regression equation yielded Beta $= .68$, $p = .14$, $d = 0.07$. With lower n's,

Figure 1

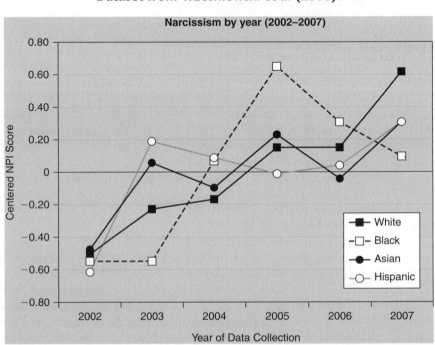

NPI scores at UC Davis 2002–2007, centered within ethnic group. Dataset from Trzesniewski et al (2008).

the *t*-tests for year among Hispanic and Black students were not significant, though the trends were in the same direction ($d = 0.14$ for Hispanics, with Beta = .72, $p = .10$; and $d = 0.10$ for Blacks, with Beta = .56, $p = .25$). Fig. 1 shows the data centered within ethnic group, illustrating the change over time within each ethnic group. Because the change was similar across ethnic groups, this is consistent with Trzesniewski et al.'s . . . finding that time by ethnicity did not produce a significant interaction.

Even when the data are collapsed across ethnicity, UC Davis students' NPI scores were higher in 2007 ($M = 15.24$, SD = 6.90) than in 2002 ($M = 14.48$, SD = 6.65), $t(5051) = 3.99$, $p < .001$, $d = 0.11$. This is a yearly change of $d = .022$, still larger than the yearly increase found in Twenge et al. . . ., and would total $d = 0.53$ over 24 years. Across all six datapoints, the Beta for year was .79, $p = .06$; using the individual-level SD, $d = 0.08$. This change is smaller than those within ethnic groups, but is still significant.

Why did Trzesniewski et al. . . . come to different conclusions?[1] Analyzing the data within ethnic groups to avoid the confound of changing popula- tions explains only some of the discrepancy. The difference in our conclusions is not due to using means vs. individual-level data, as Trzesniewski et al. . . . argued,[2] as those analyses yield identical results (e.g., for Whites, the regres- sion equation using means produces $d = 0.14$, the same as the regression equa- tion Trzesniewski et al. . . . provided to us that used individual-level data). One clear difference between our approaches is that Trzesniewski et al. . . . did not report analyses examining change over time between 2002 and 2007, only over the entire time period 1982–2007.

Because ethnic breakdowns were not available before 2002, we cannot be sure how narcissism changed at the UC campuses before that time. Although the overall mean from UC Davis in 2007 was similar to the 1979–1985 mean for UC Berkeley and UC Santa Cruz . . . , Asian-American enrollment doubled (and White enrollment was cut in half) at the UCs between the early 1980s and 2007. Raskin and Terry did not report the ethnic makeup of their sample, but Asian-Americans were 23% and Whites 61% of Berkeley undergraduates in 1983, compared to 52% Asian and 38% White in the 2007 Davis data (note that this excludes those who identified their ethnic group as "other".) This is a much larger shift in ethnic composition than that between 2002 and 2007 (from 44% to 52% Asian), and we do not know what impact these changes had on NPI scores—even for non-Asian students, if the shift in ethnic compo- sition created a different campus culture. In addition, Berkeley and Davis are different campuses with different cultures and populations; this is a particular problem because year is perfectly confounded with campus in Trzesniewski et al. . . . dataset (the two earliest datapoints are from Santa Cruz and Berkeley and the last six are from Davis). Thus the lack of change between 1979 and 2002 could be caused by the switch from one campus to another. Another problem is the small number of samples in Trzesniewski et al. . . . dataset, with just two datapoints for the 22-year period between 1979 and 2001, and only one between 1996 and 2001. This sparse coverage, combined with the changes in ethnic composition and the change in campus, make it very difficult to draw conclusions about changes in narcissism in this dataset before 2002. Another difficulty in discerning the pattern of change is that the Davis NPI means are outliers compared to means from other campuses. Recent Davis students ($M =$ 15.24) score significantly lower than recent students from other campuses [M = 17.65 for 2006 from the Twenge et al. . . . meta-analysis], $t(3625) = 9.64$, $p <$ .001, $d = .35$. This is not solely due to ethnic composition; even the White students at Davis score lower ($M = 16.42$ in 2007). Thus it is not possible to combine the Davis means with the nationwide data to examine change across both datasets; the two must be examined separately.

The 85 college student samples available nationwide show an increase in narcissism between the early 1980s and 2006. . . . The trends in our data and that of Trzesniewski et al. lead to the conclusion that narcissism increased nationwide among college students between the early 1980s and 2006 and increased at UC Davis between 2002 and 2007. . . .

Notes

1. Trzesniewski et al. . . . also reported finding no change in self-enhancement over the generations in a nationally representative dataset of high school students. Most measures of self-enhancement use the residual of subjective performance and objective performance. In this dataset, however, Trzesniewski et al. . . . relied on self-reported high school grades as the measure of "objective" performance rather than SAT scores, transcripts, or GPA reported by others. Thus it is difficult to interpret these results (see Twenge et al. . . . for further discussion of this issue).

2. Trzesniewski et al. . . . incorrectly state that cross-temporal meta-analysis [the technique used in Twenge et al. . . .] commits the ecological fallacy (or alerting correlations . . .), in which mean-level data shows larger changes because the standard deviation (SD) of groups is lower than that of individuals. However, cross-temporal meta-analysis does not calculate the effect size using the correlation or Beta. Instead, it uses the unstandardized B and the SD of the individual samples—the variance in a sample of people—*not* the SD among groups. Thus the ecological fallacy is not an issue. We use the same technique here for calculating the d for change in mean-level data regressions, relying on the individual-level SD.

M. Brent Donnellan, Kali H. Trzesniewski, Richard W. Robins

 **NO**

An Emerging Epidemic of Narcissism or Much Ado About Nothing?

0. Introduction

Twenge and colleagues have recently raised concerns about an epidemic of narcissism among today's college students and Twenge . . . has argued that this increase is an unintended effect of the self-esteem movement. In fact, Twenge . . . has suggested that, "the self-esteem movement has created an army of little narcissists." . . . In a series of articles, including a recent one entitled, "Mapping the Scale of the Narcissism Epidemic" . . ., Twenge and colleagues claim that narcissism levels have been rising dramatically over the past decade or two. . . . However, the evidentiary basis of this claim has been the subject of much controversy within the scientific literature . . . as well as in the popular media. . . . The aim of this brief report is to re-examine the evidence for secular increases in narcissism in light of the issues, criticisms, and findings presented in Twenge and Foster. . . .

1. Previous Research on Secular Changes in Narcissism

In a previous article . . ., we presented data that failed to support Twenge's . . . assertion that "narcissism is much more common in recent generations." . . . Specifically, we found nearly the same average score on the 40-item Narcissistic Personality Inventory (NPI . . .) for data collected on large samples of college students: (a) from 1979 to 1985 at the University of California (UC) Berkeley and UC Santa Cruz; (b) in 1996 at UC Berkeley; and (c) from 2002–2007 at UC Davis. In a response to Trzesniewski et al. . . .; Twenge et al. . . . re-analyzed secular trends in their meta-analytic database after restricting their analyses to the seven samples from California universities (all but one sample were from UC campuses) and replicated our original finding that college students in California have not shown an increase in narcissism. In an attempt to explain this null result, Twenge and Foster . . . speculated that the secular increase in narcissism that they believe is occurring in society as a whole has been

From *Journal of Research in Personality*, Vol. 43, 2009, pp. 498–501. Copyright © 2009 by Elsevier Ltd. Reprinted by permission.

obscured at California universities because of countervailing increases in the proportion of Asian-American students, who tend to score lower on measures of narcissism than White students.

Whether secular trends vary across racial/ethnic groups is an important question, albeit one that has been largely ignored by all of the participants in this debate . . . did not evaluate ethnicity as a moderator of secular trends in their meta-analysis). In Trzesniewski et al. . . ., we reported that Asian–Americans students scored lower on the NPI than White students, but we found no evidence that ethnicity moderated the secular trends. However, based on a reanalysis of our UC Davis data (the only data for which ethnicity was available to them), Twenge and Foster . . . concluded that narcissism levels actually increased from 2002 to 2007 for Whites and Asian Americans (but not African Americans or Latinos/as). They interpreted this result as supporting their contention that there is an epidemic of narcissism among today's college students.

The goal of this brief report is to revisit this question of whether there is an epidemic of narcissism among today's youth by examining changes in narcissism from 1996 to 2008 as a function of ethnicity using potentially more meaningful and easier to understand effect size measures. In addition, we examined whether any observed trends held across gender and across several specific facets of narcissism.

2. Method

NPI scores were drawn from prescreening sessions conducted at U.C. Berkeley in 1996 and at U.C. Davis from 2002 to 2008. We restricted the analyses to the 30,073 participants between 18 and 24 years of age who completed the NPI and self-identified their racial/ethnic background. The dataset used for some of these analyses differs from the dataset analyzed by Twenge and Foster . . . with additional data collected in 2007 ($n = 2025$) and 2008 ($n = 2405$) and with ethnicity data analyzed for the 1996 sample ($n = 571$).[1] Given the number of comparisons and the large sample sizes we set the alpha level to 0.01 to evaluate statistical significance.

3. Results

There are two general ways to analyze secular trends in narcissism. First, mean scores can be computed each year and then correlated with year of data collection. This analysis produces what is referred to as an "ecological correlation" (the N in these analyses is the number of years that data were collected). Second, the individual participants' scores can be correlated with the year each score was collected (the N in these analyses is the number of participants). This kind of analysis produces the kind of correlation coefficient that is commonly used in personality research (i.e. the unit of analysis is individual scores rather than yearly averages). Both approaches presumably reflect the degree of association between narcissism levels and year of assessment, and thus tell us something about secular trends. As we will show, however, the two approaches produce dramatically different effect sizes.

The method that Twenge and Foster . . . used to obtain their most impressive effects sizes was the ecological approach. Specifically, to test their assumption that ethnicity confounds the general trend, they predicted yearly means broken down by ethnicity from the 6 years of data collection (2002–2007) reported in Trzesniewski et al. . . . From this analysis, they reported large standardized regression coefficients (i.e. correlations) for each ethnic group ($\beta = 0.96$, 0.68, 0.72, and 0.56 for Whites, Asian Americans, Latinos/as, and African Americans, respectively). One problem with the ecological approach is that the effect size can be quite large because individual-level variability is not factored into the standardization of the regression weight.[2]

When individual-level effects were computed using the second approach, the resulting standarized coefficients (i.e., correlations) were considerably smaller ($\beta = 0.045$, 0.002, 0.021, and 0.048 for Whites, Asian Americans, Latino/a, and African Americans, respectively).[3] In contrast to Twenge and Foster's analysis of the same data, these coefficients suggest that little secular change has occurred, even when the trends were analyzed within ethnic groups. Twenge and Foster . . . suggest that these small effects could amount to potentially substantial changes if they played out at the same rate over 24 or so years. However, such an extrapolation might be unwarranted given the restricted time frame moreover, it is unclear from a "generational change" perspective why college students in 2002 or 2003 should be much different from college students in 2006 or 2007.

Based on these concerns, we evaluated within-group secular changes in narcissism by extending the sample analyzed by Twenge and Foster . . . to include data from 1996, Fall 2007, and Winter and Spring of 2008. Specifically, our goal was to examine secular trends within ethnic group, within gender, and across the NPI subscales for this longer interval. Table 1 displays mean NPI scores as a function of ethnicity and year of data collection. Averages were based on a 0–40 metric for scoring the NPI. To quantify changes over time, we calculated the individual–level correlations between NPI scores and year (1996–2008). This information is reported in row labeled $r_{overall}$. For example, the association between individual scores for Whites and year of data collection was 0.019 ($p = 0.067$) and the correlation between year of data collection and NPI score in the total sample was 0.024 ($p < 0.01$). These correlations between year and NPI scores were quite small (range = 0.019–0.044) and they provided little indication of a meaningful secular increase in narcissism from 1996 to 2008.

We next analyzed the trends separately for men and women of each ethnicity. This is an instructive analysis because Twenge et al. . . . found that only women showed a statistically significant increase in NPI scores. The correlations for women are reported in the row labeled r_{women} and the correlations for men are reported in the row labeled r_{men} For example, the correlation between individual scores for White women and year of data collection was 0.021 ($p = 0.111$), whereas the corresponding correlation for White men was 0.024 ($p = 0.184$). All of the correlations were small and none exceeded 0.10, the conventional threshold for a "small" effect. As another illustration of the magnitude of the effect, year of data collection accounted for 0.1% of the variance,

Table 1

Means, Standard Deviations, and Correlations of NPI Scores with Year of Data Collection (1996–2008), Separately for Each Ethnic Group.

Year	African-American			Asian-American			Latino/a			White			"Other"			Total Sample	
	M	SD	N	M	SD	N	M	SD	N	M	SD	N	M	SD	N	M	SD
1996	18.24	5.98	28	13.53	6.84	254	15.82	6.22	82	17.78	6.71	163	14.12	5.84	44	15.35	6.86
2002	17.38	6.55	70	13.26	6.67	1133	15.51	6.82	252	15.30	6.59	1107	16.64	7.03	535	14.85	6.84
2003	17.38	6.89	109	13.79	6.92	1818	16.32	6.65	420	15.58	6.66	1644	16.57	6.93	817	15.18	6.90
2004	17.99	7.30	92	13.64	6.87	1884	16.23	6.70	438	15.64	6.88	1505	16.54	6.90	830	15.10	6.98
2005	18.58	6.23	92	13.96	6.84	1769	16.12	6.89	437	15.96	6.87	1332	16.45	7.03	777	15.31	6.97
2006	18.24	6.48	119	13.70	6.77	2080	16.17	6.61	487	15.97	6.96	1348	16.48	6.86	924	15.19	6.94
2007	18.57	6.47	125	14.34	6.98	2171	16.40	6.61	528	16.56	7.15	1287	16.76	7.11	967	15.68	7.10
2008	18.65	5.92	48	14.33	6.73	1049	16.32	6.69	267	16.00	7.00	585	17.18	6.81	456	15.58	6.89
Overall	18.12	6.56	683	13.87	6.85	12158	16.18	6.68	2911	15.88	6.87	8971	16.61	6.95	5350	15.27	6.96
	African-American			Asian-American			Latino/a			White			"Other"			Total sample	
$r_{overall}$	0.044			0.036*			0.021			.019			0.027			0.024*	
r_{women}	0.073			0.039*			0.015			.021			0.042			0.030*	
r_{men}	0.001			0.028			0.047			.024			−0.013			0.016	

Note: $r_{overall}$ is the correlation for both men and women, whereas r_{women} is the correlation for women and r_{men} is the correlation for men.

$*p < 0.01.$

whereas gender accounted for 1.2% (i.e., 12 times as much) in a regression analysis predicting NPI scores.

It is possible that only certain facets of narcissism have been increasing over time. To explore this possibility, we computed correlations between the seven NPI subscales . . . and year of data collection, separately in the total sample and for each ethnic group. The vast majority of the 42 correlations were below 0.05 (median $r = 0.017$) and none were above 0.10 (see Table 2). Of note, the weakest correlations, hovering around zero (e.g., $r = 0.005$ in the total sample, $p = 0.351$), were found for the Entitlement subscale. Konrath, Bushman, and Campbell . . . identified Entitlement as the best predictor of laboratory aggression, even outperforming the overall NPI score. Thus, this particularly socially toxic aspect of narcissism showed no increase from 1996–2008, contrary to the characterization of the current generation of college students as "Generation Me." . . .

4. Discussion

Based on the overall pattern of results in this report, we are not convinced that there has been either a widespread or a substantial secular increase in narcissism. All of the effect sizes were well below the conventional threshold for a "small" effect and, even in our very large sample, there was no statistically detectable increase for men ($p = 0.105$) or for Latinos and African Americans ($p = 0.252$ and $p = 0.253$, respectively). Although very small effects can be highly meaningful in some contexts, in the present context, we prefer to follow recommendations by Hyde . . . who has argued that Cohen's criteria . . . (e.g., 1988) for "small" ($r = 0.10$), "medium" ($r = 0.30$), and "large" ($r = 0.50$) effects are reasonable for interpreting contentious findings such as the presence of gender differences. . . . In this case, the observed correlations are even smaller than "small," which argues for erring on the side of caution before making pronouncements about an entire generation of young adults.

Moreover, it is occasionally overlooked that the secular increase in narcissism reported by Twenge et al. . . . held only for women; the association between year and mean NPI scores was not statistically detectable for men whereas it was statistically detectable for women based on their sub-analyses of the 44 studies that had information separately reported by gender (out of 85 total studies). The present analyses further hinted at this gender difference, although the trend was miniscule even for women. Thus, even if we were to accept Twenge et al.'s claim that narcissism levels are rising, this trend seems to be restricted to women. Such an apparent boundary condition raises questions about how to best interpret the reported secular effect as scores on the NPI can reflect heightened social potency as well as more socially toxic aspects of personality. . . .

Finally, we emphasize that there is nothing in any of these data that suggests an epidemic of narcissism. Why? The NPI is measured on an arbitrary metric . . . and there is no basis for declaring when an average score indicates "excessively" high levels of the characteristic in question. In fact, even in the most recent time point . . . , when the epidemic was presumably

Table 2

Correlations of NPI Sub-Scales with Year of Data Collection (1996–2008), Separately for Each Ethnic Group.

	Authority	Exhibitionism	Superiority	Entitlement	Exploitativeness	Self-sufficiency	Vanity
African–American	0.053	0.029	0.038	−0.017	−0.008	0.070	−0.004
Asian–American	0.017	0.016	0.044*	0.006	0.029*	0.037*	0.021
Latino/a	0.002	−0.003	0.056	−0.003	0.012	0.039	−0.002
White	0.011	0.013	0.022	−0.008	0.037*	−0.007	0.026
Other	0.021	−0.003	0.040*	−0.002	0.017	0.026	0.029
Total sample	0.010	0.009	0.031*	0.005	0.024*	0.020*	0.017*

$*p < 0.01$.

raging, participants on average endorsed fewer than half (about 40%) of the narcissistic responses; whether this value should be considered high or low in an absolute sense is impossible to determine with the arbitrary metric of the NPI. Indeed, claims about an "epidemic of narcissism" essentially boil down to quite small changes over a fairly restricted range of scores all of which typically average below the midpoint of the scale. Based on these considerations, we do not believe that "epidemic" is an appropriate adjective in this context.

5. Conclusion

We continue to believe that a conservative approach is warranted with respect to the empirical status of generational increases in narcissism. Our extensive analyses of data from over 30,000 participants showed uniformly small secular trends, which failed to reach statistical significance for men, for two of the four ethnic groups, and for three of the facets of narcissism. Moreover, all of the existing NPI evidence is based on convenience (i.e., non-probability) samples, and such samples are highly problematic for making inferences about trends in the general population. Thus, evidence for an increase in narcissism is far from clear-cut and there are good reasons why researchers should be wary of labeling any apparent changes in this multifaceted dimension of personality as evidence of an epidemic. . . .

Notes

1. The 1996 data were not included in the Twenge and Foster . . . analysis because ethnicity information was not readily available when requested by Dr. Foster in February of 2008. We tracked these down in light of the Twenge and Foster . . . analysis and provided them to their team in September of 2008.

2. We are not claiming the Twenge and her colleagues are committing the *ecological fallacy* with these analyses (i.e., the error of assuming that effects at an aggregated level generalize to a lower level). Rather, we are pointing out that correlating two variables at an aggregated level yields an effect size that is quite different from the traditional correlation used in personality research, which is based on individual level data. . . . Ecological correlations are typically much larger than individual-level correlations (and can even reverse signs) and it is not clear how personality researchers should interpret the magnitude of these effects.

3. These results are based on analyses conducted using the exact same set of data analyzed by Twenge and Foster . . . , which consists of the 20,627 participants between 18 to 24 years of age who completed the NPI between 2002 and Spring of 2007 and self-identified their racial/ethnic background as African American ($n = 553$), Asian American ($n = 9969$), Latino/Latina ($n = 2,358$), or White ($n = 7,747$). These regression results were also provided to Dr. Twenge in Spring of 2008.

CHALLENGE QUESTIONS

Is There a "Narcissism Epidemic" Among Contemporary Young Adults?

- What qualifies as a "generation" of young adults? What types of social forces might have influenced the increasing emphasis on self-esteem leading to the potential for "generation me?"
- Twenge thinks that high rates of narcissism among college students relate to a gradual shift toward more emphasis on the self and individualism. Are there other factors that might contribute to her findings?
- Donnellan, Trzesniewski, and Robins suggest that any increases in narcissism seem to have mostly occurred for females rather than males. Why might there be more generational change for females?
- Some of the differences between the sides for this issue are a matter of whether to be assertive or cautious when interpreting data about generational differences. What are the relative advantages and disadvantages of each approach?

Suggested Readings

J.M. Twenge, "Generation Me, The Origins of Birth Cohort Differences in Personality Traits, and Cross-Temporal Meta-Analysis," *Social and Personality Psychology Compass* (May 2008)

M.B. Donnellan and K.H. Trzeniewski, "How Should We Study Generational 'Changes'—Or Should We? A Critical Examination of the Evidence for 'Generation Me'," *Social and Personality Psychology Compass* (September 2009)

J.M. Twenge and W.K. Campbell, *The Narcissism Epidemic: Living in the Age of Entitlement* (Free Press 2009)

J.M. Twenge, *Generation Me: Why Today's Young Americans are More Confident, Assertive, Entitled—and More Miserable than ever Before* (Free Press 2006)

K.H. Trzesniewski, M.B. Donnellan, and R.W. Robins, "Do Today's Young People Really Think They Are so Extraordinary? An Examination of Secular Changes in Narcissism and Self-Enhancement," *Psychological Science* (February 2008)

K.H. Trzesniewski, M.B. Donnellan, and R.W. Robins, "Is 'Generation Me' Really More Narcissistic than Previous Generations?" *Journal of Personality* (August 2008)

E. Russ, J. Shedler, R. Bradley, and D. Westen, "Refining the Construct of Narcissistic Personality Disorder: Diagnostic Criteria and Subtypes," *American Journal of Psychiatry* (November 2008)

J. Crocker, L. Park, "The Costly Pursuit of Self-Esteem," *Psychological Bulletin* (2004)

D. DuBois, B. Flay, "The Healthy Pursuit of Self-Esteem: Comment on and Alternative to the Crocker and Park (2004) Formulation," *Psychological Bulletin* (2004)

R. Baumeister, J. Campbell, J. Krueger, K. Vohs, "Exploding the Self-Esteem Myth," *Scientific American* (January 2005)

P. Bronson, "How Not to Talk to Your Kids: The Inverse Power of Praise," *New York Magazine* (February 9, 2007)

ISSUE 13

Are College Graduates Unprepared for Adulthood and the World of Work?

YES: Mel Levine, from "College Graduates Aren't Ready for the Real World," *The Chronicle of Higher Education* (February 18, 2005)

NO: Frank F. Furstenberg et al., from "Growing Up Is Harder to Do," *Contexts* (Summer 2004)

ISSUE SUMMARY

YES: Professor of pediatrics, author, and child-rearing expert Mel Levine argues that contemporary colleges are producing a generation of young adults who are psychologically "unready" for entering adulthood and the world of work.

NO: Sociologist Frank Furstenberg and colleagues assert that major social changes have extended the transition to adulthood, and college graduates are the group most apt to cope with these social changes.

There seems to be something attractive about idealizing previous generations. In each successive cohort, there is a group of people who are convinced that the "youth today" just are not as able as those of previous decades. This concern often relates to one of the primary tasks of early adulthood—finding one's way in the world of work. One of the traditional markers of adulthood is settling into a career, and many young adults are very focused on finding a worthwhile job. In contemporary society, however, that task is more complicated than it once was because young adults often go through extensive educational training and a succession of different jobs.

Dr. Mel Levine thinks the current generation of youth, particularly recent college graduates, are unprepared and unready to be productive members of society. In researching a book, Levine undertook interviews with employers and young adults, and persistently found that college graduates were not ready for the world of work. He lays out a series of explanations for this problem—blaming colleges, parents, and the culture at large for allowing young adults to expect that fun and gratification should be easy and without rigorous dedication.

In contrast, Frank Furstenberg and his colleagues emphasize that young adulthood today cannot be understood outside of its historical context. In fact, they suggest, what is distinctive about the current generation of youth is that they face unprecedented expectations and challenges in making the transition to adulthood. Rather than being able to seamlessly move into career and family patterns that will provide stable lives, today's young adults face the expensive and challenging task of preparing themselves to enter a stunningly complex world. From Furstenberg et al.'s perspective, college graduates are the most able to take on that task.

There is no question that the nature of early adulthood and the expectations of college have changed. Just one century ago it was only elite youth that even graduated from high school. It wasn't until the 1920s that adolescents became more likely to attend high school than immediately transition to work, apprenticeships, or family responsibilities out of childhood. It wasn't until after World War II, when the GI bill paying college tuition for returning soldiers created a massive growth in the system of higher education, that college education became broadly accessible. Now, the proportion of youth who attend college is at an all-time high. Perhaps, then, it was inevitable that the role of college in creating tomorrow's adults would become controversial and essential to thinking about lifespan development.

Considering that, can we say that college graduates are reasonably well prepared for the challenges of the contemporary world of work? Or has the changing historical context accompanied reduced expectations and dysfunctional attitudes among those in early adulthood? If you are reading this as a college student, it will be important to not get defensive; note that neither author is talking about particular college students as individuals. Instead, both are concerned with what they consider to be dominant trends affecting college students as a group. The controversy is about the nature of those dominant trends. College students may ultimately be the perfect people to comment on the influences they experience in their social world.

POINT

- Employers consistently report that their young employees are not ready to earn their place, instead expecting everything to be easy.
- Young adults admit that they are not interested in hard work required at early points of a career.
- Colleges seem overly eager to coddle students, not preparing them for the challenges of the work world.
- Parents and the culture at large are now too indulgent, leading young adults to expect that they will always be treated as special.

COUNTERPOINT

- The demands of the contemporary workplace are higher than ever, and college graduates are the best prepared.
- More young adults than ever are going to college and getting higher levels of education.
- Colleges are more accessible now than in past generations, providing opportunities to more students.
- Having a stable family life in this age requires taking longer to establish one's self in the world of work.

YES ↵

Mel Levine

College Graduates Aren't Ready for the Real World

We are witnessing a pandemic of what I call "worklife unreadiness," and colleges face a daunting challenge in immunizing students against it.

Swarms of start-up adults, mostly in their 20s, lack the traction needed to engage the work side of their lives. Some can't make up their minds where to go and what to do, while others find themselves stranded along a career trail about which they are grievously naïve and for which they lack broad preparation. Whether they spent their undergraduate or graduate years focused on a discrete pursuit—say, engineering, law, or medicine—or whether their college education was unbound from any stated career intentions, many are unprepared to choose an appropriate form of work and manage their first job experience.

In conducting interviews for my new book, *Ready or Not, Here Life Comes,* I heard repeatedly from employers that their current crop of novice employees appear unable to delay gratification and think long term. They have trouble starting at the bottom rung of a career ladder and handling the unexciting detail, the grunt work, and the political setbacks they have to bear. In fact, many contemporary college and graduate students fail to identify at all with the world of adults.

A variety of unforeseen hazards can cause an unsuccessful crossover from higher education to the workplace. Start-up adults may often not even sense that they are failing to show initiative or otherwise please their superiors. Some early-career pitfalls are unique to our times; some derive from the characteristics of individual students themselves; some are side effects of modern parenting; and others result from an educational system that has not kept pace with the era we live in. All have policy implications for higher-education leaders.

The problems start early. While many of today's young adults were growing up, their role models were each other. Kids today don't know or take an interest in grown-ups, apart from their parents, their teachers, and entertainers. That stands in contrast to previous generations, when young people "studied" and valued older people in the community.

Thus, a lot of contemporary college students are insatiable in their quest for social acceptance and close identification with an esteemed gaggle of peers. The commercialization of adolescence has further fueled a desire to be "cool" and accepted and respected within a kid culture. Some young adults become the victims of their own popularity, experiencing surges and spasms of immense yet highly brittle ego inflation. But that bubble is likely to burst in early career life, when their supervisors are not all that impressed by how well they play shortstop, how they express their taste through their earrings, or the direction in which they orient the brim of their baseball caps.

Life in the dormitory or the fraternity or sorority house no doubt perpetuates and even intensifies that pattern of overreliance on peer approval. It may also serve to cultivate an overwhelming preoccupation with body image and sexual and chemical bodily excitation—at times to the detriment of intellectual development and reality-based reflection on the future. We live in a period of college education in which the body may be the mind's No.1 rival. While that tension has always existed, our culture stresses more than ever bodily perfection, self-marketing through appearance, and physical fitness over cognitive strength. Unbridled athletic fervor may reinforce such a somatically bent collegiate culture.

Meanwhile, many college students carry with them an extensive history of being overprogrammed by their parents and their middle schools and high schools—soccer practice Monday through Saturday, bassoon lessons on Tuesday evening, square dancing on Wednesday, kung fu on Saturday afternoon, on and on. That may make it hard for them to work independently, engage in original thought processes, and show initiative.

Other students were the golden girls and boys of their high schools—popular, attractive, athletic, and sometimes scholarly insofar as they were talented test takers. Yet many never had to engage in active analytic thinking, brainstorming, creative activity, or the defense of their opinions. In quite a few instances, their parents settled all their disputes with teachers, guided (or did) their homework, and filled out their college applications. As a result, such students may have trouble charting and navigating their own course in college and beyond.

Not uncommonly, start-up adults believe that everything they engage in is supposed to generate praise and fun, as opposed perhaps to being interesting or valuable. The quest for effusive verbal feedback has been a prime motivator throughout their lives, as they have sought approval from parents, teachers, and coaches. Unbridled and sometimes unearned praise may, in fact, fuel the pressure for grade inflation in college.

Similarly, students' favorite professors may well be those whose lectures are the funniest. But what if, eight years later, their bosses have no sense of humor, and their work pales in comparison to the visual and motor ecstasy of computer games and the instantaneous satisfaction of their social and sexual conquests? They might then find themselves mentally out of shape, lacking in the capacity for hard cognitive work, and unable to engage successfully in any extended mind toil that they don't feel like doing.

On top of that, some college students are afflicted with significant underlying developmental problems that have never been properly diagnosed and managed. Examples abound, including difficulties in processing language or communicating verbally (both speaking and writing), an inability to focus attention or reason, quantitatively, and a serious lack of problem-solving skills.

We are currently encountering far more students with learning difficulties, for a multitude or reasons. Many young adults are growing up in a nonverbal culture that makes few, if any, demands on language skills, active information processing, pattern recognition, and original thinking.

The most common learning disorder among undergraduates is incomplete comprehension. Affected students have difficulty understanding concepts, terminology, issues, and procedures. Many of them succeeded admirably in high school through the exclusive use of rote memory and procedural mimicry (known in mathematics as the "extreme algorithmic approach"). So a student may have received an A in trigonometry by knowing how to manipulate cosines and tangents yet without really understanding what they represent. Such underlying deficiencies return to haunt start-up adults striving for success and recognition on the job. A young adult may be selling a product without fully understanding it, or preparing a legal brief without perceiving its ramifications.

Trouble handling the workload is an equally prevalent, and lingering, form of collegiate dysfunction that follows students into their careers. Some college students are abysmally disorganized and have serious trouble managing materials and time, prioritizing, and handling activities with multiple components that must be integrated—like writing a term paper, applying to graduate schools or prospective employers, and preparing for a final examination. Such difficulties can manifest themselves for the first time at any academic stage in a student's life, including during law, business, or medical school. The students who are burdened with them are vulnerable to dropping out, mental-health problems, and a drastic loss of motivation.

Certainly many students leave college well prepared and well informed for careers, and not every college is affected by such negative cultural forces. But work-life unreadiness is increasingly prevalent and merits the attention of faculty members and administrators. The deterrents that I have mentioned may or may not ignite implosions of grade-point averages, but they can become crippling influences in the work lives of young adults.

Although colleges can't be expected to suture all the gaps in the culture of kids, some changes merit consideration if students are to succeed after graduation. Too many start-up adults harbor serious discrepancies between what they would like to do and what they are truly capable of doing. Often they are interested in pursuits they are not good at or wired for. They opt for the wrong careers because they are unaware of their personal and intellectual strengths and weaknesses, as well as woefully uninformed about the specific job demands of their chosen trades. That combination is a time bomb set to detonate early in a career.

Therefore, colleges should re-examine the adequacy of their career-placement or career-advisory services. Those services should be able to interview students in depth, administer vocational-interest inventories, and make use of sophisticated neuropsychological tests to help floundering students formulate career aims that fit their particular skills and yield personal gratification.

Colleges can also lessen undergraduate naïveté through formal education. Within a core curriculum, perhaps offered by the psychology department, colleges should help students get to know themselves and to think about the relationship between who they are and what they think they might do with their lives. They should provide, and possibly require, courses like "Career Studies," in which undergraduates analyze case studies and biographies to explore the psychological and political nuances of beginning a career.

Students need to anticipate the challenges and agonies of work life at the bottom rungs of a tall and steep ladder. They should be taught generic career-related skills—like how to collaborate, organize and manage projects, write proposals, and decrypt unwritten and unspoken on-the-job expectations. Colleges should also offer classes that cover topics like entrepreneurialism and leadership. Further, students should also receive formal instruction, including case studies, in the pros and cons of alternative career pathways within their areas of concentration (e.g., medical practice versus health-care administration, or teaching about real estate versus pursuing a money chase in land investment).

To elucidate the specific learning problems of students who are not succeeding, colleges need to offer up-to-date diagnostic services. Those include tests to pinpoint problems with memory, attention, concept formation, and other key brain processes that will cause a career to implode whether or not a student makes it through her undergraduate years.

Faculty members should change not only what they teach but *how* they teach, to help students make a better transition to the adult world. They should receive formal training in the latest research about brain development and the learning processes that occur during late adolescence—including such key areas as higher-language functioning, frontal-lobe performance (like planning, pacing, and self-monitoring), nonverbal thought processes, memory use, and selective attention.

Professors also should base their pedagogy on some awareness of the mechanisms underlying optimal learning and mastery of their subject matter. Chemistry professors should understand and make use of the cognition of chemistry mastery, while foreign-language instructors and those conducting political-science seminars should be aware of the brain functions they are tapping and strengthening through their coursework. Current students face complex decision-making and problem-solving career challenges, but many have been groomed in high school to rely solely on rote memory—an entirely useless approach in a meaningful career.

At the same time, professors must have keen insight into the differences in learning among the students who take their courses. They should seek to offer alternative ways in which students can display their knowledge and skills. They might discover, for instance, that their tests should de-emphasize rote recall and the spewing out of knowledge without any interpretation on the part of the student.

In short, faculty members must learn about teaching. It should not be assumed that a learned person understands how people learn.

What's more, colleges should offer opportunities for scholarly research into the cognitive abilities, political strategies, and skills needed for career fulfillment in various fields. The study of success and failure should be thought of as a topic worthy of rigorous investigation at all higher-education institutions.

Finally, every college should also strive to promulgate a campus intellectual life that can hold its own against social, sexual, and athletics virtuosity. Varsity debating teams should receive vigorous alumni support and status, as should literary magazines, guest lectureships, concerts, and art exhibitions. Undergraduate institutions reveal themselves by what gets tacked up on campus bulletin boards—which often are notices of keg parties, fraternity and sorority rush events, and intramural schedules. Colleges can work to change that culture.

Our colleges open their doors to kids who have grown up in an era that infiltrates them with unfettered pleasure, heavy layers of overprotection, and heaps of questionably justified positive feedback. As a result, childhood and adolescence may become nearly impossible acts to follow.

Higher education has to avoid hitching itself to that pleasure-packed bandwagon. Otherwise, students will view the academic side of college as not much more than a credentialing process to put up with while they are having a ball for four years. Colleges must never cease to ask themselves, "What roles can and should these young adults play in the world of our times? And what must we do to prepare them?"

Frank F. Furstenberg, Jr., et al.　　　➔ **NO**

Growing Up Is Harder to Do

In the past several decades, a new life stage has emerged: early adulthood. No longer adolescents, but not yet ready to assume the full responsibilities of an adult, many young people are caught between needing to learn advanced job skills and depending on their family to support them during the transition.

In the years after World War II, Americans typically assumed the full responsibilities of adulthood by their late teens or early 20s. Most young men had completed school and were working full-time, and most young women were married and raising children. People who grew up in this era of growing affluence—many of today's grandparents—were economically self-sufficient and able to care for others by the time they had weathered adolescence. Today, adulthood no longer begins when adolescence ends. Ask someone in their early 20s whether they consider themselves to be an adult, and you might get a laugh, a quizzical look, a shrug of the shoulders, or a response like that of a 24-year-old Californian: "Maybe next year. When I'm 25."

Social scientists are beginning to recognize a new phase of life: early adulthood. Some features of this stage resemble coming of age during the late 19th and early 20th centuries, when youth lingered in a state of semi-autonomy, waiting until they were sufficiently well-off to marry, have children and establish an independent household. However, there are important differences in how young people today define and achieve adulthood from those of both the recent and the more distant past.

This new stage is not merely an extension of adolescence, as has been maintained in the mass media. Young adults are physically mature and often possess impressive intellectual, social and psychological skills. Nor are young people today reluctant to accept adult responsibilities. Instead, they are busy building up their educational credentials and practical skills in an ever more demanding labor market. Most are working or studying or both, and are developing romantic relationships. Yet, many have not become fully adult—traditionally defined as finishing school, landing a job with benefits, marrying and parenting—because they are not ready, or perhaps not permitted, to do so. For a growing number, this will not happen until their late 20s or even early 30s. In response, American society will have to revise upward the "normal" age of full adulthood, and develop ways to assist young people through the ever-lengthening transition.

Among the most privileged young adults—those who receive ample support from their parents—this is a time of unparalleled freedom from family responsibilities and an opportunity for self-exploration and development. For the less advantaged, early adulthood is a time of struggle to gain the skills and credentials required for a job that can support the family they wish to start (or perhaps have already started), and a struggle to feel in control of their lives. A 30-year-old single mother from Iowa laughed when asked whether she considered herself an adult: "I don't know if I'm an adult yet. I still don't feel quite grown up. Being an adult kind of sounds like having things, everything is kind of in a routine and on track, and I don't feel like I'm quite on track."

Changing Notions of Adulthood

Traditionally, the transition to adulthood involves establishing emotional and economic independence from parents or, as historian John Modell described it, "coming into one's own." The life events that make up the transition to adulthood are accompanied by a sense of commitment, purpose and identity. Although we lack systematic evidence on how adulthood was defined in the past, it appears that marriage and parenthood represented important benchmarks. Nineteenth-century American popular fiction, journalism, sermons and self-help guides rarely referred to finishing school or getting a job, and only occasionally to leaving home or starting one's own household as the critical turning point. On the other hand, they often referred to marriage, suggesting that marriage was considered, at least by middle-class writers, as the critical touchstone of reaching adulthood.

By the 1950s and 1960s, most Americans viewed family roles and adult responsibilities as nearly synonymous. In that era, most women married before they were 21 and had at least one child before they were 23. For men, having the means to marry and support a family was the defining characteristic of adulthood, while for women, merely getting married and becoming a mother conferred adult status. As Alice Rossi explained in 1968: "On the level of cultural values, men have no freedom of choice where work is concerned: they must work to secure their status as adult men. The equivalent for women has been maternity. There is considerable pressure upon the growing girl and young woman to consider maternity necessary for a woman's fulfillment as an individual and to secure her status as an adult."

Research conducted during the late 1950s and early 1960s demonstrated widespread antipathy in America toward people who remained unmarried and toward couples who were childless by choice. However, these views began to shift in the late 1960s, rendering the transition to adulthood more ambiguous. Psychologists Joseph Veroff, Elizabeth Douvan, and Richard Kulka found that more than half of Americans interviewed in 1957 viewed someone who did not want to get married as selfish, immature, peculiar or morally flawed. By 1976, fewer than one-third of a similar sample held such views. A 1962 study found that 85 percent of mothers believed that married couples should have children. Nearly 20 years later, just 40 percent of those women still agreed, and in 1993 only 1 in 5 of their daughters agreed. Arland Thornton and Linda Young-Demarco, who have studied attitudes toward family roles during the latter half of the 20th century, conclude that "Americans increasingly value freedom and equality in their personal and family lives while at the same time maintaining their commitment to the ideals of marriage, family, and children." While still personally committed to family, Americans increasingly tolerate alternative life choices.

To understand how Americans today define adulthood, we developed a set of questions for the 2002 General Social Survey (GSS), an opinion poll administered to a nationally representative sample of Americans every two years by the National Opinion Research Center. The survey asked nearly 1,400 Americans aged 18 and older how important each of the following traditional benchmarks was to being an adult: leaving home, finishing school, getting a full-time job, becoming financially independent from one's parents, being able to support a family, marrying and becoming a parent.

The definition of adulthood that emerges today does not necessarily include marriage and parenthood. [The] most important milestones are completing school, establishing an independent household and being employed full-time—concrete steps associated with the ability to support a family. Ninety-five percent of Americans surveyed consider education, employment, financial independence and the ability to support a family to be key steps on the path to adulthood. Nonetheless, almost half of GSS respondents do not believe that it is necessary to actually marry or to have children to be considered an adult. As a young mother from San Diego explained, having a child did not make her an adult; instead she began to feel like an adult when she realized that "all of us make mistakes, but you can fix them and if you keep yourself on track, everything will come out fine." Compared with their parents and grandparents, for whom marriage and parenthood were virtually a prerequisite for becoming an adult, young people today more often view these as life choices, not requirements.

The Lengthening Road to Adulthood

Not only are the defining characteristics of adulthood changing, so is the time it takes to achieve them. To map the changing transitions to adulthood, we also examined several national surveys that contain information on young adults both in this country and abroad. Using U.S. Census data collected as far back as 1900, we compared the lives of young adults over time. We also conducted about 500 in-depth interviews with young adults living in different parts of the United States, including many in recent immigrant groups.

Our findings, as well as the work of other scholars, confirm that it takes much longer to make the transition to adulthood today than decades ago, and arguably longer than it has at any time in America's history. [Based] on the 1960 and 2000 U.S. censuses, [there is a] large decline in the percentage of young adults who, by age 20 or 30, have completed all of the traditionally-defined major adult transitions (leaving home, finishing school, becoming financially independent, getting married and having a child). We define financial independence for both men and women as being in the labor force; however, because women in 1960 rarely combined work and motherhood, married full-time mothers are also counted as financially independent in both years.

In 2000, just 46 percent of women and 31 percent of men aged 30 had completed all five transitions, compared with 77 percent of women and 65 percent of men at the same age in 1960.

Women—who have traditionally formed families at ages younger than men—show the most dramatic changes at early ages. Although almost 30 percent of 20-year-old women in 1960 had completed these transitions, just 6 percent had done so in 2000. Among 25-year-olds (not shown), the decrease is even more dramatic: 70 percent of 25-year-old women in 1960 had attained traditional adult status, in 2000 just 25 percent had done so. Yet, in 2000, even as they delayed traditional adulthood, 25-year-old women greatly increased their participation in the labor force to levels approaching those of 25-year old men. The corresponding declines for men in the attainment of traditional adult status are less striking but nonetheless significant. For both men and women, these changes can largely be explained by the increasing proportion who go to college and graduate school, and also by the postponement of marriage and childbearing.

If we use the more contemporary definition of adulthood. . . —one that excludes marriage and parenthood—then the contrasts are not as dramatic. In 2000, 70 percent of men aged 30 had left home, were financially independent, and had completed their schooling, just 12 points lower than was true of 30-year-old men in 1960. Nearly 75 percent of 30-year-old women in 2000 met this standard, compared to nearly 85 percent of women in 1960. Nonetheless, even these changes are historically substantial, and we are not even taking into account how many of these independent, working, highly educated young people still feel that they are not yet capable of supporting a family.

The reasons for this lengthening path to adulthood, John Modell has shown, range from shifting social policies to changing economic forces. The swift transition to adulthood typical after World War II was substantially assisted by the government. The GI Bill helped veterans return to school and subsidized the expansion of education. Similarly, government subsidies for affordable housing encouraged starting families earlier. At the same time, because Social Security was extended to cover more of the elderly, young people were no longer compelled to support their parents. The disappearance or reduction of such subsidies during the past few decades may help to explain the prolongation of adult transitions for some Americans. The growing cost of college and housing forces many youth into a state of semi-autonomy, accepting some support from their parents while they establish themselves economically. When a job ends or they need additional schooling or a relationship dissolves, they increasingly turn to their family for assistance. Thus, the sequencing of adult transitions has become increasingly complicated and more reversible.

However, the primary reason for a prolonged early adulthood is that it now takes much longer to secure a full-time job that pays enough to support a family. Economists Timothy Smeeding and Katherin Ross Phillips found in the mid-1990s that just 70 percent of American men aged 24 to 28 earned enough to support themselves, while fewer than half earned enough to support a family of three. Attaining a decent standard of living today usually requires a college education, if not a professional degree. To enter or remain in the middle class, it is almost imperative to make an educational commitment that spans at least the early 20s. Not only are more Americans attending college than ever before, it takes longer to complete a degree than in years past. Census data reveal that from 1960 to 2000, the percentage of Americans aged 20, 25, and 30 who were enrolled in school more than doubled. Unlike during the 1960s, these educational and work investments are now required of women as well as men. It is little wonder then that many young people linger in early adulthood, delaying marriage and parenthood until their late 20s and early 30s.

Those who do not linger are likely those who cannot afford to and, perhaps as a result, views on how long it takes to achieve adulthood differ markedly by social class. Less-educated and less-affluent respondents—those who did not attend college and those at the bottom one-third of the income ladder—have an earlier expected timetable for leaving home, completing school, obtaining full-time employment, marriage and parenthood. Around 40 percent of the less well-off in the GSS sample said that young adults should marry before they turn 25, and one-third said they should have children by this age. Far fewer of the better-off respondents pointed to the early 20s, and about one-third of them said that these events could be delayed until the 30s. These social class differences probably stem from the reality that young people with more limited means do not have the luxury of investing in school or experimenting with complex career paths.

New Demands on Families, Schools and Governments

The growing demands on young Americans to invest in the future have come at a time of curtailed government support, placing heavy demands on families. Growing inequality shapes very different futures for young Americans with more and less privileged parents.

Early adulthood is when people figure out what they want to do and how best to realize their goals. If they are lucky enough to have a family that can help out, they may proceed directly through college, travel or work for a few years, or perhaps participate in community service, and then enter graduate or professional school. However, relatively few Americans have this good fortune. Youth from less well-off families must shuttle back and forth between work and school or combine both while they gradually gain their credentials. In the meantime, they feel unprepared for marriage or parenting. If they do marry or parent during these years, they often find themselves trying to juggle too many responsibilities and unable to adequately invest in their future. Like the mother from Iowa, they do not feel "on track" or in control of their lives.

More than at any time in recent history, parents are being called on to provide financial assistance (either college tuition, living expenses or other assistance) to their young adult children. Robert Schoeni and Karen Ross conservatively estimate that nearly one-quarter of the entire cost of raising children is incurred after they reach 17. Nearly two-thirds of young adults in their early 20s receive economic support from parents, while about 40 percent still receive some assistance in their late 20s.

A century ago, it was the other way around: young adults typically helped their parents when they first went to work, if (as was common) they still lived with their parents. Now, many young adults continue to receive support from their parents even after they begin working. The exceptions seem to be in immigrant families; there, young people more often help support their parents. A 27-year-old Chinese American from New York explained why he continued to live with his parents despite wanting to move out, saying that his parents "want me [to stay] and they need me. Financially, they need me to take care of them, pay the bills, stuff like that, which is fine."

As young people and their families struggle with the new reality that it takes longer to attain adulthood, Americans must recognize weaknesses in the primary institutions that facilitate this transition—schools and the military. For the fortunate few who achieve bachelor's degrees and perhaps go on to professional or graduate training, residential colleges and universities seem well designed. They offer everything from housing to health care while training young adults. Likewise, the military provides a similar milieu for those from less-privileged families. However, only about one in four young adults attend primarily residential colleges or join the military after high school. The other three-quarters look to their families for room and board while they attend school and enter the job market. Many of these youth enter community colleges or local universities that provide much less in the way of services and support.

The least privileged come from families that cannot offer much assistance. This vulnerable population—consisting of 10 to 15 percent of young adults—may come out of the foster care system, graduate from special education programs, or exit jails and prisons. These youth typically lack job skills and need help to secure a foothold in society. Efforts to increase educational opportunities, establish school-to-career paths, and help students who cannot afford post-secondary education must be given higher priority, even in a time of budget constraints. The United States, once a world leader in providing higher education to its citizens, now lags behind several other nations in the proportion of the population that completes college.

Expanding military and alternative national service programs also can help provide a bridge from secondary school to higher education or the labor force by providing financial credit to those who serve their country. Such programs also offer health insurance to young adults, who are often cut off from insurance by arbitrary age limits. Finally, programs for the vulnerable populations of youth coming out of foster care, special education, and mental health services must not assume that young people are fully able to become economically independent at age 18 or even 21. The timetable of the 1950s is no longer applicable. It is high time for policy makers and legislators to address the realities of the longer and more demanding transition to adulthood.

CHALLENGE QUESTIONS

Are College Graduates Unprepared for Adulthood and the World of Work?

- Assuming that most people reading this are college students themselves, how do you feel about some of the strong claims made by Mel Levine? Are you and your peers disinterested in adults outside your immediate sphere of influence? Do you and your peers prioritize physical beauty and activity over qualities of mind? Are you and your peers thinking about and preparing for the world of work and adulthood?
- If you agree with Levine, then it is important to consider why. Do you agree with the factors he identifies: excessive praise during childhood, a culture saturated with short-term gratification, a failure of colleges to make their curriculum relevant to what is needed by both youth and society?
- If you don't agree with Levine, then it is important to consider why his perspective is prominent in our culture: Why is there a widespread perception that young people in college today are at risk of not making successful transitions to the world of work and to adulthood more generally?
- Furstenberg and colleagues note that expectations are higher than ever for young adults. Are there ways in which you think that the expectations on young adults are too high?

Suggested Readings

T. Apter, *The Myth of Maturity: What Teenagers Need from Parents to Become Adults* (W. W. Norton, 2001)

J.J. Arnett, *Emerging Adulthood: The Winding Road from the Late Teens Through the Twenties* (Oxford University Press, 2004)

J.E. Cote, *Arrested Adulthood: The Changing Nature of Maturity and Identity* (New York University Press, 2000)

Institute for Research on Higher Education, "Understanding Employers' Perceptions of College Graduates," *Change* (May/June 1998)

M. Levine, *Ready or Not, Here Life Comes* (Simon & Schuster, 2005)

R.A. Settersten, F.F. Furstenberg, and R.G. Rumbaut, *On the Frontier of Adulthood: Theory, Research, and Public Policy* (MacArthur Foundation Series) (University of Chicago Press, 2005)

J. Studley, "Are Liberal Arts Dead? Far From It." *Careers and Colleges* (September–October 2003)

Is There Such a Thing as "Emerging Adulthood"?

YES: Jeffrey Jensen Arnett, from "Emerging Adulthood: What Is It, and What Is It Good For?" *Child Development Perspectives* (December 2007)

NO: Leo B. Hendry and Marion Kloep, from "Conceptualizing Emerging Adulthood: Inspecting the Emperor's New Clothes?" *Child Development Perspectives* (December 2007)

ISSUE SUMMARY

YES: Developmental psychologist Jeffrey Jensen Arnett has earned wide acclaim among scholars for defining an "emerging adulthood" as a distinctly modern stage of the life-span.

NO: Life-span research scholars Lew B. Hendry and Marion Kloep argue that defining emerging adulthood as a discrete stage provides a misleading account of the age period between the late teens and the mid- to late twenties.

Is there something different about today's young adults? Although this is a perennial question in many social and historical settings, psychologist Jeffrey Jensen Arnett thinks that the characteristics of the age period from the late teens through the mid- to late twenties in contemporary society are so distinct that they merit a new stage of life-span development. He calls this stage "emerging adulthood" and argues that it is qualitatively different from the transitional period that has long characterized life between adolescence and full adulthood. With increasing educational demands, later ages for marriage, and more instability in work, Arnett thinks that post-high school life is now a distinct time of exploration in work, relationships, and the self. While exploring options related to work and relationships may be something of a necessary process during the transition to adulthood, the prominence of self-exploration during one's twenties has raised more serious questions and concerns.

Among those interested in the study of life-span development, perhaps the most interesting question is about what qualifies as a distinct stage in the life-span? Stage theories have a long history in the study of development, including famous examples posited by Sigmund Freud, Erik Erikson, and Jean Piaget. But while those theories offer useful shortcuts for identifying important characteristics of different ages, they also may create a false sense that development occurs in orderly steps. Is there really a clear point where adulthood begins? Although we often define people by broad stages of the life-span that correspond to chronological age, we also recognize that there is much individual variation and that social markers matter as much as biological age.

It was only around the turn of the 20th century that the concept of "adolescence" as a transition period between childhood and adulthood came to be considered a distinct stage of the life-span. The need for the concept of adolescence, similar to Arnett's argument for emerging adulthood, depended on changing social conditions, including increased access to education and changing community responsibilities.

From Hendry and Kloep's perspective, however, the study of life-span development has progressed to the point where rather than adding "new" stages, it makes more sense to move away from stage theories entirely. They do acknowledge that stage theories have had some usefulness but, they note, many significant contemporary theories of development recognize that such change occurs in dynamic and non-linear ways.

The question of stages is important to the study of life-span development at all ages. In thinking about development how much attention should go to consistent patterns across broad groups of people, and how much attention should go to individual variations? While the concept of "emerging adulthood" is relatively new, and worth understanding as product of a particular cultural and historical context, being able to evaluate the concept of life-span stages is central to understanding development at any time or age.

POINT

- "Emerging adulthood" has quickly become a popular way to describe and understand the age period from the late teens through at least the mid-twenties.
- Changes in the nature of the transition between adolescence and adulthood for people growing up in modern industrialized societies necessitates marking a new life stage.
- Emerging adulthood is not an entirely discrete stage, but it is an important transition period that overlaps with both adolescence and adulthood.
- Many of the life events that used to happen in adolescence, such as the "identity crisis," have been delayed due to more extensive educational expectations and later normative ages for marriage.

COUNTERPOINT

- It is inaccurate to claim development occurs toward a comprehensive stage of adulthood since rates of development are different across domains and are reversible.
- The process of identity development does not define one stage because it is ongoing throughout the life-span.
- Generalizing about emerging adulthood discounts variations between social and cultural groups.
- Promoting emerging adulthood as a stage may mean promoting an unhealthy prolongation of wayward exploration that has negative social implications.

YES ↵

Jeffrey Jensen Arnett

Emerging Adulthood: What Is It, and What Is It Good For?

It is now 7 years since I first proposed the term *emerging adulthood* for the age period from the late teens through the mid- to late 20s (roughly ages 18–25) in an article in *American Psychologist.* . . . I had mentioned the term briefly in two previous articles . . ., but the 2000 article was the first time I presented an outline of the theory. It was not until 2004 that I proposed a full theory in a book on emerging adulthood. . . . In a short time, the theory has become widely used, not just in psychology but in many fields. At the recent Third Conference on Emerging Adulthood . . ., a remarkable range of disciplines was represented, including psychology, psychiatry, sociology, anthropology, education, epidemiology, health sciences, human development, geography, nursing, social work, philosophy, pediatrics, family studies, journalism, and law.

The swift spread of the term and the idea has surprised me because normally any new theoretical idea meets initial resistance from defenders of the reigning paradigm. Perhaps, the acceptance of emerging adulthood has been so swift because there really was no reigning paradigm. Instead, there was a widespread sense among scholars interested in this age period that previous ways of thinking about it no longer worked and there was a hunger for a new conceptualization. In any case, now that emerging adulthood has become established as a way of thinking about the age period from the late teens through at least the mid-20s, the theory is attracting commentary and critiques. . . . This is a normal and healthy part of the development of any new theory, and I welcome the exchange here with Leo Hendry and Marion Kloep.

The Configuration of Emerging Adulthood: How Does It Fit into the Life Course?

When I first proposed the theory of emerging adulthood . . . , one of my goals was to draw attention to the age period from the late teens through the mid-20s as a new period of the life course in industrialized societies, with distinctive developmental characteristics. The dominant theory of the life course in developmental psychology, first proposed by Erikson . . . postulated that adolescence, lasting from the beginning of puberty until the late teens, was

From *Child Development Perspectives*, Vol. 1, No. 2, 2007, pp. 68–72. Copyright © 2007 by Wiley-Blackwell. Reprinted by permission.

followed by young adulthood, lasting from the late teens to about age 40 when middle adulthood began. This paradigm may have made sense in the middle of the 20th century when most people in industrialized societies married and entered stable full-time work by around age 20 or shortly after. However, by the end of the century, this paradigm no longer fit the normative pattern in industrialized societies. Median ages of marriage had risen into the late 20s, and the early to mid-20s became a time of frequent job changes and, for many people, pursuit of postsecondary education or training. Furthermore, sexual mores had changed dramatically, and premarital sex and cohabitation in the 20s had become widely accepted. Most young people now spent the period from their late teens to their mid-20s not settling into long-term adult roles but trying out different experiences and gradually making their way toward enduring choices in love and work.

The theory of emerging adulthood was proposed as a framework for recognizing that the transition to adulthood was now long enough that it constituted not merely a transition but a separate period of the life course. I proposed five features that make emerging adulthood distinct: it is the *age of identity explorations,* the *age of instability,* the *self-focused age,* the *age of feeling in-between,* and *the age of possibilities.* . . . But I emphasized from the beginning that emerging adulthood is perhaps the most heterogeneous period of the life course because it is the least structured, and the five features were not proposed as universal features but as features that are more common during emerging adulthood than in other periods.

In this light, of the possible configurations A–D in Figure 1 of how emerging adulthood might fit into the adult life course, I would reject D

Figure 1

Possible Configurations of Emerging Adulthood

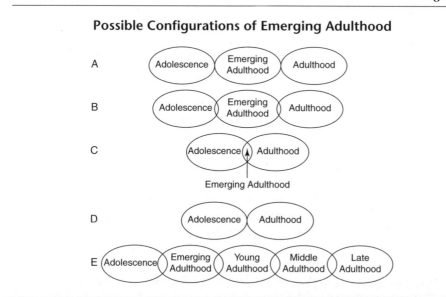

because it does not show a distinct period between adolescence and adulthood. C does not work because it slights emerging adulthood, inaccurately portraying it as a brief transition between adolescence and adulthood. A is better, but it shows the transitions from adolescence to emerging adulthood and from emerging adulthood to young adulthood as more discrete than they actually are in some respects. It applies to transitions from adolescence to emerging adulthood such as finishing secondary school and reaching the legal age of adult status, and perhaps to transitions from emerging to young adulthood such as marriage. However, B works best in my view because the five features described above are entered and exited not discretely but gradually. Furthermore, of the three criteria found in many countries and cultures to be the most important markers of reaching adult status—accepting responsibility for oneself, making independent decisions, and becoming financially independent—all are attained gradually in the course of emerging adulthood. . . .

This gradual passage from one period to the next may apply not just to emerging adulthood but to the entire adult life course. Theorists have emphasized how in recent decades the life course in industrialized societies has become increasingly characterized by *individualization,* meaning that institutional constraints and supports have become less powerful and important and people are increasingly left to their own resources in making their way from one part of the life course to the next, for better or worse. . . . Emerging adulthood is one part of this trend. So, in Figure 1, an improvement on B might be E, showing gradual transitions into and out of different periods throughout the adult life course.

Do We Really Need the Term *Emerging Adulthood*?

I believe the rapid spread of the term *emerging adulthood* reflects its usefulness and the dissatisfaction of scholars in many fields with the previous terms that had been used. There were problems with each of those terms, including *late adolescence, young adulthood, the transition to adulthood,* and *youth.* . . . *Late adolescence* does not work because the lives of persons in their late teens and 20s are vastly different from the lives of most adolescents (roughly ages 10–17). Unlike adolescents, 18- to 25-year-olds are not going through puberty, are not in secondary school, are not legally defined as children or juveniles, and often have moved out of their parents' household. *Young adulthood* does not work because it has been used already to refer to such diverse age periods, from preteens ("young adult" books) to age 40 ("young adult" social organizations). Furthermore, if 18–25 are "young adulthood," what are people who are 30, 35, or 40? It makes more sense to reserve "young adulthood" for the age period from about age 30 to about age 40 (or perhaps 45) because by age 30 most people in industrialized societies have settled into the roles usually associated with adulthood: stable work, marriage or other long-term partnership, and parenthood.

The transition to adulthood has been widely used in sociology and in research focusing mostly on the timing and sequence of transition events such as leaving home, finishing education, marriage, and parenthood. Certainly, the years from the late teens through the 20s are when the transition to adulthood takes place for most people, not only as defined by transition events but also by a more subjective sense of having reached adulthood. . . . But why call this period merely a "transition" rather than a period of development in its own right? If we state, conservatively, that it lasts 7 years, from age 18 to 25, that makes it longer than infancy, longer than early or middle childhood, and as long as adolescence. Furthermore, calling it "the transition to adulthood" focuses attention on the transition events that take place mainly at the beginning or end of the age range, whereas calling it "emerging adulthood" broadens the scope of attention to the whole range of areas—cognitive development, family relationships, friendships, romantic relationships, media use, and so on—that apply to other developmental periods as well.

Finally, *youth* has been used as a term for this period, especially in Europe but also among some American psychologists and sociologists. However, *youth* suffers from the same problem as *young adulthood,* in that it has long been used to refer to a wide range of ages, from middle childhood ("youth organizations") through the 30s. Furthermore, in its American incarnation, it was promoted by Keniston . . . on the basis of his research with student protesters in the late 1960s, and his description of it as a time of rebellion against society bears the marks of his time but does not apply widely.

Emerging adulthood is preferable because it is a new term for a new phenomenon. Across industrialized societies in the past half century, common changes have taken place with respect to the lives of young people: longer and more widespread participation in postsecondary education and training, greater tolerance of premarital sex and cohabitation, and later ages of entering marriage and parenthood. As a consequence of these changes, a new period of the life course has developed between adolescence and young adulthood. Furthermore, *emerging adulthood* reflects the sense among many people in the late teens and early 20s worldwide that they are no longer adolescent but only partly adult, emerging into adulthood but not there yet. . . .

Some aspects of the theory of emerging adulthood are likely to be modified with further research, and the main features of emerging adulthood will no doubt vary among cultures. There are certainly psychosocial differences among emerging adults related to socioeconomic status and ethnic group, and cross-national differences have only begun to be explored. . . . But there is some degree of heterogeneity in every developmental period, and overarching terms and general descriptions for those periods are nevertheless useful for understanding them. . . .

Is Emerging Adulthood Experienced Positively or Negatively by Most People?

The fact that it takes longer to reach full adulthood today than it did in the past has been subject to various interpretations, mostly negative. In American popular media, the term "quarterlife crisis" has been coined to describe the alleged difficulties experienced by emerging adults as they try to find a place in the adult world. . . . Within academia, some sociologists have asserted that

Figure 2

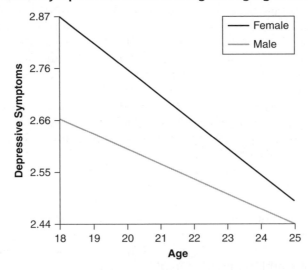

Depressive Symptoms Decline During Emerging Adulthood

Note. The sample was drawn from Grade 12 classes in six high schools in a western Canadian city, followed over the next 7 years. $N = 920$ at age 18 and 324 at age 25. The sample was diverse in socioeconomic status background; at Time 1, 10% were from families in which both parents had a university degree, and 16% had one parent with a university degree. Among the participants themselves, by age 25, 30% had a university degree, 14% had a college diploma, 24% had a technical degree, and the remaining 32% had no postsecondary educational credential. . . .

higher ages of marriage and parenthood indicate that "growing up is harder to do" than in the past.

Yet, the bulk of the evidence is contrary to these assertions. . . . Numerous studies show that for most, well-being improves during the course of emerging adulthood. An example is shown in Figures 2 and 3, which demonstrate a decline in depressive symptoms and a rise in self-esteem in a longitudinal Canadian study of emerging adults. . . . Similar results have been found in the longitudinal Monitoring the Future studies in the United States. . . . Emerging adults enjoy their self-focused freedom from role obligations and restraints, and they take satisfaction in their progress toward self-sufficiency. I think they also benefit from growing social cognitive maturity, which enables them to understand themselves and others better than they did as adolescents. . . .

Nevertheless, although I believe the notion of a "quarterlife crisis" is exaggerated, I do not dismiss it entirely. It is true that identity issues are prominent in emerging adulthood and that sorting through them and finding satisfying alternatives in love and work can generate anxiety. The idea of a "quarterlife crisis" can be seen as recognizing that the identity crisis Erikson . . . described over a half century ago as central to adolescence has now moved into emerging adulthood. It is also true that entry into the labor market is often stressful and frustrating, especially for emerging adults with limited educational credentials. . . . Furthermore, even among the most advantaged emerging

Figure 3

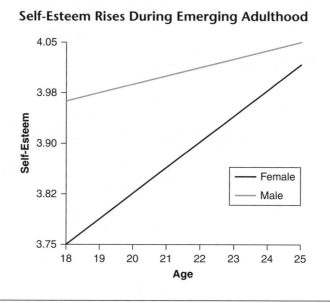

Self-Esteem Rises During Emerging Adulthood

Note. The sample was drawn from Grade 12 classes in six high schools in a western Canadian city, followed over the next 7 years. *N* = 920 at age 18 and 324 at age 25. The sample was diverse in socioeconomic status background; at Time 1, 10% were from families in which both parents had a university degree, and 16% had one parent with a university degree. Among the participants themselves, by age 25, 30% had a university degree, 14% had a college diploma, 24% had a technical degree, and the remaining 32% had no postsecondary educational credential. . . .

adults, the graduates of 4-year colleges and universities, their extraordinarily high expectations for the workplace—their aspirations of finding work that not only pays well but also provides a satisfying and enjoyable identity fit—are difficult for reality to match and often require compromises of their hopes and dreams. . . . Nevertheless, the evidence of rising well-being during the course of emerging adulthood indicates that most people adapt successfully to its developmental challenges.

Here as elsewhere, we must take into account the heterogeneity of emerging adults. Even as well-being rises for most emerging adults, some experience serious mental health problems such as major depression and substance use disorder. . . . A possible interpretation is that the variance in mental health functioning becomes broader in the course of emerging adulthood. . . . This may be because emerging adults have fewer social roles and obligations than children and adolescents, whose lives are structured by their parents and other adults, or adults (beyond emerging adulthood), whose lives are structured by work, family, and community roles and obligations. Although most emerging adults appear to thrive on this freedom, some find themselves lost and may begin to experience serious mental health problems. Emerging adults may also struggle if they are part of especially vulnerable populations, such as those aging out of foster care, coming out of the criminal justice system, or experiencing disabilities. . . .

Although I have made a case that emerging adulthood is experienced positively by most people, I hasten to add that my perspective is based mainly on my interviews and other data obtained from emerging adults in the United States and (recently) Denmark. Studies on emerging adults in other countries, such as Argentina . . ., Czech Republic . . ., and China . . . show some similarities as well as some differences. An exciting prospect for the new field of emerging adulthood is examining the forms it takes in different countries and cultures worldwide. . . .

Is Emerging Adulthood Good for Society?

Even if it is true that most people seem to enjoy their emerging adulthood, is the advent of this new period of life good for society? Certainly, there are complaints about it in American popular media. "They Just Won't Grow Up" sniggered a *TIME* magazine cover story on emerging adults in 2005. In the 2006 movie *Failure to Launch,* a young man shows so little inclination to take on adult responsibilities that his parents hire an attractive young woman to lure him out of their household. Advice writers warn that emerging adults are refusing to give up their teenage pleasures and take on adult responsibilities, with "catastrophic" results. . . .

Here, as with "quarterlife crisis," a grain of truth is exaggerated to the point of caricature. . . . It is true that many emerging adults are ambivalent about taking on adult roles and responsibilities. . . . Although they take a certain satisfaction in moving toward self-sufficiency, they also find it burdensome and onerous to pay their own bills and do all the other things their parents had always done for them. Furthermore, they often view adulthood as dull and stagnant, the end of spontaneity, the end of a sense that anything is possible.

Nevertheless, their ambivalence is not an outright refusal or rejection of adult roles. It may be that they are wise to recognize the potentials of emerging adulthood and to wait until at least their late 20s to take on the full range of adult obligations. Although adulthood may have more satisfactions and rewards than they recognize, they are right that entering adult roles of marriage, parenthood, and stable full-time work entails constraints and limitations that do not apply in emerging adulthood. Once adult roles are entered they tend to be enduring if not lifelong. It seems sensible for emerging adults to wait to enter them until they judge themselves to be ready, and meanwhile to enjoy the freedoms of emerging adulthood while they last.

It should also be added that few emerging adults fail to "grow up" and take on the responsibilities of adulthood. By age 30, three fourths of Americans are married, three fourths have at least one child, nearly all have entered stable employment, nearly all have become financially independent from their parents, and almost none live in their parents' household. . . . Similarly, by age 30 nearly all (about 90%) feel that they have fully reached adulthood, no longer feeling in-between. . . . Thus, the claim that a long and gradual process of taking on adult responsibilities during emerging adulthood results in permanent rejection of adulthood is clearly overblown. The great majority of emerging adults become contributing young adult members of society by age 30, fulfilling stable family and work roles.

Here again, my perspective is based mainly on my research with American emerging adults. However, there are some indications that similar patterns exist in most other industrialized countries, with some variations. Across industrialized societies emerging adulthood is a period of many changes in love and work but most people settle into enduring adult roles by about age 30. . . .

So, emerging adulthood may not be harmful to societies, but is it actually *good* for them? Yes and no. On the one hand, it would be nice to think that if people spend most of their 20s looking for just the right job and just the right love partner, they will have a better chance of finding happiness in love and work than if they had made long-term commitments in their late teens or very early 20s out of duty, necessity, or social pressure. On the other hand, emerging adults' expectations for love and work tend to be extremely high—not just a reliable marriage partner but a "soul mate," not just a steady job but a kind of work that is an enjoyable expression of their identity—and if happiness is measured by the distance between what we expect out of life and what we get, emerging adults' high expectations will be difficult for real life to match. So, it cannot be said with confidence that the existence of emerging adulthood ensures that most people in a society will be happier with their adult lives.

Furthermore, emerging adulthood is the peak age period for many behaviors most societies try to discourage, such as binge drinking, illegal drug use, and risky sexual behavior. . . . If people still entered adult commitments around age 20, as they did in the past, rates of risk behaviors in the 20s would undoubtedly be lower. Such behavior may be fun for emerging adults, but it can hardly be said to be good for their society. However, one way emerging adulthood is good for society is that it allows young people an extended period that can be used for post-secondary education and training that prepares them to contribute to an information and technology-based global economy.

Conclusion

Already in its short life, emerging adulthood has been shown to bear the marks of a good theory: It has generated research, ideas, and critiques that have advanced science and scholarship. Like all theories, it is an imperfect model of real life, and will no doubt be subject to alterations, revisions, and elaborations in the years to come. Especially important will be investigating the different forms it takes in cultures around the world. The theory of emerging adulthood that I have presented is offered as a starting point, and I look forward to the contributions and further advances to come, from scholars around the world. . . .

**Leo B. Hendry and
Marion Kloep**

 **NO**

Conceptualizing Emerging Adulthood: Inspecting the Emperor's New Clothes?

Academics worldwide have congratulated Arnett . . . for focusing over the last decade or so on a previously under-researched phase of the life span. Societal and economic changes and shifts inspired him to ask what these forces meant to the transition from adolescence to adulthood. Arguably, this theory has been hailed by some as the most important theoretical contribution to developmental psychology in the past 10 years. . . .

Nevertheless, in this article, we want to play the part of the little boy in Hans Christian Andersen's story who points out the Emperor's lack of clothes, because in our view, his ideas on this period of transition contain several limitations, which should be addressed if future research is to advance on firmer theoretical grounds. To examine these points, we concentrate on the following issues:

1. The configuration of adolescence, early adulthood, and adulthood.
2. Retrospect and prospect: Do we really need the term?
3. Is emerging adulthood experienced positively or negatively by most young people?
4. Is emerging adulthood good for society?

The Configuration of Emerging Adulthood

Arnett . . . is right in suggesting that the transition to adulthood has become increasingly prolonged as a result of economic changes, with many young people staying in education longer, marrying later, and having their first child later than in the past and that in present day society, it is difficult to determine when adolescence ends and adulthood begins. However, he is not the first to make this observation:

> The distinction between youth status and adult status is gradually blurring: Over the last fifteen years, the behavioural differences between youth and adults have drastically diminished. In a growing number of life spheres (sexuality, political behaviour, etc.) young people behave like adults or claim the same rights as adults. . . .

From *Child Development Perspectives,* Vol. 1, No. 2, 2007, pp. 74–78. Copyright © 2007 by Wiley-Blackwell. Reprinted by permission.

Figure 1

Arnett's Conceptualization of Emerging Adulthood

What is new in Arnett's theory is the proposal of a new stage in human development, distinct from adolescence and adulthood, overlapping with both stages (see Figure 1).

We do not agree with this model for several reasons. First, Arnett suggests that adulthood (however defined) is fully attained at a certain stage, though there is wide agreement among psychologists that development is domain specific and demonstrates plasticity. . . . Thus, not all areas of human functioning are affected to the same degree, in the same direction, or at the same time. Young people might reach adult status early in some domains, later in others, and in some aspects, never. Further, development is nonlinear and reversible. . . . Young people having reached adulthood according to their own perceptions and by societal markers may find themselves in circumstances where they have to "regress" both subjectively and objectively. For example, it is not uncommon that after cohabitation, some young people return to their familial house when the relationship breaks up, losing the feelings of independence associated with adult status. This can even happen temporarily when young (and not so young) people pursuing a career and feeling completely independent of their parents might in times of illness happily assume the role of cared-for child. . . . The transition from adolescence to adulthood is not as smooth as Arnett proposes, being domain specific, variable, and reversible.

Second, given the few, if any, normative shifts in present-day life, the search for identity is a process of recurring moratoria and achievements extending over the entire life span. . . . Fauske . . . noted that if youth can no longer be interpreted as a bridge between childhood and adulthood as two stable statuses (as Arnett proposes), there is an alternative scenario, which is some kind of perpetual youth. Adults behave like young people, undergo cosmetic surgery, return to college, fall in love with new partners, start a different career, have exciting leisure pursuits, follow youth fashions, and even give birth in advanced biological age:

> Next time you visit the supermarket, you may encounter . . . newborn infants with their mothers who are aged fifteen and sixteen and newborn infants with mothers aged thirty-five to forty. You may encounter, in fact, grandparents in their early forties as well as parents in their sixties and seventies. . . .

If there have to be stages to describe the human life course, the idea of emerging phases between them should be applied to the whole life course. In

Figure 2

Hendry and Kloep's Conceptualization of Life Transitions

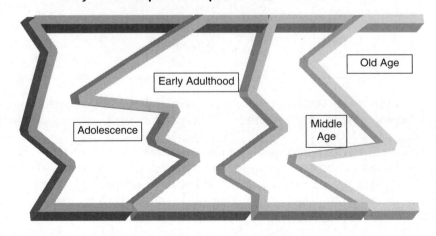

other words, most of us are almost always in the state of being in between or emerging:

> Adult life, then, is a process—a process, we must emphasise, which need not involve a predetermined series of stages of growth. The stages or hurdles, which are placed in front of people and the barriers through which they have to pass (age-specific transitions) can be shifted around and even discarded. . . .

In Figure 2, we illustrate our conceptualization of transitions (though the connections between phases should be in a continual state of dynamic fluctuation to indicate plasticity and reversibility).

Do We Really Need the Term?

Arnett . . . is right that in today's rapidly changing world, traditional developmental tasks such as gaining independence from parents, making personal living arrangements, orienting to a career, and developing new sets of relationships with parents, peers, romantic partners, and so on are differently ordered and present young people with significant challenges in gaining adult status. However, modern developmentalists have claimed that emerging adulthood is not a universal stage but depends on the cultural context in which young people develop and the social institutions they encounter. . . . Findings from studies of non-Western cultures and ethnic minorities suggest that generalizations about emerging adults do not capture the variations that exist within individuals and across cultures. . . . In many countries, young people, particularly women in rural areas, are granted no moratorium for identity exploration but glide quickly from childhood into adulthood. For example, in Turkey, the mean age for marriage is 21 years. . . . Lloyd . . . has stated that the largest generation of young people in history is now making the transition from childhood to adulthood, with 86% of this cohort, nearly 1.5 billion individuals, living in developing countries. Many of them do not experience adolescence, much less emerging adulthood!

The fact that socioeconomic conditions heavily influence the lifestyles and options of individuals in a given society is not new. Apart from Marx's well-known historic materialism, social scientists have repeatedly observed this, and Rindfuss, Swicegard, and Rosenfeld . . . stated that the life course deviates from an idealized "normal" pattern from time to time because the shaping of early adulthood is conditioned by the historical context.

To give a few examples of varying transitional pathways to adulthood with an extended period of moratorium for some, centuries ago Jane Austen wrote about how many upper class youngsters never followed an occupation and remained dependent on their parents until they died. In the same historical period, many 12-year-old children left their families to join a ship's crew or go mining or serve as maids in wealthy households, whereas some women only became "independent" adults when they married. In the political sphere, Queen Mary of Scotland married the French Dauphin (aged 14) at age 15 and a year later became Queen of France.

Considering the points above, the theory of emerging adulthood is merely a description limited to a certain age cohort in certain societies at a certain historical time with particular socioeconomic conditions. This implies that the concept will almost certainly become outdated, given that Western societies are bound to change and new cohorts emerge with different developmental characteristics in different social contexts. New technologies have an impact on young peoples' socialization and learning. There are effects of the "war on terror" on family life, a changing work–leisure balance together with demographic shifts, and increasing migration, to name but a few possible societal trends into the future that will require new theories of development.

As such, Arnett's construct of emerging adulthood does not advance our knowledge and understanding of human development. On the contrary, by elevating it to the status of a theory, we are repeating an error psychology made decades ago when it regarded male behavior as the norm. We are now in danger of having a psychology of the affluent middle classes in Western societies, with other groups being seen as deviating from that norm.

This is not a problem of Arnett's theory alone. All age-bound stage theories, from Freud to Erikson, have been criticized for being ethnocentric and having social class and gender biases. There is a great diversity among people across the life span, and as Valsiner . . . has said, whereas median trends are useful to observe, it is the error variance that is crucial to our understanding of human development. Age, like other structural variables such as gender, social class, or ethnicity, may predict, but do not explain, developmental phenomena. It is not age in itself that causes development; it is the experiences, and not necessarily associated with chronological age, that cause developmental change. Bynner . . . proposed that there is a need to

> move away from a blanket categorisation of individuals in terms of stages bounded by chronological age towards a broader conception based on a range of trajectories or pathways. . . .

In other words, how useful is it to create yet another age stage into existing theories that are neither universal nor explanatory? Rather, we need to investigate the processes and mechanisms of developmental change and abandon age stage theories altogether if we want to go beyond descriptions and seek explanations about development.

Is the Experience of Emerging Adulthood a Positive or Negative One?

Relying on young people's own optimistic perspectives of the future, Arnett . . . sees the period of emerging adulthood as mainly positive for the individual. Whether the experience of a prolonged moratorium is positive, however, depends to a large extent on what societal group they belong to and how they use this period of moratorium.

Castells . . . observed that the contemporary contours of diffuse social, economic, and cultural conditions present new challenges because people must lead their lives without a road map. In Western societies, the signposts and symbols of approaching adulthood are inconsistent and difficult for the young person to understand and interpret. These complexities led Coles . . . to compare adolescent transitions to a deadly serious game of snakes and ladders, where the main transitions are the ladders through which young people gradually move toward adult status. Although this may sound as if growing up in modern societies is risky, we often forget that many more young people survive childhood, adolescence, and emerging adulthood than in previous ages. It is true that young people are confronted with a range of challenges on their way to adulthood and that these challenges create anxieties. One of the significant contributions stage theorists have made to developmental psychology has been to pinpoint that without challenges, conflicts, and crises, there is no developmental change.

Thus, young people face a range of choices, challenges, and risks in relationships, schooling, higher education, and work. . . . Although this may open up opportunities for some, there are fewer safety nets for others, with inequalities in the distribution of resources such as social class, ethnicity, gender, health, and education . . .:

> It can be misleading to present society as changing with all elements; in effect, "marching in step". We need to recognise that the traditional routes to adulthood, with far fewer signs of its emergent status, are still very much in place. . . .

Although it may be true that independence, possibilities, and choices are available for those who can access consumer markets, this may hold only for the young person who has an income or, better yet, supportive parents: Wealthy middle-class youths do have better options. . . .

Similar to Heinz's . . . variety of pathways to occupational roles, we propose from our own research of 18- to 30-year-olds in Wales, who were either working or unemployed and not attending any school . . ., at least three broad subgroups of young people in Western societies, each experiencing the period of emerging adulthood very differently. Of these, 74% stated that they considered themselves to be adult and only 13% felt "in-between" (whereas Arnett's . . . study found 60% feeling in-between).

One of the three groups identified was in extended moratorium, which was similar to Arnett's . . . affluent, middle-class students. With parental support, they could afford a prolonged moratorium, live at home, seek new opportunities, delay in choosing a career, "have fun," and not be fully adult. Although this sounds a pleasant experience, the danger is that these young people would not develop adult skills and might experience "happy" developmental stagnation through overprotection. . . . With regard to education, Levine . . . argued that many young people in their mid-20s have not learned planning, organizational, decision-making, and interpersonal skills that are necessary for the transitions into working life. He believes that education leaves these young people unprepared to move into adulthood because they are both overindulged and pressured by parents to excel in all life domains, leaving them uncommitted to deep, focused, and detailed learning. Relatively speaking, this group is forever emerging but never adult. The increasing number of young and middle-aged adults who cannot manage their credit card debts seems to point to a lack of life skills in the wider population.

A second subgroup found in the Wales sample was disadvantaged by their lack of resources, skills, and societal opportunities, though superficially they exhibited a somewhat similar lifestyle to the more affluent subgroup, living with parents and occasionally accepting temporary unskilled jobs. The difference here was that they were in this rut not through choice but through lack of opportunities. Rather than being in a state of emerging adulthood, they were more likely in a state of "prevented adulthood" and in "unhappy stagnation." Lack of affordable housing, education, and suitable jobs prevented them from gaining independence and self-reliance. Many noted that choices and possibilities were available *but not for them,* and this was unlikely to change in the near future. Members of this group not only lacked adult skills but also felt bitter and alienated from society. In drawing attention to the economic and social factors that keep some dependent until at least their mid-20s, Côté . . . concluded that a significant number of young adults have transitional difficulties and greatest problems come to those with least economic, intellectual, and psychological resources.

Finally, there was a third, small subgroup that exhibited early maturity developed through "steeling experiences." . . . These are life events that include parental illness or divorce, having to look after younger siblings or their own children, finding a responsible job, or being forced to become financially independent because their parents could not afford to support them. . . . Growing up early added psychosocial resources and influenced their views of adult status. Barry and Nelson . . . reported that those who perceived themselves to be adult had a better sense of their own identity, were less depressed, and engaged in fewer risk behaviors than those who saw themselves as in-between.

In general, internal markers of adulthood (taking responsibility for one's actions, making independent decisions, becoming financially independent, establishing equal relations with parents) appear to be of greater salience to young people than external markers (marriage, parenthood, beginning full-time work. . . . Hence, there are several other developmental tasks than those traditionally seen as markers of adulthood. Experiencing and coping with different nonnormative shifts can enhance maturity in exactly the same way as these normative shifts achieve: These experiences are causes, not consequences, of becoming adult.

In summary, the experience of emerging adulthood depends on whether a prolonged moratorium is the result of choice or constraints and whether it is used effectively to gain experiences. Some may acquire skills for adult living, whereas others idle their time away. Overall, it seems as if the long-term consequences are more beneficial to those who do not spend lengthy years in identity exploration.

Is Emerging Adulthood Good for Society?

What might be the societal effects of young people delaying their entry into adult roles? On this we can only speculate, though Arnett makes clear that he sees it as a positive experience for young people.

Large numbers of young adults not participating in the labor market and not being economically active in their first 30 years of life (as well as in their last) would cost Western societies dearly. Some emergent adults would fail to realize their full potential throughout life because they failed to acquire skills and qualifications needed for modern living. It will certainly place large financial and emotional burdens on middle-aged parents having to support their ever-emerging children at the same time as having to care for aging parents. The current increase in divorce and the decrease in fertility rates . . . may also be a reflection of current trends in extended identity exploration. Further, emerging adults of today may not be particularly affluent parents, because they left both career and child bearing to their early 30s, and if many remain single parents, they will be unable to indulge their own children in a 30-year-long period of identity exploration. In other words, we predict that the current situation of emerging adulthood will regulate itself over time.

Already several European governments have reacted by increasing university fees, placing limits on time allowed to complete a degree course (United Kingdom and Germany), and establishing laws on cohabiting very similar to marriage laws (Ireland, United Kingdom, Sweden). These emerging adults, in extended moratorium, may also create opportunities for well-qualified non-Western immigrants within the labor markets of Western societies.

Concluding Comments

In our view, Arnett's concept does not add to our understanding of human development. Instead of simply describing the effects of certain societal conditions on certain individuals belonging to a certain cohort, we should better understand and investigate the interactive processes and mechanisms (of which societal transformation is only one) that are involved in human development. Social scientists have already moved away from age-bound stage theories toward more systemic approaches. Significant in this have been Bronfenbrenner's (1979; Bronfenbrenner & Morris, 1998) interactive micro- to macrolevel theory; Elder's (1974, 1999) emphasis on both historical time and the timing of life events; Baltes' (1987, 1997) concepts of plasticity, multidirectionality, multifunctionality, and nonlinearity; Lerner's (1985, 1998) views on proactivity and self-agency; and Valsiner's (1997) explorations of systemic developmental changes. Understanding human development and life course transitions demands that we examine the interplay among many factors and forces, including structural factors, individual agency and experience, encounters with social institutions, and cultural imperatives. This is more complex than descriptions of age stages, which cannot embrace all facets of developmental changes. In other words, contemporary developmental scientists should consider human interaction within cultural, historical, and psychosocial shifts and the peculiarities of time and place and embrace dynamic, systemic, interactive models as a way of charting and understanding development across the adolescent–adult transition and, indeed, across the whole life span (e.g., Côté, 1996, 1997; Hendry & Kloep, 2002; Magnusson & Stattin, 1998). . . .

Today, young people are increasingly required to take the initiative in forming work and personal relationships, gaining educational credentials and employment experience, and planning for their future. Those who actively address these issues with self-agency may be most likely to form a coherent sense of identity toward their subsequent life course. . . . On the other hand, an inability to shape identity is linked to heightened risks, insecurity, and stress. . . . Arnett's descriptions of a new age stage do not penetrate the layers of variations in transitional trajectories. A complementary perspective is necessary, and we would claim that a dynamic, systemic framework would suit.

To finally return to Hans Christian Andersen's story, it is fair to say that Arnett's ideas on emerging adulthood are not denuded of value. However, a new fashion designer is needed to clothe the emerging framework in the more sophisticated drapes of interactive processes and mechanisms if we are going to research and interpret the many variations within this transitional period accurately and sensitively.

CHALLENGE QUESTIONS

Is There Such a Thing as "Emerging Adulthood"?

- What is the purpose of defining life-span stages at any age? In defining stages, will we always add more or might there be cause to eliminate what used to be considered a characteristic stage of the life-span?
- What else might we call emerging adulthood? Are there other terms that might better describe aspects of this age period?
- Arnett criticizes popular claims of a "quarterlife crisis" as an exaggeration, and claims many dimensions of mental health improve during emerging adulthood. If this is the case, why has the idea of a "quarterlife crisis" achieved some popularity?
- Arnett claims that emerging adulthood leads to higher expectations in domains such as love and work, but does this seem to be a necessary result of delaying full adult responsibilities?
- Many of Hendry and Kloep's criticisms of emerging adulthood could also apply to other stages—what are the advantages and disadvantages of thinking about the lifespan in stages despite significant individual and cultural variation?

Suggested Readings

J. Arnett, *Emerging Adulthood: The Winding Road From the Late Teens Through the Twenties* (Oxford University Press, 2004)

J. Arnett and J. Tanner (eds.) *Emerging Adults in America: Coming of Age in the 21st Century.* APA Books.

P. Baltes, "Theoretical Propositions of Life-Span Developmental Psychology: On the Dynamics Between Growth and Decline." *Developmental Psychology* (September 1987)

J.C. Coleman and L.B. Hendry, *The Nature of Adolescence.* (Routledge, 1999)

A. Robbins and A. Wilner, *Quarterlife Crisis: The Unique Challenges of Life in Your Twenties,* (Tarcher, 2001).

J. Côté, *Arrested Adulthood: The Changing Nature of Maturity and Identity in the Late Modern World,* (New York University Press, 2000).

Lloyd, C.B., *Growing up Global: The Changing Transitions to Adulthood in Developing Countries,* (National Academies Press, 2005)

Internet References . . .

American Psychological Association

This Web site provides information from Division 20 of the American Psychological Association, the division focused on adult development and aging.

http://apadiv20.phhp.ufl.edu/apadiv20.htm

The Society for Research on Adult Development

The Society for Research on Adult Development brings together researchers interested in positive adult development.

http://www.adultdevelopment.org/

The Alternatives to Marriage Project

The Alternatives to Marriage Project advocates for diversity in adult relationships.

http://www.unmarried.org/

The Institute for American Values

The "Institute for American Values" promotes, among other things, marriage and traditional families.

http://americanvalues.org/

Hartford Institute for Religion Research

This Web site provides access to an encyclopedia about the role of religion in society.

http://hirr.hartsem.edu/ency/index.html

Tufts University Child and Family Web Guide

Information and links, vetted by the Eliot-Pearson Department of Child Development at Tufts University, for information about parenting.

http://www.cfw.tufts.edu/

Working Mother Magazine

The Web site for Working Mother magazine offers information and links for adult women trying to balance parenting and careers.

http://www.workingmother.com/

Parenting Blog

The author of the New York Times parenting blog, Lisa Belkin, wrote a controversial article bringing the "opt-out revolution" into popular use—and offers regular articles about issues related to balancing family with work.

http://parenting.blogs.nytimes.com/

Middle Adulthood

In conventional terms, middle adulthood is often the most productive portion of the life-span. During middle adulthood most people deeply engage with families, the world of work, and communities. As such, some versions of the life-span present middle adulthood (generally conceptualized as being between the mid-thirties and the mid-sixties) as the peak of development. But middle adulthood also produces significant challenges and new expectations. This section focuses on the relationship between healthy development and three challenges and expectations confronted by most adults in contemporary society: marriage, religion, and negotiating between career and family.

- Is the Institution of Marriage at Risk?
- Is Religion a Pure Good in Facilitating Well-Being during Adulthood?
- Are Professional Women "Opting Out" of Work by Choice?

ISSUE 15

Is the Institution of Marriage at Risk?

YES: **Andrew J. Cherlin**, from "The Deinstitutionalization of American Marriage," *Journal of Marriage and Family* (September 2004)

NO: **Frank Furstenberg**, from "Can Marriage Be Saved?" *Dissent Magazine* (Summer 2005)

ISSUE SUMMARY

YES: Sociologist Andrew J. Cherlin suggests that the institution of marriage is losing its preeminence and may become just one of many relationship options for couples.

NO: Frank Furstenberg, on the other hand, proposes that the institution of marriage will persist with appropriate government policies and support to families.

Marriage is one of the most significant markers of the adult life-span. Both historically and cross-culturally, adulthood is often defined by getting married and starting a family. In contemporary society this norm is gradually changing. While there has always been a diversity of family types, the general expectation that a person will get married immediately upon becoming an adult has waned. It is much more likely for people to wait to get married, or to not get married at all. This trend has generated tremendous controversy among those interested in considering the relationship between marriage and life-span development.

Some of the controversy derives from divorce rates that are astonishingly high. It is common to hear that half of all marriages in the United States end in divorce—though that figure is generally used more as a high-end estimate rather than the probability of any particular marriage working out. For example, by some estimates, college-educated people are half as likely to get a divorce than the less educated. Likewise, people who marry at a young age are significantly more likely to get divorced. While such statistics can be manipulated to serve varying agendas, it is true that divorce is a common outcome of contemporary marriage. And divorce is hard on people—it is hard on the people getting divorced, and it is hard on any children that may be involved. While the long-term impact of divorce is another controversial area of study, few people would argue divorce is a good outcome.

With the specter of divorce and all the other challenges to the institution of marriage, perhaps marriage will simply cease to be a central institution in contemporary society. This is the position taken by Johns Hopkins University sociologist Andrew J. Cherlin. In a broad analysis of trends in marriage, Cherlin finds a confluence of many factors that suggest the social norms surrounding marriage are irrevocably shifting. While Cherlin is wary of predicting anything with certainty because he realizes that future patterns for marriage are notoriously hard to foresee, he does persuasively illustrate trends toward an increasing diversity of relationship norms—from long-term cohabitation to same-sex marriage. Further, with the increasing social emphasis on emotional fulfillment and "expressive individualism" it may be unlikely for traditional marriage to persist as a normative part of adulthood.

Sociologist Frank Furstenberg, on the other hand, posits that marriage holds a peculiar and special place in contemporary society. While he acknowledges changing norms for marriage internationally and dramatic shifts in the United States from norms in the 1950s, he sees these more as evidence that the institution of marriage is always in flux. For Furstenberg, the key question now is how to best support marriage, and he thinks the answer lies in adequately supporting children and families. Implicit in this argument is the idea that adults will marry as long as it makes sense within their circumstance. Thus, marriage is and will likely remain the norm for adulthood.

POINT

- The social norms surrounding marriage have significantly weakened during recent decades.

- Longstanding changes in gendered divisions of labor, along with childbearing outside of marriage, have served to dramatically shift relationship possibilities.
- The relatively new growth of cohabitation and same-sex marriage have provided additional impetus for deinstitutionalization.
- All of these changes are associated with broader changes in the relatively new emphasis on romantic love and the extreme emphasis on "expressive individualism."

COUNTERPOINT

- We cannot appropriately make comparisons with the 1950s and the baby boom generation, because that was a historical anomaly. The nuclear family, other than in the 1950s, has never really been central to society.
- Family systems are always in flux—it is not just a process of one directional change.

- If we as a society invest in children and make it realistic for all families to function well, marriage will continue to be a popular institution.
- Marriage norms are not really changing much among the educated middle-class, suggesting that there is no relationship between the institution of marriage and broad social trends.

YES ↩

Andrew J. Cherlin

The Deinstitutionalization of American Marriage

This article argues that marriage has undergone a process of deinstitution-alization—a weakening of the social norms that define partners' behavior—over the past few decades. Examples are presented involving the increasing number and complexity of cohabiting unions and the emergence of same-sex marriage. Two transitions in the meaning of marriage that occurred in the United States during the 20th century have created the social context for dein-stitutionalization. The first transition, noted by Ernest Burgess, was from the institutional marriage to the companionate marriage. The second transition was to the individualized marriage in which the emphasis on personal choice and self-development expanded. Although the practical importance of mar-riage has declined, its symbolic significance has remained high and may even have increased. It has become a marker of prestige and personal achievement. Examples of its symbolic significance are presented. The implications for the current state of marriage and its future direction are discussed.

A quarter century ago, in an article entitled "Remarriage as an Incomplete Institution" (Cherlin, 1978), I argued that American society lacked norms about the way that members of stepfamilies should act toward each other. Parents and children in first marriages, in contrast, could rely on well-established norms, such as when it is appropriate to discipline a child. I predicted that, over time, as remarriage after divorce became common, norms would begin to emerge concerning proper behavior in step-families—for example, what kind of relationship a stepfather should have with his stepchildren. In other words, I expected that remarriage would become institutionalized, that it would become more like first marriage. But just the opposite has happened. Remarriage has not become more like first marriage; rather, first marriage has become more like remarriage. Instead of the institutionalization of remarriage, what has occurred over the past few decades is the deinstitutionalization of marriage. Yes, remarriage is an incomplete institution, but now, so is first marriage—and for that matter, cohabitation.

By deinstitutionalization I mean the weakening of the social norms that define people's behavior in a social institution such as marriage. In times of social stability, the taken-for-granted nature of norms allows people to go about their lives without having to question their actions or the actions of others. But when social change produces situations outside the reach of established

From *Journal of Marriage and Family*, vol. 66, September 2004, pp. 848–51, 853–861. Copyright © 2004 by National Council on Family Relations. Reprinted by permission of Blackwell Pub-lishing, Ltd. and the author.

norms, individuals can no longer rely on shared understandings of how to act. Rather, they must negotiate new ways of acting, a process that is a potential source of confict and opportunity. On the one hand, the development of new rules is likely to engender disagreement and tension among the relevant actors. On the other hand, the breakdown of the old rules of a gendered institution such as marriage could lead to the creation of a more egalitarian relationship between wives and husbands.

This perspective, I think, can help us understand the state of contemporary marriage. It may even assist in the risky business of predicting the future of marriage. To some extent, similar changes in marriage have occurred in the United States, Canada, and much of Europe, but the American situation may be distinctive. Consequently, although I include information about Canadian and European families, I focus mainly on the United States.

The Deinstitutionalization of Marriage

Even as I was writing my 1978 article, the changing division of labor in the home and the increase in childbearing outside marriage were undermining the institutionalized basis of marriage. The distinct roles of homemaker and breadwinner were fading as more married women entered the paid labor force. Looking into the future, I thought that perhaps an equitable division of household labor might become institutionalized. But what happened instead was the "stalled revolution," in Hochschild's (1989) well-known phrase. Men do somewhat more home work than they used to do, but there is wide variation, and each couple must work out their own arrangement without clear guidelines. In addition, when I wrote the article, 1 out of 6 births in the United States occurred outside marriage, already a much higher ratio than at midcentury (U.S. National Center for Health Statistics, 1982). Today, the comparable figure is 1 out of 3 (U.S. National Center for Health Statistics, 2003). The percentage is similar in Canada (Statistics Canada, 2003) and in the United Kingdom and Ireland (Kiernan, 2002). In the Nordic countries of Denmark, Iceland, Norway, and Sweden, the figure ranges from about 45% to about 65% (Kiernan). Marriage is no longer the nearly universal setting for childbearing that it was a half century ago.

Both of these developments—the changing division of labor in the home and the increase in childbearing outside marriage—were well under way when I wrote my 1978 article, as was a steep rise in divorce. Here I discuss two more recent changes in family life, both of which have contributed to the deinstitutionalization of marriage after the 1970s: the growth of cohabitation, which began in the 1970s but was not fully appreciated until it accelerated in the 1980s and 1990s, and same-sex marriage, which emerged as an issue in the 1990s and has come to the fore in the current decade.

The Growth of Cohabitation

In the 1970s, neither I nor most other American researchers foresaw the greatly increased role of cohabitation in the adult life course. We thought that, except among the poor, cohabitation would remain a short-term arrangement among childless young adults who would quickly break up or marry. But it has become a more prevalent and more complex phenomenon. For example, cohabitation has created an additional layer of complexity in stepfamilies. When I wrote my article, nearly all stepfamilies were formed by the remarriage of one or both spouses. Now, about one fourth of all stepfamilies in the United States, and one half of all stepfamilies in Canada, are formed by cohabitation rather than marriage (Bumpass, Raley, & Sweet, 1995; Statistics Canada, 2002). It is not uncommon, especially among the low-income population, for a woman to have a child outside marriage, end her relationship with that partner, and then begin cohabiting with a different partner. This new union is equivalent in structure to a step-family but does not involve marriage. Sometimes the couple later marries, and if neither has been married before, their union creates a first marriage with stepchildren. As a result, we now see an increasing number of stepfamilies that do not involve marriage, and an increasing number of first marriages that involve stepfamilies.

More generally, cohabitation is becoming accepted as an alternative to marriage. British demographer Kathleen Kiernan (2002) writes that the acceptance of cohabitation is occurring in stages in European nations, with some nations further along than others. In stage one, cohabitation is a fringe or avant garde phenomenon; in stage two, it is accepted as a testing ground for marriage; in stage three, it becomes acceptable as an alternative to marriage; and in stage four, it becomes indistinguishable from marriage. Sweden and Denmark, she argues, have made the transition to stage four; in contrast, Mediterranean countries such as Spain, Italy, and Greece remain in stage one. In the early 2000s, the United States appeared to be in transition from stage two to stage three (Smock & Gupta, 2002). A number of indicators suggested that the connection between cohabitation and marriage was weakening. The proportion of cohabiting unions that end in marriage within 3 years dropped from 60% in the 1970s to about 33% in the 1990s (Smock & Gupta), suggesting that fewer cohabiting unions were trial marriages (or that fewer trial marriages were succeeding). In fact, Manning and Smock (2003) reported that among 115 cohabiting working-class and lower middle-class adults who were interviewed in depth, none said that he or she was deciding between marriage and cohabitation at the start of the union. Moreover, only 36% of adults in the 2002 United States General Social Survey disagreed with the statement, "It is alright for a couple to live together without intending to get married" (Davis, Smith, & Marsden, 2003). And a growing share of births to unmarried women in the United States (about 40% in the 1990s) were to cohabiting couples (Bumpass & Lu, 2000). The comparable share was about 60% in Britain (Ermisch, 2001).

Canada appears to have entered stage three (Smock & Gupta, 2002). Sixty-nine percent of births to unmarried women were to cohabiting couples in 1997 and 1998 (Juby, Marcil-Gratton, & Le Bourdais, in press). Moreover, the national figures for Canada mask substantial provincial variation. In particular, the rise in cohabitation has been far greater in Quebec than elsewhere in Canada. In 1997 and 1998, 84% of unmarried women who gave birth in Quebec were cohabiting (Juby, Marcil-Gratton, & Le Bourdais). And four out of five Quebeckers entering a first union did so by cohabiting rather than marrying (Le Bourdais & Juby, 2002). The greater acceptance of cohabitation in Quebec seems to have a cultural basis. Francophone Quebeckers have substantially higher likelihoods of cohabiting than do English-speaking Quebeckers or Canadians in the other English-speaking provinces (Statistics Canada, 1997). Céline Le Bourdais and Nicole Marcil-Gratton (1996) argue that Francophone Quebeckers draw upon a French, rather than Anglo-Saxon, model of family life. In fact, levels of cohabitation in Quebec are similar to levels in France, whereas levels in English-speaking Canada and in the United States are more similar to the lower levels in Great Britain (Kiernan, 2002).

To be sure, cohabitation is becoming more institutionalized. In the United States, states and municipalities are moving toward granting cohabiting couples some of the rights and responsibilities that married couples have. Canada has gone further: Under the Modernization of Benefits and Obligations Act of 2000, legal distinctions between married and unmarried same-sex and opposite-sex couples were eliminated for couples who have lived together for at least a year. Still, the Supreme Court of Canada ruled in 2002 that when cohabiting partners dissolve their unions, they do not have to divide their assets equally, nor can one partner be compelled to pay maintenance payments to the other, even when children are involved (*Nova Scotia [Attorney General] v. Walsh*, 2002). In France, unmarried couples may enter into Civil Solidarity Pacts, which give them most of the rights and responsibilities of married couples after the pact has existed for 3 years (Daley, 2000). Several other countries have instituted registered partnerships (Lyall, 2004).

The Emergence of Same-Sex Marriage

The most recent development in the deinstitutionalization of marriage is the movement to legalize same-sex marriage. It became a public issue in the United States in 1993, when the Hawaii Supreme Court ruled that a state law restricting marriage to opposite-sex couples violated the Hawaii state constitution (*Baehr v. Lewin*, 1993). Subsequently, Hawaii voters passed a state constitutional amendment barring same-sex marriage. In 1996, the United States Congress passed the Defense of Marriage Act, which allowed states to refuse to recognize same-sex marriages licensed in other states. The act's constitutionality has not been tested as of this writing because until recently, no state allowed same-sex marriages. However, in 2003, the Massachusetts Supreme Court struck down a state law limiting marriage to opposite-sex couples, and same-sex marriage became legal in May 2004 (although opponents may eventually succeed in prohibiting it through a state constitutional amendment). The issue has developed further in Canada: In the early 2000s, courts in British Columbia, Ontario, and Quebec ruled that laws restricting marriage to opposite-sex couples were discriminatory, and it appears likely that the federal government will legalize gay marriage throughout the nation. Although social conservatives in the United States are seeking a federal constitutional amendment, I think it is reasonable to assume that same-sex marriage will be allowed in at least some North American jurisdictions in the future. In Europe, same-sex marriage has been legalized in Belgium and The Netherlands.

Lesbian and gay couples who choose to marry must actively construct a marital world with almost no institutional support. Lesbians and gay men already use the term "family" to describe their close relationships, but they usually mean something different from the standard marriage-based family. Rather, they often refer to what sociologists have called a "family of choice": one that is formed largely through voluntary ties among individuals who are not biologically or legally related (Weeks, Heaphy, & Donovan, 2001; Weston, 1991). Now they face the task of integrating marriages into these larger networks of friends and kin. The partners will not even have the option of falling back on the gender-differentiated roles of heterosexual marriage. This is not to say that there will be no division of labor; one study of gay and lesbian couples found that in homes where one partner works longer hours and earns substantially more than the other partner, the one with the less demanding, lower paying job did more housework and more of the work of keeping in touch with family and friends. The author suggests that holding a demanding professional or managerial job may make it difficult for a person to invest fully in sharing the work at home, regardless of gender or sexual orientation (Carrington, 1999).

We might expect same-sex couples who have children, or who wish to have children through adoption or donor insemination, to be likely to avail themselves of the option of marriage. (According to the United States Census Bureau [2003b], 33% of women in same-sex partnerships and 22% of men in same-sex partnerships had children living with them in 2000.) Basic issues, such as who would care for the children, would have to be resolved family by family. The obligations of the partners to each other following a marital dissolution have also yet to be worked out. In these and many other ways, gay and lesbian couples who marry in the near future would need to create a marriage-centered kin network through discussion, negotiation, and experiment.

Two Transitions in the Meaning of Marriage

In a larger sense, all of these developments—the changing division of labor, childbearing outside of marriage, cohabitation, and gay marriage—are the result of long-term cultural and material trends that altered the meaning of marriage during the 20th century. The cultural trends included, first, an emphasis on emotional satisfaction and romantic love that intensified early in the century. Then, during the last few decades of the century, an ethic of expressive individualism—which Bellah, Marsden, Sullivan, Swidler, & Tipton (1985) describe as the belief that "each person has a unique core of feeling and intuition that should unfold or be expressed if individuality is to be realized" (p. 334)—became more important. On the material side, the trends include the decline of agricultural labor and the corresponding increase in wage labor; the decline in child and adult mortality; rising standards of living; and, in the last half of the 20th century, the movement of married women into the paid workforce.

These developments, along with historical events such as the Depression and World War II, produced two great changes in the meaning of marriage during the 20th century. Ernest Burgess famously labeled the first one as a transition "from an institution to a companionship" (Burgess & Locke, 1945). In describing the rise of the companionate marriage, Burgess was referring to the single-earner, breadwinner-homemaker marriage that flourished in the 1950s. Although husbands and wives in the companionate marriage usually adhered to a sharp division of labor, they were supposed to be each other's companions—friends, lovers—to an extent not imagined by the spouses in the institutional marriages of the previous era. The increasing focus on bonds of sentiment within nuclear families constituted an important but limited step in the individualization of family life. Much more so than in the 19th century, the emotional satisfaction of the spouses became an important criterion for marital success. However, through the 1950s, wives and husbands tended to derive satisfaction from their participation in a marriage-based nuclear family (Roussel, 1989). That is to say, they based their gratification on playing marital roles well: being good providers, good homemakers, and responsible parents. . . .

Sociological theorists of late modernity (or postmodernity) such as Anthony Giddens (1991, 1992) in Britain and Ulrich Beck and Elisabeth Beck-Gernsheim in Germany (1995, 2002) also have written about the growing individualization of personal life. Consistent with the idea of deinstitutionalization, they note the declining power of social norms and laws as regulating mechanisms for family life, and they stress the expanding role of personal choice. They argue that as traditional sources of identity such as class, religion, and community lose influence, one's intimate relationships become central to self-identity. Giddens (1991, 1992) writes of the emergence of the "pure relationship": an intimate partnership entered into for its own sake, which lasts only as long as both partners are satisfied with the rewards (mostly intimacy and love) that they get from it. It is in some ways the logical extension of the increasing individualism and the deinstitutionalization of marriage that occurred in the 20th century. The pure relationship is not tied to an institution such as marriage or to the desire to raise children. Rather, it is "free-floating," independent of social institutions or economic life. Unlike marriage, it is not regulated by law, and its members do not enjoy special legal rights. It exists primarily in the realms of emotion and self-identity.

Although the theorists of late modernity believe that the quest for intimacy is becoming the central focus of personal life, they do not predict that *marriage* will remain distinctive and important. Marriage, they claim, has become a choice rather than a necessity for adults who want intimacy, companionship, and children. According to Beck and Beck-Gernsheim (1995), we will see "a huge variety of ways of living together or apart which will continue to exist side by side" (pp. 141–142). Giddens (1992) even argues that marriage has already become "just one life-style among others" (p. 154), although people may not yet realize it because of institutional lag.

The Current Context of Marriage

Overall, research and writing on the changing meaning of marriage suggest that it is now situated in a very different context than in the past. This is true in at least two senses. First, individuals now experience a vast latitude for choice in their personal lives. More forms of marriage and more alternatives to marriage are socially acceptable. Moreover, one may fit marriage into one's life in many ways: One may first live with a partner, or sequentially with several partners, without an explicit consideration of whether a marriage will occur. One may have children with one's eventual spouse or with someone else before marrying. One may, in some jurisdictions, marry someone of the same gender and build a shared marital world with few guidelines to rely on. Within marriage, roles are more flexible and negotiable, although women still do more than their share of the household work and childrearing.

The second difference is in the nature of the rewards that people seek through marriage and other close relationships. Individuals aim for personal growth and deeper intimacy through more open communication and mutually shared disclosures about feelings with their partners. They may feel justified in insisting on changes in a relationship that no longer provides them with individualized rewards. In contrast, they are less likely than in the past to focus on the rewards to be found in fulfilling socially valued roles such as the good parent or the loyal and supportive spouse. The result of these changing contexts has been a deinstitutionalization of marriage, in which social norms about family and personal life count for less than they did during the heyday of the companionate marriage, and far less than during the period of the institutional marriage. Instead, personal choice and self-development loom large in people's construction of their marital careers.

Why Do People Still Marry?

There is a puzzle within the story of deinstitutionalization that needs solving. Although fewer Americans are marrying than during the peak years of marriage in the mid-20th century, most—nearly 90%, according to a recent estimate (Goldstein & Kenney, 2001)—will eventually marry. A survey of high school seniors conducted annually since 1976 shows no decline in the importance they attach to marriage. The percentage of young women who respond that they expect to marry has stayed constant at roughly 80% (and has increased from 71% to 78% for young men). The percentage who respond that "having a good marriage and family life" is extremely important has also remained constant, at about 80% for young women and 70% for young men (Thornton & Young-DeMarco, 2001). What is more, in the 1990s and early 2000s, a strong promarriage movement emerged among gay men and lesbians in the United States, who sought the right to marry with increasing success. Clearly, marriage remains important to many people in the United States. Consequently, I think the interesting question is not why so few people are marrying, but rather, why *so many* people are marrying, or planning to marry, or hoping to marry, when cohabitation and single parenthood are widely acceptable options. (This question may be less relevant in Canada and the many European nations where the estimated proportions of who will ever marry are lower.)

The Gains to Marriage

The dominant theoretical perspectives on marriage in the 20th century do not provide much guidance on the question of why marriage remains so popular. The structural functionalists in social anthropology and sociology in the early- to mid-20th century emphasized the role of marriage in ensuring that a child would have a link to the status of a man, a right to his protection, and a claim to inherit his property (Mair, 1971). But as the law began to recognize the rights of children born outside marriage, and as mothers acquired resources by working in the paid work force, these reasons for marriage become less important. . . .

From a rational choice perspective, then, what benefits might contemporary marriage offer that would lead cohabiting couples to marry rather than cohabit? I suggest that the major benefit is what we might call *enforceable trust* (Cherlin, 2000; Portes & Sensenbrenner, 1993). Marriage still requires a public commitment to a long-term, possibly lifelong relationship. This commitment is usually expressed in front of relatives, friends, and religious congregants. Cohabitation, in contrast, requires only a private commitment, which is easier to break. Therefore, marriage, more so than cohabitation, lowers the risk that one's partner will renege on agreements that have been made. In the language of economic theory, marriage lowers the transaction costs of enforcing agreements between the partners (Pollak, 1985). It allows individuals to invest in the partnership with less fear of abandonment. For instance, it allows the partners to invest financially in joint long-term purchases such as homes and automobiles. It allows caregivers to make relationship-specific investments (England & Farkas, 1986) in the couple's children—investments of time and effort that, unlike strengthening one's job skills, would not be easily portable to another intimate relationship.

Nevertheless, the difference in the amount of enforceable trust that marriage brings, compared with cohabitation, is eroding. Although relatives and friends will view a divorce with disappointment, they will accept it more readily than their counterparts would have two generations ago. As I noted, cohabiting couples are increasingly gaining the rights previously reserved to married couples. It seems likely that over time, the legal differences between cohabitation and marriage will become minimal in the United States, Canada, and many European countries. The advantage of marriage in enhancing trust will then depend on the force of public commitments, both secular and religious, by the partners. . . .

The Symbolic Significance of Marriage

What has happened is that although the practical importance of being married has declined, its symbolic importance has remained high, and may even have increased. Marriage is at once less dominant and more distinctive than it was. It has evolved from a marker of conformity to a marker of prestige. Marriage is a status one builds up to, often by living with a partner beforehand, by attaining steady employment or starting a career, by putting away some savings, and even by having children. Marriage's place in the life course used to come before those investments were made, but now it often comes afterward. It used to be the foundation of adult personal life; now it is sometimes the capstone. It is something to be achieved through one's own efforts rather than something to which one routinely accedes. . . .

How Young Adults in General See It

The changing meaning of marriage is not limited to the low-income population. Consider a nationally representative survey of 1,003 adults, ages 20–29, conducted in 2001 on attitudes toward marriage (Whitehead & Popenoe, 2001). A majority responded in ways suggestive of the view that marriage is a status that one builds up to. Sixty-two percent agreed with the statement, "Living together with someone before marriage is a good way to avoid an eventual divorce," and 82% agreed that "It is extremely important to you to be economically set before you get married." Moreover, most indicated a view of marriage as centered on intimacy and love more than on practical matters such as finances and children. Ninety-four percent of those who had never married agreed that "when you marry, you want your spouse to be your soul mate, first and foremost." In contrast, only 16% agreed that "the main purpose of marriage these days is to have children." And over 80% of the women agreed that it is more important "to have a husband who can communicate about his deepest feelings than to have a husband who makes a good living." The authors of the report conclude, "While marriage is losing much of its broad public and institutional character, it is gaining popularity as a Super-Relationship, an intensely private spiritualized union, combining sexual fidelity, romantic love, emotional intimacy, and togetherness" (p. 13). . . .

Alternative Futures

What do these developments suggest about the future of marriage? Social demographers usually predict a continuation of whatever is happening at the moment, and they are usually correct, but sometimes spectacularly wrong. For example, in the 1930s, every demographic expert in the United States confidently predicted a continuation of the low birth rates of the Depression. Not one forecast the baby boom that overtook them after World War II. No less a scholar than Kingsley Davis (1937) wrote that the future of the family as a social institution was in danger because people were not having enough children to replace themselves. Not a single 1950s or 1960s sociologist predicted the rise of cohabitation. Chastened by this unimpressive record, I will tentatively sketch some future directions.

The first alternative is the reinstitutionalization of marriage, a return to a status akin to its dominant position through the mid-20th century. This would entail a rise in the proportion who ever marry, a rise in the proportion of births born to married couples, and a decline in divorce. It would require a reversal of the individualistic orientation toward family and personal life that has been the major cultural force driving family change over the past several decades.

It would probably also require a decrease in women's labor force participation and a return to more gender-typed family roles. I think this alternative is very unlikely—but then again, so was the baby boom.

The second alternative is a continuation of the current situation, in which marriage remains de-institutionalized but is common and distinctive. It is not just one type of family relationship among many; rather, it is the most prestigious form. People generally desire to be married. But it is an individual choice, and individuals construct marriages through an increasingly long process that often includes cohabitation and childbearing beforehand. It still confers some of its traditional benefits, such as enforceable trust, but it is increasingly a mark of prestige, a display of distinction, an individualistic achievement, a part of what Beck and Beck-Gernsheim (2002) call the "do-it-yourself biography." In this scenario, the proportion of people who ever marry could fall further; in particular, we could see probabilities of marriage among Whites in the United States that are similar to the probabilities shown today by African Americans. Moreover, because of high levels of nonmarital childbearing, cohabitation, and divorce, people will spend a smaller proportion of their adult lives in intact marriages than in the past. Still, marriage would retain its special and highly valued place in the family system.

But I admit to some doubts about whether this alternative will prevail for long in the United States. The privileges and material advantages of marriage, relative to cohabitation, have been declining. The commitment of partners to be trustworthy has been undermined by frequent divorce. If marriage was once a form of cultural capital—one needed to be married to advance one's career, say—that capital has decreased too. What is left, I have argued, is a display of prestige and achievement. But it could be that marriage retains its symbolic aura largely because of its dominant position in social norms until just a half century ago. It could be that this aura is diminishing, like an echo in a canyon. It could be that, despite the efforts of the wedding industry, the need for a highly ritualized ceremony and legalized status will fade. And there is not much else supporting marriage in the early 21st century.

That leads to a third alternative, the fading away of marriage. Here, the argument is that people are still marrying in large numbers because of institutional lag; they have yet to realize that marriage is no longer important. A nonmarital pure relationship, to use Giddens's ideal type, can provide much intimacy and love, can place both partners on an equal footing, and can allow them to develop their independent senses of self. These characteristics are highly valued in late modern societies. However, this alternative also suggests the predominance of fragile relationships that are continually at risk of breaking up because they are held together entirely by the voluntary commitment of each partner. People may still commit morally to a relationship, but they increasingly prefer to commit voluntarily rather than to be obligated to commit by law or social norms. And partners feel free to revoke their commitments at any time.

Therefore, the pure relationship seems most characteristic of a world where commitment does not matter. Consequently, it seems to best fit middle-class, well-educated, childless adults. They have the resources to be independent actors by themselves or in a democratic partnership, and without childbearing responsibilities, they can be free-floating. The pure relationship seems less applicable to couples who face material constraints (Jamieson, 1999). In particular, when children are present—or when they are anticipated anytime soon—issues of commitment and support come into consideration. Giddens (1992) says very little about children in his book on intimacy, and his brief attempts to incorporate children into the pure relationship are unconvincing. Individuals who are, or think they will be, the primary caregivers of children will prefer commitment and will seek material support from their partners. They may be willing to have children and begin cohabiting without commitment, but the relationship probably will not last without it. They will be wary of purely voluntary commitment if they think they can do better. So only if the advantage of marriage in providing trust and commitment disappears relative to cohabitation—and I must admit that this could happen—might we see cohabitation and marriage on an equal footing.

In sum, I see the current state of marriage and its likely future in these terms: At present, marriage is no longer as dominant as it once was, but it remains important on a symbolic level. It has been transformed from a familial and community institution to an individualized, choice-based achievement. It is a marker of prestige and is still somewhat useful in creating enforceable trust. As for the future, I have sketched three alternatives. The first, a return to a more dominant, institutionalized form of marriage, seems unlikely. In the second, the current situation continues; marriage remains important, but not as dominant, and retains its high symbolic status. In the third, marriage fades into just one of many kinds of interpersonal romantic relationships. I think that Giddens's (1992) statement that marriage has already become merely one of many relationships is not true in the United States so far, but it could become true in the future. It is possible that we are living in a transitional phase in which marriage is gradually losing its uniqueness. If Giddens and other modernity theorists are correct, the third alternative will triumph, and marriage will lose its special place in the family system of the United States. If they are not, the second alternative will continue to hold, and marriage—transformed and deinstitutionalized, but recognizable nevertheless—will remain distinctive.

Note

1. I thank Frank Furstenberg, Joshua Goldstein, Kathleen Kiernan, and Céline Le Bourdais for comments on a previous version, and Linda Burton for her collaborative work on the Three-City Study ethnography.

References

Baehr v. Lewin (74 Haw. 530, 74 Haw. 645, 852 P.2d 44 1993).

Beck, U., & Beck-Gernsheim, E. (1995). *The normal chaos of love*. Cambridge, England: Polity Press.

Beck, U., & Beck-Gernsheim, E. (2002). *Individualization: Institutionalized individualism and its social and political consequences*. London: Sage.

Bellah, R., Marsden, R., Sullivan, W. M., Swidler, A., & Tipton, S. M. (1985). *Habits of the heart: Individualism and commitment in America*. Berkeley: University of California Press.

Boden, S. (2003). *Consumerism, romance and the wedding experience*. Hampshire, England: Palgrave Macmillan.

Bumpass, L. L., & Lu, H.-H. (2000). Trends in cohabitation and implications for children's family contexts in the United States. *Population Studies, 54*, 19–41.

Bumpass, L. L., Raley, K., & Sweet, J. A. (1995). The changing character of stepfamilies: Implications of cohabitation and nonmarital childbearing. *Demography, 32*, 1–12.

Burgess, E. W., & Locke, H. J. (1945). *The family: From institution to companionship*. New York: American Book.

Carrington, C. (1999). *No place like home: Relationships and family life among lesbians and gay men*. Chicago: University of Chicago Press.

Cherlin, A. (1978). Remarriage as an incomplete institution. *American Journal of Sociology, 84*, 634–650.

Cherlin, A. J. (2000). Toward a new home socioeconomics of union formation. In L. Waite, C. Bachrach, M. Hindin, E. Thomson, & A. Thornton (Eds.), *Ties that bind: Perspectives on marriage and cohabitation* (pp. 126–144). Hawthorne, NY: Aldine de Gruyter.

Daley, S. (2000, April 18). French couples take plunge that falls short of marriage. *The New York Times*, pp. A1, A4.

Davis, J. A., Smith, T. W., & Marsden, P. (2003). *General social surveys, 1972–2002 cumulative codebook*. Chicago: National Opinion Research Center, University of Chicago.

Davis, K. (1937). Reproductive institutions and the pressure for population. *Sociological Review, 29*, 289–306.

England, P., & Farkas, G. (1986). *Households, employment, and gender: A social, economic, and demographic view*. New York: Aldine.

Ermisch, J. (2001). Cohabitation and childbearing outside marriage in Britain. In L. L. Wu & B. Wolfe (Eds.), *Out of wedlock: Causes and consequences of nonmarital fertility* (pp. 109–139). New York: Russell Sage Foundation.

Giddens, A. (1991). *Modernity and self-identity*. Stanford, CA: Stanford University Press.

Giddens, A. (1992). *The transformation of intimacy*. Stanford, CA: Stanford University Press.

Goldstein, J. R., & Kenney, C. T. (2001). Marriage delayed or marriage forgone? New cohort forecasts of first marriage for U.S. women. *American Sociological Review, 66*, 506–519.

Hochschild, A. (1989). *The second shift: Working parents and the revolution at home*. New York: Viking.

Jamieson, L. (1999). Intimacy transformed? A critical look at the "pure relationship." *Sociology, 33*, 477–494.

Juby, H., Marcil-Gratton, N., & Le Bourdais, C. (in press). *When parents separate: Further findings from the National Longitudinal Survey of Children and Youth*. Phase 2 research report of the project, "The Impact of Parents' Family

Transitions on Children's Family Environment and Economic Well-Being: A Longitudinal Assessment." Ottawa, Ontario: Department of Justice Canada, Child Support Team.

Kiernan, K. (2002). Cohabitation in Western Europe: Trends, issues, and implications. In A. Booth & A. C. Crouter (Eds.), *Just living together: Implication of cohabitation on families, children, and social policy* (pp. 3–31). Mahwah, NJ: Erlbaum.

Le Bourdais, C., & Juby, H. (2002). The impact of cohabitation on the family life course in contemporary North America: Insights from across the border. In A. Booth & A. C. Crouter (Eds.), *Just living together: Implications of cohabitation on families, children, and social policy* (pp. 107–118). Mahwah, NJ: Erlbaum.

Le Bourdais, C., & Marcil-Gratton, N. (1996). Family transformations across the Canadian/American border: When the laggard becomes the leader. *Journal of Comparative Family Studies, 27,* 415–436.

Lyall, S. (2004, February 15). In Europe, lovers now propose: Marry me a little. *The New York Times,* p. A3.

Mair, L. (1971). *Marriage.* Middlesex, England: Penguin Books.

Nova Scotia (Attorney General) v. Walsh. (2002). SCC 83.

Pollak, R. A. (1985). A transaction costs approach to families and households. *Journal of Economic Literature, 23,* 581–608.

Portes, A., & Sensenbrenner, J. (1993). Embedded-ness and immigration: Notes on the social determinants of economic action. *American Journal of Sociology, 98,* 1320–1350.

Smock, P. J., & Gupta, S. (2002). Cohabitation in contemporary North America. In A. Booth & A. C. Crouter (Eds.), *Just living together: Implications of cohabitation on families, children, and social policy* (pp. 53–84). Mahwah, NJ: Erlbaum.

Statistics Canada. (1997). *Report on the demographic situation in Canada 1996* (No. 91-209-XPE). Ottawa, Ontario: Statistical Reference Centre.

Statistics Canada. (2002). *Changing conjugal life in Canada* (No. 89-576-XIE). Ottawa, Ontario: Statistical Reference Centre.

Statistics Canada. (2003). *Annual Demographic Statistics, 2002* (No. 91-213-XIB). Ottawa, Ontario: Statistical Reference Centre.

Thornton, A., & Young-DeMarco, L. (2001). Four decades of trends in attitudes toward family issues in the United States: The 1960s through the 1990s. *Journal of Marriage and Family, 63,* 1009–1037.

U.S. Census Bureau. (2003b). *Married-couple and unmarried-partner households: 2000* (Census 2000 Special Reports, CENSR-5). Washington, DC: U.S. Government Printing Office.

U.S. National Center for Health Statistics. (1982). *Vital statistics of the United States, 1978* (Volume I – Natality). Washington, DC: U.S. Government Printing Office.

U.S. National Center for Health Statistics. (2003). *Births: Preliminary data for 2002.* Retrieved December 15, 2003, from . . .

Weeks, J., Heaphy, B., & Donovan, C. (2001). *Same sex intimacies: Families of choice and other life experiments.* London: Routledge.

Weston, K. (1991). *Families we choose: Lesbians, gays, kinship*. New York: Columbia University Press.

Whitehead, B. D., & Popenoe, D. (2001). Who wants to marry a soul mate? In *The state of our unions, 2001* (National Marriage Project, pp. 6–16).

Frank Furstenberg → **NO**

Can Marriage Be Saved?

A growing number of social scientists fear that marriage may be on the rocks and few doubt that matrimony, as we have known it, has undergone a wrenching period of change in the past several decades. Andrew Cherlin, a leading sociologist of the family, speaks of "the de-institutionalization of marriage," conceding a point to conservative commentators who have argued that marriage and the family have been in a state of free-fall since the 1960s.

Western Europe has experienced many of the same trends—declining rates of marriage, widespread cohabitation, and rising levels of nonmarital childbearing—but has largely shrugged them off. By contrast, concern about the state of marriage in the United States has touched a raw, political nerve. What ails marriage and what, if anything, can be done to restore this time-honored social arrangement to its former status as a cultural invention for assigning the rights and responsibilities of reproduction, including sponsorship and inheritance?

On the left side of the political spectrum, observers believe that the institutional breakdown of marriage has its roots in economic and social changes brought about by shifts in home-based production, structural changes in the economy, and the breakdown of the gender-based division of labor—trends unlikely to be reversed. The other position, championed by most conservatives, is that people have lost faith in marriage because of changes in cultural values that could be reversed or restored through shifts in the law, changes in administrative policies and practices, and public rhetoric to alter beliefs and expectations.

The Bush administration is trying to put into place a set of policies aimed at reversing the symptoms of retreat from marriage: high rates of premarital sex, nonmarital childbearing, cohabitation, and divorce. Do their policies make sense and do they have a reasonable prospect of success? To answer this question, I want to begin with the trends that Americans, including many social scientists, have found so alarming and then turn to the question of how much public policy and what kinds of policies could help to strengthen marriage.

Originally published in *Dissent Magazine,* Summer 2005, pp. 76–80. Copyright © 2005 by Foundation for Study of Independent Ideas, Inc. Reprinted by permission. www.dissentmagazine.org

Demographic Changes and Political Interpretations

When compared to the 1950s, the institution of marriage seems to be profoundly changed, but is the middle of the twentieth century an appropriate point of comparison? It has been widely known since the baby boom era that the period after the Second World War was unusual demographically: the very early onset of adult transitions; unprecedented rates of marriage; high fertility; an economy that permitted a single wage earner to support a family reasonably well; and the flow of federal funding for education, housing, and jobs distinguished the 1950s and early 1960s as a particular historical moment different from any previous period and certainly different from the decades after the Vietnam War era. For a brief time, the nuclear family in the United States and throughout much of Europe reigned supreme.

If we use the middle of the twentieth century as a comparison point, it might appear that we have been witnessing a deconstruction of the two-parent biological family en masse. But such a view is historically shortsighted and simplistic. The nuclear family, though long the bourgeois ideal, had never been universally practiced, at least as it was in the middle of the last century. Only in the 1950s—and then for a very brief time—did it become the gold standard for what constitutes a healthy family. Indeed, sociologists at that time fiercely debated whether this family model represented a decline from the "traditional" extended family. Even those who argued against this proposition could not agree whether this family form was desirable ("functional" in the language of the day) or contained fatal flaws that would be its undoing.

During the 1960s and 1970s, anthropological evidence indicated that family diversity is universal, and findings from the new field of historical demography revealed that families in both the East and the West had always been changing in response to economic, political, demographic, and social conditions. In short, the nuclear family was cross-culturally and historically not "the natural unit," that many wrongly presume today.

Although it was widely known that the family had undergone considerable changes from ancient times and during the industrial revolution, that family systems varied across culture, and that social-class differences created varied forms of the family within the same society, it was not until the 1960s, when historians began to use computers to analyze census data, that the extent of this variation came into clearer focus. For the first time, family scholars from several disciplines could see the broad outlines of a new picture of how family forms and functions are intimately related to the social, cultural, and perhaps especially the economic contexts in which household and kinship systems are embedded.

From this evidence, students of the family can assert three points. First, no universal form of the family constitutes the appropriate or normative arrangement for reproduction, nurturance, socialization, and economic support. Both across and within societies, family forms, patterns, and practices vary enormously. Second, change is endemic to all family systems, and at least in the West, where we have the best evidence to date, family systems have always been in flux. Typically, these changes create tensions and often ignite public concern. Since colonial times, the family has been changing and provoking public reaction from moralists, scientists, and, of course, public authorities. Finally, family systems do not evolve in a linear fashion but become more or less complex and more elemental in different eras or among different strata of society depending on the economic and social conditions to which families must adapt.

Does this mean that we are seeing a continuation of what has always been or something different than has ever occurred in human history—the withering of kinship as an organizing feature of human society? The decline of marriage suggests to some that this round of change is unique in human history or that its consequences for children will be uniquely unsettling to society.

Many scholars weighed in on these questions. It is fair to say that there are two main camps: (1) those who have decided that the family is imperiled as a result of changes in the marriage system, a position held by such respectable social scientists as Linda Waite, Norvel Glenn, and Judith Wallerstein; and (2) those who remain skeptical and critical of those sounding the alarm, a position held by the majority of social scientists. Many in this second camp take seriously the concerns of the "alarmists" that children's welfare may be at risk if the current family regime continues. Still, they doubt that the family can be coaxed back into its 1950s form and favor adaptations in government policy to assist new forms of the family—an approach followed by most European nations.

⋅⟨☉⟩⋅

Some portion of those skeptics are not so alarmed by changes in the family, believing that children's circumstances have not been seriously compromised by family change. They contend that children's well-being has less to do with the family form in which they reside than the resources possessed to form viable family arrangements. Lacking these resources (material and cultural), it matters little whether the children are born into a marriage, cohabitation, or a single-parent household, because they are likely not to fare as well as those whose parents possess the capacity to realize their goals.

I place myself in this latter group. Of course, children will fare better when they have two well-functioning, collaborative parents than one on average, but one well-functioning parent with resources is better than two married parents who lack the resources or skills to manage parenthood. Moreover, parents with limited cultural and material resources are unlikely to remain together in a stable marriage. Because the possession of such psychological, human, and material capital is highly related to marital stability, it is easy to confuse the effects of stable marriage with the effects of competent parenting. Finally, I believe that the best way to foster marriage stability is to support children with an array of services that assist parents and children, regardless of the family form in which they reside.

Marriage and Good Outcomes for Children

A huge number of studies have shown that children fare better in two-biological-parent families than they do in single-biological-parent families, leading most family researchers to conclude that the nuclear family is a more effective unit for reproduction and socialization. Yet this literature reveals some troubling features that have not been adequately examined by social scientists. The most obvious of these is that such findings rule out social selection.

If parents with limited resources and low skills are less likely to enter marriage with a biological parent and remain wed when they do (which we know to be true), then it follows that children will do worse in such single-parent households than in stable marriages. We have known about this problem for decades, but researchers have not been equipped adequately to rule out selection. The standard method for doing so is by statistically controlling for prior differences, but this method is inadequate for ruling out differences because it leaves so many sources of selection unmeasured, such as sexual compatibility, substance abuse, and so on. Newer statistical methods have been employed to correct for unmeasured differences, but strong evidence exists that none of these techniques is up to the challenge. Nevertheless, it is *theoretically* possible to examine social experiments such as those being mounted in the marriage-promotion campaign and assess their long-term effects on children.

Another useful approach is to examine macro-level differences at the state or national level that would be less correlated with social selection and hence more revealing of the impact of marriage arrangements on children's well-being. To date, there is little evidence supporting a correlation between family form and children's welfare at the national level. Consider first the historical data showing that children who grew up in the 1950s (baby boomers) were not notably free of problem behavior. After all, they were the cohort who raised such hell in the 1960s and 1970s. From 1955 to 1975, indicators of social problems among children (test scores, suicide, homicide, controlled-substance use, crime) that can be tracked by vital statistics all rose. These indicators accompanied, and in some cases preceded rather than followed, change in the rates of divorce, the decline of marriage, and the rise of nonmarital childbearing during this period. Conversely, there is no evidence that the cohort of children who came of age in the 1990s and early part of this century is doing worse than previous cohorts because these children are more likely to have grown up in single-parent families. Of course, compensatory public policies or other demographic changes such as small family size, higher parental education, or lower rates of poverty may have offset the deleterious effects of family form, but such an explanation concedes that family form is not as potent a source of children's well-being as many observers seem to believe.

We might also gain some purchase on this issue by comparing the success of children under different family regimes. Do the countries with high rates of cohabitation, low marriage, high divorce, and high nonmarital fertility have the worst outcomes for children? We don't know the answer to this question, but we do know that various indicators of child well-being—health, mental health, educational attainment—do show higher scores in Northern than in Southern Europe. They appear to be linked to the level of investment in children, not the family form (which is certainly more intact in Southern Europe). Still, this question deserves more attention than it has received.

Significantly, many of the countries that continue to adhere to the nuclear model have some of the world's lowest rates of fertility—a problem that seems worse in countries with very low rates of nonmarital childbearing. I am not claiming that nonmarital childbearing is necessarily desirable as a social arrangement for propping up fertility, but it is a plausible hypothesis that nonmarital childbearing helps to keep the birth rate up in countries that would otherwise be experiencing a dangerously low level of reproduction.

Finally, it is important to recognize that family change in the United States (and in most Western countries, it appears) has not occurred evenly among all educational groups. In this country, marriage, divorce, and non-marital childbearing have jumped since the 1960s among the bottom two-thirds of the educational distribution but have not changed much at all among the top third, consisting, today, of college graduates and postgraduates. Though marriage comes later to this group, they are barely more likely to have children out of wedlock, have high levels of marriage, and, if anything, lower levels of divorce than were experienced several decades ago. In other words, almost all the change has occurred among the segment of the population that has either not gained economically or has lost ground over the past several decades. Among the most socially disadvantaged and most marginalized segments of American society, marriage has become imperiled and family conditions have generally deteriorated, resulting in extremely high rates of union instability. The growing inequality in the United States may provide some clues for why the family, and marriage in particular, is not faring well and what to do about it.

Marriage and Public Policy

The logic of the Bush administration's approach to welfare is that by promoting and strengthening marriage, children's well-being, particularly in lower-income families will be enhanced. At first blush, this approach seems to make good sense. Economies of scale are produced when two adults live together. Two parents create healthy redundancies and perhaps help build social capital both within the household and by creating more connections to the community. The prevalence of marriage and marital stability is substantially higher among well-educated and more stably employed individuals than among those with less than a college education and lower incomes. Wouldn't it be reasonable to help the less educated enjoy the benefits of the nuclear family?

There are several reasons to be skeptical of this policy direction. First, we have the experience of the 1950s, when marriages did occur in abundance among low-income families. Divorce rates were extremely high during this era, and many of these families dissolved their unions when they had an opportunity to divorce because of chronic problems of conflict, disenchantment, and scarcity. In my own study of marriages of teen parents in the 1960s, I discovered that four out of every five women who married the father of their children got divorced before the child reached age eighteen; the rate of marital instability among those who married a stepfather was even higher. Certainly, encouraging marriage among young couples facing a choice of nonmarital childbearing or wedlock is not an easy choice when we know the outcome of the union is so precarious. If divorce is a likely outcome, it is not clear whether children are better off if their parents marry and divorce than remain unmarried, knowing as we do that family conflict and flux have adverse effects on children's welfare.

What about offering help to such couples before or after they enter marriage? This is a good idea, but don't expect any miracles from the current policies. Strong opposition exists to funding sustained and intensive premarital and postmarital counseling among many proponents of marriage-promotion programs. Conservative constituencies largely believe that education, especially under the aegis of religious or quasi-religious sponsorship is the best prescription for shoring up marriage. Yet, the evidence overwhelmingly shows that short-term programs that are largely didactic will not be effective in preserving marriages. Instead, many couples need repeated bouts of help both before and during marriage when they run into difficult straits. Most of these couples have little or no access to professional counseling.

The federal government has funded several large-scale experiments combining into a single program marital education or counseling *and* social services including job training or placement. These experiments, being conducted by the Manpower Research Demonstration Corporation, will use random assignment and have the best hope of producing some demonstrable outcomes. Yet, it is not clear at this point that even comprehensive programs with sustained services will be effective in increasing partner collaboration and reducing union instability.

There is another approach that I believe has a better prospect of improving both children's chances and probably at least an equal chance of increasing the viability of marriages or marriage-like arrangements. By directing more resources to low-income children regardless of the family form they live in, through such mechanisms as access to quality child care, health care, schooling, and income in the form of tax credits, it may be possible to increase the level of human, social, and psychological capital that children receive. And, by increasing services, work support, and especially tuition aid for adolescents and young adults to attend higher education, Americans may be able to protect children from the limitations imposed by low parental resources. Lending this type of assistance means that young adults are more likely to move into higher paying jobs and acquire through education the kinds of communication and problem-solving skills that are so useful to making marriage-like relationships last.

When we invest in children, we are not only likely to reap the direct benefits of increasing human capital but also the indirect benefits that will help preserve union stability in the next generation. This approach is more likely to increase the odds of success for children when they grow up. If I am correct, it probably follows that direct investment in children and youth has a better prospect of strengthening marriage and marriage-like relationships in the next generation by improving the skills and providing the resources to make parental relationships more rewarding and enduring.

So it comes down to a choice in strategy: invest in strengthening marriage and hope that children will benefit or invest in children and hope that marriages will benefit. I place my bet on the second approach.

CHALLENGE QUESTIONS

Is the Institution of Marriage at Risk?

- Cherlin finishes by providing three alternatives for the future of marriage, himself tentatively speculating that marriage may lose a special place in the United States. Which of the three alternatives do you see as most likely?
- As a general value, most people consider diversity a good thing. As such, why do some people endorse the idea that one specific type of family structure is best for adults, while others endorse a diversity of family structures?
- Despite a significant and well-intentioned push toward marriage from people promoting family values, a majority of voters in recent elections within the United States have rejected the idea of allowing homosexual couples the right to legal marriage. If marriage is good for adults, should we not allow all adults the opportunity to marry? Or would that change the nature of marriage to such a degree that it would no longer maintain its traditional value?
- If alternatives to marriage, such as cohabitation, became the norm rather than the exception, would it still be considered a negative developmental outcome?

Suggested Readings

K. Boo, "The Marriage Cure," *The New Yorker* (August 18, 2003)

A. Cherlin, "Should the Government Promote Marriage?" *Contexts* (Fall 2003)

P. England, "The Case for Marriage: Why Married People Are Happier, Healthier, and Better Off Financially," *Contemporary Sociology* (November 2001)

M. Gallagher, "The Latest War Against Marriage," *Crisis* (February 2001)

T. Huston and H. Meiz, "The Case of (Promoting) Marriage: The Devil Is in the Details," *Journal of Marriage and the Family* (November 2004)

S. Jeffrey, "The Need to Abolish Marriage," *Feminism & Psychology* (May 2004)

D. Solot and M. Miller, "Marriage-Only Forces Don't Help Today's Families," *Sojourner: The Women's Forum* (October 1999)

L. Waite and M. Gallagher, *The Case for Marriage: Why Married People Are Happier, Healthier, and Better Off Financially* (Doubleday, 2000)

L. Waite, D. Browning, W. Dohert, M. Gallagher, Y. Luo, and S. Stanley, "Does Divorce Make People Happy? Findings from a Study of Unhappy Marriages," *Institute of American Values* (2002)

ISSUE 16

Is Religion a Pure Good in Facilitating Well-Being during Adulthood?

YES: David G. Myers, from "Wanting More in an Age of Plenty," *Christianity Today* (April 2000)

NO: Julie Juola Exline, from "Stumbling Blocks on the Religious Road: Fractured Relationships, Nagging Vices, and the Inner Struggle to Believe," *Psychological Inquiry* (vol. 13, 2002)

ISSUE SUMMARY

YES: Psychologist and author David Myers asserts that religion is an antidote to the discontent many adults feel despite incredible relative material wealth.

NO: Professor of psychology Julia Juola Exline asserts that research suggesting religion to be a pure good for adult development neglects to account for the fact that it can also be a source of significant sadness, stress, and confusion.

The role of religion in lifespan development presents a challenging dilemma for social scientists: religion is clearly a huge influence upon people's lives, yet by nature that influence is difficult to quantify and measure. Further, many people simply prefer to keep their religious and spiritual lives separate from efforts to define and study the specific characteristics of the lifespan. Something about academic study often (though not always) seems to detract from the mystical power of religion. Yet, basic demographic statistics show that over 60% of Americans are active in a faith group, over 70% identify with an organized religion, and more than that consider themselves very interested in spirituality. While there is a popular trend to bemoan the loss of religion in modern society, many scholars would note that only traditionally organized religions are in decline, while American interest in spirituality may be at an all-time high.

Inevitably, despite some avoidance and trepidations, lifespan development scholars have investigated the role of religion in the lifespan. Generally steering clear of abstract spiritual questions, such as those about the nature and role of God, scholars of the lifespan tend to focus on aspects of religion that can be analyzed and measured using the methods of social science. One of those aspects is well-being in adulthood. After negotiating the challenges of childhood and youth, and settling into work and family roles, adults often find themselves addressing larger questions of meaning, purpose, and spirituality.

In the first selection David G. Myers, a prolific psychologist who has written several prominent textbooks and several other scholarly books about topics ranging from happiness to spirituality, asserts that contemporary society is incredibly well-off by structural measures such as income and material well-being. Yet, in what he calls "the American paradox," as our material well-being rises our psychological well-being is, in his reckoning, in decline. The statistics that he cites are powerful, and suggest that at a large scale level it does seem that religion and spirituality correlate with improved well-being in the form of charity, altruistic work, health, morality, and communal endeavor. In Myers's viewpoint the personal experience of religion is an overall good that can develop individuals who will improve society.

In contrast, Exline points out four very specific ways in which religion can provide individual developmental challenges. While Exline is interested in religion partially because of its powerful potential to create meaningful psychological experiences, she is wary of understanding religion as a panacea. She notes, in concordance with Myers, that significant amounts of data suggest religion and spirituality can have significant positive benefits through the lifespan. But she asserts such findings should not be oversimplified. Personal experiences of religion involve interpersonal challenges, asking hard questions about faith in the face of hardship, facing intellectual and emotional inconsistencies, and dealing with the very real potential for disappointment in adulthood.

POINT

- Although material well-being is at an all-time high, many people in contemporary Western societies indicate declining mental health that corresponds to a lack of spiritual engagement.
- Religious people tend to do better in terms of charity, altruistic work, and engaging with communities.
- Religious communities provide a rich forum for the types of social interaction that are essential to well-being.

- While religious groups have historically been associated with dramatic examples of social problems, the individual experience of religion associates with primarily positive outcomes.

COUNTERPOINT

- Many people who are spiritually engaged face hard and emotionally challenging questions about the meaning of life.

- Religion can lead people to disappointment when confronting the harsh realities of the world.

- Being part of a religious community involves facing inconsistencies between religious doctrines and personal beliefs.

- Although religion generally associates with positive characteristics, those associations do not come without significant challenge and struggle.

YES ↵

David G. Myers

Wanting More in an Age of Plenty

The Paradox of Our Time in History is that
we spend more, but have less;
we buy more, but enjoy it less.

We have bigger houses and smaller families;
more conveniences, but less time;
more medicine, but less wellness.

We read too little, watch TV too much, and pray too seldom.

We have multiplied our possessions, but reduced our values.

These are the times of tall men, and short character;
steep profits, and shallow relationships.

These are the days of two incomes, but more divorce;
of fancier houses, but broken homes.

We've learned how to make a living, but not a life;
we've added years to life, not life to years;
we've cleaned up the air, but polluted the soul.

—Excerpted from a 1999 Internet chain mailing,
usually attributed to an unknown source.

The past four decades have produced dramatic cultural changes. Since 1960 we have been soaring economically and, until recently, sinking socially. To paraphrase Ronald Reagan's famous question, "Are we better off than we were 40 years ago?" Our honest answer would be: materially yes, morally no. Therein lies the American paradox.

There is much to celebrate. We now have, as average Americans, doubled real incomes and doubled what money buys. We own twice as many cars per person, eat out two and a half times as often, and pay less than ever before (in real dollars and minutes worked) for our cars, air travel, and hamburgers. We have espresso coffee, the World Wide Web, sport utility vehicles, and caller ID.

Democracy is thriving. Military budgets are shrinking. Joblessness and welfare rolls have subsided. Inflation is down. The annual national deficit has become a surplus. The rights of women and various minorities are better protected than ever before. New drugs are shrinking our tumors, lengthening our lives, and enlarging our sexual potency. These are the best of times.

Yet by the early 1990s these had also become the worst of times. During most of the post-1960 years, America was sliding into a deepening social, and moral recession that dwarfed the comparatively milder and briefer economic recessions. Had you fallen asleep in 1960 and awakened today (even after the recent uptick in several indicators of societal health) would you feel pleased at the cultural shift? You would be awakening to a:

- Doubled divorce rate.
- Tripled teen suicide rate.
- Quadrupled rate of reported violent crime.
- Quintupled prison population.
- Sextupled (no pun intended) percent of babies born to unmarried parents.
- Sevenfold increase in cohabitation (a predictor of future divorce).
- Soaring rate of depression—to ten times the pre–World War II level by one estimate.

The National Commission on Civic Renewal combined social trends such as these in creating its 1998 "Index of National Civic Health"—which plunged southward from 1960 until the early 1990s. Bertrand Russell once said that the mark of a civilized human is the capacity to read a column of numbers and weep. Can we weep for the social recession's casualties—for the crushed lives behind these numbers?

Spiritual Hunger in an Age of Plenty

It is hard to argue with Al Gore: "The accumulation of material goods is at an all-time high, but so is the number of people who feel an emptiness in their lives." Moreover, he explained in declaring his presidential candidacy, "Most Americans are hungry for a deeper connection between politics and moral values; many would say 'spiritual values.' " There is indeed "a spiritual vacuum at the heart of American society," agreed the late Lee Atwater, George Bush's 1988 campaign manager. Having solved the question of how to make a living, having surrounded ourselves with once unthinkable luxuries—air-conditioned comfort, CD-quality sound, and fresh fruit year round—we are left to wonder why we live. Why run this rat race? What's the point? Why care about anything or anyone beyond myself?

Ronald Inglehart, a University of Michigan social scientist who follows values surveys across the Western world, discerns the beginnings of a subsiding of materialist values. Not only in Eastern Europe, where materialist Marxism is licking its wounds, but in the West one sees signs of a new generation maturing with decreasing concern for economic growth and strong defense, and with increasing concern for personal relationships, the integrity of nature, and the meaning-of life. At the peak of her fortune and fame, with 146 tennis championships behind her and married to John Lloyd, Chris Evert reflected, "We get into a rut. We play tennis, we go to a movie, we watch TV, but I keep saying, 'John, there has to be more.' "

Materialism and individualism still ride strong. For America's entering collegians, "becoming very well off financially" is still the top-rated life goal among 19 goals on an annual UCLA/American Council on Education survey; it is said to be "very important or essential" by 74 percent in 1998—nearly double the 39 percent saying the same in 1970. Yet Inglehart discerns "a renewed concern for spiritual values."

Pollster George Gallup Jr. detects the same: "One of two dominant trends in society today [along with a search for deeper, more meaningful relationships] is the search for spiritual moorings. . . . Surveys document the movement of people who are searching for meaning in life with a new intensity, and want their religious faith to grow." From 1994 to late 1998, reported Gallup, the percent of Americans feeling a need to "experience spiritual growth" rose from 54 to 82 percent. Although people in surveys exaggerate their church attendance, as they do voting, religious interests seem on an upswing. Since hitting its modern low in 1993, Gallup's "Religion in America" index has been heading upward.

This spiritual hunger is manifest all about us: in a million people annually besieging Catholic retreat centers or seeking spiritual formation guided by spiritual directors; in the NFL, where once-rare chapel services have become universal and after-touchdown kneels are almost as common as struts; in the recent surge of movies with spiritual emphases *(Dead Man Walking, The Prince of Egypt, Seven Years in Tibet)* and in television's *Touched By an Angel* reaching ratings heaven; in New Age bookstore sections devoted to angels, near-death experiences, reincarnation, astrology, and other paranormal claims; in the surge of new publications, conferences, and magazine articles on religion and science and health; in the reopening of school curricula to religion's place in history and literature; and on the Internet, where AltaVista finds "God" on 3.6 million Web pages.

The New American Dream

For Christians—people who experience spirituality in biblically-rooted faith communities—some aspects of contemporary do-it-yourself spirituality may seem gaseous, individualistic, and self-focused. Nevertheless, the essential facts are striking: while we have been surging materially and technologically we have paradoxically undergone a social and moral recession and experienced a deepening spiritual hunger. In many ways these are the best of times, yet in other ways these have been the worst of times. While enjoying the benefits of today's economic and social individualism, we are suffering the costs.

To counter radical individualism, an inclusive social renewal movement is emerging—one that affirms liberals' indictment of the demoralizing effects of poverty and conservatives indictment of toxic media models; one that welcomes liberals' support for family-friendly workplaces and conservatives' support for committed relationships; one that agrees with liberals' advocacy for children in all sorts of families and conservatives' support for marriage and coparenting.

Do we not—whether self-described liberals or conservative—share a vision of a better world? As the slumbering public consciousness awakens, something akin to the earlier civil rights, feminist, and environmental movements seems to be germinating. "Anyone who tunes in politics even for background music can tell you how the sound has changed," observes feminist columnist Ellen Goodman. Yesterday's shouting match over family values has become today's choir, she adds. When singing about children growing up without fathers, "Politicians on the right, left and center may not be hitting exactly the same notes, but like sopranos, tenors and baritones, they're pretty much in harmony." We are recognizing that liberals' risk factors (poverty, inequality, hopelessness) and conservatives' risk factors (early sexualization, unwed parenthood, family fragmentation) all come in the same package.

Whatever our differences, most of us wish for a culture that:

- Welcomes children into families with mothers and fathers who love them, and into an environment that nurtures families.
- Rewards initiative and restrains exploitative greed, thus building a strong economy that shrinks the underclass.
- Balances individual liberties with communal well-being.
- Encourages close relationships within extended families and with supportive neighbors and caring friends, people who celebrate when you're born, care about you as you live, and miss you when you're gone.
- Values our diversity while finding unity in shared ideals.
- Develops children's capacities for empathy, self-discipline, and honesty.
- Provides media that offer social scripts of kindness, civility, attachment, and fidelity.
- Regards relationships as covenants and sexuality not as mere recreation but as life-uniting and love-renewing.
- Takes care of the soul by developing a deeper spiritual awareness of a reality greater than self and of life's resulting meaning, purpose, and hope.

Thanks partly to the emerging renewal movement, several indicators of social pathology have recently shown encouraging turns. Although still at historically high levels, teen sex, pregnancy, and violence, for example, have all subsided somewhat from their peaks around 1993.

Further progress toward the new American dream requires more than expanding our social ambulance services at the base of the social cliffs. It also requires that we identify the forces that are pushing people over the cliffs. And it requires our building new guard rails at the top—by making our business and economics more family-friendly, by reforming our media, by renewing character education in our schools, and by better balancing me-thinking with we-thinking.

Are there credible grounds for adding spiritual renewal to this list? Are George W. Bush and Al Gore both right to trumpet the potential of "faith-based" reforms and social services? Or can skeptical Oxford professor Richard Dawkins more easily find evidence for seeing faith as "one of the world's great evils, comparable to the smallpox virus, but harder to eradicate"? Sifting the evidence won't decide the bigger issue of the truth of Christian claims, but it should indicate whether faith more often uplifts or debilitates.

We now have massive evidence that people active in faith communities are happier and healthier than their unchurched peers. (Recent epidemiological studies—tracking thousands of lives through years of time—reveal they even outlive their unchurched peers by several years.) Is an active faith similarly associated with social health?

God and Goodness

Asked by Gallup, "Can a person be a good and ethical person if he or she does not believe in God?," three in four Americans answered yes. Indeed, examples of honorable secularists and greedy, lustful, or bigoted believers come readily to mind. "God's will" has been used—often by those for whom religion is more a mark of group identity than of genuine piety—as justification for apartheid, for limiting women's rights, for ethnic cleansing, for gay bashing, and for war. As Madeleine L'Engle lamented, "Christians have given Christianity a bad name."

But anecdotes aside—"I can counter Jim Bakker's gold-plated bathroom fixtures with Mother Teresa, and Bible-thumping KKK members with Desmond Tutu," responds the believer—how might faith feed character? It might do so by providing a source of values. It might give us a convincing reason to behave morally when no one is looking. Lacking the ground of faith beneath our morality, cultural inertia may enable a lingering selflessness, but eventually the soil that feeds morality becomes depleted. "If there is no God, is not everything permissible?" Ivan asked in *The Brothers Karamazov*.

"The terrible danger of our time consists in the fact that ours is a cut-flower civilization," philosopher Elton Trueblood prophesied a half-century ago. "Beautiful as cut flowers may be, and much as we may use our ingenuity to keep them looking fresh for a while, they will eventually die, and they die because they are severed from their sustaining roots. We are trying to maintain the dignity of the individual apart from the deep faith that every man is made in God's image and is therefore precious in God's eyes."

Even the eighteenth-century French writer Voltaire found the influence of faith useful among the masses, even though he thought Christianity was an "infamy" that deserved crushing. "I want my attorney, my tailor, my servants, even my wife to believe in God," he wrote, because "then I shall be robbed and cuckolded less often." He once silenced a discussion about atheism until he had dismissed the servants, lest in losing their faith they might lose their morality. Although similarly skeptical of religion, biologist E. O. Wilson likewise acknowledges that "religious conviction is largely beneficent. Religion . . . nourishes love, devotion, and, above all, hope."

Faith and Character

Are Voltaire and Wilson right to presume that godliness tethers self-interest and feeds character? Seeking answers, researchers have studied not just what causes crime, but what predicts virtue. Having two committed parents, a stable neighborhood, prosocial media, and schools that teach character—all of these help. So, too, does a spiritual sense, contends Stanford psychologist William Damon. Children are "openly receptive to spiritual ideas and long for transcendent truth that can nourish their sense of purpose and provide them with a moral mission in life," he believes. "Children will not thrive . . . unless they acquire a living sense of what some religious traditions have called transcendence: a faith in and devotion to concerns that are considered larger than the self." Faith, he reports, "has clear benefits for children . . . enabling some children to adapt to stressful and burdensome life events."

The bipartisan National Commission on Children has concurred that religious faith strengthens children. "Through participation in a religious community—in communal worship, religious education, and social-action programs—children learn and assimilate the values of their faith. For many children, religion is a major force in their moral development; for some it is the chief determinant of moral behavior." Studies confirm that religious adolescents (those who say their faith is important or who attend church) differ from those who are irreligious. They are much less likely to become delinquent, to engage in promiscuous sex, and to abuse drugs and alcohol.

After analyzing data from several national studies, Vanderbilt University criminologist Byron Johnson reported that "Most delinquent acts were committed by juveniles who had low levels of religious commitment. Those juveniles whose religiosity levels were in the middle to high levels committed very few delinquent acts." Even when controlling for other factors, such as socioeconomic level, neighborhood, and peer influences, churchgoing kids rarely were delinquent.

The faith-morality relationship extends to adulthood. In their studies of Jews in Israel, Catholics in Spain, Calvinists in the Netherlands, the Orthodox in Greece, and Lutherans and Catholics in West Germany, sociologists Shalom Schwartz and Sipke Huismans consistently found that people of faith tended to be less hedonistic and self-oriented. Consistent with this observation, sociologist Seymour Martin Lipset notes that charitable giving and voluntarism are higher in America than in less religious countries.

In a 1981 U.S. Values Survey, frequent worship attendance predicted lower scores on a dishonesty scale that assessed, for example, self-serving lies, tax cheating, and failing to report damaging a parked car. Moreover, cities with high churchgoing rates tend to be cities with low crime rates. In Provo, Utah, where more than nine in ten people are church members, you can more readily leave your car unlocked than in Seattle, where fewer than a third are. Voltaire, it seems, was on to something.

Many people sense this faith-morality correlation. If your car broke down in a crime-ridden area and some strapping teenage boys approached you, asks

Los Angeles Rabbi Dennis Prager, wouldn't "you feel better to know they had just come from a Bible study?"

Faith and Altruism

So, people of faith (mostly Christians in studies to date) are, for whatever reasons, somewhat more traditionally moral—more honest and law-abiding and less hedonistic. But are they more actively compassionate? Do they really walk the love talk? Or are they mostly self-righteous hypocrites?

People often wonder about Christianity, which has a curious history of links with both love and hate. On one side are Bible-thumping slave owners, Ku Klux Klanners, and apartheid defenders. On the other are the religious roots of the antislavery movement, the clergy's leadership of the American and South African civil-rights movements, and the church's establishment of universities and Third World medical care.

A mid-century profusion of studies of religion and prejudice revealed a similarly mixed picture. On the one hand, American church members expressed more racial prejudice than nonmembers, and those with conservative Christian beliefs expressed more than those who were less conservative. For many, religion seemed a cultural habit, a part of their community tradition, which also happened to include racial segregation.

Yet the most faithful church attenders expressed less prejudice than occasional attenders. Clergy expressed more tolerance and civil-rights support than lay people. And those for whom religion was an end ("My religious beliefs are what really lie behind my whole approach to life") were less prejudiced than those for whom religion was a means ("A primary reason for my interest in religion is that my church is a congenial social activity"). Thus among church members, the devout expressed less prejudice than those who gave religion lip service. "We have just enough religion to make us hate," said the English satirist Jonathan Swift, "but not enough to make us love one another."

"Faith-based" compassion becomes even clearer when we look at who gives most generously of time and money. Fortune reports that America's top 25 philanthropists share several characteristics. They are mostly self-made, they have been givers all their lives, and "they're religious: Jewish, Mormon, Protestant, and Catholic. And most attribute their philanthropic urges, at least in part, to their religious backgrounds."

The same appears true of the rest of us. In a 1987 Gallup survey, Americans who said they never attended church or synagogue reported giving away 1.1 percent of their incomes. Weekly attenders were two and a half times as generous. This 24 percent of the population gave 48 percent of all charitable contributions. The other three-quarters of Americans give the remaining half. Followup Gallup surveys in 1990, 1992, 1994, and 1999 replicated this pattern. An estate-planning attorney at one of western Michigan's largest law firms told me that people in her highly churched area of the state are much more likely to assign part of their estate to charity than are people on the state's less religious eastern side. Much of this annual and legacy giving is not to churches. Two thirds of money given to secular charities comes from contributors who also give to religious organizations.

And of the billions given to congregations, nearly half gets donated to other organizations or allocated to nonreligious programming (and that doesn't count donations of food, clothing, and shelter by most congregations).

The faith-generosity effect extends to the giving of time:

- Among the 12 percent of Americans whom Gallup classified as "highly spiritually committed," 46 percent said they were presently working among the poor, the infirm, or the elderly—many more than the 22 percent among those "highly uncommitted."
- In a followup Gallup survey, charitable and social service volunteering was reported by 28 percent of those who rated religion "not very important" in their lives and by 50 percent of those who rated it "very important."
- In the 1992 Gallup survey, those not attending church volunteered 1.4 hours a week while those attending weekly volunteered 3.2 hours. The follow-up survey in 1994 found the same pattern, as have university-based studies.
- In yet another Gallup survey, 37 percent of those rarely if ever attending church, and 76 percent of those attending weekly, reported thinking at least a "fair amount" about "your responsibility to the poor."
- Among one notable self-giving population—adoptive parents—religious commitment is commonplace. Among a national sample, 63 percent reported attending a worship service often.

So, tell me about the generosity of someone's spirit, and you will also give me a clue to the centrality of their faith. Tell me whether their faith is peripheral or pivotal, and I will estimate their generosity.

Religious consciousness, it appears, shapes a larger agenda than advancing one's own private world. It cultivates the idea that my wealth and talents are gifts of which I am the steward. Spirituality promotes a "bond of care for others," notes Boston College sociologist Paul Schervish. Such altruism, research psychologists Dennis Krebs and Frank Van Hesteren contend, is "selfless, stemming from agape, an ethic of responsible universal love, service, and sacrifice that is extended to others without regard for merit." The religious idea of a reality and purpose beyond self would seem foundational to such "universal self-sacrificial love."

Faith-based altruism is at work here in Holland, Michigan, where the Head Start Day Care program was envisioned by a prayer group at the church where it still operates. The thriving Boys and Girls Club was spawned by the Interparish Council. Habitat for Humanity construction is mostly done by church volunteers. Our community's two main nongovernmental agencies for supporting the poor—the Community Action House and the Good Samaritan Center—were begun by churches, which continue to contribute operating funds. The local theological seminary houses the community soup kitchen. Churches fund the community's homeless shelter. Annually, more than 2,000 townspeople, sponsored by thousands more—nearly all from churches—gather for a world hunger relief walk.

If the churches of my community (and likely yours) shut down, along with all the charitable action they foster, we would see a sharp drop in beds for the homeless, food for the hungry, and services to children. Partners for Sacred Places, a nondenominational group dedicated to preserving old religious buildings, reports that nine of ten city congregations with pre-1940 buildings provide space for community programming such as food pantries, clothing closets, soup kitchens, childcare centers, recreation programs, AA meetings, and afterschool activities.

Thus, mountains of data and anecdotes make it hard to dispute Frank Emerson Andrews' conclusion that "religion is the mother of philanthropy."

To be sure, religion is a mixed bag. It has been used to support the Crusades and enslavement. But it was also Christians who built hospitals, helped the mentally ill, staffed orphanages, brought hope to prisoners, established universities, and spread literacy. It was Christians who abolished the slave trade, led civil-rights marches, and challenged totalitarianism. It was 5,000 Christians who in Le Chambon, France, sheltered Jews while French collaborators elsewhere were delivering Jews to the Nazis. The villagers, mostly descendants of a persecuted Protestant group, had been taught by their pastors to "resist whenever our adversaries will demand of us obedience contrary to the orders of the gospel." Ordered to reveal the sheltered Jews, the pastor refused, saying, "I don't know of Jews, I only know of human beings."

As the debate over government support of faith-based social services emerges—fueled by success stories such as the Rev. Eugene Rivers III's work with Boston teens, Prison Fellowship's work with inmates, and Michigan's program of connecting social-service clients with church-support groups—the church will also need to retain its prophetic voice. In Britain, which is entering a parallel national debate over "the moral and spiritual decline of the nation," the Archbishop of Canterbury, Dr. George Carey, opened "an unprecedented debate on morality" in the House of Lords in 1996 by decrying the decline of moral order and spiritual purpose and the tendency to view moral judgments as mere private taste.

Jonathan Sacks, England's Chief Rabbi, supported his compatriot:

> The power of the Judeo-Christian tradition is that it charts a moral reality larger than private inclination. . . . It suggests that not all choices are equal: some lead on to blessing, others to lives of quiet despair.
>
> It may be that religious leaders can no longer endorse, but instead must challenge the prevailing consensus—the role of the prophet through the ages. In which case the scene is set for a genuine debate between two conflicting visions—between those who see the individual as a bundle of impulses to be gratified and those who see humanity in the image of God; between those who see society as a series of private gardens of desire and those who make space for public parts which we do not own but which we jointly maintain for the sake of others and the future. No debate could be more fundamental, and its outcome will shape the social contours of the twenty-first century.

Julie Juola Exline

NO

Stumbling Blocks on the Religious Road: Fractured Relationships, Nagging Vices, and the Inner Struggle to Believe

Tossing and turning in bed, Jim finds that his mind keeps drifting to the television segment he saw on the 11:00 news. This is the third news piece that he has seen in the past year suggesting that religious involvement has benefits for health and well-being. Raised nominally Christian, Jim stopped attending church years ago. He is not even sure that he believes in God anymore, but he has been feeling troubled lately, between his arthritis flare-ups and recurring bouts of anxiety. After mulling over the pros and cons, Jim decides to give religion another try. He asks a colleague for a church recommendation and begins attending regularly. He also commits to reading his Bible each night before bed so that he can get a deeper understanding of the Christian faith. Jim does an admirable job on following through with these religious commitments. However, 6 months later, he is overcome with frustration and disappointment regarding his religious involvement. His dissatisfaction is so strong, in fact, that he decides to abandon his religious quest altogether. What could have happened? Why did Jim end up turning away from religion when he had solid reasons to pursue this coping resource? This article addresses these questions by suggesting some psychological and social stumbling blocks associated with religious belief and involvement.

Can Religion Be Good and Still Be a Locus of Strain?

Within the past decade, a wealth of evidence has accumulated to suggest positive associations between religion, physical health, and mental health. Based on these findings, scientists, scholars, and mental health professionals are beginning to take a more positive view of the role that religious belief and involvement can play in personal and social life. It is especially noteworthy that many of these pro-religion findings have emerged within the field of psychology, which has historically taken a negative or disinterested stance toward

From *Psychological Inquiry*, vol. 13, no. 3, 2002, pp. 182–188. Copyright © 2002 by Lawrence Erlbaum Associates. Reprinted by permission.

religion. The boom in pro-religion findings is likely to prove encouraging and exciting for religiously committed psychologists, providing greater freedom to discuss, study, and perhaps even advocate religious involvement.

However, to promote a balanced view of religion and well-being, it seems wise to consider some caveats and cautions. Consider one possible consequence of the current emphasis on religion, coping, and health: Might some individuals come to view religion primarily or exclusively as a personal coping mechanism? Having noted positive links between religiosity and well-being, some people might focus on only the comforting, self-affirming aspects of religious belief or involvement. Others might go a step further, thinking about religion only in terms of how it might personally benefit them or advance their interests. In one (admittedly extreme) metaphor, some people might view God as a sort of placid smiley face in the sky, advancing humanity's ongoing quest to "have a nice day."

Granted, religious belief and involvement can be powerful tools in coping with life's problems; however, religion is not merely a coping mechanism. Religion involves a quest for ultimate truth. It attempts to answer our deepest questions about life, death, and the purpose of existence. Religion also tends to be prescriptive, telling us how we should live our lives. Thus, religion is likely to make demands on us and to challenge our beliefs and actions in ways that are not always comfortable. Religion is likely to contain seeds of both pleasure and pain, as do other vitally important elements of life (e.g., work, romantic relationships, parenting). To acknowledge the problems associated with any of these pursuits does not negate the value of the pursuit, but because negative stimuli typically carry more psychological weight than positive stimuli, it seems imperative to point out some potential pitfalls that people may encounter in their religious lives.

I make a few clarifications before proceeding. Virtually all examples presented in this article emphasize Judeo-Christian religion. Many are based on Protestant Christianity, the tradition with which I identify and am most familiar. Although different religious systems will no doubt pose different dilemmas and solutions, particularly at the level of doctrine, I believe that the basic principles raised here should be common to many religions. I also note that the goal of this article is to present a series of ideas rather than a review of existing literature. Many of the ideas presented here reflect theoretical elaboration of empirical work that my colleagues and I have done. My thinking has also been directly influenced by the work of Pargament and Altemeyer and Hunsberger. The interested reader is directed to these sources and to other reviews of the field.

The goal of this article, then, is to suggest a number of social and psychological stumbling blocks that religious seekers may encounter. Four major types of stumbling blocks will be considered: interpersonal strains, negative attitudes toward God, inner struggles to believe, and problems associated with virtuous striving. Problems in any of these areas could conceivably turn people away from religion, discourage them from increasing their religious commitment, or create sources of strain and discontent regarding religion.

Interpersonal Strains Associated with Religion: Disagreement, Dissonance, and Disgust

In terms of physical and mental health, one of the primary benefits of religious involvement is that it can be a powerful source of social support. The need to belong, to have close connections with other people, is a central human motivation, and being part of a religious community can help to meet this need. Religious involvement may also provide people with the chance to help others, which can be a powerful antidote for feelings of depression and helplessness; however, if we look more closely, we can see potential for problems in the social arena surrounding religion.

Religious Disagreements

Although religious involvement can help to meet a person's need to belong, it may at the same time threaten that same need. When people choose to align themselves closely with a particular religious group or to adopt a specific set of beliefs, they increase their odds for serious disagreement with others. Such differences sometimes play out in a societal context, adding fuel to intergroup hostility and conflict, but disagreements often arise closer to home, in the circle of the believer's close relationships. If one's parents, spouse, or close friends do not share one's religious convictions, painful rifts may result.

Interfaith marriage provides one example. Although interfaith marriage has become increasingly common, up from 9% in 1965 to 52% in the late 1980s, couples in such marriages are more likely to divorce than those who share the same religious faith. Even when both partners are of the same faith, problems might arise because of differences in religious commitment levels. For example, a woman whose top priority is to love God may elicit feelings of jealousy and resentment from her husband, who now views God as an unwanted third party in the relationship. How can people cope with these religious differences in close relationships? Some may simply agree to disagree, but many religiously committed people may not be satisfied with this option. Because relationship maintenance requires sacrifice and compromise, it may seem viable to convert the unbelieving spouse or to compromise by choosing some third, "neutral ground." However, problems arise with these options as well: Many committed believers will be reluctant to shift their ideas or affiliations, and conversions to please one's romantic partner prove superficial in many cases.

Interpersonal strain may also center on specific religious doctrines, such as those regarding afterlife beliefs. Exline and Yali asked college students what percentage of people they believed were destined for heaven versus hell. To the extent that the students believed that many people were destined for hell, they reported greater social strain associated with religion. These strains included being teased about religious beliefs and behaviors, being the target of religious prejudice or discrimination, and feeling sad or anxious because friends or family members did not share their beliefs. Although preliminary, these data suggest that when disturbing beliefs about the afterlife are part of one's religious system, such beliefs may not only be personally troubling, but they may also be a locus for interpersonal strain. When religious persons believe that the high stakes of eternal destiny are involved, they may find it difficult simply to agree to disagree, especially when they care deeply about the other person.

Attempts to communicate about hell with close others will often be fraught with difficulties. Even with the best of intentions, believers are likely to offend others by insinuating that they are destined for eternal punishment. Another potential problem stems from the fact that images of hell are likely to prompt high levels of fear. Studies have suggested that extremely high levels of fear, rather than prompting behavior change, often lead to emotion-focused coping efforts as people try to defend themselves from the psychological threat. Thus, a believer who confronts another person with fiery images of hell might find that the solution backfires, as the would-be convert calms himself by avoiding all thoughts of the threatening subject.

Interpersonal strains should also surround other doctrines that take a dim view of human nature or are otherwise discordant with the climate of the broader culture. For example, modern evangelical Protestantism has often been linked with conservative political views ("the Religious Right") and with intolerance of homosexuality and abortion. In an era in which tolerance is highly valued, it will prove socially divisive to confront behaviors that are gaining social acceptance. How are believers to respond when their beliefs are socially unpopular? As suggested in the literature on outgroup behavior and prejudice in religion, one response may be to derogate and distance the self from those who do not hold the beliefs of one's group. Another option is to be open about one's views and risk offending others. A more socially comfortable option would be to focus only on points of agreement, perhaps even taking the extra step of softening one's position on controversial issues. The risk, of course, is that when people soften their position on issues central to their faith, they may compromise or misrepresent what they believe to be the truth.

Distaste toward Religious Groups or Persons

For nonbelievers or even for persons who are privately religious or spiritual, another type of interpersonal barrier could prevent them from wanting to affiliate with religious groups: They may look at the behavior of religious persons and not like what they see. Such distaste could stem from many sources. Vivid acts of terrorism and violence, ranging from racial discrimination and abortion clinic bombings to wartime atrocities, have been committed in the name of religion. Many people have observed religious hypocrisy, in which religious individuals claim to uphold high moral standards but fail to do so in their everyday lives. When high-profile religious evangelists are caught in sexual affairs, for example, people may turn to such incidents as evidence that religious people are hypocrites and fakes. Individuals who yield to religious authority (e.g., God, scripture, the Pope, other church leaders) may be viewed as ignorant by those who place higher value on other forms of persuasion, such as empirical evidence or private, common-sense philosophies of life. Religious people may also be viewed as judgmental, prudish, intolerant, and unable to have fun in life—particularly, perhaps, by persons who want to continue pleasurable habits that the religious group views as vices (e.g., sexual promiscuity, gambling, heavy alcohol use).

In short, one probable reason that people do not join religious groups is because they hold negative attitudes toward the groups. Some people might even develop stronger responses such as disgust, in which they recoil from any contact with the group. As with a food aversion, disgust might even spread to taint a person's global impressions of religion: "If that's how religious people behave, I don't want any part of it." Because feelings of disgust are often moralized, people could easily translate their disgust toward religious persons into moral disapproval. In other words, they might come to view religious people not only as unlikable but also as wrong—perhaps even as evil. By crossing the line to moral disapproval, people who dislike religious groups have a ready rationale for derogating them.

Summary

Religion, at least in its organized forms, is intimately tied with human relationships. At its best, it can be a major source of social support and a driving force behind prosocial behavior. However, the social aspect of religion can breed problems for believers and nonbelievers alike. Some people may have to overcome feelings of distaste to even consider affiliating with a religious group. Can they separate their religious ideals from the inevitable flaws that they observe among the all-too-human religious persons that they encounter? When they do make religious commitments, people may find themselves at odds with other important people in their social network who do not share their beliefs. For them, one major challenge is to participate meaningfully in their religious community without resorting to either of two extremes: outgroup derogation or watering down their beliefs.

Disappointment, Anger, and Mistrust toward God

Another major benefit of religious commitment is feeling close to God and the comfort that comes with the belief that an omnipotent being is watching over, protecting, and caring for the self. For many believers, the cultivation of an intimate relationship with God is a cornerstone of religious life. Some scholars have taken this idea a step further, conceptualizing religion as an attachment process. However, as in human relationships, a lot can go wrong in people's relationships with God. For example, some studies suggest that if people have conflicted relationships with their own fathers, they often develop negative or ambivalent feelings toward God as well. As another example, well-meaning religious parents sometimes use references to God or the Bible as self-regulation cues. For example, a parent might try to thwart a child's attempt to steal candy at the grocery store by saying "God is watching you" or quoting a Bible verse such as "Thou shalt not steal." If such statements are often used to curb misbehavior and if not tempered with positive statements about God, a child might come to see God as an oppressor primarily responsible for creating rules and policing people.

As alluded to in the previous section, both children and adults might find some aspects of God's behavior or character distasteful as they read religious texts or hear religious stories. For example, those reading the Bible may wonder this: Does God endorse killing? Why would God allow children to suffer for what their parents had done? How could a loving God send people to eternal punishment after death? For other people, the aspects of the Christian God that embody mercy and grace might be unappealing. A person who values toughness, pride, and retributive justice might be repelled by Christ's advocacy of virtues such as mercy and meekness—not to mention His own humiliating and painful death, which He accepted without protest or complaint.

Negative attitudes toward God could also stem from much more personal, intense hurts, and disappointments. In the wake of negative life events such as bereavement, illness, accidents, failures, or natural disasters, one potential response is to blame God. If God is held responsible for the act, intense feelings of mistrust, frustration, and anger can result, any of which can cause the wounded person to turn away or withdraw from God. Such pains might be especially sharp if the individual had placed hope in God, perhaps praying and trusting God for a specific outcome, only to be disappointed. We might think of such situations as parallel to those in which we feel betrayed, let down, or offended by another person, and in this case, the one who allowed our suffering could have prevented it—a thought that could fuel anger, hurt, and deep-seated grudges against God. Feelings of anger toward God have been linked with depression and anxiety and with poor coping outcomes. Some people might even decide to abandon belief altogether as a result of such incidents—a possibility that we are examining in our current research.

On the brighter side, preliminary evidence suggests that people often resolve feelings of anger toward God, and an ability to do so is associated with better mental health. How do people avoid or reduce feelings of anger at God? Although people often forgive perpetrators when they apologize or admit wrongdoing, they cannot expect such responses from God. Instead, they may have to draw on cognitive strategies. Drawing on research on interpersonal forgiveness, we might suggest that people will feel less angry toward God if they do not believe that God caused the event, if they view God's intentions as positive, or if they can see some good outcome from the incident. Also, because commitment increases the motivation to forgive, people who already feel close to God should be less likely to become angry. We are testing these hypotheses in our current research.

Another distinction made in the forgiveness literature may illuminate other problems in people's relationships with God: the distinction between *forgiveness,* which requires turning away from bitter, vengeful feelings, and *reconciliation,* which requires trust. Regardless of whether people feel angry with God, they may find it difficult to trust God. Within evangelical Christianity, for example, there is a heavy emphasis on coming to God through Christ, confessing one's sins, receiving forgiveness, and surrendering one's life to God. For some people, the prospect of admitting one's weakness and dependence on God could be intensely shaming, and regardless of whether they trust God, many individuals are likely to balk at the notion of having to come under the authority of God (and, in some cases, under the authority of religious institutions as well). For the person who takes great pride in self-reliance, personal control, and autonomy—all of which are highly valued in our Western culture—such concerns could be a substantial barrier to deepened religious commitment.

Summary

Individuals sometimes feel angry, mistrustful, or rebellious toward God. When having a close bond with God is the cornerstone of a person's religious commitment, it becomes crucial to resolve negative feelings or attitudes toward God before they undermine the relationship. People may develop negative attitudes or feelings about God in many ways, ranging from negative childhood associations to personal hurts and disappointments. Suffering persons may find it difficult to resolve anger toward God because God will not apologize to them or admit wrongdoing. To avoid holding a grudge against God, suffering persons might need to reframe hurtful events in positive ways or to remind themselves of their prior commitment to God.

The Inner Struggle to Believe: Intellectual Barriers and Dissonance

Religious beliefs help people to make sense of the world and to find a sense of meaning or purpose in existence. In fact, this meaning-making aspect of religion seems to be one of the major mediators of the association between religion and health. However, for some individuals, the answers provided by religion are not satisfactory at an intellectual or emotional level. The result might be to turn a person away from religion or, at the very least, to create cognitive dissonance about perceived inconsistencies.

Problems Faced by Nonbelievers

Studies have suggested that individuals with no childhood foundation in religion are unlikely to embrace it later in life. Young children are likely to trust what their parents tell them, and they can build worldviews consistent with their early religious learning. However, for an adult with no religious background, considering a new religious view of the world may require exceptional cognitive work. Over time, a nonbeliever will build a cognitive model of how the world works without including God in the picture, and all of these ideas may need to be revisited and challenged in order to incorporate new, God-centered ideas. Many people may not want to expend this level of effort.

Nonbelievers may also be reluctant to discard or revise their own ideas because the issues at hand are so fundamental: the purpose of life, what happens after death, who (or what) is in charge of the universe, and whether there is any reality beyond what our senses experience. Religious doctrines on these topics, faithfully accepted by believers, may not seem plausible to the nonbeliever. A religious seeker is likely to encounter many doctrines that do not offer logically consistent, coherent answers to life's difficult questions—something that a critical mind may insist on before being willing to believe.

Because many adults may find it difficult to accept religion through a purely intellectual search, we might predict that emotional pathways could serve as a shortcut to belief. For example, nonbelieving adults might be swayed by a mystical or miraculous experience by reaching a point of desperation in which they seek God's help or by finding a powerful sense of belonging within a religious group. Such emotionally charged events might provide people with a fresh incentive to adopt a particular faith, even if they have not resolved all of the intellectual fine points. Consistent with this reasoning, Altemeyer and Hunsberger found that among people with no childhood background in religion, those who embrace religion as adults often do so by means of potent social and emotional experiences. Although mainstream religions often address emotional needs, other social groups—such as cults—can also tap into emotional pathways. For a person eagerly seeking guidance, relief, or companionship, virtually any social group that promised to meet these needs could become a persuasive influence—particularly for those who are willing to suspend logic and personal judgment in the service of emotional goals.

Problems Faced by Believers

Even for individuals with some commitment to religious belief, logical stumbling points and troubling doctrines within one's religious system could be a source of cognitive dissonance. For example, many people who read the Bible (some of whom would identify themselves as Jews or Christians) are troubled by the seeming harshness and unfairness of the Old Testament world: the wars, sacrifices, punishments, and plagues that were presented as being part of God's plan for His "chosen people." Many individuals, whether Judeo-Christian or not, may find such material disturbing and inconsistent with their personal views of God. Gender-related issues often prompt dissent, as do doctrines about sexual behavior, and as mentioned earlier, our own research has suggested that Christian doctrines about hell can be a source of fear and emotional turmoil for some believers.

When people have some commitment to religion but are disturbed by specific doctrines, what are their options? For someone who already holds strongly to a religious belief system, it may be possible to tolerate some inconsistencies in religious doctrine while retaining the core beliefs of the religion and continuing to identify oneself as part of the religious group. A person within the system may be willing to suspend reasoning to some degree as an exercise of faith. Other responses might involve changing one's beliefs to reduce dissonance while still providing the benefits of religious or spiritual involvement. For example, a conservative Christian might choose to believe in heaven but not in hell. A Catholic woman may decide to go on birth control or to have an abortion, both privately and publicly disagreeing with the church's stand on these issues but still strongly identify herself as a Catholic.

Such practices might be aptly described by a term such as *cafeteria-style religion*, as they involve choosing aspects of existing religious systems that seem logical or comfortable for the self and ignoring or disbelieving those that are not. A person engaging in cafeteria-style religion might make all of his or her choices from within one religion or might choose elements from a variety of different religions. For example, a religious seeker might decide to retain a belief in Christ as an important historical figure while incorporating elements of Eastern or Native American religion into his belief system.

Another dissonance-reducing alternative to orthodox religiosity might be termed *do-it-yourself spirituality*, in which people shape spiritual beliefs and practices based on their own preferences, logic, intuition, and experience. As individualized forms of belief, both cafeteria-style religion and do-it-yourself spirituality draw people away from religious orthodoxy. More orthodox believers would thus argue that they constitute forms of self-deception, as they represent an attempt to hide the truth from oneself. However, both cafeteria-style religion and do-it-yourself spirituality would seem to be popular choices within Western culture's current postmodern ethos with its valuing of tolerance, personal freedom, subjectivity, and relativism.

Summary

When people search for answers within religion, some of them will encounter intellectual or emotional strains surrounding the belief systems themselves. Some people may simply move on, looking for another religious system that better suits them. Others will abandon the religious search altogether. Some believers, viewing apparent inconsistencies as tests of faith, learn to tolerate the resulting confusion. Another alternative is to reduce dissonance through subtle shifts of belief, undercutting orthodoxy in an attempt to create a more personally satisfying or sensible theology.

Cultivating Virtue and Confronting One's Imperfections

Another major benefit of religious involvement is that religion often encourages people to behave in virtuous ways. For example, religious beliefs can promote physical health by discouraging smoking, excessive drinking, and use of illegal drugs. Religion often encourages specific prosocial behaviors, such as forgiveness and generosity. It may also foster habits such as patience and perseverance that help people achieve their goals and regulate their emotions. Virtuous strivings are not specific to religious frameworks, of course. Anyone working toward self-improvement or following an abstract moral code could be seen as pursuing virtue. However, religion often does encourage people to reflect on their behavior and to improve it, and it is possible that virtues endorsed by religion might carry additional weight for many people because they have the backing of authority behind them.

Given that virtuous striving is an important part of religious life, what factors block the pursuit of virtue? Some barriers are motivational, in which people may not be certain that they want to cultivate certain characteristics. As evidenced by Christian virtues such as humility, meekness, gentleness, patience, and forgiveness, religious values often go against the grain of the larger culture. Because all of the virtues just listed involve some degree of self-transcendence or self-sacrifice, they may seem foolhardy to many. How are such behaviors going to fit within modern Western culture, with its emphasis on individual rights, immediate gratification, and materialism? Self-transcendent or self-sacrificing behaviors seem to invite abuse by others who are playing by a more self-serving set of rules. The pursuit of virtue may also entail giving up some favorite indulgences, which might range from overeating and sleeping in on Sundays to darker pleasures, such as revenge fantasies and slanderous gossip. Many people would prefer to follow their appetites than to pursue their virtuous counterparts, especially once deeply pleasurable (but now forbidden) habits have been established.

Even for those who earnestly desire to cultivate virtue and to improve their behavior, some degree of failure is inevitable. Virtuous behavior requires self-control, and humans are limited in their capacity for self-control. For example, consider a man who is trying to stop having thoughts of lust toward women. He is likely to face constant temptations in his environment to indulge in lust, whether by seeing scantily clad women on television and on billboards or by hearing his coworkers tell sexual jokes. He may have to fight a long-standing habit of engaging in sexual fantasies during idle moments, and in a cruel twist, research on ironic processes suggests that his very efforts to keep lusty thoughts out of his mind may make those very thoughts more likely to intrude. In a weak moment, this man is likely to give in and indulge in thoughts of lust.

As the prior example illustrates, individuals trying to control their thoughts and behaviors will often fail. Therefore, unless we are very adept at self-enhancement and self-justification, one consequence of trying to cultivate virtue is that we will be continually reminded of our shortcomings. With increased devotion and commitment to a religious system, people are likely to find more and more areas of their lives that are imperfect. Depending on how such failures are attributed, they might prompt negative outcomes such as self-condemnation, hopelessness, or perceptions of God as punitive or unforgiving toward the self. Another possibility is offered by research on abstinence violation effects: Seeing that the standard of perfection has been violated, people who fail to live up to idealistic standards may give up and indulge in more extreme misbehaviors.

Ideally, religious systems will help people to make sense of their imperfections and to use them in a positive way. Within Protestant Christianity, for example, seeing one's sins and limitations is the first step toward seeing a need for God's forgiveness and direction. Salvation is viewed as a free gift based on the God's grace and Christ's atoning sacrifice for sin, not something earned through good behavior. Virtue, rather than being seen as a cause of salvation, is viewed as a result of salvation and a person's subsequent cooperation with The Holy Spirit's ongoing work. All of these doctrines—the reality of human imperfection, the free gift of salvation, and the help of the Holy Spirit in fostering virtue—will ideally provide believers with a sense of safety and security while encouraging the further development of virtue. In reality, however, many Christians continue to dismiss their shortcomings or, at the other extreme, to condemn themselves for their mistakes.

Summary

Religion often encourages the development of virtue, which can benefit both individuals and society. However, both personal and social resistance may accompany the pursuit of virtue. Virtuous striving requires us to overcome immediate impulses to gratify or protect the self, and when people do attempt to live virtuously, failures may quickly become apparent. The ideal goal would seem to be to value virtue and to cultivate it, but without insisting on perfection.

Conclusion

Religious life is not always characterized by sunny skies. As outlined previously here, people may encounter a number of intellectual, emotional, behavioral, and social problems associated with religious commitment In spite of these problems, however, the broader picture is anything but bleak. There remains a wealth of data suggesting that religion can be a substantial positive force in personal and social life. If the problems raised in this article can be anticipated, understood, and addressed, consider some of the potential gains.

Clearly, the social world surrounding religion is far from perfect—but when people are able to unite successfully with others as part of a religious community, the sharing of values and goals may yield a sense of support, direction, and grounding that few other social ties can provide. People do experience rifts in their relationships with God, but if they can resolve their negative feelings and work to restore the relationship, a stronger bond and a more mature faith might result. Intellectual and emotional barriers may create inner conflicts about belief, but the result might be a "thinking person's faith" rather than a more passive, mindless form of devotion. Striving after virtue is difficult, especially when it confronts people with the painful reality of their imperfections, but virtuous striving might yield a more commendable life, coupled with a humble, nondefensive attitude that could serve the person well in personal, social, and spiritual contexts.

From the perspective of research and theory, an important goal for the future will be to develop empirically testable models that can help to explain when and why strain arises in religious life and how various forms of strain can best be overcome. Models of strain in religious life should complement existing frameworks on related topics such as religious coping and conversion. Some of the psychological concepts raised in this article may assist in building such frameworks. For example, future research might examine the role of self-deception in religious belief, the contrast of human relationships with relationships between humans and God, or the study of virtue and vice in a self-regulation context. Ideally, as suggested by Hill, such pursuits will not only inform the psychology of religion. Research on these religious topics may also provide fundamental insights into human nature, insights that will advance general psychological knowledge.

CHALLENGE QUESTIONS

Is Religion a Pure Good in Facilitating Well-Being during Adulthood?

- While both of these selections focus on religion and spirituality primarily in relation to a Christian tradition, the issue of religion in the adult lifespan transcends one particular faith. All of the major religious traditions share a social function of focusing communities of individuals toward mutual goals and a personal function of addressing the spiritual needs of individuals. As such, is there a universal role for religion in adult development?
- Is there something special about religion generally in the lifespan? Is religion best thought of as a broad social practice, similar to school and work, that should be analyzed for its practical contribution to development? Or is religion something more?
- The general argument that religion is good for people underlies the recent popularity of "faith-based initiatives"—public policies specifically facilitated by faith and religious groups. How might the evidence here warrant policy support for religious participation?
- Exline's perspective is based on a more theoretical approach to religious experience. What types of data might best support her position?

Suggested Readings

S. Barkan and S. Greenwood, "Religious Attendance and Subjective Well-Being Among Older Americans," *Review of Religious Research* (December 2003)

M. Hayes and H. Cowie, "Psychology and Religion: Mapping the Relationship," *Mental Health, Religion & Culture* (March 2005)

A. James and A. Wells, "Religion and Mental Health: Towards a Cognitive-Behavioral Framework," *British Journal of Health Psychology* (September 2003)

N. Krause, "God-Medicated Control and Psychological Well-Being in Late Life," *Research on Aging* (March 2005)

D. Myers, *The American Paradox: Spiritual Hunger in the Age of Plenty* (Yale University Press, 2000)

K. Pargament, "The Bitter and the Sweet: An Evaluation of the Costs and Benefits of Religiousness," *Psychological Inquiry* (2002)

L. Waite and E. Lehrer, "The Benefits from Marriage and Religion in the United States: A Comparative Analysis," *Population & Development Review* (June 2003)

ISSUE 17

Are Professional Women "Opting Out" of Work by Choice?

YES: Linda Hirshman, from "Homeward Bound," *The American Prospect Online* (November 21, 2005)

NO: Pamela Stone, from "The Rhetoric and Reality of 'Opting Out'," *Contexts* (Fall 2007)

ISSUE SUMMARY

YES: Scholar Linda Hirshman identifies as a feminist, but is frustrated with findings suggesting that successful and well-qualified women have put themselves in situations where it makes sense to prioritize parenthood over work.

NO: Sociologist Pamela Stone interviewed a different but also very successful sample of women who sacrificed careers for parenthood and found that while they perceived themselves to be making a choice, in fact they were tightly constrained by traditional gender roles and inflexible workplaces.

$\mathbf{I}$n his seminal stage theory of life-span, Erik Erikson identified the primary challenge of social development during adulthood to be negotiating between generativity and self-absorption. The concept of generativity has continued to be useful in the study of adult development: once people have begun careers and families, how do they think about generating something meaningful for future generations? Though generativity can take many forms, for many adults opportunities to generate something meaningful come primarily through work and through having children. But negotiating between devotion to one's work and to one's children is another common challenge in adulthood, and one that is particularly constrained by the changing dynamics of gendered social roles.

In recent decades, there has been a dramatic influx of women into career tracks previously reserved for men and a significant increase in two-career families. And while overall these changes have helped fulfill ideals of equal opportunity, they have also created new challenges in both work and family domains. To deal with those challenges some professional women on elite career tracks seem to be choosing family responsibilities over work, leaving scholars with new social dynamics to consider and interpret.

One interpretation of these new social dynamics is that feminism has given women the power to "choose" family over work, and a surprising number of well-educated women are availing themselves of this option. This interpretation was the basic premise of an influential and controversial *New York Times* article describing an "Opt-Out Revolution" among professional women. Provoked by that article and related claims that women may not really want to devote themselves to powerful careers even when given the option, in recent years scholars interested in adult development have investigated what sociologist Pamela Stone calls "The Rhetoric and Reality of 'Opting Out'." While there is some agreement that many professional women are prioritizing family responsibilities over their careers, there is much debate as to the scope of and rationale for those priorities.

Linda Hirshman in her article "Homeward Bound" thinks "opting out" is a real phenomenon, but disagrees with popular media suggestions that it indicates feminism was misguided. In fact, she thinks the problem is that feminism did not go far enough. Though women have an increased number of professional options, they still tend to choose less powerful careers than men and still accept that many men will "opt out" of family responsibilities because they are the primary wage earner.

While Pamela Stone also thinks feminism still has much work to do, she thinks that work should focus on changing social conditions rather than women's choices. The workplace, Stone argues, is still structured to cater to an imaginary "ideal worker" who devotes him or herself entirely to their career—and because of lingering gender roles women are more likely to be constrained by that unhealthy structure.

In terms of adult development, while generativity can take many forms—through work, or family, or community—it is interesting to consider how much choice we really have towards that end. While generativity may be a useful marker of successful adult development, it may not really be up to us.

POINT

- Though feminist movements have fostered conditions where women are well-qualified for elite jobs, women are still not moving into those jobs at the rate of men.
- When asked, many well-educated and qualified women have neglected their careers because they feel it is more important to focus on family.
- Even the most highly qualified women are deciding to stay home rather than stay in the workforce, and they do so even when offered the chance to work part time.
- For women, opting out seems to be the only choice because they disproportionately major in the liberal arts, do not focus on accumulating money and power to the same degree as men, and often end up taking on too many responsibilities within marriages.

COUNTERPOINT

- Any "choices" being made by women torn between families and careers are tightly constrained by the nature of modern workplaces.
- Among high-achieving women, there is immense social pressure to engage in very time-intensive forms of childrearing.
- Though husbands and workplaces often express support for the responsibilities of childrearing, in practice they often do not make realistic accommodations.
- Women often frame their decision to leave work as a "choice," but that is because they do not want to acknowledge the many subtle ways they are constrained.

YES

Linda Hirshman

Homeward Bound

I. The Truth About Elite Women

Half the wealthiest, most-privileged, best-educated females in the country stay home with their babies rather than work in the market economy. When in September *The New York Times* featured an article exploring a piece of this story, **"Many Women at Elite Colleges Set Career Path to Motherhood,"** the blogosphere went ballistic, countering with anecdotes and sarcasm. *Slate's* Jack Shafer accused the *Times* of **"weasel-words"** and of **publishing the same story**—essentially, **"The Opt-Out Revolution"**—every few years, and, recently, every few weeks. . . . The colleges article provoked such fury that the *Times* had to post an *explanation* of the then–student journalist's methodology on its Web site.

There's only one problem: There is important truth in the dropout story. Even *though* it appeared in *The New York Times*.

I stumbled across the news three years ago when researching a book on marriage after feminism. I found that among the educated elite, who are the logical heirs of the agenda of empowering women, feminism has largely failed in its goals. There are few women in the corridors of power, and marriage is essentially unchanged. The number of women at universities exceeds the number of men. But, more than a generation after feminism, the number of women in elite jobs doesn't come close.

Why did this happen? The answer I discovered—an answer neither feminist leaders nor women themselves want to face—is that while the public world has changed, albeit imperfectly, to accommodate women among the elite, private lives have hardly budged. The real glass ceiling is at home.

Looking back, it seems obvious that the unreconstructed family was destined to re-emerge after the passage of feminism's storm of social change. Following the original impulse to address everything in the lives of women, feminism turned its focus to cracking open the doors of the public power structure. This was no small task. At the beginning, there were male juries and male Ivy League schools, sex-segregated want ads, discriminatory employers, harassing colleagues. As a result of feminist efforts—and larger economic trends—the percentage of women, even of mothers in full- or part-time employment, rose robustly through the 1980s and early '90s.

But then the pace slowed. The census numbers for all working mothers leveled off around 1990 and have fallen modestly since 1998. In interviews, women with enough money to quit work say they are "choosing" to opt out. Their words conceal a crucial reality: the belief that women are responsible for child-rearing and homemaking was largely untouched by decades of work-place feminism. Add to this the good evidence that the upper-class workplace has become more demanding and then mix in the successful conservative cultural campaign to reinforce traditional gender roles and you've got a perfect recipe for feminism's stall.

People who don't like the message attack the data. . . .

What evidence *is* good enough? Let's start with you. Educated and afflu-ent reader, if you are a 30- or 40-something woman with children, what are you doing? Husbands, what are your wives doing? Older readers, what are your married daughters with children doing? I have asked this question of scores of women and men. Among the affluent-educated-married population, women are letting their careers slide to tend the home fires. If my interviewees are working, they work largely part time, and their part-time careers are not putting them in the executive suite.

Here's some more evidence: During the '90s, I taught a course in sexual bar-gaining at a very good college. Each year, after the class reviewed the low rewards for child-care work, I asked how the students anticipated combining work with child-rearing. At least half the female students described lives of part-time or home-based work. Guys expected their female partners to care for the children. When I asked the young men how they reconciled that prospect with the mani-fest low regard the market has for child care, they were mystified. Turning to the women who had spoken before, they said, uniformly, "But she chose it."

Even Ronald Coase, Nobel Prize–winner in economics in 1991, quotes the aphorism that "the plural of anecdote is data." So how many anecdotes does it take to make data? I—a 1970s member of the National Organization for Women (NOW), a donor to EMILY'S List, and a professor of women's studies—did not set out to find this. I stumbled across the story when, while planning a book, I happened to watch *Sex and the City*'s Charlotte agonize about getting her wedding announcement in the "Sunday Styles" section of *The New York Times*. What better sample, I thought, than the brilliantly educated and accomplished brides of the "Sunday Styles," circa 1996? At marriage, they included a vice president of client communication, a gastro-enterologist, a lawyer, an editor, and a marketing executive. In 2003 and 2004, I tracked them down and called them. I interviewed about 80 percent of the 41 women who announced their weddings over three Sundays in 1996. Around 40 years old, college graduates with careers: Who was more likely than they to be reaping feminism's promise of opportunity? Imagine my shock when I found almost all the brides from the first Sunday at home with their children. Statistical anomaly? Nope. Same result for the next Sunday. And the one after that.

Ninety percent of the brides I found had had babies. Of the 30 with babies, five were still working full time. Twenty-five, or 85 percent, were not working full time. Of those not working full time, 10 were working part time but often a long way from their prior career paths. And half the married women with children were not working at all.

And there is more. In 2000, Harvard Business School professor Myra Hart surveyed the women of the classes of 1981, 1986, and 1991 and found that only 38 percent of female Harvard MBAs were working full time. A 2004 survey by the Center for Work-Life Policy of 2,443 women with a graduate degree or very prestigious bachelor's degree revealed that 43 percent of those women with children had taken a time out, primarily for family reasons. Richard Posner, federal appeals-court judge and occasional University of Chicago adjunct professor, reports that "the [*Times*] article confirms—what everyone associated with such institutions [elite law schools] has long known: that a vastly higher percentage of female than of male students will drop out of the workforce to take care of their children."

How many anecdotes to become data? The 2000 census showed a decline in the percentage of mothers of infants working full time, part time, or seeking employment. Starting at 31 percent in 1976, the percentage had gone up almost every year to 1992, hit a high of 58.7 percent in 1998, and then began to drop—to 55.2 percent in 2000, to 54.6 percent in 2002, to 53.7 percent in 2003. Statistics just released showed further decline to 52.9 percent in 2004. Even the percentage of working mothers with children who were not infants declined between 2000 and 2003, from 62.8 percent to 59.8 percent.

Although college-educated women work more than others, the 2002 census shows that graduate or professional degrees do not increase work-force participation much more than even one year of college. When their children are infants (under a year), 54 percent of females with graduate or professional degrees are not working full time (18 percent are working part time and 36 percent are not working at all). Even among those who have children who are not infants, 41 percent are not working full time (18 percent are working part time and 23 percent are not working at all).

Economists argue about the meaning of the data, even going so far as to contend that more mothers are working. They explain that the bureau changed the definition of "work" slightly in 2000, the economy went into recession, and the falloff in women without children was similar. However, even if there wasn't a falloff but just a leveling off, this represents not a loss of present value but a loss of hope for the future—a loss of hope that the role of women in society will continue to increase.

The arguments still do not explain the absence of women in elite workplaces. If these women were sticking it out in the business, law, and academic worlds, now, 30 years after feminism started filling the selective schools with women, the elite workplaces should be proportionately female. They are not. Law schools have been graduating classes around 40-percent female for decades—decades during which both schools and firms experienced enormous growth. And, although the legal population will not be 40-percent female until 2010, in 2003, the major law firms had only 16-percent female partners, according to the American Bar Association. It's important to note that elite workplaces like law firms grew in size during the very years that the percentage of female graduates was growing, leading you to expect a higher female employment than the pure graduation rate would indicate. The Harvard Business School has produced classes around 30-percent female. Yet only 10.6 percent of Wall Street's corporate officers are women, and a mere nine are Fortune 500 CEOs. Harvard Business School's dean, who extolled the virtues of interrupted careers on *60 Minutes*, has a 20-percent female academic faculty.

It is possible that the workplace is discriminatory and hostile to family life. If firms had hired every childless woman lawyer available, that alone would have been enough to raise the percentage of female law partners above 16 percent in 30 years. It is also possible that women are voluntarily taking themselves out of the elite job competition for lower status and lower-paying jobs. Women must take responsibility for the consequences of their decisions. It defies reason to claim that the falloff from 40 percent of the class at law school to 16 percent of the partners at all the big law firms is unrelated to half the mothers with graduate and professional degrees leaving full-time work at childbirth and staying away for several years after that, or possibly bidding down.

This isn't only about day care. Half my *Times* brides quit *before* the first baby came. In interviews, at least half of them expressed a hope never to work again. None had realistic plans to work. More importantly, when they quit, they were already alienated from their work or at least not committed to a life of work. One, a female MBA, said she could never figure out why the men at her workplace, which fired her, were so excited about making deals. "It's only money," she mused. Not surprisingly, even where employers offered them part-time work, they were not interested in taking it.

II. The Failure of Choice Feminism

What is going on? Most women hope to marry and have babies. If they resist the traditional female responsibilities of child-rearing and householding, what Arlie Hochschild called "The Second Shift," they are fixing for a fight. But elite women aren't resisting tradition. None of the stay-at-home brides I interviewed saw the second shift as unjust; they agree that the household is women's work. As one lawyer-bride put it in explaining her decision to quit practicing law after four years, "I had a wedding to plan." Another, an Ivy Leaguer with a master's degree, described it in management terms: "He's the CEO and I'm the CFO. He sees to it that the money rolls in and I decide how to spend it." It's their work, and they must do it perfectly. "We're all in here making fresh apple pie," said one, explaining her reluctance to leave her daughters in order to be interviewed. The family CFO described her activities at home: "I take my [3-year-old] daughter to all the major museums. We go to little movement classes."

Conservatives contend that the dropouts prove that feminism "failed" because it was too radical, because women didn't want what feminism had to offer. In fact, if half or more of feminism's heirs (85 percent of the women in my *Times* sample), are not working seriously, it's because feminism wasn't radical enough: It changed the workplace but it didn't change men, and, more importantly, it didn't fundamentally change how women related to men.

The movement did start out radical. Betty Friedan's original call to arms compared housework to animal life. In *The Feminine Mystique* she wrote, "[V]acuuming the living room floor—with or without makeup—is not work that takes enough thought or energy to challenge any woman's full capacity. . . . Down through the ages man has known that he was set apart from other animals by his mind's power to have an idea, a vision, and shape the future to it . . . when he discovers and creates and shapes a future different from his past, he is a man, a human being."

Thereafter, however, liberal feminists abandoned the judgmental starting point of the movement in favor of offering women "choices." The choice talk spilled over from people trying to avoid saying "abortion," and it provided an irresistible solution to feminists trying to duck the mommy wars. A woman could work, stay home, have 10 children or one, marry or stay single. It all counted as "feminist" as long as she *chose* it. (So dominant has the concept of choice become that when Charlotte, with a push from her insufferable first husband, quits her job, the writers at *Sex and the City* have her screaming, "I choose my choice! I choose my choice!")

Only the most radical fringes of feminism took on the issue of gender relations at home, and they put forth fruitless solutions like socialism and separatism. We know the story about socialism. Separatism ran right into heterosexuality and reproduction, to say nothing of the need to earn a living other than at a feminist bookstore. As feminist historian Alice Echols put it, "Rather than challenging their subordination in domestic life, the feminists of NOW committed themselves to fighting for women's integration into public life."

Great as liberal feminism was, once it retreated to choice the movement had no language to use on the gendered ideology of the family. Feminists could not say, "Housekeeping and child-rearing in the nuclear family is not interesting and not socially validated. Justice requires that it not be assigned to women on the basis of their gender and at the sacrifice of their access to money, power, and honor."

The 50 percent of census answerers and the 62 percent of Harvard MBAs and the 85 percent of my brides of the *Times* all think they are "choosing" their gendered lives. They don't know that feminism, in collusion with traditional society, just passed the gendered family on to them to choose. Even with all the day care in the world, the personal is still political. Much of the rest is the opt-out revolution.

III. What Is to Be Done?

Here's the feminist moral analysis that choice avoided: The family—with its repetitious, socially invisible, physical tasks—is a necessary part of life, but it allows fewer opportunities for full human flourishing than public spheres like the market or the government. This less-flourishing sphere is not the natural or moral responsibility only of women. Therefore, assigning it to women is unjust. Women assigning it to themselves is equally unjust. To paraphrase, as Mark Twain said, "A man who chooses not to read is just as ignorant as a man who cannot read."

The critics are right about one thing: Dopey *New York Times* stories do nothing to change the situation. Dowd, who is many things but not a political philosopher, concludes by wondering if the situation will change by 2030. Lefties keep hoping the Republicans will enact child-care legislation, which probably puts us well beyond 2030. In either case, we can't wait that long. If women's flourishing does matter, feminists must acknowledge that the family is to 2005 what the workplace was to 1964 and the vote to 1920. Like the right to work and the right to vote, the right to have a flourishing life that includes but is not limited to family cannot be addressed with language of choice.

Women who want to have sex and children with men as well as good work in interesting jobs where they may occasionally wield real social power need guidance, and they need it early. Step one is simply to begin talking about flourishing. In so doing, feminism will be returning to its early, judgmental roots. This may anger some, but it should sound the alarm before the next generation winds up in the same situation. Next, feminists will have to start offering young women not choices and not utopian dreams but *solutions* they can enact on their own. Prying women out of their traditional roles is not going to be easy. It will require rules—rules like those in the widely derided book *The Rules*, which was never about dating but about behavior modification.

There are three rules: Prepare yourself to qualify for good work, treat work seriously, and don't put yourself in a position of unequal resources when you marry.

The preparation stage begins with college. It is shocking to think that girls cut off their options for a public life of work as early as college. But they do. The first pitfall is the liberal-arts curriculum, which women are good at, graduating in higher numbers than men. Although many really successful people start out studying liberal arts, the purpose of a liberal education is not, with the exception of a miniscule number of academic positions, job preparation.

So the first rule is to use your college education with an eye to career goals. Feminist organizations should produce each year a survey of the most common job opportunities for people with college degrees, along with the average lifetime earnings from each job category and the characteristics such jobs require. The point here is to help women see that yes, you can study art history, but only with the realistic understanding that one day soon you will need to use your arts education to support yourself and your family. The survey would ask young women to select what they are best suited for and give guidance on the appropriate course of study. Like the rule about accepting no dates for Saturday after Wednesday night, the survey would set realistic courses for women, helping would-be curators who are not artistic geniuses avoid career frustration and avoid solving their job problems with marriage.

After college comes on-the-job training or further education. Many of my *Times* brides—and grooms—did work when they finished their educations. Here's an anecdote about the difference: One couple, both lawyers, met at a firm. After a few years, the man moved from international business law into international business. The woman quit working altogether. "They told me law school could train you for anything," she told me. "But it doesn't prepare you to go into business. I should have gone to business school." Or rolled over and watched her husband the lawyer using his first few years of work to prepare to go into a related business. Every *Times* groom assumed he had to succeed in business, and was really trying. By contrast, a common thread among the women I interviewed was a self-important idealism about the kinds of intellectual, prestigious, socially meaningful, politics-free jobs worm their incalculably valuable presence. So the second rule is that women must treat the first few years after college as an opportunity to lose their capitalism virginity and prepare for good work, which they will then treat seriously.

The best way to treat work seriously is to find the money. Money is the marker of success in a market economy; it usually accompanies power, and it enables the bearer to wield power, including within the family. Almost without exception, the brides who opted out graduated with roughly the same degrees as their husbands. Yet somewhere along the way the women made decisions in the direction of less money. Part of the problem was idealism; idealism on the career trail usually leads to volunteer work, or indentured servitude in social-service jobs, which is nice but doesn't get you to money. Another big mistake involved changing jobs excessively. Without exception, the brides who eventually went home had much more job turnover than the grooms did. There's no such thing as a perfect job. Condoleezza Rice actually wanted to be a pianist, and Gary Graffman didn't want to give concerts.

If you are good at work you are in a position to address the third undertaking: the reproductive household. The rule here is to avoid taking on more than a fair share of the second shift. If this seems coldhearted, consider the survey by the Center for Work-Life Policy. Fully 40 percent of highly qualified women with spouses felt that their husbands create more work around the house than they perform. According to Phyllis Moen and Patricia Roehling's *Career Mystique,* "When couples marry, the amount of time that a woman spends doing housework increases by approximately 17 percent, while a man's decreases by 33 percent." Not a single *Times* groom was a stay-at-home dad. Several of them could hardly wait for Monday morning to come. None of my *Times* grooms took even brief paternity leave when his children were born.

How to avoid this kind of rut? You can either find a spouse with less social power than you or find one with an ideological commitment to gender equality. Taking the easier path first, marry down. Don't think of this as brutally strategic. If you are devoted to your career goals and would like a man who will support that, you're just doing what men throughout the ages have done: placing a safe bet.

In her 1995 book, *Kidding Ourselves: Babies, Breadwinning and Bargaining Power,* Rhona Mahoney recommended finding a sharing spouse by marrying younger or poorer, or someone in a dependent status, like a starving artist. Because money is such a marker of status and power, it's hard to persuade women to marry poorer. So here's an easier rule: Marry young or marry much older. Younger men are potential high-status companions. Much older men are sufficiently established so that they don't have to work so hard, and they often have enough money to provide unlimited household help. By contrast, slightly older men with bigger incomes are the most dangerous, but even a pure counterpart is risky. If you both are going through the elite-job hazing rituals simultaneously while having children, someone is going to have to give. Even the most devoted lawyers with the hardest-working nannies are going to have weeks when no one can get home other than to sleep. The odds are that when this happens, the woman is going to give up her ambitions and professional potential.

It is possible that marrying a liberal might be the better course. After all, conservatives justified the unequal family in two modes: "God ordained it" and "biology is destiny." Most men (and most women), including the liberals, think women are responsible for the home. But at least the liberal men should feel squeamish about it.

If you have carefully positioned yourself either by marrying down or finding someone untainted by gender ideology, you will be in a position to resist bearing an unfair share of the family. Even then you must be vigilant. Bad deals come in two forms: economics and home economics. The economic temptation is to assign the cost of child care to the woman's income. If a woman making $50,000 per year whose husband makes $100,000 decides to have a baby, and the cost of a full-time nanny is $30,000, the couple reason that, after paying 40 percent in taxes, she makes $30,000, just enough to pay the nanny. So she might as well stay home. This totally ignores that both adults are in the enterprise together and the demonstrable future loss of income, power, and security for the woman who quits. Instead, calculate that all parents make a total of $150,000 and take home $90,000. After paying a full-time nanny, they have $60,000 left to live on.

The home-economics trap involves superior female knowledge and superior female sanitation. The solutions are ignorance and dust. Never figure out where the butter is. "Where's the butter?" Nora Ephron's legendary riff on marriage begins. In it, a man asks the question when looking directly at the butter container in the refrigerator. "Where's the butter?" actually means butter my toast, buy the butter, remember when we're out of butter. Next thing you know you're quitting your job at the law firm because you're so busy managing the butter. If women never start playing the household-manager role, the house will be dirty, but the realities of the physical world will trump the pull of gender ideology. Either the other adult in the family will take a hand or the children will grow up with robust immune systems.

If these prescriptions sound less than family-friendly, here's the last rule: Have a baby. Just don't have two. Mothers' Movement Online's Judith Statdman Tucker reports that women who opt out for child-care reasons act only after the second child arrives. A second kid pressures the mother's organizational skills, doubles the demands for appointments, wildly raises the cost of education and housing, and drives the family to the suburbs. But cities, with their Chinese carryouts and all, are better for working mothers. It is true that if you follow this rule, your society will not reproduce itself. But if things get bad enough, who knows what social consequences will ensue? After all, the vaunted French child-care regime was actually only a response to the superior German birth rate.

IV. Why Do We Care?

The privileged brides of the *Times*—and their husbands—seem happy. Why do we care what they do? After all, most people aren't rich and white and heterosexual, and they couldn't quit working if they wanted to.

We care because what they do is bad for them, is certainly bad for society, and is widely imitated, even by people who never get their weddings in the *Times*. This last is called the "regime effect," and it means that even if women don't quit their jobs for their families, they think they should and feel guilty about not doing it. That regime effect created the mystique around *The Feminine Mystique,* too.

As for society, elites supply the labor for the decision-making classes—the senators, the newspaper editors, the research scientists, the entrepreneurs, the policy-makers, and the policy wonks. If the ruling class is overwhelmingly male, the rulers will make mistakes that benefit males, whether from ignorance or from indifference. Media surveys reveal that if only one member of a television show's creative staff is female, the percentage of women on-screen goes up from 36 percent to 42 percent. A world of 84-percent male lawyers and 84-percent female assistants is a different place than one with women in positions of social authority. Think of a big American city with an 86-percent white police force. If role models don't matter, why care about Sandra Day O'Connor? Even if the falloff from peak numbers is small, the leveling off of women in power is a loss of hope for more change. Will there never again be more than one woman on the Supreme Court?

Worse, the behavior tarnishes every female with the knowledge that she is almost never going to be a ruler. Princeton President Shirley Tilghman described the elite colleges' self-image perfectly when she told her freshmen last year that they would be the nation's leaders, and she clearly did not have trophy wives in mind. Why should society spend resources educating women with only a 50-percent return rate on their stated goals? The American Conservative Union carried a column in 2004 recommending that employers stay away from such women or risk going out of business. Good psychological data show that the more women are treated with respect, the more ambition they have. And vice versa. The opt-out revolution is really a downward spiral.

Finally, these choices are bad for women individually. A good life for humans includes the classical standard of using one's capacities for speech and reason in a prudent way, the liberal requirement of having enough autonomy to direct one's own life, and the utilitarian test of doing more good than harm in the world. Measured against these time-tested standards, the expensively educated upper-class moms will be leading lesser lives. At feminism's dawning, two theorists compared gender ideology to a caste system. To borrow their insight, these daughters of the upper classes will be bearing most of the burden of the work always associated with the lowest caste: sweeping and cleaning bodily waste. Not two weeks after the Yalie flap, the *Times* ran a story of moms who were toilet training in infancy by vigilantly watching their babies for signs of excretion 24-7. They have voluntarily become untouchables.

When she sounded the blast that revived the feminist movement 40 years after women received the vote, Betty Friedan spoke of lives of purpose and meaning, better lives and worse lives, and feminism went a long way toward shattering the glass ceilings that limited their prospects outside the home. Now the glass ceiling begins at home. Although it is harder to shatter a ceiling that is also the roof over your head, there is no other choice. . . .

Pamela Stone   ➡ **NO**

The Rhetoric and Reality of "Opting Out"

*P*rofessional women who leave the workforce may have fewer options than it seems. What does that tell us about work in America today?

As a senior publicist at a well-known media conglomerate, Regina Donofrio had one of the most coveted, glamorous jobs in New York. A typical workday might include "riding around Manhattan in limousines with movie stars." She loved her job, had worked "a long time," and felt "comfortable" in it. So when the time came to return to work after the birth of her first child, Regina did not hesitate. "I decided I would go back to work, because the job was great, basically," she told me.

Before long, Regina found herself "crying on the train," torn between wanting to be at home with her baby and wanting to keep up her successful, exciting career. She started feeling she was never in the right place at the right time. "When I was at work, I should have been at home. When I was at home, I felt guilty because I had left work a little early to see the baby, and I had maybe left some things undone." Ever resourceful, she devised a detailed job-share plan with a colleague who was also a first-time mother. But their proposal was denied. Instead, Regina's employer offered her more money to stay and work full time, and Regina left in a huff, incensed that her employer, with whom she had a great track record, would block her from doing what she wanted to do—continue with her career and combine it with family.

Despite mainstream media portrayals to the contrary, Regina's reasons for quitting are all too typical of what I found in my study of high-achieving, former professionals who are now at-home moms. While Regina did, in fact, feel a strong urge to care for her baby, she decided to quit because of an inflexible work-place, not because of her attraction to home and hearth. She gave up her high-powered career as a last resort, after agonized soul-searching and exhausting her options. Her story differs from the popular depiction of similar, high-achieving, professional women who have headed home. Media stories typically frame these women's decisions as choices about family and see them as symptomatic of a kind of sea-change among the daughters of the feminist revolution, a return to traditionalism and the resurgence of a new feminine mystique.

The quintessential article in this prevailing story line (and the one that gave the phenomenon its name) was published in 2003 by the *New York*

Times's work-life columnist, Lisa Belkin, titled "The Opt-Out Revolution." "Opting out" is redolent with overtones of lifestyle preference and discretion, but Regina's experience counters this characterization; her decision to quit was not a lifestyle preference, nor a change in aspirations, nor a desire to return to the 1950s family. Regina did not "opt out" of the workplace because she chose to, but for precisely the opposite reason: because she had no real options and no choice.

High-achieving women's reasons for heading home are multilayered and complex, and generally counter the common view that they quit because of babies and family. This is what I found when I spoke to scores of women like Regina: highly educated, affluent, mostly white, married women with children who had previously worked as professionals or managers and whose husbands could support their being at home. Although many of these women speak the language of choice and privilege, their stories reveal a choice gap—the disjuncture between the rhetoric of choice and the reality of constraints like those Regina encountered. The choice gap reflects the extent to which high-achieving women like Regina are caught in a double bind: spiraling parenting (read "mothering") demands on the homefront collide with the increasing pace of work in the gilded cages of elite professions.

Some Skepticism

I approached these interviews with skepticism tempered by a recognition that there might be some truth to the popular image of the "new traditionalist." But to get beyond the predictable "family" explanation and the media drumbeat of choice, I thought it was important to interview women in some depth and to study women who, at least theoretically, could exercise choice. I also gave women full anonymity, creating fictitious names for them so they would speak to me as candidly as possible. The women I interviewed had outstanding educational credentials; more than half had graduate degrees in business, law, medicine, and other professions, and had once had thriving careers in which they had worked about a decade. By any measure, these were work-committed women, with strong reasons to continue with the careers in which they had invested so much. Moreover, they were in high-status fields where they had more control over their jobs and enjoyed (at least relative to workers in other fields) more family-friendly benefits.

While these women had compelling reasons to stay on the job, they also had the option not to, by virtue of their own past earnings and because their husbands were also high earners. To counter the potential criticism that they were quitting or being let go because they were not competent or up to the job, I expressly chose to study women with impeccable educational credentials, women who had navigated elite environments with competitive entry requirements. To ensure a diversity of perspectives, I conducted extensive, in-depth interviews with 54 women in a variety of professions—law, medicine, business, publishing, management consulting, nonprofit administration, and the like—living in major metropolitan areas across the country, roughly half of them in their 30s, half in their 40s.

To be sure, at-home moms are a distinct minority. Despite the many articles proclaiming a trend of women going home, among the demographic of media scrutiny—white, college-educated women, 30–54 years old—fully 84 percent are now in the workforce, up from 82 percent 20 years ago. And the much-discussed dip in the labor-force participation of mothers of young children, while real, appears to be largely a function of an economic downturn, which depresses employment for all workers.

Nevertheless, these women are important to study. Elite, educated, high-achieving women have historically been cultural arbiters, defining what is acceptable for all women in their work and family roles. This group's entrance into high-status, formerly male professions has been crucial to advancing gender parity and narrowing the wage gap, which stubbornly persists to this day. At home, moreover, they are rendered silent and invisible, so that it is easy to project and speculate about them. We can see in them whatever we want to, and perhaps that is why they have been the subject of endless speculation—about mommy wars, a return to traditionalism, and the like. While they do not represent all women, elite women's experiences provide a glimpse into the work-family negotiations that all women face. And their stories lead us to ask, "If the most privileged women of society cannot successfully combine work and family, who can?"

Motherhood Pulls

When Regina initially went back to work, she had "no clue" that she would feel so torn. She advises women not to set "too much in stone," because "you just don't know, when a human being comes out of your body, how you're going to feel." For some women, the pull of children was immediate and strong. Lauren Quattrone, a lawyer, found herself "absolutely besotted with this baby. . . . I realized that I just couldn't bear to leave him." Women such as Lauren tended to quit fairly soon after their first child was born. For others, like Diane Childs, formerly a nonprofit executive, the desire to be home with the kids came later. "I felt that it was easy to leave a baby for twelve hours a day. That I could do. But to leave a six-year-old, I just thought, was a whole different thing."

But none of these women made their decisions to quit in a vacuum. In fact, they did so during a cultural moment when norms and practices for parents—mothers—are very demanding. These women realized they would rear children very differently from the way their own mothers raised them, feeling an external, almost competitive pressure to do so. Middle- and upper-middle-class women tend to be particularly mindful of expert advice, and these women were acutely aware of a well-documented intensification in raising children, which sociologist Sharon Hays calls an "ideology of intensive mothering." This cultural imperative, felt by women of all kinds, "advises mothers to expend a tremendous amount of time, energy and money in raising their children."

A corollary is what Annette Lareau terms "concerted cultivation," a non-stop pace of organized activities scheduled by parents for school-age children. Among the women I spoke to, some, like Diane, felt the urgency of "concerted cultivation" and reevaluated their childcare as the more sophisticated needs of their older children superseded the simpler, more straightforward babysitting and physical care required for younger children. Marina Isherwood, a former executive in the health care industry, with children in the second and fourth grades, became convinced that caregivers could not replace her own parental influence:

> There isn't a substitute, no matter how good the child-care. When they're little, the fact that someone else is doing the stuff with them is fine. It wasn't the part that I loved anyway. But when they start asking you questions about values, you don't want your babysitter telling them. . . . Our children come home, and they have all this homework to do, and piano lessons and this and this, and it's all a complicated schedule. And, yes, you could get an au pair to do that, to balance it all, but they're not going to necessarily teach you how to think about math. Or help you come up with mnemonic devices to memorize all of the countries in Spain or whatever.

Because academic credentials were so important to these women's (and their husband's) career opportunities, formal schooling was a critical factor in their decisions to quit. For some, the premium they placed on education and values widened the gap between themselves and their less educated caregivers.

Depending on the woman, motherhood played a larger or smaller role in her decision whether and when to quit. Children were the main focus of women's caregiving, but other family members needed care as well, for which women felt responsible. About 10 percent of the women spoke of significant elder-care responsibilities, the need for which was especially unpredictable. This type of caregiving and mothering made up half of the family/career double bind. More important, though, motherhood influenced women's decision to quit as they came to see the rhythms and values of the workplace as antagonistic to family life.

Workplace Pushes

On top of their demanding mothering regime, these women received mixed messages from both their husbands and their employers. Husbands offered emotional support to wives who were juggling career and family. Emily Mitchell, an accountant, described her marriage to a CPA as "a pretty equal relationship," but when his career became more demanding, requiring long hours and Saturdays at work, he saw the downside of egalitarianism:

> I think he never minded taking my daughter to the sitter, that was never an issue, and when he would come home, we have a pretty equal relationship on that stuff. But getting her up, getting her ready, getting himself ready to go into work, me coming home, getting her, getting her to bed, getting unwound from work, and then he would come home, we'd try to do something for dinner, and then there was always

something else to do—laundry, cleaning, whatever—I think he was feeling too much on a treadmill.

But husbands did little to share family responsibilities, instead maintaining their own demanding careers full-speed ahead.

Similarly, many workplaces claimed to be "family friendly" and offered a variety of supports. But for women who could take advantage of them, flexible work schedules (which usually meant working part-time) carried significant penalties. Women who shifted to part-time work typically saw their jobs gutted of significant responsibilities and their once-flourishing careers derailed. Worse, part-time hours often crept up to the equivalent of full time. When Diane Childs had children, she scaled back to part time and began to feel the pointlessness of continuing:

> And I'm never going to get anywhere—you have the feeling that you just plateaued professionally because you can't take on the extra projects; you can't travel at a moment's notice; you can't stay late; you're not flexible on the Friday thing because that could mean finding someone to take your kids. You really plateau for a much longer period of time than you ever realize when you first have a baby. It's like you're going to be plateaued for thirteen to fifteen years.

Lynn Hamilton, an M.D., met her husband at Princeton, where they were both undergraduates. Her story illustrates how family pulls and workplace pushes (from both her career and her husband's) interacted in a marriage that was founded on professional equality but then devolved to the detriment of her career:

> We met when we were 19 years old, and so, there I was, so naive, I thought, well, here we are, we have virtually identical credentials and comparable income earnings. That's an opportunity. And, in fact, I think our incomes were identical at the time I quit. To the extent to which we have articulated it, it was always understood, well, with both of us working, neither of us would have to be working these killer jobs. So, what was happening was, instead, we were both working these killer jobs. And I kept saying, "We need to reconfigure this." And what I realized was, he wasn't going to.

Meanwhile, her young daughter was having behavioral problems at school, and her job as a medical director for a biomedical start-up company had "the fax machine going, the three phone lines upstairs, they were going." Lynn slowly realized that the only reconfiguration possible, in the face of her husband's absence, was for her to quit.

Over half (60 percent) of the women I spoke to mentioned their husbands as one of the key reasons why they quit. That not all women talked about their husbands' involvement, or lack thereof, reveals the degree to which they perceived the work-family balancing act to be their responsibility alone. But women seldom mentioned their husbands for another reason: they were, quite literally, absent.

Helena Norton, an educational administrator who characterized her husband as a "workaholic," poignantly described a scenario that many others took for granted and which illustrates a pattern typical of many of these women's lives: "He was leaving early mornings; 6:00 or 6:30 before anyone was up, and then he was coming home late at night. So I felt this real emptiness, getting up in the morning to, not necessarily an empty house, because my children were there, but I did, I felt empty, and then going to bed, and he wasn't there."

In not being there to pick up the slack, many husbands had an important indirect impact on their wives' decisions to quit. Deferring to their husbands' careers and exempting them from household chores, these women tended to accept this situation. Indeed, privileging their husbands' careers was a pervasive, almost tacit undercurrent of their stories.

When talking about their husbands, women said the same things: variations on "he's supportive," and that he gave them a "choice." But this hands-off approach revealed husbands to be bystanders, not participants, in the work-family bind. "It's your choice" was code for "it's your problem." And husbands' absences, a direct result of their own high-powered careers, put a great deal of pressure on women to do it all, thus undermining the façade of egalitarianism.

Family pulls—from children and, as a result of their own long work hours, their husbands—exacerbated workplace pushes; and all but seven women cited features of their jobs—the long hours, the travel—as another major motivation in quitting. Marketing executive Nathalie Everett spoke for many women when she remarked that her full-time workweek was "really 60 hours, not 40. Nobody works nine-to-five anymore."

Surprisingly, the women I interviewed, like Nathalie, neither questioned nor showed much resentment toward the features of their jobs that kept them from fully integrating work and family. They routinely described their jobs as "all or nothing" and appeared to internalize what sociologists call the "ideal worker" model of a (typically male) worker unencumbered by family demands. This model was so influential that those working part time or in other flexible arrangements often felt stigmatized. Christine Thomas, a marketing executive and job-sharer, used imagery reminiscent of *The Scarlet Letter* to describe her experience: "When you job share, you have 'MOMMY' stamped in huge letters on your forehead."

While some women's decisions could be attributed to their unquestioning acceptance of the status quo or a lack of imagination, the unsuccessful attempts of others who tried to make it work by pursuing alternatives to full-time, like Diane, serve as cautionary tales. Women who made arrangements with bosses felt like they were being given special favors. Their part-time schedules were privately negotiated, hence fragile and unstable, and were especially vulnerable in the context of any kind of organizational restructuring such as mergers.

The Choice Gap

Given the incongruity of these women's experiences—they felt supported by "supportive" yet passive husbands and pushed out by workplaces that once prized their expertise—how did these women understand their situation? How did they make sense of professions that, on the one hand, gave them considerable status and rewards, and, on the other hand, seemed to marginalize them and force them to compromise their identity as mothers?

The overwhelming majority felt the same way as Melissa Wyatt, the 34-year-old who gave up a job as a fund-raiser: "I think today it's all about choices, and the choices we want to make. And I think that's great. I think it just depends where you want to spend your time." But a few shared the outlook of Olivia Pastore, a 42-year-old ex-lawyer:

> I've had a lot of women say to me, "Boy, if I had the choice of, if I could balance, if I could work part-time, if I could keep doing it." And there are some women who are going to stay home full-time no matter what and that's fine. But there are a number of women, I think, who are home because they're caught between a rock and a hard place. . . . There's a lot of talk about the individual decisions of individual women. "Is it good? Is it bad? She gave it up. She couldn't hack it," . . . And there's not enough blame, if you will, being laid at the feet of the culture, the jobs, society.

My findings show that Olivia's comments—about the disjuncture between the rhetoric of choice and the reality of constraint that shapes women's decisions to go home—are closer to the mark. Between trying to be the ideal mother (in an era of intensive mothering) and the ideal worker (a model based on a man with a stay-at-home wife), these high-flying women faced a double bind. Indeed, their options were much more limited than they seemed. Fundamentally, they faced a "choice gap": the difference between the decisions women could have made about their careers if they were not mothers or caregivers and the decisions they had to make in their circumstances as mothers married to high-octane husbands in ultimately unyielding professions. This choice gap obscures individual preferences, and thus reveals the things Olivia railed against—culture, jobs, society—the kinds of things sociologists call "structure."

Overall, women based their decisions on mutually reinforcing and interlocking factors. They confronted, for instance, two sets of trade-offs: kids versus careers, and their own careers versus those of their husbands. For many, circumstances beyond their control strongly influenced their decision to quit. On the family side of the equation, for example, women had to deal with caregiving for sick children and elderly parents, children's developmental problems, and special care needs. Such reasons figured in one-third of the sample. On the work side, women were denied part-time arrangements, a couple were laid off, and some had to relocate for their own careers or their husbands'. A total of 30 women, a little more than half the sample, mentioned at least one forced-choice consideration.

But even before women had children, the prospect of pregnancy loomed in the background, making women feel that they were perceived as flight risks. In her first day on the job as a marketing executive, for example, Patricia Lambert's boss asked her: "So, are you going to have kids?" And once women did get pregnant, they reported that they were often the first in their office, which made them feel more like outsiders. Some remarked that a dearth of role models created an atmosphere unsympathetic to work-family needs. And as these women navigated pregnancy and their lives beyond, their stories revealed a latent bias against mothers in their workplaces. What some women took from this was that pregnancy was a dirty little secret not to be openly discussed. The private nature of pregnancy thus complicated women's decisions regarding their careers once they became mothers, which is why they often waited until the last minute to figure out their next steps. Their experiences contrasted with the formal policies of their workplaces, which touted themselves as "family friendly."

The Rhetoric of Choice

Given the indisputable obstacles—hostile workplaces and absentee husbands—that stymied a full integration of work and family, it was ironic that most of the women invoked "choice" when relating the events surrounding their decision to exit their careers. Why were there not more women like Olivia, railing against the tyranny of an outmoded workplace that favored a 1950s-era employee or bemoaning their husbands' drive for achievement at the expense of their own?

I found that these women tended to use the rhetoric of choice in the service of their exceptionality. Women associated choice with privilege, feminism, and personal agency, and internalized it as a reflection of their own perfectionism. This was an attractive combination that played to their drive for achievement and also served to compensate for their loss of the careers they loved and the professional identities they valued. Some of these women bought into the media message that being an at-home mom was a status symbol, promoted by such cultural arbiters as *New York Magazine* and the *Wall Street Journal*. Their ability to go home reflected their husbands' career success, in which they and their children basked. Living out the traditional lifestyle, male breadwinner and stay-at-home-mom, which they were fortunate to be able to choose, they saw themselves as realizing the dreams of third-wave feminism. The goals of earlier, second-wave feminism, economic independence and gender equality, took a back seat, at least temporarily.

Challenging the Myth

These strategies and rhetoric, and the apparent invisibility of the choice gap, reveal how fully these high-achieving women internalized the double bind and the intensive-mothering and ideal-worker models on which it rests. The downside, of course, is that they blamed themselves for failing to "have it all" rather than any actual structural constraints. That work and family were incompatible was the overwhelming message they took from their experiences. And when they quit, not wanting to burn bridges, they cited family obligations as the reason, not their dissatisfaction with work, in accordance with social expectations. By adopting the socially desirable and gender-consistent explanation of "family," women often contributed to the larger misunderstanding surrounding their decision. Their own explanations endorsed the prevalent idea that

quitting to go home is a choice. Employers rarely challenged women's explanations. Nor did they try to convince them to stay, thus reinforcing women's
perception that their decision was the right thing to do as mothers, and perpet-
uating the reigning media image of these women as the new traditionalists.

Taken at face value, these women do seem to be traditional. But by reject-
ing an intransigent workplace, their quitting signifies a kind of silent strike.
They were not acquiescing to traditional gender roles by quitting, but voting
with their feet against an outdated model of work. When women are not pos-
ing for the camera or worried about offending former employers (from whom
they may need future references), they are able to share their stories candidly.
From what I found, the truth is far different and certainly more nuanced than
the media depiction.

The vast majority of the type of women I studied do not want to
choose between career and family. The demanding nature of today's parenting puts added pressure on women. Women do indeed need to learn to be
"good enough" mothers, and their husbands need to engage more equally in
parenting. But on the basis of what they told me, women today "choose" to
be home full-time not as much because of parenting overload as because of
work overload, specifically long hours and the lack of flexible options in their
high-status jobs. The popular media depiction of a return to traditionalism is
wrong and misleading. Women are trying to achieve the feminist vision of
a fully integrated life combining family and work. That so many attempt to
remain in their careers when they do not "have to work" testifies strongly to
their commitment to their careers, as does the difficulty they experience over
their subsequent loss of identity. Their attempts at juggling and their plans to
return to work in the future also indicate that their careers were not meant to
be ephemeral and should not be treated as such. Rather, we should regard their
exits as the miner's canary—a frontline indication that something is seriously
amiss in many workplaces. Signs of toxic work environments and white-collar
sweatshops are ubiquitous. We can glean from these women's experiences the
true cost of these work conditions, which are personal and professional, and,
ultimately, societal and economic.

Our current understanding of why high-achieving women quit—based
as it is on choice and separate spheres—seriously undermines the will to
change the contemporary workplace. The myth of opting out returns us to
the days when educated women were barred from entering elite professions
because "they'll only leave anyway." To the extent that elite women are arbiters of shifting gender norms, the opting out myth also has the potential to
curtail women's aspirations and stigmatize those who challenge the separate-
spheres ideology on which it is based. Current demographics make it clear
that employers can hardly afford to lose the talents of high-achieving women.
They can take a cue from at-home moms like the ones I studied: Forget opting
out; the key to keeping professional women on the job is to create better, more
flexible ways to work. . . .

CHALLENGE QUESTIONS

Are Professional Women "Opting Out" of Work by Choice?

- Much of the debate in this issue is about how much choice people really have in the face of broader social forces—during adult development how much is really up to the individual and how much is constrained by social norms and structures?
- Why does Hirshman claim that when successful women end up devoting more time to family than to work it is bad for society as a whole? Do you agree?
- Stone notes that many of the women she interviewed perceived their leaving work as a choice, but Stone thinks they were wrong. When researching adult life choices, how much should a scholar trust the perceptions of the people themselves?
- While Hirshman thinks improving options for successful women is up to the women themselves, and Stone thinks it is up to the workplace, what do you think needs to change if women are to really have choices in their adult development?
- Both authors implicitly dismiss the idea that women may "naturally" take more interest in childrearing. Why? Are there reasons to believe otherwise?

Suggested Readings

L. Belkin, "The Opt-Out Revolution," *The New York Times Magazine* (October 26, 2003)

E.J. Graff, "The Opt-Out Myth," *Columbia Journalism Review* (March/April 2007)

L.R. Hirshman, *Get to Work: A Manifesto for Women of the World* (Viking Adult, 2006)

P. Stone, *Opting Out?: Why Women Really Quit Careers and Head Home* (University of California Press, 2008)

L. Morgan Steiner, *Mommy Wars: Stay-at-Home and Career Moms Face Off on Their Choices, Their Lives, Their Families* (Random House, 2006)

M. Blair-Loy, *Competing Devotions: Career and Family among Women Executives* (Harvard University Press, 2003)

C. Percheski, "Opting Out? Cohort Differences in Professional Women's Employment Rates from 1960 to 2005." *American Sociological Review* (June 2008)

A. Hochschild. *The Second Shift* (Viking, 1989)

J.A. Jacobs and K. Gerson, *The Time Divide: Work, Family and Gender Inequality* (Harvard University Press, 2004)

Internet References . . .

National Institute on Aging

The National Institute on Aging Web site offers health and research information related primarily to the science of later adulthood.

http://www.nia.nih.gov/

AARP

The AARP is a nonprofit organization organized to help "people 50 and over improve the quality of their lives," and offers related research information on its Web site.

http://www.aarp.org/research/

The Urban Institute

The Web site for the Urban Institute provides research based information related to retirement and contemporary society.

http://www.urban.org/retirement_policy/

Trinity University

An academic's site with references to information about "social gerontology" or the study of sociological aspects of old age.

http://www.trinity.edu/~mkearl/geron.html

Alzheimer's Association

At this Alzheimer's Association Web site there is a wide-range of information about Alzheimer's Disease and related dementias (including "Mild Cognitive Impairment").

http://www.alz.org/alzheimers_disease.asp

Snenscence.info

A Web site with links to information about research into mostly biological aspects of aging.

http://www.senescence.info/

The American Geriatric Society Foundation for Health in Aging

The American Geriatric Society Foundation for Health in Aging works to connect aging research and practice.

http://www.healthinaging.org/

Research on Euthanasia

Information and links for "research on euthanasia, physician-assisted suicide, living wills, [and] mercy killing."

http://www.euthanasia.com/

Ethics Matters on Euthanasia

Resources and links related to euthanasia and end-of-life decisions focused particularly on ethics.

http://ethics.sandiego.edu/Applied/Euthanasia/

Later Adulthood

*T*he central question for thinking about later adulthood, generally defined as the period of life after retirement age, is whether it is an inevitable period of decline or merely a period of adaptation? While we often think of old age as a time of deterioration, research suggests that most people in this stage actually adjust to the challenges of aging reasonably well. Yet there are unquestionable challenges, including changing social roles, the eventual decline of cognitive functioning, and the inevitability of death. The issues in this section consider each of these challenges in turn, while broadly addressing the nature of old age as a time of continuing development.

- Is More Civic Engagement Among Older Adults Necessarily Better?
- Is "Mild Cognitive Impairment" Too Similar to Normal Aging to be a Relevant Concept?
- Should the Terminally Ill Be Able to Have Physicians Help Them Die?

ISSUE 18

Is More Civic Engagement Among Older Adults Necessarily Better?

YES: Sheila R. Zedlewski and Barbara A. Butrica, from "Are We Taking Full Advantage of Older Adults' Potential?" *Perspectives on Productive Aging* (Number 9, December 2007)

NO: Marty Martinson, from "Opportunities or Obligations? Civic Engagement and Older Adults," *Generations* (Winter 2006–2007)

ISSUE SUMMARY

YES: Urban Institute researchers Sheila R. Zedlewski and Barbara A. Butrica, writing as part of a broader project to investigate the changing nature of retirement, argue that promoting civic engagement is good for both individuals and society.

NO: Critical gerontologist Marty Martinson acknowledges that promoting civic engagement in old age can be useful, but suggests that it also serves to shift attention away from broader social problems and responsibilities toward individuals who may or may not benefit from conventional civic engagement.

The American population and the world population are both aging. People are living longer, and spending more time in the stage generally described as old age. With more people living longer and longer there has been increasing interest in the field of "gerontology," which is defined as "the comprehensive study of aging and the problems of the aged" (according to the Merriam-Webster Dictionary). This definition points out the traditional emphasis in gerontology on problems, deriving from a general assumption that old age is a period of inevitable decline. In response to this assumption, many gerontologists have tried to address ways that old age can be re-conceptualized in more optimistic terms. One such effort has involved promoting older adults as a resource toward the civic good. But it turns out that overly optimistic conceptions of old age may have as many problems as overly pessimistic ones.

In work that some scholars describe as the "new gerontology" attention has been devoted toward focusing less on fixing the problems of old age and more on promoting "successful aging." One of the tenants of "successful aging" is to emphasize the importance of staying active and engaged during older adulthood.

While this emphasis may seem uncontroversial, critical gerontologists have pointed out that not all people have the option of staying active in old age. Critical scholars suggest that emphasizing activity as the basis for "successful aging" risks promoting a "new ageism" that discriminates against people who have been confronted by significant challenges through their lives.

Nevertheless, many organizations and public policy efforts have taken up the call of the "new gerontology" to promote ways that older adults can and should stay active. The selection from Zedlewski and Butrica is one example, deriving from a project by the Urban Institute to promote "productive aging." In their review of research and literature about ways that civic engagement during older adulthood might influence well-being, they find only positive effects—there is, for example, a clear correlation between good health and being engaged with activities such as work and volunteering.

But scholars know that correlation does not necessarily equal causation, and Marty Martinson points out that the relationship between active civic engagement in old age and well-being may be due to social forces rather than individual choices. Martinson defines civic engagement "broadly to include not only formal volunteering, but also things like political activism, caregiving, and community organizing," yet she notes that much public policy takes civic engagement to focus only on volunteerism in service of institutional goals. Acknowledging that civic engagement can have some benefits, Martinson raises questions about whether more is always better and whether older adults are just being expected to offer free labor. These questions are well worth considering for our aging society and for the study of life-span development—should old age just be about continuing adult-like productivity, or does the nature of older adulthood offer something different?

POINT

- Staying engaged with work and volunteering in old age has significant benefits for both individuals and communities.

- There are many capable older adults who could be more involved than they currently are, and many would benefit economically.

- Civic engagement offers a sense of purpose, social status, and better health by encouraging social interactions and access to resources.

- With changing economic climates, there are likely to be more opportunities for non-physically demanding jobs and for non-profit volunteer work.

COUNTERPOINT

- While civic engagement among older adults has some value, people too often think about it simply as an individual choice without recognizing the structural forces that shape the nature of old age.

- By suggesting that civic engagement makes life meaningful for older adults, the implication is that without such engagement old age is meaningless—ignoring viable roles with less direct economic value such as caregiving and political activism.

- Promoting civic engagement in old age may end up obliging people to burdensome work at all ages, and may promote negative stigmas for people who are unable to stay productive.

- Emphasizing volunteer civic engagement can serve to diminish the responsibility of governments and institutions for addressing social problems.

YES ⟵

**Sheila R. Zedlewski and
Barbara A. Butrica**

Are We Taking Full Advantage of Older Adults' Potential?

Staying engaged in work and formal volunteer activities at older ages significantly benefits the health and well-being of the volunteers themselves, the organizations that count on them, the people served by those organizations, and the economy. Yet, numerous studies show many older adults, especially those in low-income groups, sit out these opportunities. Why isn't completely clear. Do some older Americans simply prefer to relax and spend time with family, friends, and hobbies after long and sometimes stressful years on the job? Do such personal challenges as poor physical or mental health or limited skills keep them from connecting? Or are opportunities scarce or out of sync with older adults' preferences?

The answers to these questions have broad and pressing policy implications. In 2008, the oldest baby boomers will start turning 62—the age at which many people retire. Since this cohort is 76 million people strong, the societal and economic payoffs for encouraging boomers to stay engaged could be enormous.

Using data from the 2004 Health and Retirement Study, we estimate the potential for increasing engagement among adults 55 and older. We define engagement as working for pay or volunteering for an organization, and summarize the literature that documents the key benefits of engagement at older ages. We then examine engagement rates among older adults and the characteristics that distinguish the engaged from the unengaged, highlighting income differences. We then estimate which and how many unengaged older adults would most likely benefit from increased engagement opportunities. Finally, we ask how well demand for older workers and volunteers is likely to mesh with supply.

We find enormous potential for increasing the number of engaged older Americans. More than 10 million healthy older adults with no caregiving responsibilities, including 3.6 million low-income individuals, are now on the sidelines. Over half of these able seniors are under age 75, and 9 out of 10 have worked before. And recent surveys indicate that this larger group is interested in both paid work and volunteer opportunities. Given this untapped potential, shortages of volunteers and workers should prompt employers and nonprofits to court this talent. That said, public policies that boost engagement among interested low-income seniors—who have the most to gain—may also be needed to ensure broad participation.

The Payoff to Engagement

Research increasingly documents how engagement in work and formal volunteer activities benefits the participants, the recipients of volunteer services, and the economy. Those who regularly work or volunteer enjoy better health and live longer, thanks to stimulating environments and a sense of purpose. Recipients of volunteer services, especially children, benefit from interactions with older adults. In addition, older adults' volunteer activities are what make many nonprofits viable. And older Americans' work and volunteering boost economic vitality.

Engagement Improves Health Status

A raft of recent studies documents the benefits of formal volunteer activities on older adults' health. . . . Using multiple data sources and methods, 10 studies published since 1999 document the significant positive associations between volunteer activity and decreased mortality and depression, improved health and strength, greater happiness, and enhanced cognitive ability.

Research on work also tends to find positive effects. Calvo . . . shows that paid work at older ages reduces morbidity and improves health. Following a sample of early retirees for 30 years, Tsai and coauthors . . . find that this group had higher morbidity rates than workers who retired later. In the same vein, Dhaval, Rashad, and Spasojevic . . . find that complete retirement (defined in most such studies as withdrawal from paid work) takes a toll on physical and mental health. In contrast, Charles . . . finds that retirement improves mental health, while Bound and Waidmann . . . find that retiring has little effect on health either way. Gallo and coauthors . . . show that involuntary job loss at older ages decreases well-being.

Investigations of why engagement improves health and mortality generally point to increased cognitive activity, exposure to stimulating environments, and social interactions. . . . Enhanced social status . . . and greater access to social, psychological, and material resources can also play a role. . . . Some activities help older adults develop knowledge and skills that boost their self-images and mental outlooks. . . . Greenfield and Marks . . . document that formal volunteering helps older adults mitigate the loss of a sense of purpose.

Engagement Provides Social and Economic Benefits

Children, in particular, benefit from older adults' engagement, especially in educational activities. . . . The evaluation of the Family Friends program found that volunteer home visitors age 55 and older significantly reduced hospitalization rates among chronically ill and disabled children and improved the overall well-being of parents and families. . . . When adolescents with behavioral problems or struggles in school were linked with older mentors in the Across Ages program, they showed improved class attendance, more positive attitudes toward school, and reductions in substance use. . . . More generally, Wheeler, Gorey, and Greenblatt . . . reviewed 37 studies across a variety of program models and found that 85 percent of the individuals served by older adults showed significantly improved results.

Nonprofits increasingly rely on volunteers, a significant portion of whom are older adults. Over 6 in 10 nonprofits report working with volunteers between the ages of 65 and 74. . . . Volunteers who manage or deliver social services allow nonprofits to save money and get more done, extending the reach of their staff and stabilizing their resources. . . .

Finally, both paid work and formal volunteer activities benefit the economy. Johnson and Schaner . . . value formal volunteering activities among older adults at $44.3 billion in 2002. Paid work also increases the retirement security of older adults. Even a few additional years can significantly boost retirement income, especially among lower-paid workers. . . .

Today's Engagement Patterns

More than half of adults age 55 and older formally engaged in paid or volunteer work in 2004 (table 1). About 2 in 5 worked for pay and 1 in 3 volunteered for organizations. Compared with higher-income older adults, considerably smaller shares of low-income older adults worked for pay

Table 1

Activities of Adults Ages 55 and Older in 2004, by Income Level and Engagement Status (percent)

	Total	Low Income	Higher Income
Type of formal engagement			
Any	57	33	65*
Work	39	15	46*
Volunteering	34	23	37*
Type of informal engagement			
Any	67	55	71*
Informally volunteering	52	38	57*
Providing care	39	32	41*
Population (000s)	63,952	16,307	47,645

Source: Authors' estimates from the 2004 Health and Retirement Study.

Note: The universe is respondents ages 55 and older in 2004.

*Mean value for the low-income group is significantly different from the comparable mean value for the higher-income group at the 10 percent level or better. Results are based on a total, unweighted sample size of 15,871.

(15 percent versus 46 percent) or volunteered for organizations (23 percent compared with 37 percent). In 2004, two-thirds of older adults also volunteered informally by helping their neighbors or caring for a family member. Higher-income older adults informally volunteered more often than their low-income counterparts.

How older adults spend their time may reflect differences in their personal traits and job experiences (table 2). Engaged older adults tend to be younger, healthier, and better-educated than same-age adults who choose not to work or volunteer. For example, more than half of engaged older adults are under age 65, in very good to excellent health, and have some education beyond high school. Nearly two-fifths have managerial or professional experience. In contrast, only 1 in 4 of the unengaged report being very healthy, 3 in 10 have more than a high school degree, and 1 in 5 has managerial experience.

Race and ethnic differences between the engaged and the unengaged are relatively small, though statistically significant. Also, there is little urban/ rural difference between the engaged and the unengaged, countering some worries that older adults in rural areas have fewer chances for work or volunteer activities. Access to transportation does differ significantly between the two groups; 92 percent of engaged adults own a vehicle, compared with 77 percent of the unengaged.

What Is the Potential?

A large share of older adults continues to work or volunteer, but many more still don't. Adults with the lowest rate of participation tend to have lower incomes, less education, and more physically demanding jobs. Getting this group to stay engaged requires both a strong demand for older workers and volunteers and a large supply of willing and able individuals. Fortunately, the evidence is positive for both supply and demand.

Demand Is Strong

Toossi . . . at the Bureau of Labor Statistics projects a 15 million–person increase in the labor force between 2004 and 2014. Adults age 55 and older will account for 11 million, or 73 percent, of this increase. Additionally, Johnson, Mermin, and Resseger . . . show a more favorable job climate for older workers, as the physical demands of most U.S. jobs decline. Yet, as the authors point out, older adults, particularly those with limited education who worked in physically demanding jobs, may need job training to update their skills.

Nonprofit organizations will likely need more workers and volunteers, owing to the government's increasing reliance on nonprofits to deliver public services. Tierney . . . expects nonprofits will grow because of projections of large future donations and wealth transfers. Between 2002 and 2004, the nonprofit paid and volunteer workforce grew by 5.3 percent, compared with an overall employment decline of 0.2 percent. . . . The bulk of nonprofit opportunities are in human services and, more particularly, in health services. Also,

Table 2

Characteristics of Adults Ages 55 and Older in 2004, by Formal Engagement Status (percent)

	Total	Engaged	Unengaged
Age			
55–64	45	59	27*
65–74	29	26	32*
75+	26	15	40*
Health status			
Fair/poor	28	17	42*
Good	31	31	32
Excellent/very good	41	52	26*
Depressed			
Yes	13	8	20*
No	79	86	71*
Race/ethnicity			
White, non-Hispanic	83	85	80*
Black, non-Hispanic	9	8	10*
Hispanic	6	5	8*
Other race	2	2	3
Educational attainment			
High school or less	56	46	71*
More than high school	44	54	29*
Occupation of longest job			
Manager, professional	31	38	21*
Sales, clerical, service	36	37	36
Operator, craftsperson	28	24	33*
Never worked	5	1	10*
Urban/rural			
Urban	47	47	47
Suburban	21	21	22*

Continued

Table 2 (Continued)

Characteristics of Adults Ages 55 and Older in 2004, by Formal Engagement Status (percent)

	Total	Engaged	Unengaged
Rural	32	32	32
Own a vehicle			
Yes	86	92	77*
No	14	8	23*
Family income			
Low income	25	15	40*
Higher income	75	85	60*
Population (000s)	63,952	36,449	27,503

Source: Authors' estimates from the 2004 Health and Retirement Study.

Notes: The universe is respondents ages 55 and older in 2004. Engaged is defined as working or formally volunteering. Occupation is based on those with nonmissing values.

*Mean value for the engaged is significantly different from the comparable mean value for the unengaged at the 10 percent level or better. Results are based on a total, unweighted sample size of 15,871.

nonprofits are experiencing shortages in executive skills. As the nonprofit sector grows and seasoned executives retire, these shortages are expected to worsen. . . .

Supply Is Ample

Older adults want to work and volunteer, according to recent surveys. . . . Boomers say they plan to work well into their 60s and 70s. . . . Some will continue working because of a growing insecurity about retirement income, including changes to the Social Security retirement age, the decline in employer-sponsored pensions, and the erosion in retiree health benefits. The desire to continue working is also a desire to stay involved; most older adults say they plan to work longer because their work interests them, not out of economic necessity. . . .

More than half of adults age 55 and older who do not volunteer indicate some interest in volunteering now or in the future. . . . Surveys document boomers' strong interest in the nonprofit sector. . . . One survey by VolunteerMatch . . . found that white-collar workers and women were most likely to express interest in volunteer opportunities. Many potential volunteers said they want to work on causes that matter to them (56 percent) and to use their skills (35 percent); convenience (43 percent) and flexible scheduling (46 percent) were also deemed important.

We expect that the older adults most willing and able to stay engaged are healthy and free of caregiving responsibilities. Out of 27.5 million unengaged older adults, 8.7 million report good health and 7.2 million report excellent health (table 3). Also, 18.4 million of the unengaged have no family caregiving responsibilities. All told, 10.3 million unengaged older adults had good or better health and no caregiving responsibilities in 2004, including 3.6 million low-income persons. These adults could be targeted for new engagement opportunities.

More than half of the most able unengaged older adults are relatively young (age 55 to 74), including 44 percent of the low-income group and 55 percent of the higher-income group. About 1 in 3 have more than a high school degree, but the share drops to 1 in 5 for those in the low-income group. Many adults with more than a high school education have managerial or professional experience (3.6 million, or 17 percent of the entire unengaged group), skills often sought by nonprofits. In contrast, most of those with only a high school education had careers in services (such as sales or clerical work) or as operators and craftspeople. Only 9.4 percent of the most able unengaged adults had never worked, including 7.5 percent of those in the low-education group and 1.9 percent of those in the high-education group.

Potential workers and volunteers are a geographically diverse group, with nearly half living in urban areas. Table 3 also shows the percent of older adults volunteering informally, as a potential indicator of their propensity to enjoy formal volunteer positions. About 4 out of 10 older adults, including 35 percent of those with low incomes and 41 percent of those with higher incomes, report helping their neighbors and friends.

The number and profile of healthy, unengaged older adults with no current caregiving responsibilities demonstrate ample opportunity for engaging greater numbers of older adults. Many have sales and clerical experience, skill sets that will grow in demand with the rise of service occupations and nonprofit agencies. Others who worked in more physically demanding jobs, such as craftspeople or machine operators, may need job training outside their fields to find more opportunities to work and volunteer.

Discussion and Next Steps

More than 10 million healthy older adults without caregiving responsibilities do not engage in paid work or formal volunteering. More than half of these able adults are under age 75, and more than 9 out of 10 have some paid work experience. Recent surveys show that many of these individuals would enjoy a paid work or volunteer position. Low-income individuals—3.6 million strong—would especially benefit from the additional dividend of extra income from paid work.

Opportunities for older boomers seeking volunteer or paid work are ample, but policy interventions are needed to engage a larger share of those with limited education and work experience not well matched to high-growth job and volunteer opportunities. Particularly needed is more funding for training programs that target low-income older adults and broader communication networks that connect older adults to available volunteer and work

Table 3

Demographic Characteristics of Unengaged Adults
Ages 55 and Older, 2004

	All Unengaged (000s)	Most Able: Good to Excellent Health and Without Caregiving Responsibilities		
		All	Low Income	Higher Income
Population (000s)	27,503	10,337	3,561	6,775
Total (Percent)		100.0	100.0	100.0
Age				
55–64	7,535	19.2	17.8	20.0
65–74	8,868	31.8	26.5	34.6
75+	11,101	48.9	55.7	45.4
High school or less				
Manager, professional	1,683	8.2	7.5	8.6
Sales, clerical, service	6,654	27.4	31.1	25.4
Operator, craftsman	7,100	24.3	29.8	21.4
Never worked	1,997	7.5	12.5	4.8
More than high school				
Manager, professional	3,631	17.0	6.1	22.7
Sales, clerical, service	2,330	9.2	6.8	10.5
Operator, craftsman	1,043	4.6	3.7	5.1
Never worked	367	1.9	2.5	1.6
Urban/rural				
Urban	12,826	47.9	41.0	51.6
Suburban	5,995	21.8	21.2	22.1
Rural	8,682	30.3	37.9	26.3
Informally volunteer				
No	17,551	60.9	65.0	58.8
Yes	9,952	39.1	35.0	41.2

Continued

Table 3 (Continued)

Demographic Characteristics of Unengaged Adults
Ages 55 and Older, 2004

	All Unengaged (000s)	Most Able: Good to Excellent Health and Without Caregiving Responsibilities		
		All	Low Income	Higher Income
Characteristics used to Identify most able Health status				
Fair/poor	11,596	0.0	0.0	0.0
Good	8,699	56.0	61.2	53.2
Excellent/very good	7,208	44.1	38.8	46.8
Provide care				
No	18,429	100.0	100.0	100.0
Yes	9,074	0.0	0.0	0.0
Family income				
Low income	10,866	34.5	100.0	0.0
Higher income	16,637	65.6	0.0	1.6

Source: Authors' estimates from the 2004 Health and Retirement Study.

Note: The universe is respondents ages 55 and older in 2004. Unengaged is defined as not working or formally volunteering. Occupation is based on those with nonmissing values. The sample size for the total unengaged population is 7,560.

opportunities. Public-sponsored outreach to older adults on the advantages of engagement while receiving Social Security benefits is also needed.

Policymakers must understand the payoffs of keeping older adults engaged. Longer careers increase retirement incomes, generate greater tax revenue, and reduce net Social Security payouts. Increased volunteerism improves physical and mental health, potentially reduces public health care costs, and benefits those receiving the services older adults provide. Investments in training older adults for new work and volunteer opportunities will have large personal, community, and national economic rewards. . . .

Marty Martinson

➡ **NO**

Opportunities or Obligations? Civic Engagement and Older Adults

Last spring, Meredith Minkler and I presented our critical perspective on the promotion of civic engagement and older adults at the Joint Conference of the American Society on Aging and the National Council on Aging. With all the current enthusiasm and support for civic engagement initiatives among gerontologists, academics, and others working with or in behalf of older adults, I was surprised, pleased, and a bit curious that almost all the chairs in our presentation room were filled. Preparing for an audience that would not necessarily agree with our position, Meredith joked with the group about how we were grateful that the conference organizers had given us a room with two exit doors behind the podium, in case we needed to make a quick escape. I similarly began the presentation with a quote from Maggie Kuhn . . . who, as the founder of the Gray Panthers, encouraged others to "Stand before the people you fear and speak the truth, even if your voice shakes." . . . While I was not truly fearful of the audience, evoking Kuhn's words was a way to acknowledge our contrarian perspective and of inviting the group to contemplate our questions about the promotion of late-life civic engagement. I hoped to broaden the discussion, which had thus far remained fairly limited in its scope.

Our concerns and critique resonated with many, including those who, like Meredith and me, are deeply involved in programs that support volunteerism among older adults. It is with their inspiration, and a desire to keep these critical questions on the table while the promotion of civic engagement moves ahead, that I write this essay.

My goal here is not in any way to disparage civic engagement (which I define broadly to include not only formal volunteering, but also things like political activism, caregiving, and community organizing) for and by older adults. I firmly believe in the value of such activity, be it on the individual, community, or policy level. Rather, my intent here is to look more closely at the context in which this promotion of civic engagement has emerged and how the discourse around it affects and reflects meanings being constructed and experienced about aging.

I use a critical approach to unpack some of the assumptions embedded in the civic engagement movement that have thus far been taken for granted. As the critical gerontologists Carroll Estes, Simon Biggs, and Chris Phillipson . . .

From *Generations*, Winter 2006–2007, pp. 59–65. Copyright © 2007 by American Society on Aging. Reprinted by permission.

write, "a critical approach, then, sees 'common sense' about age as a starting point, not as an answer in itself." . . .

In the case of civic engagement, if it is "common sense" that such engagement is good for older adults and for society, it is important that we ask how that came to be and who decided it is true. From there, we can explore other important questions: For example, What assumptions are being made in the promotion of civic engagement about the roles older adults might or should play in society? What expectations are being created for older adults and internalized by them? What happens to those who cannot or do not fulfill these roles and expectations, who are they likely to be, and will they experience adverse consequences because they do not fit into these roles? What types of civic engagement are being promoted and what types are being played down? And finally, who is served by the promotion of these types of civic engagement?

This article is a follow-up to previous work in which Meredith Minkler and I, as "loving critics," used a critical gerontology framework to explore the political and economic context in which the new emphasis on civic engagement is situated, the roles older adults are being encouraged to play as community volunteers within that context, and the possible exclusionary effect on older adults who do not play these roles. . . .

In this article, I again use a critical gerontology approach, with its overlapping perspectives from political economy and from the humanities, to more closely examine the potential impact of this burgeoning movement on images and perceptions of aging and of what it means to grow old. As gerontologists, we must consider the possible consequences of the current framing and promotion of late-life civic engagement in order to best develop and support civic opportunities for those older adults who take a civic-engagement path, while also supporting and honoring other experiences of aging.

Framework of Critical Gerontology

Using a critical gerontology approach allows us to explore the ways in which political, economic, and social structures affect the aging processes of the diverse population. Estes, Biggs, and Phillipson . . . have described this critical framework as "one diat goes beyond everyday appearances and the unreflective acceptance of established positions. It examines the structural inequalities that shape the everyday experience of growing old." . . . In order to move beyond the individual focus of traditional gerontology, critical gerontology considers "the critical role of social policy and social institutions in structuring and restructuring the life course and the meanings of old age." . . . This is not to say that the aging individual is without agency, but rather that structural forces affect how people see and experience themselves as aging beings as they internalize, wrestle with, and integrate these forces and ideologies into a sense of self and others. In considering the civic engagement initiatives of the national gerontological associations as well as those emerging from the 2005 White House Conference on Aging, this critical gerontology framework allows us to understand the ways in which these social policies and programs are situated within a specific political, economic, and socio-historical context and how the policies and programs both shape and are shaped by meanings ascribed to aging through the opportunities they create, the messages they promote, and the alternatives they ignore.

Politics of Retrenchment

Useful insights regarding how the emerging discourse on civic engagement and older Americans contributes to particular meanings of aging can be gained by using two interrelated paths of critical gerontology: a political-economy approach, which identifies how socio-structural factors influence aging . . . , and a humanities-based one, which explores aging and old age on a relational and personal level, from the inside out. . . . As examined in previous work . . . , the political economy lens reveals how the current push for civic engagement and volunteerism among older Americans is situated within the politics of retrenchment that began in earnest in the Reagan years and have since been a central feature of American political and economic life. With the introduction of the anti-welfare-state agenda of the Reagan administration, which included major cutbacks in federal spending on social programs and services, came a particular framing of the value of volunteerism in the United States. President George H. W Bush's 1989 inaugural address spoke volumes about how responsibility for managing budgetary shortfalls—and their disastrous social consequences—would henceforth be shifted to the American people and away from the government:

> My friends, we have work to do. There are the homeless, lost and roaming. There are the children who have nothing, no love, no normalcy. There are those who cannot free themselves of enslavement to whatever addiction—drugs, welfare, the demoralization that rules the slums. The old solution, the old way, was to think that public money alone could end these problems. But we have learned that is not so . . . We have more will than wallet; but will is what we need. . . . We will turn to the only resource we have that in times of need always grows—the goodness and the courage of the American people. . . .

This presidential speech exemplifies a politically conservative, individualistic view of volunteerism that places the responsibility for solving social problems on the shoulders of American volunteers while government retreats. The diminished federal funding for social services and public programs that has been a hallmark of political life beginning in the 1980s and continuing through today, has placed increasingly greater responsibilities on already deficit-ridden states and municipalities, which often then turn to individuals, families, and volunteerism to help take up the slack. George H. W. Bush put forth a call for a certain type of civic engagement—volunteerism in service and social programs serving the country's most vulnerable residents—while simultaneously reducing or eliminating federal funds for those services and programs.

Now in the new millennium, older adults are being called upon to embrace civic engagement as a meaningful and beneficial activity. Given that many older adults are among the most vulnerable Americans affected by years of budget cuts, what does it mean to be asking them to fill these gaps?

Emergence of Active, Successful, and Productive Aging Models

Along with cuts in social programs, increased privatization of services, and a growing emphasis on individual responsibility, a contentious discourse has emerged regarding the consequences of the rapidly aging U.S. population for society. The "apocalyptic demography" scenario . . ., embraced by the media, many policy makers, and others for the past three decades, presents the aging of America as a foreboding economic and social catastrophe, with precious resources being engulfed by burdensome and greedy older adults and their skyrocketing health-care costs. . . .

Gerontologists, including researchers and practitioners, have moved quickly to counter these negative images with the presentation of "active aging," "successful aging," and "productive aging" models. These models highlight involvement, mobility, and productivity as means for older people to maintain independence and thus prove the value and worthiness of the older adult population to the larger society. In turn, a number of critical gerontologists have joined the discourse by presenting eloquent critiques of these models. . . . Such critiques assert that in their well-intended attempts to present alternative scenarios to the negative images of older adults, proponents of the active, successful, and productive aging models have shaped cultural norms of aging that are limited, exclusive, and even oppressive.

For example, Stephen Katz unpacks the "gerontological nexus connecting activity, health, and successful aging" in Western societies . . . by examining the ways in which neoliberal policies, emphasizing individual responsibility amid declining government programs and services for the most vulnerable populations (many of whom are older adults), have created "market-driven programs to 'empower' older individuals to be active to avoid the stigma and risks of dependency." . . . In doing so, he asserts, "positive agendas based on activity and mobility can downplay traditionally crucial values such as wisdom and disengagement by translating the latter into 'problems' of inactivity and dependency." . . .

Estes, Biggs, and Phillipson . . . further point out how active, successful, and productive aging models, created with the good intention of countering negative stereotypes, actually serve to maintain the inequities of the status quo by providing homogenized models of aging that emphasize individual responsibility while ignoring structural inequities that affect people's life-course experiences and their likelihood of fitting into these glorified ways of being old.

Estes and her colleagues assert that the productive aging scenario in particular, with its ideal of aging constructed "through the lens of economic usefulness" . . ., presents an especially troubling model as it links individualistic solutions to the very market economy that has penalized and discriminated against older adults and other vulnerable groups. Furthermore, the productive ideal is culturally irrelevant or inappropriate for some subpopulations and leaves out other ways of aging that exist outside this mainstream notion of productivity.

These concerns are echoed by Martha Holstein . . ., who identifies the particularly "troubling implications" of the productive aging scenario for women who have traditionally carried the unacknowledged burden of caregiving responsibilities throughout their lives. By suggesting that old age must involve continued productivity, women are further burdened with expectations to continue in this role throughout their lives. In addition, Holstein asserts, the emphasis on productivity may "impose negative value on those who are not productive in the traditional sense or who do not maintain youthful vigor and independence. It can also intensify the prejudice that already marks social attitudes toward the elderly who have physical and mental impairments." . . .

Making a similar point in their critique of the concept of successful aging within gerontology, Holstein and Minkler . . . describe how such models ignore socio-cultural and environmental influences on the life course that create opportunities for some and limitations for others. In viewing aging processes through such an individualistic lens, proponents of successful aging may perpetuate a kind of victim-blaming for those older adults who do not age "successfully." As Holstein and Minkler assert:

> By suggesting that the great majority of those elders in wheelchairs could indeed have been on cross-country skis had they but made the right choices and practiced the right behaviors can burden rather than liberate older people . . . [C]oncepts such as successful aging are marked by important and unacknowledged class, race and gender concerns that result in further marginalizing the already marginalized . . .

Civic Engagement as Another Permutation

Civic engagement is being presented as yet another strategy for promoting health among older adults while countering images of decline and loss and addressing societal anxieties about "greedy geezers" . . . and a shrinking workforce. As such, the strategy raises questions and concerns similar to those expressed about the active, successful, and productive aging models. Proponents of civic engagement have described older adults as "a growing yet largely untapped civic resource for responding to community needs through both paid and unpaid work." . . . They have asserted that this resource of aging Americans can address the desperate need to fill the gaps in services left underfunded by government while also helping to address labor shortages anticipated with the mass retirement of baby boomers. Furthermore, civic engagement initiatives are put forth as providing "opportunities for greater fulfillment and purpose in later years." . . .

Calling upon older (and younger) Americans to be involved in their communities, and suggesting that such involvement can be meaningful both in individual and community terms, is certainly justifiable. However, the unintended consequences of framing a desirable old age within the boundaries of civic engagement are troubling. Given that civic engagement among older adults has primarily been put into practice as volunteerism . . ., what we are seeing is the placement of volunteer activity within the productive aging paradigm as a means of justifying older adults' existence, addressing society's ills, and shaping meanings of old age through "productive" roles. Civic engagement, in the form of volunteerism, is presented as a way of attaining validity in a society that values productivity and individualism over other ways of being and relating. Any lifestyle outside of that productive paradigm is unwittingly discouraged and therefore read as undesirable. Civic engagement is also promoted as a means of finding purpose and meaning in the later years—with the promoters defining that purpose in very specific ways. While attempting to counter ageist stereotypes, this promotion of civic engagement thus framed may serve to further enforce such stereotypes by inadvertently suggesting that without productive activity, older adults have no purpose.

In his critical examination of the social policies and public discourse promoting volunteerism in the U.K., the U.S., and other Western societies, the writer Simon Biggs . . . describes how these policies force older adults to struggle with placing themselves within or outside of restrictive definitions of aging. He asserts, "For older people, a narrative is emerging of social value through work or near-work situations. If you are active, volunteering and mentoring are identified as legitimized fields of social inclusion." . . . Less visible activities such as caregiving and activities like political activism, which Biggs called delegitimized, are absent from this civic engagement agenda: "This story of late life development . . . has little place for dissident or alternative pathways for self and social development other than through work." . . .

Civic Engagement as One Path of Many

Any promotion of civic engagement must be developed with thoughtful attention to the audience—who it speaks to and who it doesn't. As with promotion of the active and productive aging models, which, perhaps inadvertently, creates a kind of outsider or deviant status for those who do not fit the model, proponents of civic engagement must recognize that not all older adults can or will choose a civic engagement path. As the political analysts Ramakrishnan and Baldassare have aptly noted, "although civic engagement may involve acts of individual choice, these choices are often structured by various social, economic and institutional factors." . . .

Thus, poverty, education, cultural norms, mental or physical disabilities, family obligations, and other factors will influence whether or not an older adult engages in volunteerism. Elevating civic engagement as an ideal for aging may further marginalize those people who, for any number of reasons, are not civically engaged and thus do not reflect that ideal.

In addition, as efforts are made to expand opportunities for civic engagement for those who do choose such a path, the realm of activities visibly encompassed by this term must also be expanded beyond traditional notions of volunteerism in the service or private sector.

Political activism, for example, is another type of activity that has dramatic public consequences and therefore ought to be embraced in the realm of civic engagement. I was pleased to see political engagement included in the working definition of civic engagement for this issue of *Generations,* especially given that political activism has been largely ignored in civic engagement promotions to date. The danger in promoting service volunteerism as the only type of desirable civic involvement and ignoring the value of political participation is that doing so may reinforce a trend among the citizenry to shy away from political involvement and replace efforts to create systemic change upstream with one-on-one efforts downstream. . . .

Such community service is of course valuable, but localized efforts will not address the societal ills that many civic engagement proponents suggest they will. As Theiss-Morse and Hibbing . . . assert, "Volunteering in a soup kitchen will help hungry individuals in a town but will do nothing to address broader problems of homelessness and poverty." . . . We would all be at much greater risk of losing an essential safety net for our increasingly diverse aging population were it not for the thousands of older Americans who have worked tirelessly as political activists to defend the preservation of Social Security. And it is notable that they have done so even though recently proposed changes will not have any effect on their own generation's benefits. Such civic engagement efforts that directly address the structural inequities of our society must be celebrated and supported for the scale of their public consequences, especially for society's most vulnerable groups.

Finally, the option of not being involved in civic engagement as an older adult must be honored. As Biggs notes, "There is an astonishing absence of diversity in policies that assume that everyone from a white male in his fifties to a black woman in her nineties has the same personal and social priorities." . . . We as gerontologists can learn far more about aging and be better advocates for older adults by recognizing the multiple ways in which people experience late life—be they active, inactive, dependent, independent, civically engaged or not. David Lynch's stunning 1999 movie, *The Straight Story,* presents another model: Alvin Straight, a 73-year-old farmer (played by the 79-year-old Richard Farnsworth) who travels on a lawn mower from Iowa to Wisconsin to visit his estranged brother, who has fallen ill. As we watch Alvin's slow journey, we discover how much more he sees from his decelerated vantage point. When a younger woman speeding past him at seventy-five miles per hour hits a deer (her fifth deer murder that week), Alvin stops to roast the deer and then honors it by placing its antlers on the front of his cross-country lawn mower. Later, when his vehicle breaks down along the road, he simply sits there quietly rather than immediately jumping up and trying to fix it. After some time, and with encouragement from a passing gray-haired tractor driver, he turns the key again and the lawn mower starts up.

Lessons on the advantages of moving slowly, and of aging outside the mainstream of a productive, active, competitive market economy, are found in the faces of Alvin Straight and of many other aging Americans. Let us not assume that aging looks just one way, that all baby boomers are alike, or that older adults need some packaged program in order to find purpose and meaning in their lives. Rather, let us honor the many ways in which people age, recognize and seek to address inequities faced by those who have been particularly marginalized throughout the life course, and celebrate community involvement in all its manifestations without asserting such involvement as the ideal way of growing old. . . .

CHALLENGE QUESTIONS

Is More Civic Engagement Among Older Adults Necessarily Better?

- This issue has significant public policy implications in that retirement is often guided by legal guidelines; what is the role of developmental research in shaping public policy agendas relevant to old age?
- Zedlewski and Butrica note that more "higher-income" adults stay engaged in old age, and argue that low-income older adults constitute a missed opportunity. Why might this class difference exist, and what are alternative explanations for its consequences?
- Though Martinson is specifically addressing old age, how might her critique of volunteerism as a trend that addresses immediate needs at the expense of deeper structural problems apply at other stages of the life-span?
- Why do we mandate a specific retirement age when there is so much individual variation in people's capabilities during old age? How might developmental perspectives contribute to thinking about the appropriate time to retire?

Suggested Readings

M. Martinson and M. Minkler, "Civic Engagement and Older Adults: A Critical Perspective," *The Gerontologist* (June 2006)

R.B. Hudson, "Aging in a Public Space: The Roles and Functions of Civic Engagement," *Generations* (Winter 2006–2007)

J.W. Rowe and R.L. Kahn, *Successful Aging* (Pantheon, 1998)

M.B. Holstein and M. Minkler, "Self, Society, and the 'New Gerontology'," *The Gerontologist* (December 2003)

J. Birren, K. Schaie, *Handbook of the Psychology of Aging* (Academic Press, 2005)

M.R. Gillick, *The Denial of Aging—Perpetual Youth, Eternal Life and Other Dangerous Fantasies* (Harvard University Press 2006)

P. Baltes, J. Smith, "New Frontiers in the Future of Aging: From Successful Aging of the Young Old to the Dilemmas of the Fourth Age," *Gerontology* (March/April, 2003)

G.E. Vaillant, *Aging Well: Surprising Guideposts to a Happier Life from the Landmark Harvard Study of Adult Development* (Little, Brown, 2002)

ISSUE 19

Is "Mild Cognitive Impairment" Too Similar to Normal Aging to be a Relevant Concept?

YES: Janice E. Graham and Karen Ritchie, from "Mild Cognitive Impairment: Ethical Considerations for Nosological Flexibility in Human Kinds," in *Philosophy, Psychiatry, & Psychology* (March 2006)

NO: Ronald C. Petersen, from "Mild Cognitive Impairment Is Relevant," in *Philosophy, Psychiatry, & Psychology* (March 2006)

ISSUE SUMMARY

YES: Philosophers Janice E. Graham and Karen Ritchie raise concerns that rigidly defining Mild Cognitive Impairment (MCI) as a disorder associated with aging artificially creates the harmful impression that the conditions of old age are merely biomedical problems.

NO: Medical doctor and researcher Ronald C. Petersen has been a prominent proponent of defining MCI as an intermediate stage between normal aging and Alzheimer's disease. In this selection he counters Graham and Ritchie by emphasizing the usefulness of MCI as a diagnosis.

Among the sometimes scary aspects of growing old is the prospect of cognitive decline—the gradual loss of intellectual functioning. Studying cognitive and intellectual changes over the life-span has thus been an important area for researchers learning about old age. Over decades of study a general picture has emerged with some consistency. We know, for example, that dramatic cognitive decline is not an inevitable fact of aging, although in some ways our intellectual functioning does inevitably change with time. We also know that not all cognitive and intellectual functioning reacts to aging in the same way.

But we also know that many older adults do experience some degree of cognitive impairment, and that extreme forms such as Alzheimer's disease are a very real problem for our aging population. Alzheimer's disease is the most common type of dementia, which is a general category of enduring cognitive problems that most often occurs during older adulthood. Most forms of dementia, including Alzheimer's disease, are impossible to cure and difficult to diagnose. Despite much attention from researchers and practitioners, there is no single diagnostic test that conclusively defines types of dementia. As such, some scholars worry that focusing on the biomedical aspects of dementia create a misleading sense that there is a clear distinction between it and normal aging.

Janice E. Graham and Karen Ritchie are among the concerned scholars. When they promote "nosological flexibility," they are referring specifically to nosology as the medical science responsible for classifying diseases. Though such classification may seem to be a simple matter of putting physical symptoms together with labels and definitions, in fact it can be a complex process of interpreting biological and social realities. Graham and Ritchie point out that the relatively new diagnosis of Mild Cognitive Impairment (MCI) offers a challenging example of these complexities. From their perspective, MCI is too similar to normal aging and too poorly understood to merit a distinct diagnosis. In fact, by presenting MCI as an established disorder, Graham and Ritchie are concerned that older adults may be misled by pharmaceutical concerns and doctors towards the conclusion that slight degrees of memory loss or minor deficits in information processing indicate the start of a devastating illness.

Ronald C. Petersen, a medical doctor and researcher at the Mayo Clinic in Minnesota, is more focused on using the diagnosis of MCI to help make progress against more intractable problems such as Alzheimer's. Petersen is often credited with defining MCI as a disorder, and thus has a vested stake in this controversy. But he also makes the quite reasonable claim that simply because a disorder is complex does not mean it is not a disorder. Throughout the life-span, from childhood behavioral problems to adult struggles with mental health, developmental characteristics regularly tread a fine line between "normal" and "abnormal." As such, thinking about MCI as either a part of or deviation from "normal aging" also provides a valuable opportunity to think through what exactly is "normal" in older adulthood.

POINT

- The concept of MCI as a clear disorder is not true to the reality that age-related cognitive decline comes in many diverse forms; MCI in some cases may be early stage dementia, but it is impossible to be sure.

- There is a risk of MCI as a diagnosis being driven more by marketing and the pharmaceutical industry than by actual processes of aging.

- There are few benefits to defining MCI as a clinical disorder, but the costs negatively label people even when they may be simply experiencing normal aging.

- Labeling MCI creates a false sense that it is a "purely biological" disorder requiring medical and pharmaceutical attention rather than social investment.

COUNTERPOINT

- The construct of MCI is actually flexible enough to account for a variety of causes and consequences, and while defining MCI it has been important to make clear distinctions between normal and abnormal aging processes.

- Despite claims that the pharmaceutical industry drives the definition of MCI, most research on the condition has originated in non-profit settings.

- Focusing on MCI before it becomes full Alzheimer's disease or dementia may allow for early intervention that can prevent cognitive decline during old age.

- Just because treating conditions such as MCI is complicated does not mean we avoid characterizing and diagnosing those conditions.

YES ↵

Janice E. Graham and
Karen Ritchie

Mild Cognitive Impairment: Ethical Considerations for Nosological Flexibility in Human Kinds

. . . This paper examines mild cognitive impairment (MCI), an emerging classification that does not meet all the criteria for dementia, and explores the advantage of allowing nosological flexibility between normal and pathologic definitions associated with aging-related modifications in cognitive performance. We frame the origins of the concept of MCI, and the problems with the premature application of criteria, within a nosological phenomenon: the drive to define a heterogeneous condition as a reified disease entity works against both scientific discovery and human compassion. Who "calls" MCI, and for what reasons? What reliability and validity does this designation have?

The social and ethical implications of identifying and treating those speculated to have an early form of inevitable dementia, a kind of disorder more remarkable for its variability than its predictability . . ., demands attention. Any diagnostic decision is based on anecdotal evidence of improvement or decline, and/or measurements calculated from scientifically standardized instruments. No matter what the source, these everyday and scientific explanatory models serve particular purposes and interests. When potential treatments become available, we must be sure that the market does not determine nosology. We need to examine the possibility that MCI is principally an entity defined to create a market for a product of unknown value.

The micromoral social worlds where decision making takes place contain vulnerable individuals and groups . . ., but the worlds of leading researchers driven by their colleagues' results, and busy clinicians dependent on pharmaceutical representatives, are also laden with opinion and belief. Diagnostic evidence may come from scientific research, a clinician's anticipation of treatment success, or a sufferer's hopes and fears. Research-clinicians, though trying to relieve suffering, may be contributing to premature and speculative hype.

Origins of the Mild Cognitive Impairment Concept

Chronic cognitive deficits, in the absence of neurodegenerative disorder, have been documented since Aristotle as an inevitable feature of the aging process. Such deficits are commonly associated with difficulties in the performance of daily activities. Clinical interest in such conditions has mainly centered on differentiating them from potentially treatable disorders such as depression, metabolic disorders, and toxic reactions and also from early stage neurodegeneration. These subclinical cognitive symptoms are principally distinguished from neurodegenerative disorders such as Alzheimer's disease (AD) by their far slower progression, and by their milder impact on daily performance, linguistic and visuospatial functions. Nevertheless, recent research into the nature and long-term prognosis of aging-related modifications in cognitive performance has begun to question the extent to which these changes may be considered normal. This questioning is refected in the evolution of a nosology for these subclinical alterations.

In keeping with the notion that mild cognitive deficits are a common feature of aging, early definitions were based on the comparative performance of young and elderly cohorts on a limited number of cognitive tests. Recognizing particular clinical populations using these concepts began with Kral's . . . concept of benign senescent forgetfulness. Later, Crook et al. . . . defined *age-associated memory impairment* (AAMI) as changes in subjective complaints of memory loss in elderly persons measured by a decrement of at least one standard deviation on a formal memory test in comparison with means established for young adults. Blackford and La Rue . . . refined the excessive inclusiveness of Crook's criteria. They defined their concept of "late-life forgetfulness" as performance between one and two standard deviations below the mean on at least fifty percent of a battery of at least four tests. Flicker, Ferris, and Reisberg . . . grappled with the normal–dementia divide. Levy et al. . . . introduced *aging-associated cognitive decline,* a concept that stipulated that the deficit should be defined in reference to norms for the elderly and not for young adults. This point signaled a subtle conceptual shift: MCI s are still judged as normal, but they are now to be compared to an "optimum" level of functioning.

Subclinical cognitive deficit in the elderly had become a clinical entity even in the absence of any specific therapeutic management. Recognition by the major international classifications of disease—of subclinical cognitive deterioration linked to the normal aging process—began with the appearance in DSM-IV (American Psychiatric Association [APA] . . .) of *age-related cognitive decline* (ARCD). It refers to an objective decline in cognitive functioning caused by the physiologic process of aging for which no clinical criteria or cognitive testing procedures are specified. Subsequent attempts to operationalize ARCD using data from two general population studies in France and the United States have concluded that the concept has little value either in predicting clinical outcomes or in identifying comparable populations for research purposes.

As research into the causes of dementia and cerebrovascular disease began to shed new light on the etiology of aging-related neuronal decline, it became evident that many of the physiologic abnormalities seen in these pathologies were also present to a lesser extent in subjects identified as having a normal aging-related cognitive disorder. Consequently elderly persons with subclinical cognitive deficits have become the subject of neurologic and geriatric research that seeks to discover whether cognitive deficits of this type may be caused by treatable pathologic processes. Alternative concepts have subsequently appeared in the literature linking cognitive disorder to various forms of under-lying pathology. As an example of this research, the tenth revision of the *International Classification of Diseases* . . . lists *mild cognitive disorder* (MCD). MCD refers to disorders of memory, learning, and concentration, often accompanied by mental fatigue, which must be demonstrated by formal neuropsychological testing and attributable to cerebral disease or damage, or systemic physical disease known to cause dysfunction. MCD is secondary to physical illness or impairment, excluding dementia, amnesic syndrome, concussion, or postencephalitic syndrome. The concept of MCD, which was principally developed to describe the cognitive consequences of autoimmune deficiency syndrome, but was then expanded to include other disorders in which cognitive change is secondary to another disease process, is applicable to all ages, not just the elderly. In practice, attempts to apply MCD criteria to population studies of elderly persons suggest it to be of limited value in this context; it has doubtful validity as a nosological entity for this age group. . . . The DSM IV . . . has proposed a similar entity, namely, *mild neurocognitive disorder* (MNCD), which encompasses not only memory and learning difficulties, but also perceptual–motor, linguistic, and central executive functions. Although the concepts proposed by the two international classifications—MCD and MNCD—do not provide sufficient working guidelines for application in a research context, they do give formal recognition to subclinical cognitive disorder as a pathologic state requiring treatment and as a source of handicap, and are thus likely to be important within a legal context.

A provisional classification, in this case meant specifically for elderly populations, is *cognitive impairment—no dementia* (CIND). CIND was developed within the context of the Canadian Study of Health and Aging (CSHA) with an epidemiologic view to research rather than clinical treatment. It is defined by reference to neuropsychological testing and clinical examination. . . . As with MCD and MNCD, persons with CIND are considered to have cognitive impairment attributable to an underlying physical disorder, but they may also have "circumscribed memory impairment," a modifed form of AAMI that accords with Blackford and LaRue's revisions. . . . CIND encompasses a wider range of underlying etiologies such as delirium, substance abuse, and psychiatric illness. MCD, MNCD, and CIND are constructs that have been developed principally for research. They consider cognitive disorder in the elderly as heterogeneous and not necessarily progressive. Their treatment should be determined by the nature of the underlying primary systemic disease. Operational concepts intended for research afford them an heuristic utility unconstrained by the clinical need to relieve symptoms. The first long-term prospective studies of subclinical cognitive disorders suggested that they are not benign, with many neurologists arguing that they are principally, if not exclusively, early stage dementia. These studies mark a complete turn around in the conceptualization of mild aging-related cognitive deficits: whereas in the 1990s, dementia was generally considered to constitute an upward extension of a "normal" process of progressive aging-related cognitive deterioration, subclinical cognitive deficit was now conceptualized as a downward extension of dementia.

In 1997, Petersen et al. proposed diagnostic criteria for a new category, MCI, defined as complaints of defective memory and demonstration of abnormal memory functioning for age, with normal general cognitive functioning and conserved ability to perform activities of daily living. Importantly, MCI was considered to be a prodrome of AD. Neurologists accepted MCI in theory; a period of early cognitive disability in which intellectual difficulties did not yet reach formal diagnostic levels for dementia was self-evident. But MCI criteria were difficult to apply in practice; too much depended on individual clinical judgment and ability to differentiate MCI at one point in time from cohort effects and low intelligence. A later study refined the initial definition by referring to memory impairment beyond that expected for both age and education level. . . . An alternative approach has been to simply define MCI in terms of early stage dementia.

Problems with the Application of Mild Cognitive Impairment Criteria

The identification of subjects for research and treatment for MCI has been problematic owing to the lack of a working definition based on designated cognitive tests and other clinical measures. The result has been that population prevalence, the clinical features of subjects identified with MCI, and their clinical outcomes, vary widely between studies and even within studies where there has been longitudinal follow-up. . . . It is also unclear whether MCI should include any form of cognitive change or whether it should be confined exclusively to isolated memory impairment as initially defined. Although there is some evidence that a purely amnesic syndrome may exist . . . , it appears in only a very small proportion (six percent) of elderly persons with cognitive deficit when the full range of cognitive functions are examined.

An MCI consensus group meeting in Chicago . . . concluded that subjects with MCI should be considered to have a condition that is different from normal aging and is likely to progress to AD at an accelerated rate; however, they may also progress to another form of dementia or improve. This group thus proposed subtypes of MCI according to type of cognitive deficit and clinical outcome distinguishing MCI amnestic (MCI with pronounced memory impairment progressing to AD), MCI multiple domain (slight impairment across several cognitive domains leading to AD, vascular dementia or stabilizing in the case of normal brain aging changes), and MCI single non-memory domain (significant impairment in a cognitive domain other than memory leading to AD or another form of dementia). It has subsequently been suggested that MCI be further subdivided according to the suspected etiology of the cognitive impairment in keeping with international classifications of dementing disorders: for example, MCI-AD, MCI-LBD, MCI-FTD, and so on. However, this proposal is complicated by more recent neuroradiologic and post mortem research that suggests the borderline between the principal forms of dementia (AD, vascular, Lewy body, and frontotemporal) is problematical and calls for a revision of dementia nosology. . . .

Although early identification of memory and language disorders might well mark individuals likely to manifest AD . . ., other forms of dysfunction are also likely to signal early pathologies worthy of clinical observation. To date, evidence supports the prognostic irrelevance of MCI subcategories in identifying specific entities predictive of dementia. . . . Some individuals diagnosed with early cognitive impairment in CSHA did not progress to dementia, and others were diagnosed five years later as having no cognitive impairment. A longitudinal study of a general population sample with subclinical cognitive deficits has demonstrated multiple patterns of cognitive change with variable clinical outcomes including dementia, depression, and cardiovascular and respiratory disorders, as well as dementia. . . . Current criteria for MCI pick up all these causes. Should researchers only be focusing on cases at risk of evolving toward AD? Even if we could do these studies based on the identification of MCI in general practice (and it is here that subjects will be principally presenting if a treatment is ever available), results suggest that current criteria have poor predictive validity for dementia in this setting and, applying theoretical criteria for the establishment of a formal diagnostic category, that MCI cannot be considered to be a separate clinical entity. . . .

Mapping Nosologies to Flexible Concepts

Although the recognition of MCI as a pathology marks an early step toward the recognition of nondementia cognitive disorder as an important clinical problem with a potential for treatment, it does not yet meet the criteria for a formal nosological entity. . . . Useful conceptual taxonomies should be able to accommodate more flexible kinds. Clinical research on MCI focuses narrowly on forms that lead to AD, the specter of which drives researchers, policymakers, and the public . . . to identify research subjects earlier. The expansion of the potentially affected population coincidentally provides a potential pharmaceutical market of from one quarter to one half of the population over sixty-five.

Ian Hacking's writing on natural and human kinds and his concept of "dynamic nominalism" can inform this discussion. The concept shows how new objects can be introduced into the world; these facts and categories are both socially created and real. Hacking describes the effects of this phenomenon,

> People classified in a certain way tend to conform to or grow into the ways that they are described; but they also evolve in their own ways, so that the classifications and descriptions have to be constantly revised. . . .

How might Hacking's looping of cause and effect, the way observation and identification changes the subject under study, affect those subjects who are identified early? Furthermore, how might those who escape this surveillance fare? How can the diagnosis of MCI be sustained when it has such poor predictive validity? Case identification remains a key issue in MCI as it did in dementia. . . . Accommodating the effects of education continues to require special screening and diagnostic criteria. Cognitive decline in both the normal and CIND groups is associated with older age, lower MMSE, and education, and increased functional impairment at baseline. . . . Concern about missed cases in MCI research outweighs concern about including individuals who are not cognitively impaired (false positives).

Dynamic nominalism stresses how much the act of classifying people changes both the classifier and the subject of classification. . . . Abnormal must predicate normal as a deviation from it, yet some absolute state of normal is itself simply constructed from an averaging of the cases selected. This paradox prompted Schneider to differentiate disease from abnormal variations in the early half of the last century, and both Canguilhem . . . and Foucault . . . to challenge the presumed stability of normal health. Recently, Davis has creatively employed the paradox to address the dynamic flexibility of health as a "plurality of possibilities and potential transitions to new norms." . . . New norms represent flexible adaptation to a new environment. Flexibility as a marker for health can be usefully compared to frailty, a benign accumulation of comorbidities and progressing severity. . . . But the progression from healthy flexibility to frailty is neither linear nor inevitable; it is less a paradigmatic dualism of incommensurable biological and social factors than a balancing board with often undetectable weights dropped on and off and interacting synergistically and antagonistically with one another. . . .

Although individuals do age, and they do become subject to pathologic processes marked by inadaptability and disease, evidence suggests that there is considerable deviation in cognitive impairment within and among individuals. In contrast to Davis's view . . . that dementia "tolerates no deviation" different processes may well play varying roles; cognitive degeneration is neither inevitable nor "natural" and it remains subject to interpretation, for example, by ascertainment bias. An individual identified as having MCI might embody behavioral symptoms that are a response to the diagnosis itself. These characteristics, in turn, are associated with progressive decline (i.e., agitation, irritation, depression, apathy). Moreover, the worried well may turn to self-monitoring, evaluating, discussing, and further data gathering. The act of identifying provides a comfortable prompt category and repository for information. What would be normal in the unhailed . . . , serves to reinforce pathology. Researchers, clinicians, patient advocates, or pharmaceutical companies can then mobilize these new human kinds to exert influence on policy decisions. . . .

MCI, like the dementias that it is presumed to precede, is a heterogeneous condition with no certain biomarker or known etiology. At this stage, MCI still incorporates multiple patterns of pathologic, cognitive, behavioral, and functional criteria. Useful conceptual nosologies should be able to accommodate a plurality of causal explanations as they consolidate research operational definitions with empirical evidence to build new models to explore etiologies. Although suggesting causal subtypes of MCI, Petersen's . . . focus on Alzheimer's disease constrains his "MCI" to a specific ontological passage, and should perhaps more accurately be identified as "mild AD." As noted, clinical research is focused on forms of MCI that lead to AD. Practical kinds offer a way out of this etiologically constrained box. They accommodate dimensional approaches and combine theoretical and empirical evidence to help us understand cognitive impairment and cognitive decline within a complex matrix of social and biological determinants of health. . . .

Technical, Social, and Corporate Relationships

The pathologic process of neurodegeneration is situated in sociodegeneration, or what Davis . . . refers to as *socioneurologic degeneration*. The quality of disintegrating relationships defies a simple normative–pathologic dualism. These relationships only have meaning, can only be defined in historically contextualized complex exchanges of shared memories and experiences, social interactions that are situated, embodied expressions of agency. . . . The persistence in viewing cognitive impairment as a purely biological process, as a natural kind that sits in contrast to some ideal normal healthy state, lacks internal validity—the complex heterogeneities of a variable sociodegenerative process incorporate redundancies, synergies and antagonisms of intricately woven biocultures. . . . For Canguilhem . . ., pathology was a product of the clinical encounter, the therapeutic intervention between a doctor and patient. If only recognized upon the clinician's diagnosis, then pathology or disease have no relevance or meaning beyond that clinical encounter. Over half a century ago, Kurt Schneider suggested that suffering be a criterion for pathology. . . . Is the diagnosis of MCI cause for more suffering?

Treatments for cognitive impairment show only modest benefits in individuals with dementia . . . and, therefore, have given rise to a need to show efficacy through new clinically meaningful treatment outcomes. Clinicians are using qualitative methods to ground their judgments in refined operational definitions and criteria that evoke patient and caregiver perceptions, meaningfulness, and hope for symptomatic relief in anticipation of a progressive decline in memory, thought, and action. Tests such as the MMSE and ADAS-Cog are cognitive scales with an emphasis on logical and linguistic dimensions. These standardized packages categorically reify some evoked pathology . . . in a person who then too easily becomes a Clinical Dementia Rating Scale 2, MMSE 15, ADAS-Cog 47; these categories contribute little insight into person-hood or identity. The real, clinically meaningful markers are localized in actions and relationships . . .—working, doing housework, canning fruit with a daughter, washing oneself in front of a mirror, walking the dog along a worn mnemonic path. Such everyday activities received scant attention before their affectual qualities were realized to mark a potential "treatment success" whose documentation as "clinically meaningful" might further the treatment's sales. This clinical turn places patient desires and expectations at the top of clinical management and treatment goals and it is an important and worthy movement; nevertheless, we need to reflect on the reasons for it and who profits from it.

We are now in the midst of a quiet revolution, as the desires and responses of the patient as subject, if not quite participant, are brought into focus. At the heart of the issue remains measurement. Formerly, the hold of quantitative psychometric and biometric gatekeepers, there is a growing body of research that measures qualitative everyday events and the values that individuals attach in the context of their socioneurodegeneration. Efforts to assess these measures are continuing. . . . But with earlier ascertainment of subtle cognitive impairments and the availability of questionable techniques to link individual responder subtypes to therapies . . . comes a responsibility.

The 1990s saw a turn away from a command and control regulatory apparatus. The U.S. Food and Drug Administration, concerned that pharmaceutical companies might not be rigorous enough in their testing procedures when it set out standardized criteria for measuring efficacy . . ., adopted partnerships with sponsor companies and now relies almost exclusively on company data to show efficacy and safety. There is a pressure to get products to the market faster. Rather than relying on objective psychometric measures of efficacy, as was outlined by the committee in 1990, there are increasing calls to adopt more clinically meaningful outcomes . . . that necessarily require a different approach to measurement. Research-clinicians and industry now ask what the quantitative data actually mean in everyday life. They look to patient expectations to measure success. Whether the rush to market has an effect on the methods and findings of these studies and whether data are subject to equally rigorous critical appraisals requires further analysis. New operational definitions require evidence that stand up to standards of accountability, reliability, and validity; consensus decisions to adopt these methods must be subject to scrutiny.

But what happens when new operational criteria and methods are proposed that equate treatment improvement to maintenance or "staying the same"? A common sense argument is constructed that accepts no further decline as a positive finding for an elderly person. Clinicians elicit narrative meaning from their patients; the existing assessment tools that cannot establish efficacy for a treatment get replaced by patient testimonials; panels of scientists agree that no decline is improvement. They form consensus committees, publish practice guidelines, set international standards and authorize this paradox. Moreover, the emotionally resonant influence of personal testimonies from sufferers is used as evidence. A constellation of signs, symptoms, and social and technical relations are being mapped based on patient and caregiver hopes and fears, not the least of which is the concern about affordable access to their only hope. The noise from these heterogeneous sociotechnical relations creates accounts that cannot make sense. . . . Pharmaceutical grammar (in the form of hopes and fears and treatment success) feeds clinician desires to assist the sufferer who wants access to anything that might possibly work. If treatment effect is to be used to identify the category boundaries for practical kinds, but operational definitions for response continue to be diluted to maintenance, they may well mimic the variable states found in untreated Alzheimer's patients. . . . A vulnerable incipient disease population can be created by excessively loose inclusion criteria. . . .

Although the pharmaceutical industry may be pushing the treatment of MCI at a pace that is detrimental to clinical validity, it must be acknowledged that it is fulfilling its role as a market provider. It has played an important role, responding rapidly to changing social attitudes toward aging and a demand for increasing intervention to improve quality of life in the elderly, in the face of a lagging public health policy that has, for too long, neglected psychogeriatrics. Although it has promoted these causes to their shareholders gain, it is clearly the role of the clinicians implicated in industrial research, and not the industry itself, to ensure that the clinical limits of trial outcomes are adequately discussed.

Despite poor clinical predictive validity, MCI has market appeal to an anxious public. Personal testimonies of modest results risks exaggerating the efficacy of treatments, but it also overlooks the fact that many people do not respond to treatment. In identifying subgroups who may be more prone to treatment effects than others, researchers could underestimate the true potential of a therapy by averaging results across heterogeneous patient subgroups. Although MCI cannot be considered a formal nosological entity (it is rather a heterogeneous syndrome in which dementia is "nested"), it is being treated as though it were and may thus risk being used as a diagnosis in a legal sense—as such it could be evoked in damages, to exclude persons from responsibilities and services (notably elderly care admission) or employment. On the other hand, we have to be careful—MCI is important socially: we are no longer saying that cognitive decline is just normal aging, which the elderly have to tolerate (thus also underlying common attitudes to the elderly as incompetent), but that they should be investigated as practical kinds. Various treatments that might be detected using more flexible nosologies, which allow researchers and clinicians to understand more practical kinds better, might be actively sought. The cholinesterase inhibitors may be only one approach among many provided we are clearer about who we are giving them to and why. . . .

Ronald C. Petersen → **NO**

Mild Cognitive Impairment Is Relevant

Graham and Ritchie . . . have contributed a scholarly document that implores us to reexamine nosological categories and certain diagnostic outcomes. They have chosen mild cognitive impairment (MCI) as the target of their scrutiny and have raised several interesting issues. I would like to comment on their approach and suggest that MCI is a useful clinical entity that does serve a practical function and hopefully will lead to a better quality of life for aging persons.

There are several clarifications concerning the construct of MCI that need to be emphasized. Graham and Ritchie have asserted that all persons with MCI eventually evolve to Alzheimer's disease (AD) and have claimed that this is the inevitable outcome of the disorder. Although it is true that many of the early studies on MCI focused on the amnestic subtype as a precursor to AD . . ., subsequent work has expanded the construct to include prodromal forms of other disorders. . . . As such, the construct of MCI has become flexible in recent years to account for alternative types of intermediate cognitive impairment.

The authors state that MCI addresses those individuals speculated to have an inevitable dementia. Certainly, we do not presume that dementia is inevitable in the aging process; rather, we posit that if certain criteria are fulfilled in persons who are aging, the likelihood of a person progressing to a certain type of dementia is quite high. As such, this is an important precondition about which to learn, because interventional strategies may be available.

Graham and Ritchie argue that some cognitive changes with aging are "normal" and trying to classify these individuals as "abnormal" is performing a disservice to much of the aging population. We draw an important distinction between the cognitive changes of normal aging, as they are recognized to exist, and what we feel constitutes the pathologic changes of MCI. We believe that the abnormal cognitive function found in MCI has a high probability of progressing to a greater degree of cognitive dysfunction in a relatively short period of time and these behavioral changes are accompanied by pathologic brain changes that are manifested on magnetic resonance imaging scans, positron emission tomography scans, cerebrospinal fuid biomarkers, and autopsy studies. . . . This type of progression is in contradistinction to other individuals who are experiencing cognitive changes of normal aging. These individuals do not progress rapidly to greater degrees of impairment and autopsy studies

From *Philosophy, Psychiatry & Psychology,* March 2006, pp. 45–49. Copyright © 2006 by Johns Hopkins University Press. Reprinted by permission.

reveal that their brains do not harbor the pathologic changes found in the MCI population. . . .

The cognitive and behavioral changes accompanying persons with MCI are devastating and cannot be ascribed to "senility" or "He is just getting old." It is a mistake to imply that by labeling people with a condition such as MCI we are doing them a disservice. Most of these individuals are seeking medical attention for their perceived difficulties. Consequently, addressing these concerns and educating the individuals on the implications of their symptoms are important services. Although we may not have adequate therapies at present, this does not imply that we should ignore the symptoms.

We cannot treat many conditions at present, yet we do not avoid the opportunity to characterize the condition and make a diagnosis. Even if this were part of the aging process, this does not mean that we should ignore the disability and refuse to treat it. Most individuals develop an inflexibility of their optical lenses as they age, yet corrective lenses of one type or another are believed to be extremely beneficial at alleviating this disability associated with the aging phenomenon. No one would argue that it is inappropriate to treat this condition because it is "just a part of aging."

It should be noted that I have stressed the situation in which individuals are seeking medical attention for their cognitive concerns. It is quite a different situation if an investigator were proactively to enroll a subject in, for example, an epidemiologic study and then label subjects as having some type of disorder such as MCI. In this instance, the individual subject is not seeking attention for any medical concerns and consequently it is inappropriate to intrude proactively on their daily activities and put a research label on them. This is particularly important while MCI is still evolving with regard to its refinement, and as such has not been completely delineated. However, in the clinical situation whereby an individual is seeking medical attention, the responsibility of the evaluating clinician is quite different.

Graham and Ritchie strongly imply that the entire research and clinical enterprise in MCI is driven by the pharmaceutical industry. Statements such as ". . . the possibility that MCI is principally an entity defined to create a market for a product of unknown value . . ." . . . are false and an inappropriate indictment of the research community. Virtually all of the MCI research that has emanated from the Mayo Clinic has been supported by the National Institute on Aging (NIA). Similarly, most of the major longitudinal studies on which these data are based—the Religious Order Study, the Cache County Study, the Cardiovascular Health Study, and the Monongahela Valley Epidemiologic Study—are all federally funded. These investigators do not have ties to the pharmaceutical industry. Furthermore, the MCI criteria currently in place have been adopted by federally funded agencies to promote research such as the NIA-sponsored Alzheimer's Disease Centers research program and the NIA-supported Alzheimer's Disease Neuroimaging Initiative. . . . To imply that this work is driven by pharmaceutical interests to create a market for marginally effective products is a distortion of the intents of the academic community.

Our work in Rochester, Minnesota, grew out of a longitudinal study on aging and dementia in which we observed individuals who exhibited cognitive concerns and impaired performance through a longitudinal follow-up study. We appreciated that these individuals progressed more rapidly to dementia and particularly AD than would be expected solely on the basis of aging. This observation led us to codify the criteria for these subjects and perform a longitudinal observational study. After many years of scrutiny, it became apparent that these individuals were progressing more rapidly than would be expected on the basis of age, and that this condition likely was the clinical precursor of dementia. There was no influence from the pharmaceutical industry in the design, execution, analysis, or reporting of these data. Yet, Graham and Ritchie would assert that the entire MCI research enterprise was spawned by the pharmaceutical industry.

This is not to say that the pharmaceutical industry has not appreciated this line of research as a marketing opportunity, and partnerships have developed between federally funded grants and industry, for example, the Alzheimer's Disease Cooperative Study, in an attempt to develop treatments for this condition. As such, with appropriate oversight and scrutiny, the public is likely to benefit from a combination of resources of these two partners. Having said that, when the Alzheimer's Disease Cooperative Study reported its MCI treatment trial involving donepezil and vitamin E, the final analysis, interpretation, and reporting of the data were under the auspices of the Alzheimer's Disease Cooperative Study without pharmaceutical company authorship. . . . Strict guidelines were in place in the Alzheimer's Disease Cooperative Study restricting the key investigators from having collaborative relationships with sponsoring pharmaceutical companies. Consequently, these assertions are false and distracting from the essential discussion.

Claiming that MCI research is the product of the pharmaceutical industry would be tantamount to saying that the diagnosis, cognitive impairment—no dementia (CIND) from the Canadian Study of Health and Aging was motivated by the development of a market for the pharmaceutical industry. CIND has not been the study of clinical trials because the overall concept lacks the specificity required to test certain pharmaceutical interventions. However, some Canadian researchers have defined subcategories of CIND that are virtually identical to the subtypes of MCI, and hence have demonstrated the utility and similarity of these two constructs. . . .

Graham and Ritchie claim that the identification of MCI subtypes for research and treatment has been problematic. That is, in part, true. However, with increasing attention and education of clinicians, these subjects are being recognized at an increasing rate. The threshold for detection of a meaningful cognitive impairment is shifting toward lesser degrees of impairment, and subjects are being recognized at earlier stages. A significant number of people with full-blown dementia still go unrecognized in general practice, and this problem would be magnified as one considers milder degrees of impairment. Yet, the threshold is moving and many individuals in general clinical practice are now becoming aware of more subtle forms of impairment and national organizations such as the American Academy of Neurology have recommended that clinicians identify these individuals because they are at increased risk of progressing to dementia. . . . With increased refinement of the criteria including subtypes and etiologies, a great deal of the variability among the studies in the literature can be avoided.

An issue raised by Graham and Ritchie concerns the worry that the act of classifying might alter the classifier and the subject of the classification. This is a relevant and valid; since both the classifier and the classified are probably changed by the process. However, one can look at this issue from a positive as well as a negative perspective. That is, as noted, as clinicians become more aware of the subtleties involved in identifying early impairment, they may refine their own techniques for classification. In a similar fashion, the process of classifying may well have an impact on the subjects of that classification system. Investigators have a moral responsibility for monitoring the labels they place on individuals and this needs to be respected. On the one hand, some individuals appreciate the classification of concerns about their own symptoms, although we must be concerned that labeling people with a condition that is still under refinement may be problematic. We need to caution people about the uncertainties involved in the classification system and indicate the research that is underway. Nevertheless, if this is done in a responsible fashion, this should not dissuade the clinician from exploring new constructs that may be of potential benefit to their patients.

Finally, Graham and Ritchie claim that conceptual nosologies should accommodate a plurality of causal explanations. The authors criticize MCI as a heterogeneous condition as if that were a detrimental quality. They claim that the depiction of MCI is driven only by a treatment focus. Once again, this appears to be an oversimplification of the issues. MCI is by definition heterogeneous because in its broadest sense, it is a precursor to a variety of dementing illnesses. If dementia is characterized by a loss of cognitive capacity of a sufficient degree to impair daily function, then by definition, there must be multiple causes. As we know, from many of the diagnostic manuals, dementia is the first step in a multilayered process of arriving at an ultimate diagnosis. Once the diagnosis of dementia is made, then the clinician must decide the etiology of that dementing syndrome, for example, degenerative, vascular, metabolic, or traumatic. After that determination is made, then a specific diagnosis can be entertained, such as AD, frontotemporal dementia, dementia with Lewy bodies, or vascular dementia.

In a similar vein, if many of these conditions have a prodromal state (e.g., MCI), then MCI should have multiple causations as well. Therefore, the most recent iteration of the MCI diagnostic process includes a specification of a particular subtype based on clinical features such as amnestic or nonamnestic and single or multiple domains. This type of clinical classification leads the process in the direction of diagnostic specificity. However, stopping at this stage produces variability in the longitudinal outcomes of the various clinical subtypes. That is, if a study only classifies the subjects syndromically, then one would expect variable outcomes owing to the multitude of etiologies that could produce the clinical syndrome. Therefore, when an epidemiologic study claims that the syndrome of MCI is "unstable" because some subjects get better and some get worse, this is what one would expect. This is not a problem with the MCI entity itself. Some persons with a memory impairment caused by an evolving degenerative condition will likely get worse; others with the same clinical syndrome caused by depression or medication would be expected to improve once the offending cause has been eliminated. This is not an indictment of the construct of MCI; rather, this variable outcome is to be expected if the consideration of an etiology of the syndrome is not considered. This would be analogous to someone making the diagnosis of dementia and then claiming that dementia is unstable because all of the cases do not ultimately turn out to be AD. Dementia can have multiple etiologies in a similar fashion to the broad syndromic definition of MCI. Therefore, after the designation of the clinical syndrome is made, the clinician must assess the likely etiology. If an amnestic MCI subtype is determined and the likely cause is believed to be cerebral degeneration, then and only then can the specificity of amnestic MCI leading to AD be determined.

All this is to say that MCI does accommodate a plurality of causal explanations and the result and heterogeneity of the construct is a positive attribute. When MCI diagnostic algorithms are utilized to their fullest extent, they do exhibit the appropriate sensitivity and specificity to make the construct a useful clinical tool.

In closing, it is probably quite obvious that I am not a philosopher. The arguments of Graham and Ritchie are forceful and well expressed. Ultimately, I must classify myself as a pragmatist. I believe we can contest these issues interminably, probably to little avail. It is my contention that data will ultimately settle the issues. Prospectively designed longitudinal studies employing the most recent iteration of the diagnostic schemes and tools for MCI will determine the ultimate utility of the construct. Finally, I would contend that although academic exchanges are useful to clarify the issues, the final determination regarding the viability of the construct will be made by the clinicians and patients themselves. If clinicians find the construct of MCI useful, predictive, and helpful with patients, and if patients similarly find the construct explanatory and useful in communicating with each other and with their physicians, then the construct will prevail. At the very least, the construct of MCI has spawned a great deal of interest, debate, and research and that in and of itself is likely useful. . . .

CHALLENGE QUESTIONS

Is "Mild Cognitive Impairment" Too Similar to Normal Aging to be a Relevant Concept?

- What are the relative advantages and disadvantages to "creating" disorders associated with the declines of aging before fully understanding their cause and treatment?
- At present there are few treatments for cognitive decline, and no "cures" for Alzheimer's disease. How might this create a contentious situation for pharmaceutical companies and doctors working with older adults?
- Graham and Ritchie identify MCI as part of a broader problem where complex changes with age are defined as exclusively bio-medical concerns. What other changes and characteristics might also fit as part of this problem?
- Petersen claims that he is more of a pragmatist than a philosopher, and argues that MCI is a pragmatic diagnosis. What are the relative advantages and disadvantages to approaching the study of older adulthood as a pragmatist?
- These selections are primarily concerned with the way professionals define and think about MCI. How might those considerations relate to the actual experience of older adults confronting cognitive impairment?

Suggested Readings

R.C. Petersen and D.S. Knopman, "MCI is a clinically useful concept," *International Psychogeriatrics* (September 2006)

P.J. Visser and H. Brodaty, "MCI is not a clinically useful concept," *International Psychogeriatrics* (September 2006)

R.C. Petersen, *Mild Cognitive Impairment: Aging to Alzheimer's Disease* (Oxford University Press, 2003)

P.J. Whitehouse and D. George, *The Myth of Alzheimers: What You Aren't Being Told About Today's Most Dreaded Diagnosis* (St. Martin's Press, 2008)

S. Artero and K. Ritchie, "The Detection of Mild Cognitive Impairment in the General Practice Setting," *Aging and Mental Health* (Issue 4, 2003)

D.H. Davis, "Dementia: Sociological and Philosophical Constructions," *Social Science & Medicine* (January 2004)

J.C. Hughes, "Views of the Person with Dementia," *Journal of Medical Ethics* (April 2001)

K. Schaie, *Developmental Influences on Adult Intelligence: The Seattle Longitudinal Study* (Oxford University Press, 2005)

A. Kramer and S. Willis, "Enhanc7ing the Cognitive Vitality of Older Adults," *Current Directions in Psychological Science* (October 2002)

ISSUE 20

Should the Terminally Ill Be Able to Have Physicians Help Them Die?

YES: Richard T. Hull, from "The Case for Physician-Assisted Suicide," *Free Inquiry* (Spring 2003)

NO: Margaret A. Somerville, from "The Case against Euthanasia and Physician-Assisted Suicide," *Free Inquiry* (Spring 2003)

ISSUE SUMMARY

YES: Philosopher Richard T. Hull claims that allowing physician-assisted suicide will appropriately give control over dying to patients and families rather than medical professionals.

NO: Ethicist Margaret Somerville instead asserts that allowing euthanasia oversimplifies the complex issues at the end of life, and allows people to ignore the imperative of providing appropriate care.

Although the end of life is inevitable, it is rarely simple. For those concerned with lifespan development, the end of life is embedded with complicated meanings and values that reflect broader attitudes toward human life. These meanings and values are starkly evident in the debate about physician-assisted suicide, which has been intermittently sparked by maneuvering about the legality of allowing doctors to help end a life. The most prominent example is the state of Oregon's "death with dignity" law, which was first passed in 1994 but has been a source of long-running controversy.

While there are important and complicated legal issues surrounding laws such as Oregon's "death with dignity," such laws also raise important questions for scholars interested in lifespan development. The end of life has always had important symbolic meaning, but has become more contentious with advanced technology that allows for prolonged life in ways distinct through human history. For much of the twentieth century, scholars focused primarily about how to prolong life, rather than focusing on what the possibility of technologically prolonging life meant to individuals. In her famous 1969 book *On Death and Dying*, however, Elisabeth Kübler-Ross brought widespread attention to death as a meaningful psychological process. Though Kübler-Ross's specific ideas have since proved controversial in their own right, they have led to important thinking about what qualifies as a "good death."

Many scholars consider a central element for a "good death" to be a situation where an individual is able to die with a sense of the dignity that comes from having some control. In his article, philosopher Richard T. Hull argues that such dignity is best accommodated by making physician-assisted suicide a legal option. As he has watched the debate about physician-assisted suicide, Hull has seen medical professionals becoming more attuned to the needs of those who are dying. He feels that people at the end of life deserve to have their needs met, and that giving them the power to choose the way they will die is the best method toward that end.

Ethicist Margaret A. Somerville, on the other hand, asserts that physician-assisted suicide is profoundly disrespectful to the meaning of death. She asserts that allowing physicians to actively assist people in death goes against any version of civilized morality, and holds dangerous implications for a just society. Rather than giving power to dying patients, Somerville argues that physician-assisted suicide takes away the moral authority that comes with being responsible for ethical care. Her perspective provides an intriguing endpoint for this book because it points out the interesting ways in which our attitudes toward death reflect our broader perspectives on the meaning of life.

POINT	COUNTERPOINT
• Allowing physician-assisted suicide forces the medical community to attend appropriately to pain management at the end of life.	• It is wrong to kill someone no matter the circumstances.
• Without choices about how to die, people at the end of life are left without any power for self-determination and humanity.	• Legalizing physician-assisted suicide has broad and dangerous social implications.
• There has been inadequate management of suffering for years.	• Decisions surrounding death are symbolic of how we think about the importance of human life, and as such must be cautious and respectful rather than technologically efficient.
• There are many cases of people choosing to die with honor, such as soldiers in battle, yet we do not condemn that choice.	• Allowing physician-assisted suicide will invite abuse of end-of-life regulations.
• The fact that physicians can withdraw life support means that we already condone medical professionals being involved with the end of life.	• Prohibiting physician-assisted suicide will erode public trust in doctors.

YES ↵

Richard T. Hull

The Case for Physician-Assisted Suicide

In early 1997, the medical community awaited the U.S. Supreme Court's decision in *Vacco* v. *Quill*. Ultimately the high court would overturn this suit, in which doctors and patients had sought to overturn New York's law prohibiting physician-assisted suicide. But it was fascinating to see how much attention physicians suddenly paid to the question of pain management while they were waiting.

Politicians and physicians alike felt shaken by the fact that the suit had made it as far as the Supreme Court. Medical schools scrutinized their curricula to see how, if at all, effective pain management was taught. The possibility that physician-assisted suicide would be declared as much a patient's right as the withdrawal of life-sustaining technology was a clarion call that medicine needed to "houseclean" its attitudes toward providing adequate narcotics for managing pain.

The ability to demand physician aid in dying is the only resource dying patients have with which to "send a message" (as our public rhetoric is so fond of putting it) to physicians, insurers, and politicians that end-of-life care is inadequate. Far too many patients spend their last days without adequate palliation of pain. Physicians sensitive to their cries hesitate to order adequate narcotics, for fear of scrutiny by state health departments and federal drug agents. Further, many physicians view imminent death as a sign of failure in the eyes of their colleagues, or just refuse to recognize that the seemingly endless variety of tests and procedures available to them can simply translate into a seemingly endless period of dying badly. Faced with all this, the ability to demand—and receive—physician aid in dying may be severely compromised patients' only way to tell caregivers that something inhumane stalks them: the inhumanity of neglect and despair.

Many physicians tell me that they feel it is an affront to suppose that their duty to care extends to a duty to kill or assist in suicide. If so, is it not even more an affront, as dying patients and their families tell me, to have to beg for increases in pain medication, only to be told that "We don't want to make you an addict, do we?" or that "Doctor's orders are being followed, and Doctor can't be reached to revise them." If apologists for the status quo fear that a slippery slope will lead to voluntary euthanasia, then nonvoluntary euthanasia, the proponents of change already know that we've been on a slippery slope of inadequate management of suffering for decades.

Let's examine some of the stronger arguments against physician-assisted suicide—while keeping in mind that these arguments may not be the deepest reasons some people oppose it. My lingering sense is that the unspoken problem with physician-assisted suicide is that it puts power where opponents don't want it: in the hands of patients and their loved ones. I want to see if there are ways of sorting out who holds the power to choose the time and manner of dying that make sense.

> *1. Many severely compromised individuals, in their depression, loneliness, loss of normal life, and despair, have asked their physicians to assist them in dying. Yet later (after physicians resisted their requests and others awakened them to alternative opportunities) they have returned to meaningful lives.*

No sane advocate of physician-assisted suicide would deny the importance of meeting the demand to die with reluctance and a reflective, thorough examination of alternative options. The likelihood of profound mood swings during therapy makes it imperative to distinguish between a patient's acute anguish of loss and his or her rational dismay at the prospect of long-term descent into the tubes and machines of intensive care.

But note that, in stories like the above, it is the very possibility of legal physician-assisted suicide that empowers patients to draw attention to their suffering and command the resources they need to live on. Patients who cannot demand to die can find their complaints more easily dismissed as "the disease talking" or as weakness of character.

> *2. Medicine would be transformed for the worse if doctors could legally help patients end their lives. The public would become distrustful, wondering whether physicians were truly committed to saving lives, or if they would stop striving as soon as it became inconvenient.*

Doubtless there are physicians who, by want of training or some psychological or moral defect, lack the compassionate sensitivity to hear a demand for aid in dying and act on it with reluctance, only after thorough investigation of the patient's situation. Such physicians should not be empowered to assist patients to die. I would propose that this power be restricted to physicians whose primary training and profession is in pain management and palliation: they are best equipped to ensure that reasonable alternatives to euthanasia and suicide are exhausted. Further, patients' appeals for assisted suicide should be scrutinized by the same institutional ethics committees that already review requests for the suspension of life-sustaining technology as a protection against patient confusion and relatives' greed.

> *3. Euthanasia and physician-assisted suicide are incompatible with our obligations to respect the human spirit and human life.*

When I hear *all* motives for euthanasia and physician-assisted suicide swept so cavalierly into the dustbin labeled Failure to Respect Human Life, I'm prompted to say, "Really? *Always?*" Those same opponents who find physician-assisted suicide appalling will typically excuse, even acclaim, self-sacrifice on behalf of others. A soldier throws himself on a grenade to save his fellows. A pedestrian leaps into the path of a truck to save a child. Firefighters remain in a collapsing building rather than abandon trapped victims. These, too, are decisions to embrace death, yet we leave them to the conscience of the agent. Why tar all examples of euthanasia and physician-assisted suicide with a common brush? Given that we do not have the power to ameliorate every disease and never will, why withhold from individuals who clearly perceive the financial and emotional burdens their dying imposes on loved ones the power to lessen the duration and extent of those burdens, in pursuit of the values they have worked to support throughout their lives?

Consider also that some suffering cannot be relieved by any means while maintaining consciousness. There are individuals, like myself, who regard conscious life as essential to personal identity. I find it nonsensical to maintain that it is profoundly morally *preferable* to be rendered comatose by drugs while awaiting life's "natural end," than to hasten death's arrival while still consciously able to embrace and welcome one's release. If I am irreversibly comatose, "I" am dead; prolongation of "my life" at that point is ghoulish, and I should not be required to undergo such indignity.

Finally the question, "What kind of life is worth living?" is highly personal. There are good reasons patients diagnosed with a wide range of conditions might not wish to live to the natural end of their diseases. How dare politicians and moralists presume to make these final judgments if they don't have to live with the results? Of course, every demand for physician-assisted suicide must be scrutinized, and determined to be fully informed. To withhold aid in dying beyond that point is, first, barbarically cruel. Second, it only increases the risk that individuals determined to end their lives will attempt to do so by nonmedical means, possibly endangering others or further magnifying their own suffering.

> 4. *The time-honored doctrine of double effect permits administering pain-relieving drugs that have the effect of shortening life, provided the intent of the physician is the relief of the pain and not the (foreseen) death of the patient. Isn't that sufficient?*

Others may find comfort in the notion that the intention of the agent, not the consequences of his or her action, is the measure of morality. I do not. In any case, preferences among ethical theories are like preferences among religious persuasions: no such preference should be legislated for all citizens. For the thinker who focuses on consequences rather than intentions, the fact that we permit terminal care regimens to shorten life *in any context* shows that the line has already been crossed. The fact that physicians must, at the insistence of the competent patient or the incompetent patient's duly appointed surrogate, withdraw life-sustaining technology shows that physicians *can* assist patient suicides and can perform euthanasia on those fortunate enough to be dependent on machines. It becomes a matter of simple justice—equal protection before the law—to permit the same privileges to other terminal patients. That the U.S. Supreme Court has ruled against this argument did not dissuade the citizens of the State of Oregon from embracing it. States like New York that have turned back such initiatives must bear the shame of having imposed religious majorities' philosophies on all who suffer.

Margaret Somerville

NO

The Case against Euthanasia and Physician-Assisted Suicide

There are two major reasons to oppose euthanasia. One is based on principle: it is wrong for one human to intentionally kill another (except in justified self-defense, or in the defense of others). The other reason is utilitarian: the harms and risks of legalizing euthanasia, to individuals in general and to society, far outweigh any benefits.

When personal and societal values were largely consistent with each other, and widely shared because they were based on a shared religion, the case against euthanasia was simple: God or the gods (and, therefore, the religion) commanded "Thou shalt not kill." In a secular society, especially one that gives priority to intense individualism, the case for euthanasia is simple: Individuals have the right to choose the manner, time, and place of their death. In contrast, in such societies the case against euthanasia is complex.

Definitions

Definitions are a source of confusion in the euthanasia debate—some of it deliberately engendered by euthanasia advocates to promote their case.[1] Euthanasia is "a deliberate act that causes death undertaken by one person with the primary intention of ending the life of another person, in order to relieve that person's suffering."[2] Euthanasia is not the justified withdrawing or withholding of treatment that results in death. And it is not the provision of pain relief, even if it could or would shorten life, provided the treatment is necessary to relieve the patient's pain or other serious symptoms of physical distress and is given with a primary intention of relieving pain and not of killing the patient.

Secular Arguments against Euthanasia

1. *Impact on society.* To legalize euthanasia would damage important, foundational societal values and symbols that uphold respect for human life. With euthanasia, how we die cannot be just a private matter of self-determination and personal beliefs, because euthanasia "is an act that requires two people to make it possible and a complicit society to make it acceptable."[3] The prohibition on intentional

From *Free Inquiry*, Spring 2003, pp. 33–34. Copyright © 2003 by Margaret Somerville. Reprinted by permission.

killing is the cornerstone of law and human relationships, emphasizing our basic equality.[4]

Medicine and the law are the principal institutions that maintain respect for human life in a secular, pluralistic society. Legalizing euthanasia would involve—and harm—both of them. In particular, changing the norm that we must not kill each other would seriously damage both institutions' capacity to carry the value of respect for human life.

To legalize euthanasia would be to change the way we understand ourselves, human life, and its meaning. To explain this last point requires painting a much larger picture. We create our values and find meaning in life by buying into a "shared story"—a societal-cultural paradigm. Humans have always focused that story on the two great events of each life, birth and death. Even in a secular society—indeed, more than in a religious one—that story must encompass, create space for, and protect the "human spirit." By the human spirit, I do not mean anything religious (although this concept can accommodate the religious beliefs of those who have them). Rather, I mean the intangible, invisible, immeasurable reality that we need to find meaning in life and to make life worth living—that deeply intuitive sense of relatedness or connectedness to others, the world, and the universe in which we live.

There are two views of human life and, as a consequence, death. One is that we are simply "gene machines." In the words of an Australian politician, when we are past our "best before" or "use by" date, we should be checked out as quickly, cheaply, and efficiently as possible. That view favors euthanasia. The other view sees a mystery in human death, because it sees a mystery in human life, a view that does not require any belief in the supernatural.

Euthanasia is a "gene machine" response. It converts the mystery of death to the problem of death, to which we then seek a technological solution. A lethal injection is a very efficient, fast solution to the problem of death—but it is antithetical to the mystery of death. People in postmodern societies are uncomfortable with mysteries, especially mysteries that generate intense, free-floating anxiety and fear, as death does. We seek control over the event that elicits that fear; we look for a terror-management or terror-reduction mechanism. Euthanasia is such a mechanism: While it does not allow us to avoid the cause of our fear—death—it does allow us to control its manner, time, and place—we can feel that we have death under control.

Research has shown that the marker for people wanting euthanasia is a state that psychiatrists call "hopelessness," which they differentiate from depressions[5]—these people have nothing to look forward to. Hope is our sense of connection to the future; hope is the oxygen of the human spirit.[6] Hope can be elicited by a sense of connection to a very immediate future, for instance, looking forward to a visit from a loved person, seeing the sun come up, or hearing the dawn chorus. When we are dying, our horizon comes closer and closer, but it still exists until we finally cross over. People need hope if they are to experience dying as the final great act of life, as it should be. Euthanasia converts that act to an act of death.

A more pragmatic, but nevertheless very important, objection to legalizing euthanasia is that its abuse cannot be prevented, as recent reports on euthanasia in the Netherlands have documented.[7] Indeed, as a result of this evidence some former advocates now believe that euthanasia cannot be safely legalized and have recently spoken against doing so.[8]

To assess the impact that legalizing euthanasia might have, in practice, on society, we must look at it in the context in which it would operate: the combination of an aging population, scarce health-care resources, and euthanasia would be a lethal one.

2. *Impact on medicine.*[9] Advocates often argue that euthanasia should be legalized because physicians are secretly carrying it out anyway. Studies[10] purporting to establish that fact have recently been severely criticized on the grounds that the respondents replied to questions that did not distinguish between actions primarily intended to shorten life—euthanasia—and other acts or omissions in which no such intention was present—pain-relief treatment or refusals of treatment—that are not euthanasia.[11] But even if the studies were accurate, the fact that physicians are secretly carrying out euthanasia does not mean that it is right. Further, if physicians were presently ignoring the law against murder, why would they obey guidelines for voluntary euthanasia?

Euthanasia "places the very soul of medicine on trial."[12] Physicians' absolute repugnance to killing people is necessary if society's trust in them is to be maintained. This is true, in part, because physicians have opportunities to kill not open to other people, as the horrific story of Dr. Harold Shipman, the British physician–serial killer, shows.

How would legalizing euthanasia affect medical education? What impact would physician role models carrying out euthanasia have on medical students and young physicians? Would we devote time to teaching students how to administer death through lethal injection? Would they be brutalized or ethically desensitized? (Do we adequately teach pain-relief treatment at present?) It would be very difficult to communicate to future physicians a repugnance to killing in a context of legalized euthanasia.

Physicians need a clear line that powerfully manifests to them, their patients, and society that they do not inflict death; both their patients and the public need to know with absolute certainty—and to be able to trust—that this is the case. Anything that would blur the line, damage that trust, or make physicians less sensitive to their primary obligations to protect life is unacceptable. Legalizing euthanasia would do all of these things.

Conclusion

Euthanasia is a simplistic, wrong, and dangerous response to the complex reality of human death. Physician-assisted suicide and euthanasia involve taking people who are at their weakest and most vulnerable, who fear loss of control or isolation and abandonment—who are in a state of intense "pre-mortem loneliness"[13]—and placing them in a situation where they believe their only alternative is to be killed or kill themselves.

Nancy Crick, a sixty-nine-year-old Australian grandmother, recently committed suicide in the presence of over twenty people, eight of whom were members of the Australian Voluntary Euthanasia Society. She explained: "I don't want to die alone." Another option for Mrs. Crick (if she had been terminally ill—an autopsy showed Mrs. Crick's colon cancer had not recurred) should have been to die naturally with people who cared for her present and good palliative care.

Of people who requested assisted suicide under Oregon's Death with Dignity Act, which allows physicians to prescribe lethal medication, 46 percent changed their minds after significant palliative-care interventions (relief of pain and other symptoms), but only 15 percent of those who did not receive such interventions did so.[14]

How a society treats its weakest, most in need, most vulnerable members best tests its moral and ethical tone. To set a present and future moral tone that protects individuals in general and society, upholds the fundamental value of respect for life, and promotes rather than destroys our capacities and opportunities to search for meaning in life, we must reject euthanasia.

Notes

1. Margaret Somerville, "Death Talk: The Case Against Euthanasia and Physician-Assisted Suicide" (Montreal: McGill Queen's University Press, 2001), p. xiii.

2. Ibid.

3. D. Callahan, "When Self-Determination Runs Amok," *Hastings Center Report* 1992, 22(2): 52–55.

4. House of Lords. Report of the Select Committee on Medical Ethics (London: HMSO, 1994).

5. H.M. Chochinov, K.G. Wilson, M. Enns, et al. "Depression, Hopelessness, and Suicidal Ideation in the Terminally Ill," *Psychosomatics* 39 (1998): 366–70, "Desire for Death in the Terminally Ill," *American Journal of Psychiatry* 152 (1995): 1185–1191.

6. Margaret Somerville, *The Ethical Canary: Science, Society and the Human Spirit* (Toronto: Viking/Penguin, 2000).

7. K. Foley and H. Hendin, editors, *The Case Against Assisted Suicide: For the Right to End-of-Life Care* (Baltimore: The Johns Hopkins University Press, 2002).

8. S.B. Nuland, "The Principle of Hope," *The New Republic* OnLine 2002: May 22.

9. This section is based on Margaret Somerville, "'Death Talk': Debating Euthanasia and Physician-Assisted Suicide in Australia," *AMAJ* February 17, 2003.

10. H. Kuhse, P. Singer, P. Baume, et al. "End-of-Life Decisions in Australian Medical Practice," *Med J Aust* 166 (1997): 191–96.

11. D.W. Kissane, "Deadly Days in Darwin," K. Foley, H. Hendin, editors, *The Case Against Assisted Suicide: For the Right to End-of-Life Care,* pp. 192–209.

12. W. Gaylin, L. Kass, E.D. Pellegrino, and M. Siegler, "Doctors Must Not Kill," *JAMA* 1988; 259:2139–2140.

13. J. Katz, *The Silent World of Doctor and Patient* (New York: Free Press, 1984).

14. K. Foley and H. Hendin. "The Oregon Experiment," in K. Foley, H. Hendin, editors, *The Case Against Assisted Suicide: For the Right to End-of-Life Care,* p. 269.

CHALLENGE QUESTIONS

Should the Terminally Ill Be Able to Have Physicians Help Them Die?

- Both sides agree that improved palliative care and pain management are essential for end-of-life care. Why do you think the medical system is not effective with such types of care?
- Both sides imply that our attitudes toward the process of death reflect broader attitudes toward the life-span. What are some attitudes about life-span development embedded in this issue, and why do they matter?
- Hull argues that allowing physician-assisted suicide has the somewhat paradoxical effect of improving the amount of attention we pay to the dying process. Why is the dying process so hard for people to acknowledge as important and complex?
- Sommerville argues that it is wrong to kill no matter the circumstances. Have social changes and technological possibilities changed the meaning of similar moral codes?
- Life-span development scholars often refer to the idea that society has a responsibility to ensure people experience a "good death." What do you think a "good death" might look like?

Suggested Readings

I. Dowbiggin, *A Merciful End: The Euthanasia Movement in Modern America* (Oxford University Press, 2002)

R. Henig, "Will We Ever Arrive at the Good Death?" from *The New York Times Magazine* (August 7, 2005)

S. Kaufman, *And a Time to Die: How American Hospitals Shape the End of Life* (University of Chicago Press, 2006)

D. Kuhl, *What Dying People Want: Practical Wisdom for the End of Life* (Public Affairs, 2003)

S. Nuland, *How We Die: Reflections on Life's Final Chapter* (Knopf, 1994)

M. Webb, *The Good Death: The New American Search to Reshape the End of Life* (Bantam, 1997)

Contributors to This Volume

EDITOR

ANDREW M. GUEST is a developmental psychologist and faculty member in the department of social and behavioral sciences at the University of Portland. He has research experience investigating development in impoverished communities, studying culture in relation to social development during middle childhood, and evaluating the influence of extracurricular activities during adolescence. He also has experience working with programs focused on enhancing life-span development for disadvantaged populations in the United States, Malawi, Mexico, and Angola. He received a B.A. from Kenyon College in psychology, an M.S. from Miami University in sports studies, and a M.A. and Ph.D. from the University of Chicago's Committee on Human Development.

AUTHORS

JEFFREY JENSEN ARNETT is a research professor in the department of psychology at Clark University. He has done extensive scholarly work on the concept of "emerging adulthood" as a life-span stage between adolescence and adulthood, including publishing a book titled *Emerging Adulthood: The Winding Road from the Late Teens Through the Twenties.*

GWEN J. BROUDE teaches developmental psychology and cognitive science at Vassar College and is the director of the college's Cognitive Science Program. She is the editor of cross-cultural encyclopedias on growing up and marriage, family, and relationships.

PHYLLIDA BROWN is a writer based in the UK who has specialized in science journalism.

BARBARA A. BUTRICA is a labor economist and senior research associate at The Urban Institute who has done a great deal of research about retirement-related issues.

ANDREW J. CHERLIN is the Benjamin H. Griswold, III, Professor of Public Policy in the department of sociology at the Johns Hopkins University. He is an expert on the sociology of the family and is the author of the text *Public and Private Families: An Introduction.*

M. BRENT DONNELLAN is a faculty member in the department of psychology at Michigan State University. His research focuses on social and personality factors associated with transitions across the life-span.

JACQUELYNNE S. ECCLES is the McKeachie-Pintrich Distinguished University Professor of Psychology and Education at the University of Michigan. She is a national expert on adolescent development and a past president of the Society for Research on Adolescence.

PAUL EHRLICH is the Bing Professor of Population Studies in the department of biological sciences at Stanford University. He is an expert in population and natural resource issues and is a prominent voice in concerns about global overpopulation.

JULIE JUOLA EXLINE is a member of the department of psychology at Case Western Reserve University. Dr. Exline specializes in research about religious and spiritual struggles as they relate to morality and humanity's relationship with God.

THE FEDERAL TRADE COMMISSION BUREAU OF ECONOMICS STAFF is part of the United States government agency responsible for ensuring consumer protection and competitive business practices. The Bureau of Economics is specifically charged with analyzing the impacts of regulations on consumers and competition.

MARCUS FELDMAN is a professor of biological sciences at Stanford University, with primary research focusing on the interaction of biological and cultural evolution.

CONTRIBUTORS

JOSHUA D. FOSTER is a social psychologist and faculty member at the University of South Alabama. His research focuses on the self, personality, and relationships.

MICHAEL FUMENTO is an author, journalist, and attorney specializing in science and health issues. He has written for numerous newspapers and magazines, and his work has been nominated for the National Magazine Award.

FRANK F. FURSTENBERG, JR. is a professor of sociology and a research associate in the Population Studies Center at the University of Pennsylvania. He has been chair of the MacArthur Foundation Research Network on the Transition to Adulthood and co-editor of *On the Frontiers of Adulthood: Theory, Research, and Public Policy.*

HOWARD GARDNER is professor of cognition and education at the Harvard Graduate School of Education and founder of *Project Zero*, a research group to aid development of personalized curriculum designed for multiple intelligences (the theory Gardner is most known for). Winner of numerous honors in the fields of education and psychology, Garner is also author of more than twenty books.

JANICE E. GRAHAM is a medical anthropologist and Canada Research Chair in Bioethics at Dalhousie University in Halifax Nova Scotia. Her work takes an interdisciplinary approach to cultural, technical, and moral issues as related to health.

ELIZABETH HAMEL is associate director, public opinion and survey research for the Kaiser Family Foundation.

ANGEL L. HARRIS is on the faculty of Princeton University in the department of sociology. His research focuses on academic inequality.

JUDITH RICH HARRIS has psychology degrees from Brandeis and Harvard Universities and has authored several textbooks in developmental psychology, most notably *The Child* and *Infant and Child*. She writes extensively about child environments, parenting, and the nature-vs.-nurture question.

LEO B. HENDRY is a professor of psychology at the University of Glamorgan in Cardiff, Wales, where he is also a founding member of the Lifespan Research Centre. He has done extensive research and writing about lifespan development in diverse international contexts.

LINDA HIRSHMAN is a freelance writer, and former Allen/Berenson Distinguished Visiting Professor of Philosophy and Women's Studies at Brandeis University. Hirshman also taught and practiced law in Chicago.

RICHARD T. HULL is professor emeritus of philosophy at the State University of New York at Buffalo and an expert on biomedical ethics.

THE KAISER FAMILY FOUNDATION is a non-profit foundation that describes itself as "a non-partisan source of facts, information, and analysis for policymakers, the media, the health care community, and the public."

MARION KLOEP is a professor in psychology and co-director of the Centre for Lifespan Research at the University of Glamorgan in Cardiff, Wales. Her main research interests are in adolescence, but she also investigates adulthood and old age.

MEL LEVINE is the author of numerous books and articles, and is a founding member of Bringing Up Minds—which uses science to help parents and children dealing with "puzzling individual variations in children's 'brain wiring'." Dr. Levine has also been a professor of pediatrics at the University of North Carolina School of Medicine.

JOSEPH L. MAHONEY is a developmental psychologist and faculty member in the department of education at the University of California, Irvine. He was formerly on the psychology faculty at Yale, and edited the book *Organized Activities as Contexts of Development*.

MICHAEL MALES is a senior researcher for the Center on Juvenile and Criminal Justice and the online information service YouthFacts.org. He has also worked widely with youth and community programs and taught sociology at the University of California.

GARY F. MARCUS is the director of the NYU Center for Child Language and a professor of psychology at New York University. His books include *Kluge, The Birth of the Mind, The Algebraic Mind,* and *The Norton Psychology Reader*.

MARTY MARTINSON is a public health scholar and critical gerontologist examining the ethics and ideals of aging as they may exclude or devalue certain groups of older adults.

JULIA MOSKIN is a writer and journalist for the *New York Times* who writes primarily about food and dining.

DAVID G. MYERS is a social psychologist with research interests in happiness and spiritual well-being. A professor of psychology at Hope College, Meyers has written several popular psychology textbooks and multiple other scholarly books.

RONALD C. PETERSEN is a medical doctor, researcher, and director of the Mayo Clinic's Alzheimer's Disease Research Center. His scholarly work focuses on aging, mild cognitive impairment, dementia, Alzheimer's disease, and neuroimaging.

STEVEN PINKER is a specialist in language and cognition and professor of psychology at Harvard University. His books include *How the Mind Works* and *The Blank Slate*.

C. CYBELE RAVER is a faculty member in applied psychology at New York University and the director of NYU's Institute of Human Development and Social Change. She previously held faculty positions at the University of Chicago and Cornell University, with research focusing primarily on the well-being of children and families.

KAREN RITCHIE is a neuropsychologist and epidemiologist. She is currently a research director with the French National Institute of Medical Health and Medical Research.

VICTORIA RIDEOUT is a vice president for media and public education at the Kaiser Family Foundation, where she directs the Program for the Study of Entertainment Media and Health.

MICHAEL ROBB studies the media and children's development, having previously worked in the television industry doing educational outreach for children's programming.

RICHARD W. ROBINS is a professor of psychology at the University of California, Davis. His research explores self and other perceptions.

ALVIN ROSENFELD graduated from Harvard Medical School and works in private practice doing child and adult psychiatry. He is also an associate psychiatrist at Massachusetts General Hospital and serves on the Board of Governors for Harvard Medical School's Center for Mental Health and Media.

MARGARET SOMERVILLE is a professor in the Faculty of Medicine at McGill University in Montreal, Quebec, Canada. She is also the founding director of the McGill Centre for Medicine, Ethics and Law.

ELIZABETH S. SPELKE is the Marshall L. Berkman Professor of Psychology at Harvard University and is an award winning scholar with particular expertise in infant cognitive development.

LAURENCE STEINBERG is the Distinguished University Professor and Laura H. Carnell Professor of Psychology at Temple University. He is a prodigious scholar of adolescence and author of several hundred articles along with the leading college textbook on adolescent development.

PAMELA STONE is professor of sociology and a fellow in the Gender Equity Program at Hunter College. She has published widely on gender issues related to employment and work-family balance.

THE U.S. DEPARTMENT OF HEALTH AND HUMAN SERVICES is the United States government agency responsible for public health and social services. The department oversees several hundred programs, many of which serve disadvantaged populations.

KALI H. TRZESNIEWSKI is a faculty member in the department of psychology and director of the Life Span Development Lab at the University of Western Ontario.

JEAN TWENGE is a faculty member in the department of psychology at San Diego State University. Her recent book, co-authored with W. Keith Campbell, is titled *The Narcissism Epidemic: Living in the Age of Entitlement*.

ELLEN WARTELLA is Distinguished Professor of Psychology at the University of California, Riverside. She has researched and written widely about children and media, serves on the Board of Trustees of Sesame Workshop, and is a member of the National Academy of Sciences Board on Children Youth and Families.

ROGERS H. WRIGHT is a clinical psychologist and a fellow of the American Psychological Association.

SHEILA R. ZEDLEWSKI is the director of The Urban Institute's Income and Benefits Policy Center and has been involved with research projects related to retirement policy.

ZERO TO THREE is a not-for-profit organization working to promote the healthy development of infants and toddlers.

EDWARD F. ZIGLER is emeritus director of the Zigler Center in Child Development and Social Policy at Yale University. Zigler is the author of several books, including *Children's Play* and *The First Three Years and Beyond*, and was closely involved with developing the federal Head Start pre-school program.